# PRIVATE STOCK
# COOKBOOK

# PRIVATE STOCK
# COOKBOOK

## The United Airlines Friendship Guild of the Children's Orthopedic Hospital and Medical Center

Proceeds to benefit the Children's Orthopedic
Hospital and Medical Center

PEANUT BUTTER
PUBLISHING

Mercer Island, Washington

Illustrations & cover design: Neil Sweeney
Cover photography: Kenneth Redding
Typesetting: Charles Heim & Nancy Mattson
Copy editing: Lisa Ford

ISBN 0-89716-109-2

# DEDICATION

The United Airlines Friendship Guild dedicates this cookbook to Children's Orthopedic Hospital and Medical Center in recognition of its significance as a major regional, non-profit pediatric medical center. Established in 1907 as a 7-bed ward in Seattle General Hospital, this vast network now provides health care to children from all over the world with a 200-bed hospital, over 50 outpatient clinics and numerous specialty services. But in the last seventy-five years one policy has not changed, the tradition that the doors are open to all children, regardless of race, creed or ability to pay.

All proceeds from the sale of this book will be donated to Children's Orthopedic Hospital and Medical Center to support and salute its ongoing medical and humanitarian accomplishments.

# CONTENTS

Preface . . . . . . . . . . . . . . . . . . . . . . . . . . . . . . . . . . . . ix
Acknowledgments . . . . . . . . . . . . . . . . . . . . . . . . . . . xi
Appetizers . . . . . . . . . . . . . . . . . . . . . . . . . . . . . . . . . 1
Beverages . . . . . . . . . . . . . . . . . . . . . . . . . . . . . . . . 33
Seafood . . . . . . . . . . . . . . . . . . . . . . . . . . . . . . . . . . 43
Poultry . . . . . . . . . . . . . . . . . . . . . . . . . . . . . . . . . . 89
Meat . . . . . . . . . . . . . . . . . . . . . . . . . . . . . . . . . . . 127
Eggs & Cheese . . . . . . . . . . . . . . . . . . . . . . . . . . . 179
Pasta & Rice . . . . . . . . . . . . . . . . . . . . . . . . . . . . . 191
Vegetables . . . . . . . . . . . . . . . . . . . . . . . . . . . . . . 205
Salads . . . . . . . . . . . . . . . . . . . . . . . . . . . . . . . . . . 227
Soups . . . . . . . . . . . . . . . . . . . . . . . . . . . . . . . . . . 259
Sauces & Relishes . . . . . . . . . . . . . . . . . . . . . . . . . 273
Breads . . . . . . . . . . . . . . . . . . . . . . . . . . . . . . . . . . 291
Desserts & Sweets . . . . . . . . . . . . . . . . . . . . . . . . . 319
About United's Chefs . . . . . . . . . . . . . . . . . . . . . . . 383
Recipe Index . . . . . . . . . . . . . . . . . . . . . . . . . . . . . 393

# PREFACE

TWO YEARS AGO, Seattle employees of United Airlines formed a guild to support the Children's Orthopedic Hospital and Medical Center in Seattle, Washington. Like other children's hospitals located throughout the country, Children's is a non-profit operation which depends largely on private donations and the fund raising activities of organizations such as ours to stay open and continue its care and research. Many children visit the medical center because of crippling or hard-to-treat diseases, and without this facility, and its generous free-care program, medical treatment for them would not be possible.

Our desire in establishing the guild was to help make it possible for children to receive the medical care they need. All the proceeds from this cookbook, one of our fund raising projects, will be donated to that end.

Included are over 650 of our employees' favorite recipes, some of which come from the kitchens of United's senior executives and management personnel. Additionally, over 150 of the recipes were contributed by executive chefs from each of United's kitchens nationwide. The extensive backgrounds of these men, most of whom are European-born and educated, are outlined in the back of the book. Many of them have served royalty, heads of state, presidents and famous entertainment personalities. Many have worked in world-famous hotels and resorts in Europe and in well-known American dining rooms such as those in the Westin, Sheraton and Hilton hotels. The majority of their recipes presented here are from their own personal collections.

Each recipe was lovingly donated to provide you with culinary enjoyment, and to provide children with good health.

*Susan Warren*
*Chairman*
*Cookbook Committee*

# ACKNOWLEDGMENTS

A year and a half has passed from the time we decided to put this cookbook together until it finally went to press. That moment would not have arrived without the help and dedication of a number of people who either worked on, or closely with, the Cookbook Committee.

First, my heartfelt thank you to all the employees who responded to our request for favorite recipes. We received over 1400, which made the selection of recipes the most difficult decision about the book. I regret that we were unable to publish them all but wish to thank each and every one of you for your support.

Each of our chefs deserves special mention for giving away his culinary secrets. I would especially like to thank John Wolfsheimer in San Francisco who always found time to talk to me and Bruno Good in Seattle who helped in many extra ways.

Several more people come to mind who deserve special thanks, for without them this book would not have been possible: Sheldon Best, Regional Vice President, for his full support; Bill Fudge, Reservations Support Manager, for his writing expertise, advice and constant faith in us; and a special thank you to Jack Gamble of our Public Relations Department in Chicago, for financial and intellectual contributions.

Many hours were spent in transcribing, typing and proofreading the recipes submitted. Those long hours at the typewriter, burning the midnight oil, were donated by Karen Fudge, Arlene McEachern and Kathy Ideta.

A special recognition to Eastman Kodak for their generous contribution toward our publicity.

Last, but not least, thanks to Cookbook Committee members Randy Greseth and Kathy Birkner, as well as to Dan Smith, and everyone else who believed in and supported us. The final outcome has been well worth it all.

# APPETIZERS

### Bruno's Cheese Fondue

1 clove garlic
1 ½ cups dry white wine
1 lb. imported Swiss cheese,
    grated
1 tsp. cornstarch

1 Tbsp. kirsch, cognac or
    brandy
Pinch of nutmeg
2 loaves hard-crust French
    bread, cut into
    bite-size pieces

Rub an enameled metal casserole with the garlic. Pour in the wine and set over low heat. Heat until air bubbles rise to the surface; add the cheese by handfuls, stirring constantly with a wooden spoon until the cheese melts. Dissolve the cornstarch in the kirsch, add to the cheese mixture and stir again for 2 to 3 minutes. Season with the nutmeg. Place the casserole on the table on a hot plate or over an alcohol burner to keep the mixture faintly bubbling. Spear the bread on forks and dip into the cheese.

Serves 6.

Bruno Good
Executive Chef
Seattle Food Services

### Rhinelander Cheese Fondue

1 cup sauterne or chablis
1 Tbsp. butter
1 tsp. garlic powder
¼ tsp. MSG
Dash of white pepper

Dash of nutmeg
5 cups grated processed
    (American) Swiss cheese
½ loaf rye bread, cubed
½ loaf French bread, cubed

Combine the wine, butter and seasonings with 2 cups water and bring to a boil. Add the cheese and place in a double boiler over heated water. Stir thoroughly until blended into a smooth, thick sauce. Transfer to a fondue pot and serve with the bread cubes.

Fran Christensen
Reservations

## Voilà la Fondue de la Gruyère

*As you might expect from a Swiss chef, Willi Niederer's choice for a quick and easily prepared party treat is bubbling fondue. He recommends serving it with a good bottle of chilled white wine such as Emerald Dry, Fendant or Johannisberg Riesling. And for after dinner, a little Swiss schnapps!*

*3 cups dry white wine*
*2 cloves garlic, finely chopped*
*2 lbs. imported Swiss Gruyère,*
  *grated*

*1 Tbsp. cornstarch*
*¼ cup plus 2 Tbsp. kirsch*
*Fresh pepper*
*French bread, cut into 1" cubes*

In a fondue pot, heat the wine just to the boiling point, but do not boil. Add the garlic, then slowly add the cheese, stirring constantly with a wooden spoon until the cheese is creamy and barely simmering. Blend the cornstarch with the kirsch and slowly add to the fondue. Season with fresh pepper and stir until the mixture bubbles. Serve with the French bread. Keep the fondue hot but not simmering; if it becomes thick, add a little more wine.

*Serves 6.*

Willi Niederer
Executive Chef
San Francisco Food Services

## Crab Fondue

*1 (8-oz.) pkg. cream cheese,*
  *softened*
*2 Tbsp. finely diced onion*
*Dash of pepper*

*1 (7-oz.) can or 1 cup fresh*
  *crab, drained and flaked*
*1 Tbsp. milk*
*½ tsp. creamed horseradish*
*⅓ cup slivered almonds*

Stir the cream cheese and add the remaining ingredients except the almonds. Bake at 375° for 15 minutes. Sprinkle the almonds on top.

Julie Jacobson
Reservations

## Shrimp Fondue

1 can shrimp soup, undiluted
1 (8-oz.) pkg. cream cheese

1 small can shrimp
French bread

Combine the soup and cheese in a pan and heat until melted. Add the shrimp and heat through. Transfer to a fondue pot. Serve with French bread, cut in chunks.

Sally Keenan
Inflight Services

## Cheese Fondue

1 large clove garlic
2 cups Neuchâtel or other dry
   white wine
1 lb. 2 oz. Jarlsberg, Gruyère or
   natural Swiss cheese (use a
   half-and-half combination
   of 2 cheeses)
¼ cup flour

¼ tsp. salt
¼ tsp. pepper
¼ tsp. nutmeg
¼ cup kirsch

1 loaf sourdough or other
   hard-crust white bread,
   cut into 1" cubes

Rub an earthenware fondue dish generously with the garlic clove; let stand for 10 minutes. Add the wine and heat slowly over the fondue dish burner. Shred the cheeses and mix lightly with the flour. When the wine bubbles and the bubbles rise to the surface (do not boil), add the cheese mixture a handful at a time, stirring with a wooden spoon or paddle until each handful melts. Continue until all the cheese is added. Add the seasonings and kirsch; stir well. Adjust the burner flame to low, but keep the fondue slowly bubbling. Provide fondue forks for dipping the bread and serve.

Note: If the fondue becomes too thick, add a little hot wine.

Serves 4.

Jerry F. Boyer
Executive Chef
Newark Food Services

## Avocado Dip

1 (8-oz.) pkg. Philadelphia
   cream cheese
1 pint sour cream
3 Tbsp. mayonnaise
⅓ to ½ cup avocado puree

1 tsp. chopped chives
Tabasco sauce to taste
Worcestershire sauce to taste
Salt and pepper to taste

Cut the cheese into chunks, place in a mixing bowl and beat at low speed until creamy. Add the remaining ingredients and mix again for 5 minutes. Place in the refrigerator for 1 hour and then serve with your favorite chips or garden fresh vegetables such as cucumbers, carrots, celery, zucchini and cauliflower.

George J. Mendreshora
Executive Chef
Honolulu Food Services

## Hot Pepper Bean Dip

1 (3-oz.) pkg. cream cheese
1 to 4 canned hot chili
   peppers, chopped
¼ tsp. salt

1 tsp. Worcestershire sauce
¼ tsp. garlic salt
1 (16-oz.) can chili beans

Bring the cream cheese to room temperature. Remove the stems from the chili peppers and rinse. Combine the cheese, peppers, salt, Worcestershire sauce and garlic salt in a blender and whirl until smooth. Drain the beans, discarding the liquid, turn into blender and whirl until well mixed. Serve with corn chips.

Dottie Martin

## Hot Dip

4 (8-oz.) pkg. cream cheese
1 Tbsp. milk
1 Tbsp. plus 1 tsp. minced onion
1 cup sour cream
1 tsp. garlic powder

4 oz. chipped beef,
   finely scissored
1 cup chopped pecans
¼ cup butter
1 tsp. salt

In a blender or mixer, combine all the ingredients except the pecans, butter and salt. Place the mixture in a 9" x 13" pan. Sauté the pecans in the butter and salt. Pour over the mixture and bake at 350° for 25 to 30 minutes. Serve with chips.

*This may be refrigerated until ready to bake.*

Sue Crane
Reservations

## Bean Dip

1 cup cooked red beans
1 green chili, seeded and
   cut up
1 tsp. chili powder

½ tsp. cumin
1 to 2 Tbsp. tomato sauce
2 Tbsp. raw onion
¼ cup cubed sharp cheese

Put all the ingredients in a blender except the cheese. Blend until mushy, add the cheese. Cook over low heat until smooth. Serve with Doritos.

Janis Sisley
Reservations

## Crab Dip #1

1 (8-oz.) pkg. cream cheese
1 to 3 Tbsp. heavy cream
½ tsp. creamed horseradish
2 Tbsp. finely chopped onion

¼ tsp. salt
Dash of pepper
½ lb. Dungeness crab
⅓ cup sliced almonds

Cream together the cream cheese and cream. Stir in the remaining ingredients except the almonds. Pour into a casserole dish and bake at 375° for 15 minutes or until bubbly. Transfer to a chafing dish. Just before serving, sprinkle with the almonds.

*Note: For a different taste, add 1 tsp. Worcestershire sauce and a shake of hot sauce.*

John & Sid Reed
Fran Christensen
Karen Bixler
Reservations

## Crab Dip #2

1 (6½-oz.) can crabmeat
1 cup mayonnaise
1 cup cocktail sauce

Worcestershire sauce
Garlic salt
Tabasco sauce

Drain the crabmeat and combine with the mayonnaise and cocktail sauce. Add the Worcestershire sauce, garlic salt and Tabasco sauce to taste.

Linda Stevens
Reservations

## Crab Dip #3

1 (8-oz.) pkg. cream cheese,
  softened
¼ can tomato soup
1 cup mayonnaise
1 tsp. horseradish
1 tsp. lemon juice

2 to 3 tsp. Worcestershire
  sauce
1 (6½-oz.) can crabmeat
Salt and pepper
MSG

Combine the first 6 ingredients. Stir in the crabmeat. Add the salt, pepper and MSG to taste.

Janis Sisley
Reservations

## Shrimp Dip

1 (8-oz.) pkg. cream cheese
¼ cup Kraft creamy-style
  French dressing
¼ cup catsup
1 tsp. instant onion

1 can shrimp, drained
Dash of Worcestershire sauce
Dash of Tabasco sauce
Dash of lemon juice

Mix all the ingredients together and chill well before serving.

John & Sid Reed
Reservations

## Crab Guacamole

2 avocados
3 Tbsp. lemon juice
1 cup cooked crabmeat
2 Tbsp. minced hot green
   chilies
1 clove garlic, minced

Salt and pepper to taste
2 Tbsp. minced green onion
½ tomato, peeled, seeded
   and chopped
½ tsp. ground coriander seed

Cut the avocados in half, remove the pits and scoop out the pulp with a spoon. Place in a bowl and mash with a fork. Blend in the remaining ingredients. Serve as a dip with tortilla chips or spoon into the avocado shells and serve as a 1st course.

Jan Rowley
Reservations

## Taco Dip

2 large tomatoes, chopped
4½ oz. black olives, chopped
4 mild pickled peppers,
   chopped

¼ onion, chopped
1 tsp. garlic salt
1 tsp. chili powder
3 Tbsp. oil

Mix all the ingredients together and marinate overnight. Serve with Doritos.

Karen Fudge
Regional Sales

## Fiesta Dip

1 can enchilada dip
1 can guacamole dip
Chopped red onions
Chopped tomatoes

1 can chopped green chilies
1¼ cups grated cheddar
   cheese

Layer all the ingredients on a serving plate and serve with Doritos or king-size Fritos.

James M. Guyette
Vice President-Personnel

## Pineapple Cheese Spread

2 (8-oz.) pkg. cream cheese,
   softened
1 (8½-oz.) can crushed
   pineapple, drained

1 cup chopped pecans
½ cup chopped green peppers
2 Tbsp. chopped green onion
1 tsp. Lawry's seasoned salt

Mix together all the ingredients. Pack in a crock and refrigerate or roll the mixture in a ball and cover with more pecans. Serve with crackers.

*Makes 5 cups.*

Sue McCaffray
Reservations

## Liverwurst and Beer Dip

1 lb. liverwurst
1 (8-oz.) pkg. cream cheese
1 Tbsp. Worcestershire sauce

½ cup sour cream
½ cup beer (approx.)

Begin with all the ingredients at room temperature. Mash the liverwurst. Stir in the cream cheese, Worcestershire sauce and sour cream. Blend well until smooth. Gradually add the beer until the mixture is smooth and of dip consistency. Serve with party rye slices, crackers or raw vegetables.

Ken Christensen
Operations Planning

## Creamy Chutney and Nut Spread

2 (8-oz.) pkg. cream cheese,
   softened
½ cup chutney

½ cup chopped toasted
   almonds
1 tsp. curry powder
½ tsp. dry mustard

Mix all the ingredients together well. Pack in a crock or deep dish. Chill. Serve with crackers or use to stuff celery.

Lillian Warren

## Chili Con Queso

1 large onion
1 Tbsp. butter
2 (16-oz.) cans peeled whole
  tomatoes
1 tsp. cumin powder
1 tsp. oregano

3 small cans Ortega chili
  peppers, finely chopped
1 lb. sharp cheddar cheese,
  grated
1 lb. Velveeta cheese, grated

Finely chop the onion and sauté in the butter in a large saucepan. Add the tomatoes, cumin, oregano and chili peppers. Cook, stirring frequently, over medium heat for 1 hour or more until the mixture thickens. Gradually stir in the cheeses and cook until melted. Serve with corn chips or Doritos.

Susan Warren
Reservations

## Shrimp Pâté

½ cup butter
½ lb. raw shrimp
Pinch of ground mace
Dash of Tabasco sauce

Salt
Freshly ground black pepper
2 Tbsp. sherry

Melt half the butter in a skillet and sauté the shrimp in it for 2 to 3 minutes, depending on size, until they are cooked and turn bright pink. Halfway through cooking, sprinkle the shrimp with the mace, Tabasco sauce, salt and plenty of pepper. When cooked, drain the shrimp, reserving the butter, peel and finely chop them or work a few at a time in a blender. Combine with the reserved butter and the sherry. Adjust the seasoning and pack into a dish or crock. Melt the remaining butter. Pour it over the pâté to seal and chill. Serve with hot toast or crackers.

*The pâté will keep, covered, in the refrigerator for 1 to 2 days.*

Virginia Hansen

## Quick Chicken Pâté

2 slices bacon, diced
4 oz. liver sausage or
   Braunschweiger
1 cup finely chopped, cooked
   chicken

1 clove garlic, crushed
1 tsp. finely chopped
   parsley
1 tsp. finely chopped chives
Salt and pepper to taste

Fry the bacon for about 5 minutes over medium heat. Pour off the fat and blend it with the liver sausage. Add the bacon, chicken, garlic, parsley and chives. Season with salt and pepper. Blend well. Pack into a dish, cover and chill for at least 30 minutes. Serve on warm toast squares.

## Lobster Pâté

1 (8-oz.) pkg. cream cheese,
   softened
¼ cup dry white wine
½ tsp. onion salt

½ tsp. seasoned salt
⅛ tsp. dill weed
1 ½ cups finely chopped
   lobster meat

Beat the cheese and wine until smooth and creamy. Blend in the salts and dill weed. Add the lobster. Cover and refrigerate for several hours or overnight. Serve with crackers.

Jackie Partlow
Reservations

## Cheese Balls

½ cup butter or margarine
1 cup flour
1 cup grated cheddar cheese

1 cup Rice Krispies
1 tsp. baking powder
Dash of Tabasco sauce

Mix all the ingredients together. Make into small balls. Flatten with a fork. Place on a baking sheet and bake at 350° for 10 minutes. Serve hot or cold.

Sally Keenan
Inflight Services

## Cheese Delights

12 slices white bread
1 cup butter
1 cup cream cheese

2 cups cottage cheese
½ cup grated Romano cheese
3 eggs

Cut the corners off the bread. Roll each slice thin with a rolling pin. Melt the butter and dip each slice of bread in the butter. Press each slice into a 12-cup muffin tin. Cream together the cheeses and eggs. Fill each bread cup about three-fourths full. Bake at 375° for 25 to 30 minutes or until golden brown. Serve hot.

*If you have any filling left, roll out more bread and fill another muffin tin.*

Fran Christensen
Reservations

## Hot Ryes

1 cup finely grated Swiss
   cheese
¼ cup cooked, crumbled
   bacon
1 (4½-oz.) can chopped
   ripe olives

¼ cup minced green onions
   or chives
1 tsp. Worcestershire sauce
¼ cup mayonnaise
1 loaf party rye or
   pumpernickel bread

Mix together all the ingredients except the bread. Spread on the bread and bake at 375° for 10 to 15 minutes or until browned.

*These may be frozen after baking and later reheated.*

*Makes 36 hors d'oeuvres.*

Sue McCaffray
Reservations

☞ *Cheese grates more readily if chilled first.*

## French Bread with a Twist

1½ cups mayonnaise
¾ cup finely chopped onions
¾ cup Parmesan cheese

1 Tbsp. Worcestershire sauce
1 loaf French bread

Mix all the ingredients together except the bread. Cut the bread loaf in half lengthwise, spread the mixture over the bread and warm at 350° until the bread is heated through.

Lillian Warren

## Pepper Jelly Canapés

1 cup diced green peppers
2½ Tbsp. Tabasco sauce
1½ cups cider vinegar
6½ cups sugar

3 oz. Certo
Cream cheese
Biscuits or wafers
Watercress sprigs

Place the green peppers, Tabasco sauce and cider vinegar in a food processor with a metal blade and blend for a few seconds. In a 6-quart, heavy-duty saucepan, combine with the sugar and bring to a rolling boil that cannot be stirred down over high heat. Remove from the heat for 10 minutes, skim off the froth, stir in the Certo and seal in 6 to 7 half-pint, heated, sterilized jars. To serve, form a border of cream cheese on your favorite biscuit or wafer. Fill the center with a small amount of pepper jelly and garnish with a sprig of watercress.

Jerry F. Boyer
Executive Chef
Newark Food Services

## Flintstone Bread

2 cups sour cream
2 cups mayonnaise
2 Tbsp. parsley
2 Tbsp. diced onion
1 Tbsp. Beau Monde
    seasoning

3 pkg. chipped beef
1 loaf Flintstone bread
    (French bread baked in
    a can)

Combine the first 6 ingredients. Slice off the top of the bread and hollow out the inside to make a "bucket." Spoon the sour cream mixture into the bread and serve. To eat, tear off pieces of the "bucket" and dip in the sour cream mixture.

Janet Vitcovich
Reservations

## Egg Rolls

1 cup finely chopped shrimp
½ lb. pork, very finely chopped
2 tsp. salt
1 tsp. MSG
1 large pinch of black pepper
1 tsp. sesame seed oil
2 egg whites

1 Tbsp. cornstarch
¾ cup flour
2 heaping Tbsp. baking powder
Oil
5 whole eggs
2 egg yolks

Combine the shrimp, pork, 1 scant tsp. salt, MSG, pepper and sesame seed oil. Stir the egg whites into it, add the cornstarch and mix well; set aside. Combine the flour, baking powder, 1 tsp. salt and 1⅛ cups water; set aside. Heat a small amount of oil in a frying pan over medium heat. Meanwhile, combine in a bowl the whole eggs and egg yolks and stir thoroughly. When the oil is hot, reduce the heat and pour ¼ of the egg mixture into the frying pan; tilt the pan until the egg thoroughly covers the bottom. When the egg solidifies, flip over and cook for a few more seconds. Set the cooked egg on a platter and cook the remainder of the eggs in fourths. Spread ¼ of the shrimp filling on each cooked egg and roll up to resemble a jelly roll. Set each of these egg rolls in a separate steamer. Pour 1" of water into a wok. Cover and let heat until it steams, then stack the steamers on top of each other and set in a wok; steam for 7 minutes. Remove and cut the egg rolls diagonally into ½" slices. Dip the slices in the flour batter and drop in a 350° fryer; cook for 3 minutes or until golden brown. Drain and serve hot.

Susan Warren
Reservations

## Smoked Eggs

¼ cup soy sauce
1 tsp. sugar
½ tsp. salt

½ tsp. liquid smoke
4 eggs, hard-cooked
and shelled

Combine the soy sauce, sugar, salt, liquid smoke and ¼ cup water in a small bowl. Pour over the eggs and marinate at room temperature for 2 to 3 hours or more, turning the eggs frequently. Drain. Cut into wedges and serve.

Geri Shippee
Reservations

## Fillings for Stuffed Eggs

Mix any of the following with hard-cooked egg yolks and spoon into the halved whites.

*Crisply fried, crumbled bacon and chopped chutney.*

*Chopped, cooked lobster meat, Dijon mustard and capers (optional).*

*Black caviar, fresh lemon juice and grated onion.*

*Chopped ham, mustard, parsley, fresh dill and freshly grated lemon rind.*

*Minced, smoked salmon, grated onion, capers, lemon juice, mayonnaise and freshly ground pepper.*

*Sour cream, dill weed, mashed anchovies, chopped chives, parsley, salt and pepper.*

*Minced, cooked ham, minced sweet pickles, mayonnaise, Dijon mustard, salt and pepper.*

Sue McCaffray
Reservations

## Scotch Eggs

6 eggs, hard-cooked and
    well chilled
1 lb. bulk sausage meat
2 Tbsp. finely chopped parsley
½ tsp. ground sage
¼ tsp. pepper

¼ cup flour
2 eggs, beaten
½ to ¾ cup packaged bread
    crumbs
Vegetable oil

Peel the hard-cooked eggs. Combine the sausage, parsley, sage and pepper in a large mixing bowl, mixing well. Divide the meat mixture into 6 equal portions. Press the meat mixture around the eggs with your hands, keeping an oval shape. Sprinkle the flour over the eggs, coating lightly on all the sides. Dip into the eggs and then roll in the bread crumbs. Heat the vegetable oil to 350° in a deep fryer or deep, heavy saucepan. Cook, one egg at a time, for about 4 to 5 minutes or until well browned. Drain on paper toweling, cool and refrigerate.

Annemarie Fleming
Reservations

## Deviled Sweet and Sour Eggs

6 eggs, hard-cooked
¼ tsp. salt
⅛ tsp. pepper
¼ tsp. dry mustard

2 Tbsp. sugar
2 Tbsp. vinegar
1 Tbsp. mayonnaise

Halve the eggs and set the whites aside. Add the remaining ingredients to the yolks and mash together. Spoon into the halved whites.

Geri Shippee
Reservations

## Sweet-Sour Sausage Balls

4 lbs. bulk pork sausage
4 eggs, slightly beaten
1½ cups soft bread crumbs
3 cups catsup

¾ cup firmly packed
    brown sugar
½ cup white wine vinegar
½ cup soy sauce

Mix together the sausage, eggs and bread crumbs. Using the palms of your hands, shape the mixture into balls. Bake at 500° on a rimmed baking sheet for 7 minutes or until browned. Combine the catsup, brown sugar, vinegar and soy sauce. Set in a saucepan and heat through. Put the sausage balls in a pot or casserole. Pour the sauce over the meatballs. Heat through. Serve hot.

*Refrigerate or freeze the sausage balls in the sauce.*

Beth DiPasquale
Help Desk

## Marinated Bacon Wraps

*1 (8-oz.) can water chestnuts*      *½ lb. lean bacon*
*1 cup soy sauce*

Cut the water chestnuts in half and marinate in the soy sauce for 1 hour. Cut the raw bacon strips into thirds. Wrap a bacon strip around each water chestnut and secure with a toothpick. Place on a cookie sheet and broil until the bacon is done, about 4 to 5 minutes. Serve hot or cold.

Susan Warren
Reservations

## Bacon Roll-Ups

*1 (8-oz.) pkg. crescent rolls*      *½ lb. bacon, cooked and*
*½ cup sour cream*           *crumbled*
*½ tsp. onion salt*

Separate the rolls. Combine the remaining ingredients and spread on the rolls. Cut each into thirds and roll up. Bake at 375° for 12 to 15 minutes.

*Makes 24 roll-ups.*

Sue McCaffray
Reservations

## Scottish Sausage Rolls

8 oz. flaky or shortcrust pastry          1 egg, beaten (or milk)
¾ lb. sausage meat

Roll the pastry out to ⅛" thickness on a floured board and cut into rectangles. Put a roll of sausage meat in each pastry rectangle; roll up. Moisten the edges of the pastry with water to seal. Make 3 cuts on the top of each roll. Place on a baking tray and brush with the egg. Bake at 425° on the top rack for 20 minutes.

Great for snacks or parties.

Makes 8 to 10 rolls.

Margaret Hamilton
Inflight Services

## Chicken Livers with Mushrooms

½ cup butter                          ¾ lb. button mushrooms
5 shallots, sliced                     1 Tbsp. flour
1½ lbs. chicken livers, halved         ½ cup Madeira wine
Salt and pepper                        2 Tbsp. chopped parsley

In a large skillet over medium heat, melt half the butter. Add the shallots and sauté until golden. Add the livers. Sauté until well browned, stirring constantly. Add salt and pepper to taste. Remove the shallots and livers, wipe the skillet with a paper towel. Return the skillet to high heat. Add the remaining butter and sauté the mushrooms quickly, stirring constantly. When the mushrooms turn slightly brown, reduce the heat, sprinkle the flour over the mushrooms, stirring constantly, and add the wine. Cook for a few minutes. Return the shallots and livers to the pan and blend thoroughly. Check the seasoning. To serve, place in a chafing dish or serving bowl and sprinkle the parsley over.

Kathy Pickering
Reservations

### Stuffed Chicken Wings

12 chicken wings
½ lb. fresh ground pork
½ tsp. salt
1 to 2 tsp. soy sauce
½ tsp. MSG

1 (4-oz.) can water chestnuts,
   finely chopped
3 to 4 bamboo shoots,
   finely chopped

Prepare the chicken wings by cutting off the wing tip at the joint. Discard the wing tip and remove the smaller bone of the second joint by snapping off, twisting and loosening the tendon and tissue. Make a pocket by loosening the skin from the meat in the section from which the bone was removed. Put the pork in a skillet and cook slowly. Add the salt, soy sauce and MSG and remove from the heat. Add the water chestnuts and bamboo shoots, mixing thoroughly. Stuff the wings, using about 2 Tbsp. pork mixture per wing. The stuffed wing should assume a triangular shape. Salt the wings lightly and place in a baking pan. Bake at 325° to 350° for 30 to 40 minutes, basting occasionally with additional soy sauce to glaze the wings.

*This is a tedious recipe, but the results are very rewarding.*

Richard D. Tabery
Senior Vice President
Maintenance Operations Division

### Chinese Barbequed Spareribs

1 side pork spareribs                    ¼ can Hoisin sauce

Place the two half-slabs of ribs on a roasting rack set in a baking pan. Coat the ribs generously with the Hoisin sauce; place in the oven and bake at 375° for 2 hours. Slice between each rib with a sharp knife. Serve as an hors d'oeuvre or as a main dish.

*Ask your butcher to cut the entire slab in half cross-wise to the bones. Hoisin sauce is available in the Asian grocery sections of some supermarkets or in any Asian grocery store.*

Kathy Fong
Manager
Reservations Sales

### Baked Oysters Maxine

1 Tbsp. chopped dry shallots
Butter
1 lb. crabmeat, in chunks
2 Tbsp. chopped ripe olives
4 cups **Mornay Sauce** (see
    index)

1 heaping Tbsp. Dijon mustard
Salt
Rock salt
Oysters on the half-shell
White wine
Grated Parmesan cheese

Sauté the shallots in butter. Add the crabmeat, olives, **Mornay Sauce** and mustard. Sprinkle with salt to taste. Remove from the heat and keep warm. Fill a small baking dish with the rock salt and heat under the broiler. Place the open-shell oysters on the rock salt, sprinkle with wine and place under the broiler. Poach the oysters for 3 to 4 minutes. Remove and cover each oyster with the crab mixture, then sprinkle with the Parmesan cheese. Return to the broiler until browned. Serve at once.

Pamela Shamsid-Deen
Reservations

### Crab Mousse

1 (6-oz.) pkg. cream cheese
1 cup mayonnaise
1 cup finely chopped celery
6 green onions, chopped
1 pkg. Knox gelatin
2 tsp. boiling water

¾ (6-oz.) can cream of
    mushroom soup
1 (6-oz.) can crab, drained
Lettuce leaves
Parsley

Mix the cream cheese, mayonnaise, celery and onions together. Dissolve the gelatin in the boiling water. Heat the soup to boiling, add the gelatin and remove from the heat. Slowly stir the soup into the cream cheese mixture, then add the crab. Stir well. Pour into a mold greased with vegetable oil and chill until set. Turn out on a bed of lettuce leaves, garnish with parsley. Serve with crackers or on toast.

Gail Workman
Reservations

## Mrs. Ritchie's Hot Crab Soufflé

8 slices white bread
2 cups crab or shrimp
½ cup mayonnaise
1 onion, chopped
½ to 1 green pepper, chopped
1 cup chopped celery

4 eggs
3 cups milk
1 can cream of mushroom
  soup
Grated cheese
Paprika

Dice half the bread and put in the bottom of a baking dish. Mix the crab, mayonnaise, onion, green pepper and celery together. Spread over the diced bread. Trim the crusts from the remaining bread and place the slices over the crab mixture; mix the eggs and milk together and pour over the crab. Refrigerate overnight. Bake at 325° for 15 minutes. Remove from the oven and spoon the soup over the top. Cover with grated cheese and paprika. Bake at 325° for 1 hour more. Good served with sliced, baked ham, a tossed green salad and garlic bread.

Serves 12.

Lou Gardiner
Reservations

## Crab Crunchies

1 (6½-oz.) can snow crab
1 (3-oz.) pkg. cream cheese,
  softened
½ tsp. garlic powder

½ (8-oz.) pkg. won ton
  wrappers
Oil for frying

Mix together the crab, cheese and garlic powder. Place ½ to 1 tsp. of the mixture in the center of each wrapper. Dampen the 2 adjacent edges with water. Fold in half diagonally to form a triangle. Press tightly along the edges to seal. Deep fry to a golden brown. Serve at once with Chinese hot mustard and toasted sesame seeds.

Yvonne Erickson
Reservations

### Hot Crab Appetizer

1 (8-oz.) pkg. cream cheese
¾ to 1 cup flaked crabmeat
2 Tbsp. instant minced onion
1 Tbsp. milk

½ tsp. prepared horseradish
¼ tsp. salt
Dash of pepper
Paprika

Combine all the ingredients except the paprika. Mix until well blended. Spoon the mixture into an ungreased, 8", glass pie pan. Sprinkle paprika on top. Bake at 350° for 15 minutes. Serve with crackers.

John & Sid Reed
Reservations

### Nordic Shrimp Delights

¼ cup butter or margarine
1 lb. medium shrimp, shelled
and deveined
1½ cups sliced mushrooms
½ cup sliced green onions
2 Tbsp. chopped parsley

½ tsp. salt
¼ tsp. pepper
¼ tsp. paprika
1½ cups shredded Jarlsberg
cheese

In a large skillet, melt the butter. Add and sauté the shrimp, mushrooms, onions, parsley, salt, pepper and paprika over medium-high heat for about 3 minutes or until the shrimp are tender and pink. Spoon the shrimp mixture into 6 greased, shell-shaped ramekins or small baking dishes. Sprinkle the cheese over, covering the shrimp mixture entirely. Place on a baking sheet and broil 4" from the heat for 7 to 8 minutes or until the cheese is golden. Serve immediately.

Serves 6.

Ray Stokes
Retired Supervisor
Reservations

## Smoked Herring with Horseradish Cream

4 smoked herring filets
¼ cup heavy cream
2 to 3 tsp. lemon juice
2 tsp. grated horseradish

1 tsp. tarragon vinegar
Salt and pepper
½ cucumber
Lemon slices

If the herring is heavily smoked, soak it in water for several hours. Drain, dry, remove the skin and break into bite-size pieces. Blend the heavy cream with the lemon juice, horseradish and vinegar and season to taste with salt and pepper. Cut the unpeeled cucumber into thin slices and use to line individual, shallow serving dishes. Mix the herring carefully into the dressing and pile into the center of the cucumber slices. Top each portion with a lemon slice. Serve with buttered whole wheat bread or melba toast.

Pamela Shamsid-Deen
Reservations

## Salmon Cheese Appetizer

1 (7¾-oz.) can salmon,
    drained
1 (8-oz.) pkg. cream cheese,
    at room temperature
¼ cup crumbled blue cheese
1 Tbsp. grated onion
2 Tbsp. chopped parsley

1 Tbsp. lemon juice
½ tsp. anchovy paste
    (optional)
¼ tsp. pepper
1 tsp. Worcestershire sauce
Parsley

Mix all the ingredients together until smooth. If desired, first rub the mixing bowl with a cut clove of garlic. Mold the mixture in a small bowl lined with plastic wrap. Chill for 2 to 3 hours. Unmold to serve and garnish with parsley. Serve with crackers, toast rounds or thinly sliced rye bread.

*Makes about 2 cups.*

Kay Lund
Director of Consumer Affairs
Chicago, Illinois

### Salmon Fritters

Vegetable oil
1 (16-oz.) can salmon, drained
   and flaked
1 cup buttermilk baking mix
1 egg
½ tsp. salt

1 tsp. dill weed
1 Tbsp. lemon juice
2 Tbsp. sliced green onion
   with tops
2 Tbsp. finely chopped
   green pepper

Pour the oil into a skillet or large saucepan to a depth of 2" to 3". Heat to 365° on a deep fat frying thermometer. Combine all the remaining ingredients in a large bowl. Drop by tablespoons, a few at a time, into the hot fat. Fry, turning once, until golden brown, about 2 minutes. Drain.

*Makes about 24 fritters.*

Annemarie Fleming
Reservations

### Salmon Party Mound

2 cups canned salmon
1 (8-oz.) pkg. cream cheese
1 Tbsp. lemon juice
2 tsp. grated dried onion
1 tsp. horseradish

¼ tsp. salt
¼ tsp. liquid smoke
½ cup chopped pecans
3 Tbsp. snipped parsley

Drain and flake the salmon. Mix together well the cream cheese, lemon juice, onion, horseradish, salt and liquid smoke; add the salmon and chill. Combine the pecans and parsley and shape into a ball. Roll the salmon in the nut mixture and chill again. Serve with Triscuits or other crackers.

Pearl Yamamoto
Supervisor

### Poor Man's Smoked Salmon

1 (16-oz.) can salmon
1 (8-oz.) pkg. cream cheese
1 Tbsp. lemon juice
1 Tbsp. minced onion

1 tsp. horseradish
¼ tsp. commercial smoked
   flavoring
¼ tsp. salt

Drain the salmon. Combine with the remaining ingredients and chill for 3 hours. Divide into 2 portions and roll into logs. Serve on toast or crackers or with corn chips and potato chips.

*Note: For extra flavor, roll the salmon logs in nuts.*

Nola Sears
Reservations

## Salmon Sandwich Loaf

2 (16-oz.) cans salmon
2 cups chopped celery
1 cup chopped walnuts
¾ cup mayonnaise
1 loaf French bread

3 dill pickles, sliced
   lengthwise
1 red onion, sliced into rings
Spinach leaves

Drain and flake the salmon. Combine with the celery, walnuts and mayonnaise. Chill. Cut the bread in half lengthwise and remove a small amount of the center. Spread each half with the salmon mixture. Cut each half into 12 slices crosswise. Serve with the pickle slices, onion rings and spinach leaves.

*Makes approximately 12 servings.*

## Salmon Dreams

16 slices white bread
¼ cup butter
1 (7¾-oz.) can salmon
2 oz. cream cheese
1 Tbsp. grated cheddar cheese

Salt and pepper
1 egg
1 Tbsp. milk
Paprika
Fat or oil for frying

Cut 16 circles from the bread with a 2" biscuit cutter. Butter each circle. Drain the salmon, remove the skin and bones. Mash with a fork, stir in the cheeses. Season with salt and pepper. Spread on half the circles. Cover with the other half and press firmly together. Beat the egg and milk. Season with salt, pepper and paprika to taste. Dip the sandwiches in the mixture and sauté both sides in hot fat or oil until crisp and golden. Drain on crumpled paper towels. Serve at once.

## Escargot

36 canned snails
36 snail shells
1 cup butter
3 Tbsp. chopped parsley

2 Tbsp. chopped shallots
1 clove garlic, crushed
¼ tsp. salt
Ground pepper to taste

Wash and dry the snails and shells. Cream the butter. Add the parsley, shallots, garlic, salt and pepper. Mix well. Insert the snails in the shells as far as possible. Fill most of the shells with the butter mixture. Place in a dish with the open side up. Put the remaining butter mixture in the dish. Bake at 450° for 10 minutes.

Fran Christensen
Reservations

## Artichoke Squares

3 (6-oz.) jars marinated
   artichoke hearts
1 clove garlic, crushed
½ cup chopped onions
4 eggs
¼ cup bread crumbs

½ lb. sharp cheddar cheese,
   grated
2 Tbsp. minced fresh parsley
½ tsp. salt
⅛ tsp. oregano
⅛ tsp. pepper
⅛ tsp. Tabasco sauce

Drain the oil from 1 jar artichoke hearts into a 12" skillet. Sauté the garlic and onions in the oil over medium heat for 5 minutes. Set aside. Drain the oil from the remaining artichoke hearts. Chop the hearts finely and set aside. In a medium bowl, beat the eggs until foamy. Blend in the bread crumbs, cheese, parsley and seasonings. Add the chopped artichokes and stir. Add the onions and garlic. Mix and spoon into a 9" x 9" pan. Bake at 325° for 30 minutes. Cool and cut into 2" squares. Heat again for 10 to 12 minutes before serving.

*Reserve the oil from the 2nd jar of artichoke hearts and use as a dressing for tossed green salad.*

Cindy Hibbert
Apollo Systems

## Mrs. Di's Antipasto

2 lbs. cauliflower, broken into
   florets
1 lb. French carrots, cut into
   chunks (optional)
2 lbs. mushrooms, cleaned
   and sliced
Oil
4 (14-oz.) bottles Heinz catsup
1½ cups apple cider vinegar
1½ cups olive oil
2 lbs. canned small green
   beans, drained
2 lbs. green peppers, cut into
   strips
1 lb. pimentos, drained and cut
   into strips (if unavailable,
   use sweet red peppers)

2 lbs. small whole onions,
   precooked or canned and
   drained
2 lbs. mixture of pitted ripe
   olives and stuffed green
   olives
2 lbs. dill pickles, cut into
   strips
½ lb. canned anchovies,
   fileted
4 (7-oz.) cans tuna packed
   in oil
2 cans artichoke hearts,
   cut into quarters (optional)

Parboil the cauliflower for 3 minutes and the carrots for 2 minutes; drain each and set aside. Sauté the mushrooms in a little oil; set aside. Place the catsup, vinegar and olive oil in a large pan, bring to a boil, reduce the heat and simmer for 10 minutes. Add the cauliflower, carrots, beans, green peppers and pimentos; simmer for 10 minutes. Add the onions, olives and dill pickles; simmer for 5 minutes. Add the remaining ingredients (be sure to include the oils from the tuna and anchovies for flavor) and cook for 14 minutes. Spoon into hot, sterilized jars and process for 20 minutes or store in the refrigerator up to 2 weeks. Serve chilled.

Beth DiPasquale
Help Desk

## Spinach and Cheese Squares

½ cup butter
3 eggs
1 cup flour
1 cup milk
1 tsp. salt

1 tsp. baking powder
1 lb. Monterey Jack cheese,
   grated
4 cups chopped fresh
   spinach

Melt the butter in a 9" x 13" pan. Beat the eggs. Add the flour, milk, salt and baking powder. Add the cheese and spinach, mixing well. Spread into the pan and bake at 350° for 35 minutes. Cool for 30 minutes before serving. Cut into squares.

*These freeze well in plastic bags.*

*Makes 40 squares.*

Sue McCaffray
Reservations

## Stuffed Mushrooms with a View

*30 medium mushrooms*
*½ cup chopped green onions*
*1 clove garlic, minced*
*5 Tbsp. butter*
*1 tsp. dried marjoram,*
  *crushed*
*1 cup finely chopped, cooked*
  *ham*

*½ tsp. salt*
*½ cup saltine cracker crumbs*
*¼ cup dry white wine*
*1 Tbsp. snipped parsley*
*1 egg, beaten*
*3 Tbsp. freshly grated*
  *Parmesan cheese*

Clean the mushrooms by gently wiping the caps with a damp paper towel. Remove the stems from mushrooms, reserving the caps, and chop the stems into small pieces. In a saucepan, cook the chopped stems, green onions and garlic in 2 Tbsp. butter until the onions are limp. Remove from the heat, stir in the marjoram, ham, salt, cracker crumbs, wine, parsley and egg until blended; set aside. Melt the remaining 3 Tbsp. butter in a saucepan, add the mushroom caps and turn in the butter to coat. Place the mushrooms on a tray of heavy-duty aluminum foil, cavity side up, and mound the ham mixture into each cap, pressing in firmly. (At this point you may cover and refrigerate until the next day.) Before cooking, sprinkle the cheese over the mushrooms. Place the foil tray on a barbeque grill over medium coals. Grill until the mushrooms are tender, 15 to 20 minutes.

*Makes 10 servings.*

## Stuffed Celery Hors D'Oeuvres

½ lb. bleu cheese
1 (8-oz.) pkg. cream cheese

½ cup butter
Celery stalks

Mix the cheeses and butter together until pulverized, then place in a pastry bag with a star tube tip. Using only tender stalks, wash the celery thoroughly, dry on a towel and fill with the mixture. (Work rapidly as the base softens very quickly.) Refrigerate until ready to serve.

Emile LeBoulluec
Executive Chef
Boston Food Services

## Zucchini Appetizer

6 eggs, slightly beaten
½ cup vegetable oil
1 cup Bisquick
½ tsp. salt
½ tsp. seasoned salt
½ tsp. Italian seasoning
Dash of pepper
1 clove garlic, finely chopped

2 Tbsp. snipped parsley
½ cup grated Parmesan
   cheese
½ cup finely chopped onions
3 cups unpared, thinly sliced
   zucchini (about 4 small
   zucchini)

Mix all the ingredients together and spread in a 9" x 13" pan. Bake at 375° for 25 minutes or until golden brown. Cut into 1" x 2" squares, on a diagonal.

Makes about 4 dozen.

Arlene McEachern
Public Affairs

## French-Fried Vegetables

1 cup beer
2 cups flour (approx.)
1 cup Parmesan cheese
2 (8-oz.) cans artichoke
   hearts, drained and halved

1 large head cauliflower,
   broken into florets
3 large zucchini, cut into
   1" slices
Oil
Salt

Combine the beer, 1½ cups flour and Parmesan cheese to make a batter. Coat the vegetables with additional flour and shake off the excess. Dip the vegetable pieces in the batter and fry in oil in a deep fryer set at 375° until golden brown. Drain on unglazed brown paper. Salt gently to taste.

Kathy Pickering
Reservations

## Ham-Filled Mushroom Caps

1 lb. small whole mushrooms
¼ cup butter, melted
2 cups ground, cooked ham

½ cup sour cream
2 Tbsp. minced chives
6 pitted ripe olives, sliced

Remove the stems from the mushrooms and chop enough stems to make 1 cup. Lightly sauté the caps in the butter and arrange in a greased baking pan. Mix together 1 cup chopped mushroom stems, the ham, sour cream and chives. Pile inside the caps. Bake at 350° for 10 minutes. Garnish with the olives.

Kathy Pickering
Reservations

## Sausage-Stuffed Mushrooms

2 lbs. medium or large fresh
   mushrooms
White wine

¾ lb. sausage
Garlic salt

Wash the mushrooms and pat dry. Remove the stems and place the mushrooms on a cookie sheet, stem side up. Fill each cavity with a little wine. Roll the sausage into small balls. Place a sausage ball on each mushroom. Sprinkle with garlic salt. Broil in the oven until the sausage is done, about 3 minutes. Serve hot.

Susan Warren
Reservations

## Brandied Mushrooms and Cream

1 lb. mushrooms, cleaned
   and sliced
¼ cup plus 2 Tbsp. butter
1 cup dry sherry

¼ cup brandy
½ cup heavy cream
Dash of salt

Simmer the mushrooms in the butter and sherry until the liquid is nearly evaporated. Add the brandy, heat and ignite. Heat the cream, add the salt and pour over the mushrooms. Serve on toast triangles or with toothpicks.

Sue McCaffray
Reservations

## Crab-Stuffed Mushrooms

36 large fresh mushrooms
1 (7½-oz.) can crabmeat,
   drained and flaked
1 Tbsp. snipped parsley

½ cup mayonnaise
¼ tsp. dry mustard
1 tsp. pimento

Clean the mushrooms by gently wiping the caps with a damp paper towel. Remove the stems. Combine the remaining ingredients. Fill each mushroom with the crab mixture. Bake at 375° for 8 to 10 minutes.

Yvonne Erickson
Reservations

---

☞ When boiling onions or cabbage, boil a little vinegar in a separate saucepan to freshen the air of the vegetable odor.

# BEVERAGES

## Chevoney

1 oz. Galliano                    ½ oz. vodka
½ oz. Grand Marnier               1 scoop vanilla ice cream

Combine all the ingredients in a blender and blend quickly. Serve in chilled champagne glasses.


## Crème De Cacao Nightcap

1¼ cups milk                      5 Tbsp. sugar
½ cup plus 1 Tbsp. crème          ¼ cup whipped cream
  de cacao                        Unsweetened cocoa
¼ cup California brandy

Heat the milk, 4 oz. crème de cacao, brandy and 3 Tbsp. sugar until hot. Do not boil. Combine the 1 Tbsp. crème de cacao, 2 Tbsp. sugar and the whipped cream. Pour the milk mixture into small cups or glasses, top with the whipped cream mixture and sprinkle cocoa on top.

*Makes 2 cups.*

Fran Christensen
Tour Desk


## Velvet Hammer Drink

1 pint vanilla ice cream          1 oz. Cointreau or Triple Sec
2 oz. brandy                      1 oz. crème de cacao

Place all the ingredients in a blender and blend until creamy. Serve immediately.

*Serves 4 to 6.*

Jan Taylor
Reservations

## Egg Nog

6 large eggs, separated
6 heaping Tbsp. sugar
2 cups heavy cream

1 cup bourbon
Nutmeg

Beat the egg yolks until thick and lemon colored; do not overbeat. Gradually fold in the sugar and refrigerate. Beat the egg whites until very stiff and refrigerate. Whip the cream and refrigerate. Very slowly fold the bourbon into the yolks with a slotted spoon, then slowly fold the yolk mixture into the egg whites. Slowly fold in the whipped cream; do not overfold. Drop by spoonfuls into cups and sprinkle with nutmeg.

*So thick you can eat it with a spoon!*

Fran Christensen
Tour Desk

## Kahlua

4 cups sugar
4 cups boiling water
⅔ cup freeze-dried coffee

1 fifth vodka or brandy
1 vanilla bean
Dark bottles

Stir the sugar into the water and continue to boil for 10 minutes. Let the mixture cool, add the coffee and liquor. Chop the vanilla bean into 15 pieces and divide among the bottles. Divide the liquor among the bottles, cork and store for 4 to 5 weeks, shaking occasionally.

*Note: The longer it ages, the better it is.*

Janet Wanink
Gladys Tyo
Jan Taylor
Reservations

## Orange Liqueur

3 navel oranges                           1½ cups sugar
3 cups vodka

Pare the rinds from the oranges and use the oranges for other purposes. Blot the rinds on a paper towel to remove the oil. Put 2 cups vodka and the rinds in a quart jar. Cover and store for 2 to 3 days. Remove the rinds and add the sugar, shaking or stirring until the sugar dissolves. Add the remaining vodka, stir until clear and store for 1 week.

*If you don't like the alcohol bite, add a few drops of vanilla extract.*

Jan Taylor
Reservations

## Peach Margarita

¼ to ½ cup fresh peaches        ½ oz. Triple sec
½ oz. fresh lemon juice          1 oz. peach brandy
1 oz. Tequila                          Crushed ice

Pour the fruit, juice and liquors over the ice, strain and serve.

*Serves 1.*

Gail Workman
Reservations

## Punch with a Punch

2 fifths rum                             2 cups sugar
1 bottle brandy                       1 cup lemon juice
½ cup apricot, peach or           1 cup water
   blackberry brandy

Combine all the ingredients in a punch bowl, add ice and serve.

Rick Sanders
Reservations

### Rum Punch

2½ cans frozen lemonade
2½ cans frozen orange juice
6 cups water

1½ cups Rose's sweetened
   lime juice
4 to 5 cups rum or vodka
12 cups ginger ale

Combine all the ingredients in a large punch bowl, add ice and serve.

Janis Sisley

### Uncle Norm's Rum Slush

1 (6-oz.) can frozen limeade
6 oz. rum

4 (6-oz.) cans 7-Up

Combine all the ingredients, stir lightly and freeze. Serve in sherbet glasses.

Norm Groesbeck
Reservations

### Holiday Punch

3 pieces crystallized ginger
1 (3") stick cinnamon
8 whole cloves
3 to 4 cardamon seeds
6 lemons

6 small oranges
1 gallon apple cider
1 quart pineapple juice
½ tsp. salt
1 quart rum

Tie the spices in a bag of fine cheesecloth. Peel and cut the lemons and oranges into thin slices and add to the cider and pineapple juice. To this mixture, add the spice bag and bring to a very low, simmering boil. Simmer and stir slowly for 15 minutes; then add the salt and stir vigorously. Just before serving, add the rum. Serve hot.

This is similar to the old English Wassail-type punch.

Makes 40 to 50 servings.

Cindy Herter
Help Desk

### Hot Buttered Rum

2¼ cups packed brown sugar
3½ cups packed powdered
  sugar
2 cups butter
1 to 3 tsp. nutmeg

1 to 3 tsp. cinnamon
1 quart vanilla ice cream,
  softened
Rum

Cream together the sugars and butter until smooth. Add the spices and stir in the ice cream. Store in a tightly sealed bowl in the freezer until ready to use. For 1 serving, put 2 Tbsp. mix in a mug, add 1 oz. rum and stir. Add boiling water to fill the cup. Stir and sprinkle nutmeg on the top.

*The batter will keep for up to 6 months in the freezer.*

Yvonne Erickson
Dorothy Stitt
Reservations
Kathy Morgan
Inflight Services

### Tom and Jerry Batter

3½ cups packed powdered
  sugar
3 eggs, separated

Rum, brandy or whiskey
Hot milk or water
Nutmeg

Add the powdered sugar to the egg yolks and beat well. Beat the egg whites until stiff and fold into the yolks. To make 1 serving, place 1 Tbsp. or more of this mixture in a mug, add 1 oz. liquor and stir. Fill the mug with with hot milk or water, stir again and grate nutmeg on top.

*Note: Leave out the booze and kids love it!*

Dorothy Stitt
Reservations

## Hot Spiced Apple Cider

10 cups apple cider
1 tsp. cinnamon
1 tsp. allspice
¼ tsp. nutmeg

5 tsp. sugar (for larger
quantities, use only ¼ tsp.
sugar per cup)

Combine all the ingredients and put into the basket of a coffee maker (use a paper or cloth filter in the basket). Perk until the cider is done and the fragrance permeates the room.

*Makes 10 cups.*

Tim Walker
Reservations

## Schweizer Gluhwein
### (Swiss Hot Wine)

½ cup sugar
1 cup water
4 (⅛") lemon slices
½ medium bay leaf

1 clove
2 (2" to 3") cinnamon sticks
4 cups red or white wine

Combine the first 6 ingredients and cook for 5 minutes. Add the wine and heat to a high temperature but do not boil. Cover and let stand for 5 minutes before serving.

*Note: To kill a cold, drink 2 cups hot **Gluhwein**, put on flannel pajamas and hit the sack. You will feel much better in the morning.*

Paul Steuri
Executive Chef
Omaha Food Services

☞ *A dash of salt added to coffee which has been cooked too long or re-heated will freshen the taste.*

## Champagne Punch

4 bottles champagne
Juice of 12 lemons
¾ cup bar sugar

1 fifth gin
1 ice block
Lemon slices (optional)

Combine the first 4 ingredients in a punch bowl and add ice. Garnish with lemon slices, if desired.

Fran Christensen
Tour Desk

## Orange Julius

1 (6-oz.) can frozen orange
   juice
1 cup milk
1 cup water

½ cup sugar
1 tsp. vanilla
10 to 12 ice cubes

Combine all the ingredients in a blender, cover and blend until smooth, about 30 seconds. Serve immediately.

Makes 6 cups.

Nola Sears
Reservations

## Wassail

2 quarts sweet cider
2 cups orange juice
1 cup lemon juice
2½ cups pineapple juice

4 sticks cinnamon
12 whole cloves
½ cup sugar or to taste

Combine all the ingredients and simmer for 15 minutes; do not boil. Serve hot.

Serves 24.

Lillian Warren

## Spiced Tea

*2 cups sugar*
*12 cups water*
*3 cinnamon sticks*
*Juice of 4 oranges*

*Juice of 3 lemons*
*1 large can pineapple juice*
*2 cups boiling water*
*3 tea bags*

Combine and boil the sugar, 4 cups water and cinnamon sticks for 5 minutes. Mix and add the remaining ingredients. Serve hot.

*May be stored together for up to 2 weeks in the refrigerator.*

*Serves 15 to 25.*

Janis Sisley

☞ *When preparing iced tea always allow it to cool at room temperature before refrigerating to prevent it from becoming cloudy.*

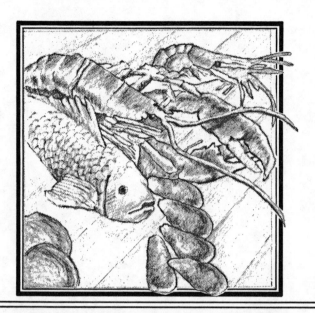

# SEAFOOD

## Crabmeat Imperial

½ cup chopped green peppers
3 Tbsp. butter
½ tsp. salt
¼ tsp. black pepper
1 tsp. Worcestershire sauce
¼ tsp. dry mustard
¼ cup mayonnaise

1 lb. cooked fresh crabmeat
   or an equal amount of
   shrimp, scallops or halibut
⅓ cup chopped pimentos
⅔ cup soft bread crumbs
½ tsp. paprika

Sauté the peppers in 1 Tbsp. butter. Add the salt, pepper, Worcestershire sauce, mustard and mayonnaise. Add the crabmeat and place the mixture in a casserole dish. Melt the remaining butter and combine with the pimentos, bread crumbs and paprika. Sprinkle on top of the casserole. Bake at 350° for about 30 minutes.

Serves 4.

Annemarie Fleming
Reservations

## King Crab Legs Parmesan

3 Tbsp. chopped onion
1 cup butter
3 Tbsp. flour
1½ cups half & half
1 cup grated Parmesan cheese
1½ lbs. crab legs, in 1½"
   sections

½ tsp. crushed fresh garlic
Juice of 1 lemon
½ cup white wine
1 tsp. Worcestershire sauce
2 Tbsp. chopped fresh parsley
Cheese croutons

Sauté the onion in the butter until transparent. Add the flour, stirring well. Slowly pour in the half & half, stirring constantly until thickened. Stir in the Parmesan cheese until it melts. Add the crab, garlic, lemon juice, wine and Worcestershire sauce. Heat through, stirring gently. Garnish with the parsley and croutons. This dish is excellent served over rice.

Serves 6.

Gail Workman
Reservations

## Crab Imperial

¼ cup clarified butter
¾ cup finely chopped onions
2 Tbsp. finely diced green
    pepper
2 Tbsp. chopped chives
1 tsp. dry mustard
Dash of cayenne pepper
1 lb. crabmeat

Buttered bread crumbs

**Cream Sauce:**
¼ cup butter
¼ cup flour
1 cup half & half
1 cup milk
Salt and white pepper to taste

Heat the butter in a skillet, add the onions and green pepper and sauté gently until soft; do not brown the vegetables. Then mix in the **Cream Sauce**, add the chives, mustard and cayenne pepper and fold in the crabmeat. Heap the mixture onto lightly greased, individual serving shells or ramekins and top with buttered crumbs. Bake at 425° for 15 minutes or until brown and bubbly.

**Cream Sauce:** Heat the butter in a thick-bottomed saucepan; add the flour and cook over low heat, stirring constantly, for 8 to 10 minutes; do not allow the roux to brown. Heat the cream and milk to boiling, then stir the hot liquid into the roux gradually, beating briskly until the sauce is thickened and smooth. Simmer for 5 minutes, stirring occasionally; bring to a boil and strain. Season to taste with salt and white pepper.

Serves 4.

Jerry F. Boyer
Executive Chef
Newark Food Services

## Trader Vic's Crab Crepes Bengal

1 lb. crabmeat
1 Tbsp. plus 1 tsp. minced
    shallots
Butter
2 Tbsp. curry powder
½ tsp. salt
⅛ tsp. pepper

½ tsp. Worcestershire sauce
1 cup dry white wine
2½ cups white wine béchamel
12 crepes
½ cup **Hollandaise Sauce**
    (see index)
¼ cup heavy cream, whipped

Remove any bits of shell from the crabmeat and sauté with the shallots in butter for 1 minute. Add the curry powder, salt, pepper, Worcestershire sauce and wine; boil for 3 minutes or until the wine is reduced by one-half. Stir in 2 cups béchamel. Prepare the crepes. Place 1 heaping Tbsp. of crab filling in the center of each crepe. Shape each crepe into a roll 1½" in diameter and place seam side down, side by side, in a shallow baking pan. Combine the ½ cup béchamel, **Hollandaise Sauce** and whipped cream and spoon over the crepes. Broil until the sauce is glazed and tinged with brown, about 3 to 4 minutes.

*Note: When preparing the béchamel, be sure to substitute white wine for the milk or cream.*

*Makes 4 dinner servings, 6 luncheon servings or 10 to 12 appetizer servings.*

Trader Vic's
Seattle, Washington

## Crab Broil

1 cup grated cheddar cheese
2 tsp. butter
½ cup milk

1 cup Dungeness crab or
  1 (8-oz.) can crab
2 tsp. Worcestershire sauce
6 English muffins, split

Heat the cheese in the butter and milk until well blended. Add the crab and Worcestershire sauce. Spread on the muffin halves and broil until brown.

*Borrowed from the Rainier Club, Seattle, Washington.*

R. L. Mangold
Senior Vice President & General Manager
Division Headquarters-New York

## Crabmeat Dewey

2 lbs. shelled Alaskan
  crabmeat
½ cup butter
½ lb. fresh mushrooms, sliced
2 small green peppers, diced
1 (4-oz.) jar pimentos, drained
  and diced
½ medium onion, chopped
1 cup white wine
Salt and pepper to taste

½ tsp. Maggi seasoning
2 Tbsp. Aunt Penney's
  Hollandaise sauce
1 tsp. chives

**Cream Sauce:**
½ cup butter
1½ Tbsp. flour
3 cups milk, scalded
Salt to taste

Dice the crabmeat into bite-size pieces. In the butter, sauté the mushrooms, green peppers, pimentos and onion. Add the crabmeat and bake at 325° for 3 minutes. Deglaze with the wine and allow the wine to reduce. Add the **Cream Sauce**, season with salt and pepper and the Maggi seasoning and simmer slowly for 5 minutes. Just before serving, top with the Hollandaise sauce and chives. Serve with rice or potatoes.

**Cream Sauce:** Melt the butter and stir in the flour. Stir constantly with a wire whisk for 3 minutes. Add the milk, stir for an additional 2 minutes and add some salt to taste. Strain the cream sauce if it is lumpy.

For a tangier taste, add 1 tsp. Coleman's dry mustard and 2 tsp. prepared mustard with the sauce and seasonings.

Serves 6.

John H. Wolfsheimer
Executive Chef
San Francisco Food Services

☞ Before scalding milk, rinse the pan in cold water to avoid coating.

### Scalloped Clams

*¼ cup plus 3 Tbsp. butter*
*½ cup toasted bread crumbs*
*1 cup cracker crumbs*
*¼ tsp. paprika*
*Salt and pepper*

*2 cups finely chopped clams*
*2 Tbsp. minced shallots or*
  *scallions*
*3 Tbsp. minced parsley*
*½ cup light cream*

Mix ¼ cup plus 2 Tbsp. butter with the bread and cracker crumbs and paprika. Add salt and pepper to taste. Set aside ⅓ cup of the mixture. Combine the remaining mixture with the clams and shallots or scallions. Add the parsley. Spoon into a greased baking dish. Sprinkle with the reserved crumb mixture. Pour in the cream. Dot with the remaining butter. Bake at 375° for 20 to 25 minutes.

Virginia Hansen

### Puget Sound Clams in Shells

*2 (6½- or 7-oz.) cans minced*
  *or chopped clams*
*¾ lb. shell macaroni*
*2 to 3 cloves garlic, minced*
*½ cup grated Parmesan*
  *cheese*

*⅓ cup chopped parsley*
*¼ cup melted margarine or*
  *butter*
*½ tsp. salt*
*⅛ tsp. pepper*

Drain the clams and reserve the liquid. Cook the macaroni according to the package directions. Meanwhile, in a 2-quart saucepan, cook the clam liquid with the garlic over low heat until it is reduced by half. Drain the macaroni well. Combine the macaroni and clams with the clam liquid. Add the cheese, parsley, margarine, salt and pepper and heat through. If desired, portion the mixture into 6 (8-oz.) individual baking shells or ramekins. Garnish with additional Parmesan cheese and broil for 2 to 3 minutes until lightly browned.

*Makes 6 entrée servings or 12 appetizer servings.*

Pamela Shamsid-Deen
Reservations

## Lobster Newburg #1

¼ cup plus 1 Tbsp. butter
2 cups raw lobster meat
1 tsp. salt
¼ tsp. Tabasco sauce
⅓ cup cognac

1½ cups heavy cream
3 egg yolks
¾ tsp. lobster coral, cooked
   and forced through a fine
   wire sieve (optional)

Heat the butter in a medium skillet and sauté the lobster with the salt and Tabasco sauce for about 4 minutes. Heat the cognac, ignite and pour over the lobster. Heat the cream and egg yolks in a double boiler over hot water, stirring constantly until the mixture coats the spoon. Add the lobster and heat through, being certain that the hot water under the mixture does not boil. Correct the seasoning and sprinkle with the lobster coral. Place in a pastry shell or the center of a rice ring.

Serves 4.

Jerry F. Boyer
Executive Chef
Newark Food Services

## Lobster Newburg #2

Meat of 2 (1¼-lb.) Northern
   lobsters
¼ cup butter
⅛ tsp. paprika
1 Tbsp. flour (Wondra
   works best)
½ cup light cream

⅓ cup dry sherry
¾ cup milk
2 egg yolks, beaten
Salt
White pepper
2 to 4 slices bread, toasted

Cut the lobster into ½" slices. Melt the butter in a heavy skillet, add the lobster and paprika and sauté for 1 minute. Set aside. Dissolve the flour in the cream and combine with the sherry and milk over medium heat. Slowly bring to a boil. Stir a small amount of the hot cream sauce into the egg yolks, then slowly drizzle the remaining yolks into the cream sauce. Cook only until the sauce begins to bubble around the edges and to thicken. Overcooking will cause this sauce to curdle. Remove from the heat, add salt and pepper to taste. Arrange the lobster on toast points, pour the sauce over and serve.

*Serves 2 to 4.*

David Rieman
Passenger Service

## Lobster Thermidor

4 (1½-lb.) whole live lobsters
1 stalk celery, sliced
1 carrot, sliced
1 large onion, diced
2 bay leaves
Juice of 2 lemons
Salt and pepper to taste
Butter
6 shallots, chopped
12 mushrooms, diced
1 tsp. paprika

3 oz. brandy
½ tsp. chopped fresh tarragon
½ tsp. dry English mustard
½ tsp. chopped parsley
2 cups **Cream Sauce**
  (see index)
3 pats of butter
2 tsp. Bovril or other
  meat glaze
Grated Parmesan cheese

Make a court bouillon by boiling approximately 3 quarts water in a large pan and adding the lobster, celery, carrot, onion, bay leaves, lemon juice and salt; reduce the heat and simmer for 20 minutes. Remove the lobster and let cool, split in half lengthwise. Remove the pouch and discard, remove the meat and dice into ¾" squares. Using the butter, sauté the shallots and mushrooms in a pan. Add the lobster meat, sprinkle with the paprika and deglaze with the brandy. Simmer covered for 2 minutes. Add the tarragon, mustard, parsley, **Cream Sauce**, pats of butter and Bovril; season with salt and pepper. Refill the lobster shells with the meat and sauce, sprinkle grated Parmesan cheese on top. Place under the broiler and glaze until golden brown. Serve piping hot.

John H. Wolfsheimer
Executive Chef
San Francisco Food Services

## Hangtown Fry

¾ lb. canned, fresh or frozen
    medium Pacific oysters
3 slices bacon, cut into
    1" pieces
8 eggs
½ tsp. salt
Dash of pepper

½ cup dry bread or cracker
    crumbs
⅓ cup flour
¼ cup milk
2 Tbsp. melted margarine or
    cooking oil
2 tsp. minced parsley
6 lemon wedges

Thaw the oysters if frozen and drain well. Fry the bacon in a 10" skillet until crisp, remove and drain on absorbent paper. Reserve the bacon drippings. Combine the eggs with salt and pepper and ¼ cup water; beat lightly and set aside. Combine the crumbs and flour. Dip the oysters in the milk and roll in the crumb mixture. Heat the margarine and reserved bacon drippings over medium heat. Fry the oysters in the hot fat for 2 to 3 minutes or until lightly browned. Sprinkle the bacon over the oysters, then pour the egg mixture over the bacon and oysters. Cook over low heat, gently lifting the edge of the omelet with a spatula to allow the uncooked egg to flow to the bottom of the skillet. Cook just until the eggs are set. Sprinkle with the parsley before serving. If preferred, loosen the omelet around the edge of the pan; fold and roll onto a heated platter and sprinkle with the parsley. Serve with the lemon wedges.

Makes 6 servings.

Jackie Partlow

## Zucchini Boats with Lobster

3 zucchini
2 cups white wine
1 Tbsp. oil
1 tomato, chopped
1 onion, chopped
2 to 3 Tbsp. chopped parsley
Pinch of thyme
1 Tbsp. lemon juice
1 bay leaf
Salt and pepper to taste

½ cup sliced artichoke hearts
½ cup sliced mushrooms
1 to 1½ cups cooked lobster
    meat (approx.)
1½ cups mayonnaise
1 Tbsp. chopped, cooked
    spinach
2 Tbsp. catsup
Shredded lettuce

Peel the zucchini and cut in half lengthwise, scoop out the centers. In a frying pan, heat the wine, oil, tomato, onion, 1 to 2 Tbsp. parsley, thyme, lemon juice, bay leaf, salt and pepper. Place the zucchini halves in the wine mixture, cover and cook just until tender. Remove the zucchini halves and chill. To serve, layer the center of each zucchini with the following in this order: 1 slice artichoke heart, 1 Tbsp. sliced mushrooms, 4 pieces lobster meat. Then cover 2 zucchinis with green mayonnaise, 2 with red mayonnaise and 2 with plain white mayonnaise. Make green mayonnaise by blending 6 Tbsp. mayonnaise with 1 Tbsp. spinach and 1 Tbsp. parsley. Make red mayonnaise by blending 6 Tbsp. mayonnaise with 2 Tbsp. catsup. Serve the boats on a tray of shredded lettuce. The tray can be garnished with sliced or cherry tomatoes, hard-cooked eggs, lemon wedges and cooked asparagus spears.

Jackie Partlow

## Cape Cod Scallops Denise

*1 lb. Cape Cod scallops*
*1 Tbsp. chopped shallots*
*¾ cup butter (approx.)*
*⅓ cup Noilly Prat vermouth*
*½ cup white wine*

*1 cup all-purpose flour*
*1 cup light cream*
*½ cup sliced mushrooms*
*¼ lb. bay shrimp, cooked*

Sauté the scallops and shallots in a small amount of butter. Add the vermouth and white wine; cover and simmer for a few minutes. Remove the scallops and place in the original shells. Reduce the liquid by one-half. Mix together ½ cup butter and the flour and cook over low heat for a few minutes to make a roux. Gradually add the roux and cream to the wine sauce, cook and stir to desired thickness. Add the mushrooms and shrimp and bring to a quick boil. Remove from the heat and sprinkle with the butter. Pour the sauce over the scallops and serve.

*Serves 6.*

Duri Arquisch
Executive Chef
Salt Lake City Food Services

## Quenelles of Scallops Nantua

¼ cup butter
1 cup milk
½ cup all-purpose flour
1 lb. deep sea scallops
1 Tbsp. chopped onion
Dash of nutmeg
1½ tsp. chives
⅛ tsp. white pepper
½ tsp. Maggi seasoning

¾ tsp. salt
2 Tbsp. cream
3 egg whites
1 cup white wine
1 bay leaf
½ medium onion, sliced
1½ Tbsp. fresh lemon juice
1½ Tbsp. grated lemon rind

Melt the butter in the milk and bring to the boiling point. Add the flour and beat this batter with a wooden spoon over low heat for 3 minutes, as for cream puff batter. Remove and let cool. Grind the raw scallops through a meat grinder (set on the same size as for hamburger) and place the ground scallops together with the cream puff batter in an electric mixer. Add the chopped onion, nutmeg, chives, pepper, Maggi seasoning and salt. Mix at medium speed. Combine the cream and the egg whites and add to the batter in thirds, allowing the batter to absorb all the liquid before adding more. Whip thoroughly for at least 5 minutes. Portion onto a wax paper-lined sheet pan by means of a pastry bag into 2-oz. rounded mounds. Set in the freezer for 1 hour. Remove the wax paper and place the frozen quenelles in a greased, shallow pan. Add the wine, 1 cup water, the bay leaf, sliced onion, lemon juice and rind. Cover the pan with foil, then bake at 375° for 25 minutes; strain the juices and use as sauce.

*Makes 15 (2-oz.) quenelles.*

John H. Wolfsheimer
Executive Chef
San Francisco Food Services

☞ *When food gets scorched, set the pan immediately in cold water to remove the burned taste from the food that was not scorched.*

## Baked Scallop Casserole

1 quart scallops, chopped
1 to 1½ cups light cream
6 cups soft bread crumbs
1 cup butter, melted

2 tsp. salt
½ tsp. pepper
2 Tbsp. celery seed
Paprika

Arrange the scallops in a greased, 11½" x 7½" x 1½" baking dish; pour over half the cream. Toss the remaining ingredients together except the remaining cream and paprika and sprinkle over the scallops. Pour the cream on top. Sprinkle with paprika. Bake uncovered at 400° for about 30 minutes.

Serves 8.

Mikele McKnight
Reservations

## Scallops Meunière

8 (2- to 2½-oz.) deep sea
    scallops
Salt and pepper to taste
1 Tbsp. flour
2 eggs, beaten

½ cup butter
1 tsp. chopped parsley
1 tsp. capers
Juice of 2 lemons

Pound the scallops with a wooden mallet to about 4" thickness to break down the fibers. Season with salt and pepper, dredge in the flour on both sides, dip in the eggs and sauté in ¼ cup butter on both sides until browned. Remove from the heat. Brown the remaining butter and add to it the parsley, capers and lemon juice. Pour the sauce over the scallops and serve piping hot.

Serves 4.

John H. Wolfsheimer
Executive Chef
San Francisco Food Services

## Shrimp de Jonghe

2 lbs. medium-large shrimp,
  cooked
1 cup butter
1½ cups milk, heated
1 cup toasted bread crumbs
½ cup finely minced parsley

1 clove garlic, minced
1½ tsp. salt
⅛ tsp. freshly ground pepper
¼ cup freshly grated
  Parmesan cheese

Sauté the shrimp in ¼ cup butter over medium heat for 2 minutes. Place in a shallow, 2-quart casserole. Pour the milk over the bread crumbs and mix well with a fork. Let the mixture stand until it is the consistency of thick custard. (If it is too thick, add more milk.) Add the parsley, garlic, salt, pepper and ½ cup softened butter to the milk and crumbs. Mix thoroughly and spread over the shrimp. Sprinkle with the Parmesan cheese. Drizzle with ¼ cup melted butter and bake at 350° for 30 minutes. Place under a broiler for several minutes to brown lightly. Watch closely to avoid burning.

Marianne Shute

## Crepes Diplomat

2 cups flour
2 eggs
2 to 3 cups milk
Salt and pepper to taste

**Filling:**
¼ cup butter
2 cups bay shrimp
1 tsp. paprika
1 oz. blended bourbon
½ cup cream sauce

¼ cup half & half
Salt and pepper to taste

**Sauce:**
2 Tbsp. butter
1 tsp. paprika
1 oz. blended bourbon
¾ cup cream sauce
½ cup half & half
Salt and pepper to taste

Blend together the flour, eggs, milk and salt and pepper and stir until smooth. If the mixture is too thick, add more milk. Cook 8 very thin cakes on both sides in a 5" omelette pan. Fill each pancake with filling and roll. Place in a serving dish, 2 crepes per person, pour the sauce over and serve.

**Filling:** Melt the butter in a skillet, add the shrimp and paprika. Sauté lightly, douse with the bourbon and flame to evaporate the alcohol. Add the cream sauce and half & half and season with salt and pepper.

**Sauce:** Over medium heat, melt the butter and add the paprika, mixing well. Add the bourbon, flame and add the remaining ingredients, whipping to a smooth sauce.

*Note: The cream sauce should be made from roux, milk and chicken broth.*

*Serves 4.*

Erich Dorfhuber
Executive Chef
Portland Food Services

## Shrimp Saganaki

*1 lb. raw medium shrimp*
*1 (8-oz.) pkg. frozen artichoke*
*    hearts or 1 can artichoke*
*    hearts, halved*
*¼ cup olive oil*
*¼ lb. small whole*
*    mushrooms*

*2 cloves garlic, finely minced*
*½ tsp. salt*
*Freshly ground pepper*
*½ tsp. crumbled dried oregano*
*2 Tbsp. lemon juice*
*2 Tbsp. finely chopped parsley*

Peel and devein the shrimp. Blanch the artichoke hearts in boiling, salted water for 2 minutes; drain. Heat the oil in a frying pan, add the shrimp and mushrooms and cook, stirring until the shrimp turn pink. Add the artichoke hearts, garlic, salt, pepper and oregano, heat through. Sprinkle with the lemon juice and stir to blend. Sprinkle with the parsley.

*Serve in a heat-proof dish over a candle-warmer.*

Beth DiPasquale
Apollo Systems

### Shrimp Casserole Harpin

2½ lbs. shrimp
1 Tbsp. lemon juice
3 Tbsp. salad oil
1 cup uncooked rice
2 Tbsp. butter
¼ cup chopped green peppers
¼ cup chopped onions
1 tsp. salt

½ tsp. pepper
½ tsp. mace
¼ tsp. cayenne pepper
1 (10-oz.) can tomato soup
1 cup heavy cream
½ cup sherry
¾ cup slivered blanched
  almonds

Cook the shrimp in boiling, salted water for 5 minutes; drain. Place in a 2-quart casserole and sprinkle with the lemon juice and oil. Cook the rice and drain. Refrigerate everything. About 1 hour and 10 minutes before serving, in the butter, sauté the green peppers and onions, then combine with the rice, salt, pepper, mace, cayenne pepper, soup, cream, sherry and ½ cup almonds. Add to the shrimp in the casserole. Bake uncovered at 350° for 35 minutes. Top with the remaining almonds and a few of the shrimp. Bake for 20 minutes more or until the mixture is bubbly and the shrimp are slightly browned.

Serves 6 to 8.

Gail Workman
Reservations

### Sweet and Sour Shrimp

½ cup brown sugar
¼ cup cornstarch
1 tsp. salt
1 cup vinegar
1 Tbsp. soy sauce

2 (20-oz.) cans pineapple
  chunks
2 green peppers, cut into strips
3 medium onions, cut into
  rings
2 lbs. shrimp, cooked

Combine the brown sugar, cornstarch, salt, vinegar and soy sauce in a saucepan. Drain the pineapple syrup and add enough water to make 2 cups liquid. Stir into the brown sugar mixture. Cook until slightly thickened, stirring constantly. Add the green peppers, onions and pineapple chunks and cook for 3 minutes. Remove from the heat, add the shrimp and let stand for 10 minutes. Before serving, return to the heat and bring to the boiling point, stirring constantly. Serve over white rice. Garnish with raisins and slivered almonds, if desired.

### Shrimp Arnaud

¼ cup cider vinegar
½ cup olive oil
2 Tbsp. Catarain's prepared
   Creole mustard
4 green onions with tops,
   finely minced
½ stalk celery, finely minced

Salt and pepper to taste
2 tsp. paprika
3 lbs. shrimp, boiled
   and peeled
Shredded lettuce
Thin tomato slices

Thoroughly mix together the first 7 ingredients in a large bowl. Stir the shrimp into the sauce and toss, making sure all are well coated. Chill thoroughly for at least 2 hours (preferably overnight). To serve, place shredded lettuce and tomato slices on individual, ice-cold salad plates and top with the marinated shrimp.

*Note: The secret to this delicious dish is in thoroughly marinating the shrimp with the dressing so that the fish absorbs the unique flavor of the sauce. And to create the unique flavor of the sauce, the mustard must be Catarain's prepared Creole mustard.*

W. Reichmuth
Executive Chef
Chicago Food Services

### Shrimp Poulette

1 Tbsp. finely chopped onion
1 Tbsp. butter
2 Tbsp. canned diced
   mushrooms
12 raw medium shrimp
¼ cup dry white wine

Dash of lemon juice
Salt and white pepper to taste
Pinch of thyme
Beurre Manié
¼ cup half & half
1 Tbsp. finely chopped parsley

Smother the onion in the butter for 1 minute in a saucepan. Add the mushrooms, shrimp, wine, lemon juice, salt, pepper and thyme; cover and simmer until the shrimp are cooked. Remove the shrimp and cook the remaining liquid for 5 minutes. Then whip the Beurre Manié, one tsp. at a time, into the sauce until it is of desired consistency. Return the shrimp to the sauce, cook for 2 to 3 minutes, add the half & half and parsley and heat thoroughly (do not boil). Serve as an entrée with a rice pilaf, a fresh vegetable and a cold bottle of wine or alone as a hot dish on a buffet.

*Note: Beurre Manié can be made by combining equal parts of softened butter and flour, pressing it into a roll and tearing off parts as needed.*

Paul Steuri
Executive Chef
Omaha Food Services

## Mahi Mahi Espagnola

6 (5-oz.) boneless pieces
  Mahi Mahi
1 Tbsp. salt
Dash of white pepper
Juice of 1 lemon
¾ cup Gold Medal Flour, sifted

½ cup butter
1 ¼ cups **Espagnola Sauce**
  (see index)
6 (½-oz.) slices provolone
  cheese
Melted butter

Season the Mahi Mahi with salt, pepper and lemon juice. Drench in the flour and sauté in the butter. Place the well-done Mahi Mahi on a cookie sheet. Pour the **Espagnola Sauce** over the Mahi Mahi, cover with the provolone cheese and sprinkle with melted butter. Lightly bake in the oven. Serve with parsleyed potatoes.

*Serves 6.*

Erwin Alt
Executive Chef
Chicago Food Services

## Fried Mahi Mahi in Macadamia Nut Sauce

5 (¼-lb.) boneless, skinless
  Mahi Mahi fish filets
Salt and pepper to taste
¼ cup flour
1 cup margarine
Freshly chopped parsley

**Macadamia Nut Sauce:**
2 Tbsp. cornstarch
1 cup chicken stock, chilled
¾ tsp. butter
Salt and pepper
1 ½ Tbsp. lemon juice
½ cup chopped macadamia
  nuts

Season the fish with salt and pepper and dip into the flour. Sauté in the margarine in a skillet until golden brown on both sides. Bake at 300° for 8 minutes or until the fish is done. Remove and place on a warm serving platter. Pour the sauce over and sprinkle with parsley. Serve hot.

**Macadamia Nut Sauce:** Dissolve the cornstarch in ¼ cup chicken stock. Bring the remaining chicken stock and the butter to a boil and add salt and pepper to taste. With a wire whisk, whip the cornstarch into the stock, cook for 1 minute, then add the lemon juice and macadamia nuts.

*Serves 5.*

John H. Wolfsheimer
Executive Chef
San Francisco Food Services

## Mahi Mahi Pacific

*¼ cup butter*
*1 Tbsp. chopped onion*
*4 (5-oz.) Mahi Mahi filets*
*Salt and pepper to taste*
*⅔ cup dry white wine*
*Buttered parchment paper*
*⅔ (10½-oz.) can white sauce*

*½ cup heavy cream*
*1 Tbsp. chives*
*Worcestershire sauce to taste*
*Lemon juice to taste*
*8 canned medium mushroom heads*

Melt the butter in a skillet and sprinkle in the onion. Place the fish filets on top; season with salt and pepper. Pour the wine over, cover with the parchment paper and poach for 5 to 8 minutes, until the fish is done. Remove from the pan and place on a serving dish. Simmer until the juices reduce by half. Add the white sauce and fold in the cream and chives. Season to taste with salt, pepper, Worcestershire sauce and lemon juice. Place 2 mushroom heads on each filet, pour the sauce over and serve.

*Serves 4.*

Rolf Conrad
Executive Chef
Denver Food Services

### Finest Barbequed Salmon

1 large salmon filet
Butter
Salt and pepper to taste
Green onions, finely diced

Dark brown sugar
1 lemon, thinly sliced
Paprika

Filet the salmon and remove all the bones. Line a cookie sheet with foil. Place the salmon on the foil and butter it just as you would a slice of bread. Then sprinkle salt and pepper over. Sprinkle with the green onions and then liberally apply the sugar. Lay the lemon slices over and sprinkle with paprika. Place on a grill and barbeque for approximately 40 minutes.

*Especially good if cooked in a Weber kettle. Soak hickory chips in water. Just before putting the fish on the grill, put the chips on the fire.*

Pat Shea

### Barry's Baked or Barbequed Salmon

1 salmon
2 Tbsp. butter
¼ cup lemon juice
2 cloves garlic (approx.)

2 oz. vermouth
1 tsp. parsley
1 lemon, thinly sliced
1 medium onion, thinly sliced

Cut the salmon down the center and lay it open flat. Remove all the bones and trim the edges. Make a sauce by melting the butter and adding the lemon juice, garlic to taste, vermouth and parsley. Lay the salmon out, meat side up, on a piece of aluminum foil that is large enough to wrap the entire fish. Layer with the lemon and onion slices, pour the sauce over and wrap the foil around the salmon, sealing all the edges. Make a 1½" slit in the top of the foil to allow ventilation. Bake at 350° for 25 minutes or until the salmon flakes easily.

For barbequed salmon, follow the above procedures exactly, except wrap the fish closely in the foil and do not cut a ventilation slit. Place the meat side down on the barbeque grill over medium coals and cook for 10 minutes. Turn the salmon over on the grill, open up the foil to expose the salmon completely and crimp the edges to hold in the juices.

Add alderwood chips to the fire and raise the grill up to about 8" over the coals. Cook for another 30 minutes and add more alderwood as needed.

Barry Gardiner
Reservations

## Filet of Salmon Marguerite

4 (8-oz.) boneless, skinless
    salmon filets
2 Tbsp. chopped onion
½ cup butter
1 bay leaf
1 cup dry white wine
2 oz. shrimp meat

¼ lb. fresh or canned
    mushroom buttons
2 Tbsp. flour
½ cup heavy cream
1 tsp. chopped chives
½ tsp. Maggi seasoning
Salt and pepper

Place the fish in a shallow cooking pan that can be covered; sprinkle 1 Tbsp. onion over. Melt 2 Tbsp. butter and brush over the fish. Add the bay leaf and wine. Bring to a boil, cover the pot and simmer for 12 minutes. Remove the filets to a hot platter and keep the juices hot. In another pan sauté the remaining onion until transparent in 3 Tbsp. butter. Add the shrimp and mushrooms; then add the juices from the poached fish and simmer slowly for 5 minutes. Melt the remaining butter and add the flour to it, stirring to make a paste. Whisk this into the fish sauce (it should have the thickness of a heavy cream soup). Add the heavy cream and continue to simmer for an additional 2 minutes. Add the chives and Maggi seasoning and salt and pepper to taste. Pour the sauce over the fish filets and serve piping hot. Best served with boiled potatoes but other starches can be selected as desired.

Makes 4 servings.

John H. Wolfsheimer
Executive Chef
San Francisco Food Services

## Cheese-Stuffed Baked Salmon with Mushrooms

1 (6-lb.) salmon
2 cups grated Velveeta cheese
1 tsp. salt
⅛ tsp. pepper
½ tsp. thyme
3 Tbsp. lemon juice

½ can flat beer
3 Tbsp. butter
6 lemon slices
½ onion, thinly sliced
½ lb. fresh mushrooms

Wash the fish inside and out and pat dry. Combine the cheese, salt, pepper and thyme. Place the fish on a double thickness of heavy foil. Mound the cheese mixture in the fish cavity and sprinkle with 1 Tbsp. lemon juice. Pour the beer over the fish and dot the top with the butter, lemon and onion slices, mushrooms and the remaining lemon juice. Bring the foil together over the fish and secure. Set on a cookie sheet and bake at 375° for 1 hour. Remove the cheese stuffing before serving and use as an accompaniment.

Note: To barbeque, prepare as above and barbeque for 20 minutes on each side or until the fish flakes easily.

Lillian Warren

## Poached Salmon with Cucumber Sauce

1½ Tbsp. salt
2 Tbsp. lemon juice
1 bay leaf
6 fresh salmon steaks
1 cup grated, unpeeled
  cucumber
½ cup sour cream
¼ cup mayonnaise

1 Tbsp. minced parsley
2 tsp. grated onion
2 tsp. cider vinegar
¼ tsp. salt
Pinch of black pepper
1 lemon, quartered
2 tomatoes, quartered

In a large skillet, heat 4 cups water with the salt, lemon juice and bay leaf to boiling. Simmer 3 of the salmon steaks at a time in the liquid for 10 minutes. Remove the steaks with a large slotted spoon or spatula and chill well. To make the sauce, combine all the remaining ingredients except the lemon and tomatoes and chill until serving. At serving time, arrange the salmon on a platter or board, garnish with the lemon and tomato quarters and serve with the cucumber sauce.

Dottie Martin

## Salmon Steaks à la Crème

*6 (1" thick) salmon steaks*
*Salt and pepper*

*2½ cups light cream (approx.)*
*1 small bay leaf*

Wipe the steaks with a damp cloth and season with salt and pepper to taste. Place the fish in a greased baking dish large enough to hold the fish in a single layer. Pour over enough cream to cover the fish. Lay a bay leaf on top, cover with foil and bake in the center of the oven at 375° for 20 minutes, basting if necessary.

## Salmon Lasagna Pinwheels

*1 (15½-oz.) can salmon*
*1½ cups coarsely chopped*
  *spinach*
*¼ cup chopped green onions*
*1½ cups ricotta cheese*
*⅓ cup grated Parmesan*
  *cheese*
*1 egg*
*½ tsp. salt*
*¼ tsp. garlic powder*

*12 lasagna noodles*

**Cheese Sauce:**
*¼ cup butter or margarine,*
  *melted*
*¼ cup flour*
*Half & half*
*½ tsp. salt*
*1 cup shredded Swiss cheese*
*¼ cup grated Parmesan*
  *cheese*

Drain and flake the salmon, reserving the liquid. Combine the salmon, spinach, green onions, ricotta and Parmesan cheese, egg, salt and garlic and mix well. Cook the noodles according to the package directions and drain. Divide the filling into 12 parts and spread on the noodles. Roll up pinwheel fashion and set aside. Pour half the **Cheese Sauce** into the bottom of an 11" x 7" x 1¾" baking dish. Place the noodles on end in the baking dish. Cover with the remaining sauce and bake at 375° for 30 minutes or until golden and bubbly.

**Cheese Sauce:** Combine the butter or margarine with the flour. Add half & half to the reserved salmon liquid to measure 2 cups. Gradually add the liquid to the butter and flour mixture. Cook until thickened and smooth, stirring constantly. Add the remaining ingredients and continue cooking until the cheese melts.

*Serves 6.*

Annemarie Fleming
Reservations

## Potlatch Salmon

6 (5- to 6-oz.) fresh or frozen
  salmon or other fish steaks
1 Tbsp. juniper berries
  (approx. 50)
¼ cup salad oil

2 tsp. salt
⅛ tsp. pepper
6 lemon or lime wedges
Mayonnaise

Thaw the fish if frozen. Lightly crush the juniper berries and push 6 to 8 berries into each steak. Coat the fish with the oil to prevent sticking, sprinkle each fish with the salt and pepper and grill over hot coals for 5 to 6 minutes on each side. Garnish with the lemon wedges and mayonnaise.

*The fish may be broiled or pan fried for approximately the same length of time.*

*Makes 6 servings.*

Janis Sisley

## Salmon Loaf with Sour Cream Sauce

2 Tbsp. salad oil
¾ cup finely chopped celery
½ cup chopped onions
1 (8-oz.) can salmon or equal
  amount of freshly cooked
  salmon
1 egg, slightly beaten
1 can evaporated milk
1 cup fine bread crumbs
1 tsp. salt

¼ tsp. pepper

**Sour Cream Sauce:**
½ cup mayonnaise
¼ cup sour cream
1 Tbsp. lemon juice
1 Tbsp. milk
2 tsp. dill weed
½ tsp. sugar
½ tsp. salt

Prepare at least 1½ hours before serving. Pour the oil into a 2-quart saucepan and sauté the celery and onions over medium heat until tender, about 10 minutes. Remove from the heat, add the salmon and its liquid, egg, milk, bread crumbs, salt and pepper. Mix until smooth. Grease a 6" x 3½" loaf pan and spoon the mixture into the pan. Bake at 350° for 50 minutes. Remove the loaf from the pan. Serve either hot or cold with the **Sour Cream Sauce**.

**Sour Cream Sauce:** Combine all the ingredients and mix well. The sauce may be refrigerated before serving.

Fran Christensen
Reservations

## Salmon Romanoff St. George

1 (16-oz.) can salmon
1 cup sour cream
1 cup small-curd creamed
  cottage cheese
2 Tbsp. margarine or butter
½ cup chopped green onions
  with tops
½ cup chopped fresh
  mushrooms or 1 (2-oz.) can
  chopped mushrooms,
  drained

1 clove garlic, minced
2 Tbsp. all-purpose flour
1 (10-oz.) pkg. frozen green
  peas, thawed and drained
¼ tsp. salt
⅛ tsp. liquid hot pepper sauce
3 cups cooked noodles or
  6 servings of toast or crepes
Sour cream (optional)
Red caviar (optional)

Drain the salmon and reserve the liquid; discard the skin and flake the meat. Combine the salmon with the sour cream and cottage cheese. Melt the margarine in the top of a double boiler. Add the onions, mushrooms and garlic, cook over low heat for about 10 minutes or until the onions are transparent. Add the flour and gradually stir in the salmon liquid. Cook over hot water in a double boiler until the mixture is thickened, stirring occasionally. Add the salmon mixture, peas, salt and hot pepper sauce. Cook until the peas are tender, about 10 minutes. Serve over noodles or toast or use as a filling for crepes. Serve with sour cream and red caviar.

*Makes 6 servings.*

Jackie Partlow

## Salmon Loaf

3 egg whites, stiffly beaten
1 can celery soup
3 egg yolks, slightly beaten
2 tsp. chopped pimento
2 Tbsp. parsley
1 Tbsp. lemon juice

Dash of pepper
1 cup cracker crumbs
¼ cup chopped onions
2 cups finely flaked fish
4 thin lemon slices

Combine all the ingredients except the lemon slices. Bake at 350° for 45 minutes. Garnish with lemon slices.

Ina Nelson
Reservations

## Smelt Almondine

18 smelt
¼ cup plus 2 Tbsp. light cream
Flour seasoned with salt,
    pepper and paprika

¼ cup plus 2 Tbsp. butter
1 Tbsp. olive oil
1 cup sliced almonds

Lightly wash the smelt in cold water. Split, remove the entrails, cut off the heads and pat dry. Dip the smelt in the cream and roll in the flour. Melt the butter in a heavy skillet and add the olive oil. Sauté the smelt for 4 minutes on each side, remove the fish from the pan and keep warm. In the same skillet, increase the heat slightly and sauté the almonds until brown. Sprinkle the smelt with almonds and pan drippings.

Effie Johnston

☞ Boil several cloves in a cup of water to rid the house of objectionable food odors, especially of seafood.

## Trout Almondine

*A collection of recipes to enhance the enjoyment of fish cookery would be incomplete without the classic Trout Almondine.*

| | |
|---|---|
| ¾ tsp. salt | Flour |
| 1 cup whole milk | Butter |
| 6 (8-oz.) dressed trout | ⅓ cup blanched almonds |

Combine the salt and milk. Dip the trout in the milk, roll in flour and brown in butter over medium heat. Place the trout on a warm platter. In the same pan, add 3 more Tbsp. butter. Add the almonds, stir and cook until they are brown. Sprinkle over the trout and serve at once.

*Serves 6.*

Sarina Ames, Jr.
Reservations

## Mountain Trout Sauté Temple Square

| | |
|---|---|
| 8 (8-oz.) trout | 2 Tbsp. salad oil |
| Salt and pepper | ⅓ cup fresh lemon juice |
| ½ cup milk | 1 tsp. Worcestershire sauce |
| Flour | 16 mint leaves |
| 8 bacon slices, crisply fried (reserve drippings) | ½ cup fresh butter |

Thoroughly clean and scrape the fish. Season with salt and pepper, dip in the milk and roll in flour. Sauté the fish in the bacon drippings and oil in an iron skillet, browning well on both sides. Remove the trout to an ovenproof plate, pour the lemon juice and Worcestershire sauce over and place the mint leaves on top. Set in the oven to keep warm. Brown the butter. When ready to serve, pour the butter over the fish and garnish with the bacon slices. Serve with boiled potatoes.

*Serves 8.*

Duri Arquisch
Executive Chef
Salt Lake City Food Services

## Sautéed Trout Bretonne

8 boneless trout
Salt and white pepper to taste
¼ cup lemon juice
¾ cup flour
¾ cup melted butter
½ lb. fresh julienne of carrots
½ lb. fresh julienne of celery

½ lb. fresh mushrooms, sliced
1 Tbsp. chopped parsley

**Lemon Butter:**
1 cup butter
¼ cup plus 2 Tbsp. lemon juice

Cut off the head and tail of each fish and cut the fish in half lengthwise. Sprinkle with salt, pepper and some lemon juice, drench in the flour and fry in some butter. Sauté the carrots, celery and mushrooms in the remaining butter and lemon juice until tender. Add salt and pepper to taste. Garnish the trout with parsley and serve with the **Lemon Butter**.

**Lemon Butter:** Melt the butter in a pan until clear. Drain off the milky part and discard. Add the lemon juice to the clear butter and mix well.

Serves 8.

Erich Dorfhuber
Executive Chef
Portland Food Services

## Stuffed Trout with Butter Sauce

4 (8-oz.) boneless trout
Seasoned flour
1 Tbsp. butter

**Stuffing:**
½ cup finely chopped onions
¼ cup finely chopped celery
¼ cup finely chopped green
  peppers
2 Tbsp. sweet butter
1 cup soft bread crumbs
1 egg

1 tsp. thyme
1 cup chicken stock

**Butter Sauce:**
¼ cup flour, sifted
2 Tbsp. butter
2 cups boiling water
3 egg yolks
¼ cup cream
Juice of ¼ lemon
½ cup plus 2 Tbsp. sweet
  butter

Dip the trout in seasoned flour and shake to remove excess flour. Place the butter in a preheated pan, add the trout and brown on both sides. Remove the trout from the pan, fill with stuffing and place in a greased dish. Bake at 350° for 15 minutes. Spoon the **Butter Sauce** over and serve.

**Stuffing:** Sauté the onions, celery and green peppers in the butter for approximately 5 minutes. Add the bread crumbs, egg and thyme and mix well, then add the chicken stock. Place in a baking pan, cover and bake at 350° for 20 minutes.

**Butter Sauce:** Combine the flour and butter and dilute in the water. Stir briskly until very well blended. Immediately add the egg yolks, cream and lemon juice. Strain through a very fine strainer and finish with the sweet butter.

Rolf Conrad
Executive Chef
Denver Food Services

## Stuffed Rainbow Trout with Mushrooms

*1 ½ tsp. salt*
*6 rainbow trout, dressed*
*4 cups soft bread crumbs*
*½ cup plus 2 Tbsp. butter*
*1 cup sliced fresh mushrooms*

*½ cup sliced green onions*
*½ cup chopped parsley*
*1 (2-oz.) jar pimentos, chopped*
*1 ½ Tbsp. lemon juice*
*½ tsp. thyme*

Sprinkle 1 tsp. salt evenly over the inside and outside of the fish. Sauté the bread crumbs in the ½ cup butter until lightly browned, stirring frequently. Add the mushrooms and onions and cook until the mushrooms are tender. Add the ½ tsp. salt, parsley, pimentos, lemon juice and thyme and toss lightly. Stuff the fish with the dressing and arrange in a well-greased baking pan. Brush with 2 Tbsp. melted butter. Bake at 350° for 25 to 30 minutes or until the fish flakes easily when tested with a fork.

Susan Warren
Reservations

## Baked Cod

4 small pieces cod
1 (16-oz.) can stewed
  tomatoes

1 large onion, sliced
¼ cup melted butter
Salt and pepper

Filet the fish and place in a greased baking dish. Spread the tomatoes over the fish. Cover with the onion slices. Pour the melted butter over. Add salt and pepper to taste. Bake at 350° for 30 minutes, basting occasionally with the sauce in the pan. Serve with rice and green peas.

*Quick and easy to prepare, especially for single guys!*

Mike Dearing
Reservations

## Baked Fish in Mustard Sauce

1 lb. frozen fish filets, thawed
  only until able to separate
½ cup safflower or other
  mayonnaise
2 Tbsp. Viennese or French
  brown prepared mustard

¼ cup chopped onions
1 Tbsp. parsley flakes or
  chopped fresh parsley
¼ tsp. thyme

Place a layer of half the fish in a greased, shallow baking dish. Mix the rest of the ingredients together and spread one-half over the fish. Repeat with the remaining fish and sauce. Bake uncovered at 400° for 20 to 25 minutes. Do not overcook.

Ann Atwood
Reservations

## White Fish en Casserole

2 lbs. white fish (halibut, sole,
  lingcod, etc.)
¼ cup butter
1 Tbsp. finely chopped onion
1¾ cups heavy cream

Juice of ½ lemon
2 tsp. paprika
¼ lb. mushrooms, sliced
¾ cup peeled shrimp

Skin the fish and place in a buttered casserole. Bake at 350° for 15 minutes. Remove the fish from the oven and sprinkle with the onion. Combine the cream and lemon juice and pour over the fish. Dust with paprika, cover with a lid or foil and bake at 350° for 20 minutes, basting twice. Combine the mushrooms with the shrimp and sprinkle over the casserole. Bake for 15 minutes more, basting twice.

## Poached White Fish with Cucumber Sauce

4 to 6 white fish filets
1 tsp. salt
2 peppercorns
3 lemon slices
3 sprigs parsley
1 bay leaf

**Cucumber Sauce:**
¼ cup vegetable oil
2 Tbsp. flour
2 cups milk

3 egg yolks, slightly beaten
1 medium cucumber, peeled,
  seeded and diced into
  ½" cubes
1 (4½-oz.) can shrimp,
  coarsely chopped
1 tsp. salt
½ tsp. Tabasco sauce
½ tsp. nutmeg
⅛ tsp. pepper

Fill a large, deep skillet with about 1½ cups water and bring to a boil. Add the remaining ingredients. Cover and simmer for 4 to 6 minutes or until the fish flakes easily when tested with a fork. Remove the fish carefully with a spatula and serve immediately with the warm **Cucumber Sauce**.

**Cucumber Sauce:** Blend the oil and flour together in a saucepan until smooth. Slowly and thoroughly stir in the milk. Bring to a boil over low heat, stirring constantly; boil for 1 minute. Remove from the heat and gradually stir at least half the hot sauce into the egg yolks. Then blend the yolks into the hot mixture in the saucepan. Boil for 1 minute more, stirring constantly. Remove from the heat and add the remaining ingredients.

Fran Christensen
Reservations

## Baked Fish au Gratin

2 lbs. white fish filets
8 thin slices cheddar cheese
1 tsp. thyme or oregano
¼ cup chopped parsley
1 cup chopped onions

2 Tbsp. vegetable oil
2 Tbsp. flour
1 tsp. salt
⅛ tsp. pepper
1 cup milk

Place half the filets in a greased, 9" x 9" baking dish and cover with half the cheese. Then add another layer of fish and cheese. Sprinkle with the thyme and parsley. Sauté the onions in the oil over medium heat until they are clear and lightly browned. Blend in the flour, salt and pepper. Slowly stir in the milk and bring to a boil over low heat, stirring constantly. Boil for 1 minute. Pour the sauce over the fish and bake at 400° for 20 to 30 minutes.

Fran Christensen
Reservations

## Butterfish in Spanish Sauce

1½ lbs. fresh or frozen Pacific
    butterfish or other fish filets
2 Tbsp. margarine or butter
1 cup chopped onions
½ cup chopped green peppers

1 (1-lb.) can tomatoes,
    undrained and chopped
1 tsp. salt
⅛ tsp. pepper

Thaw the fish if frozen and cut into 4 portions. In a saucepan melt the margarine, add the onions and green peppers and cook until tender. Stir in the tomatoes, salt and pepper; cover and simmer for 8 to 10 minutes. Place the fish in a saucepan, spoon the sauce over, cover and cook for 8 to 10 minutes or until the fish flakes easily when tested with a fork.

Makes 4 servings.

# Hawaiian Kabobs Teriyaki

2 lbs. fresh or frozen cod or
  other thick fish filets
1 (16-oz.) can pineapple
  chunks
½ cup soy sauce
¼ cup sherry (optional)
2 Tbsp. brown sugar

1 Tbsp. freshly grated ginger
  root or 1 tsp. ground
  ginger
1 tsp. dry mustard
1 clove garlic, crushed
1 green pepper, cut into
  1" squares
3 cups cooked rice (optional)

Thaw the fish if frozen and cut into 1" cubes. Drain the pineapple, reserving ¼ cup of the juice. Combine the juice, soy sauce, sherry, brown sugar, ginger, mustard and garlic. Pour the marinade over the fish; cover and refrigerate for at least 1 hour. Drain the fish, reserving the marinade. Thread the fish, pineapple chunks and green pepper alternately on skewers. Cook over hot coals or under the broiler, 4" to 5" from the heat source, for 4 to 5 minutes, while basting with the marinade. Turn and cook for 4 to 5 minutes more or until the fish flakes easily when tested with a fork. Serve as an entrée on a bed of rice or alone as an appetizer.

For an extra festive touch, place a flower on the end of the skewer after cooking.

Makes 6 entrée servings or 18 to 20 appetizers.

Janis Sisley
Reservations

☞ Peel garlic cloves and store them in olive oil in the refrigerator. This keeps them fresh, and the oil can later be used in salad dressing.

## Shrimp-Stuffed Flounder

1 large or 2 small flounder
Salt
½ cup chopped green onions
¼ cup minced green peppers
½ cup minced celery
1 clove garlic, minced
¼ cup butter
1 cup boiling water

1 cube chicken bouillon
2 cups plain stuffing mix
1 Tbsp. chopped parsley
1 egg, beaten
1 cup small shrimp, cooked
Pepper
Paprika
Lemon juice

Make a pocket in the side of the flounder and season with salt. Sauté the onions, peppers, celery and garlic in half the butter; set aside. Pour the water over the bouillon, add the stuffing and parsley and toss well. Cool slightly, then stir in the egg, sautéed vegetables and shrimp. Season to taste with salt and pepper. Stuff the fish, place in a greased pan and cover with foil. Bake at 350° for 30 minutes. Brush with the remaining butter. Sprinkle with the paprika and lemon juice. Bake uncovered for 10 minutes more.

Serves 2.

Pamela Shamsid-Deen
Reservations

## Flounder Provencale

6 (4-oz.) flounder filets
¼ cup butter
¼ cup chopped onions
1 clove garlic, minced
1 (16-oz.) can tomatoes,
  chopped

1 (3-oz.) can chopped
  mushrooms
¼ cup dry white wine
6 lemon wedges
Parsley

Wash and dry the fish; lay out flat. Dot with butter, roll up and secure with toothpicks. Combine and place the remaining ingredients in a 13" x 9" casserole. Add the fish. Bake until the fish flakes.

Other types of white fish can be substituted for the flounder.

Andrea Meyer
Reservations

## Golden Puffs of Fried Flounder

2 eggs, separated
2 Tbsp. flour
1 tsp. salt
¾ cup olive oil

1½ lbs. flounder filets,
  cut into 4" x 3" pieces
6 fresh lemon wedges

Beat the egg whites until stiff. Beat the yolks until thick; stir in the flour and salt. Gently fold in the stiffly beaten whites until well blended. Heat the olive oil in a 10" skillet until tiny bubbles form around the edge. Dip each piece of fish into the batter and place in the hot oil until golden brown. Carefully turn and cook until golden on the other side. Serve immediately with the lemon wedges.

Serves 6.

Tim Walker
Reservations

## Halibut Alyeska

4 Pacific halibut filets
Dry white wine
2 to 3 scallions, chopped
Pinch of dry mustard

¾ cup sour cream
¾ cup mayonnaise
Grated Parmesan cheese

Marinate the halibut in the wine for 3 hours; drain. Transfer the filets to a casserole dish, sprinkle with the scallions and mustard. Thoroughly combine the sour cream and mayonnaise and pour the mixture over the halibut. Bake at 350° for 30 minutes. Turn off the oven, sprinkle the cheese over the casserole and return to the oven until the cheese melts. Cool slightly before serving. Serve with Grey Riesling wine, salad and French bread.

Note: Use different cheeses for variety.

Dave Hall
Manager of Systems and Implementation
Apollo Travel Systems

# Sourdough Fried Fish with Blueberry Sauce

**Sourdough:**
½ cup **Sourdough Starter**
  (see index)
1 cup lukewarm water
1 ¼ cups flour

**Batter:**
¼ cup milk or cream
1 egg, beaten
1 Tbsp. sugar
1 Tbsp. vegetable oil
½ tsp. baking soda
½ tsp. salt

**Fish:**
2 lbs. lingcod or other thick
  fish filets
1 tsp. salt
¼ tsp. pepper
½ cup flour
Fat

**Blueberry Sauce:**
2 cups blueberries
¼ to ⅓ cup sugar
2 cinnamon sticks
2 Tbsp. fresh lemon juice
1 tsp. cornstarch

Combine the sourdough ingredients, cover and let stand overnight. When ready to cook, mix together the batter ingredients and stir into the refrigerated sourdough batter; let stand and bubble for 10 minutes. Cut the fish into serving-size portions, sprinkle with the salt and pepper, coat with the flour and dip into the sourdough batter. Fry in a large, deep skillet with fat approximately 2" deep, turning once until both sides are brown and the fish flakes easily when tested with a fork. Drain on absorbent paper. Serve with the hot **Blueberry Sauce**.

**Blueberry Sauce:** In a saucepan combine the blueberries, ½ cup water, the sugar and cinnamon. Heat to simmering, stirring until the sugar is dissolved; simmer for 5 minutes more. Stir in the lemon juice. Blend the cornstarch and 1 Tbsp. water together, then add to the sauce, stirring constantly. Heat to boiling and boil for 2 minutes, stirring constantly.

*Makes 6 servings.*

Jackie Partlow

## Sashimi

1 lb. white Daikon radishes
⅓ small carrot
1 lb. very fresh tuna filets
1 Tbsp. plus 1 tsp. water

1 Tbsp. plus 1 tsp. Wasabi powder
Soy sauce
Parsley sprigs

Peel the radishes and shred into long, fine, grass-like strands. Peel and shred the carrot the same way, mix with the radishes, place in ice water and set aside. Rinse the fish in cold water and pat dry with towels. Cut off and discard any dark portions (in red-fleshed fish, these will be almost black). If the fish is wide, cut into strips 1½" to 2" wide. Place the filets on a cutting board and, using a very sharp, thin-bladed knife, cut across the grain into ⅛" thick slices. (All the slices should be uniformly cut in size and thickness to keep the flavor fresh.) Handle no more than necessary. Drain the radish-carrot mixture thoroughly, pat dry and arrange on a chilled serving plate. Transfer the fish slices with a spatula to the serving plate, arrange in 2 rows over the radishes, leaving about one-third of the vegetable mixture exposed. Gradually add the water to the Wasabi powder, blending into a smooth paste. Cover and let stand for 5 to 8 minutes. Place this Wasabi paste and the soy sauce in serving dishes at the side and garnish with parsley. Set out small sauce dishes for mixing Wasabi paste with soy sauce, if desired.

*Note: Wasabi powder is a hot, green horseradish; if unavailable, substitute pastes can be made by combining 1 Tbsp. plus 1 tsp. dry English mustard with 1 Tbsp. water, or by slightly draining 2 Tbsp. prepared horseradish or by serving freshly grated ginger root. The radishes can be substituted with 3 cups finely shredded cabbage or iceberg lettuce. The tuna can also be substituted or combined with other red fish like bluefin or yellowfish or with white fish like albacore, white seabass or halibut.*

**Sashimi** *is considered a delicacy of the Orient and is highly favored by gourmets.*

*Serves 4 as an entrée or 6 to 8 as an appetizer.*

Oswald M. Gnigler
Executive Chef
Las Vegas Food Services

### Filet of Sole Veronique

| | |
|---|---|
| 2 lbs. fresh or frozen rex or Dover sole or other fish filets | 1 cup white seedless grapes (¼ lb.) |
| 2 Tbsp. lemon juice | ¼ tsp. fines herbes |
| 2 tsp. salt | 3 Tbsp. margarine or butter |
| 1 cup dry white wine | 2 Tbsp. flour |

Thaw the fish if frozen. Cut into serving-size portions, sprinkle the lemon juice and salt over and arrange in a well-greased, 10" skillet in 1 or 2 layers. Combine the wine, grapes and fines herbes. Pour over the fish and heat to simmering. Cover and poach for about 5 minutes or until the fish flakes easily when tested with a fork. Carefully remove the sole, reserving the liquid, and drain on absorbent paper. Transfer the fish to an ovenproof platter, strain the grapes from the liquid and reserve for garnish. In a separate pan, melt the margarine and blend in the flour. Add the reserved liquid gradually and cook until thick and smooth, stirring constantly. The sauce should be light; add more wine, if necessary. Pour the sauce over the fish and garnish with the reserved grapes. The fish may be heated under the broiler until lightly browned.

*Shortcut Method: Poach the fish and fresh grapes. Remove the fish from the poaching liquid and spread canned Hollandaise sauce over the fish. Broil until hot and lightly browned. Garnish with the reserved grapes.*

*Note: This recipe is best prepared with fresh grapes, but canned grapes may be used out of season. Do not poach canned grapes.*

Makes 4 servings.

Virginia Hansen

### Ocean Perch Almondine

| | |
|---|---|
| 6 (6-oz.) fresh or frozen perch filets | 2 Tbsp. butter |
| Lemon juice | ⅔ cup slivered blanched almonds |
| ½ cup milk | Salt and pepper to taste |
| Flour | Chopped parsley |

If frozen, thaw the filets; dip in lemon juice and the milk and roll in flour. Sauté in the butter until browned on both sides and remove to a hot platter. Add the almonds to the pan and let brown very quickly. Add salt and pepper, a dash of lemon juice and the chopped parsley and pour the hot butter over the filets.

*Serves 6.*

Duri Arquisch
Executive Chef
Salt Lake City Food Services

## Filet of Red Snapper Palos Verdes

¾ cup butter
6 (8-oz.) red snapper filets
½ cup sliced shallots
1 tsp. sliced garlic
½ tsp. cayenne pepper
1 Tbsp. salt
½ tsp. thyme leaves
1 bay leaf

½ cup chopped parsley
1 cup diced celery
½ tsp. saffron
4 tomatoes, peeled and sliced
2 cups dry white wine
2 cups **Fish Stock** (see index)
¼ cup plus 2 Tbsp. lemon juice
1 cup white bread crumbs

Butter the bottom of a large, shallow, ovenproof fish pan with half the butter and lay the filets in it lengthwise. Sprinkle over the fish the shallots, garlic, cayenne pepper, salt, thyme, bay leaf, parsley, celery, saffron and tomatoes. Add the wine, **Fish Stock** and lemon juice, cover securely with aluminum foil and bring to a boil on top of the stove. Remove the foil and sprinkle the bread crumbs over the fish. Dot with the remaining butter, replace the foil and bake at 450° for 30 minutes. Remove the foil and cook for 5 minutes more or until the top browns. Serve with rice or potatoes and a vegetable of your choice.

*Serves 6.*

Raoul F. Delbol
Executive Chef
Los Angeles Food Services

## Sole au Gratin with Shrimp Sauce

2 lbs. sole filets, halved
¼ cup dry sherry
2 Tbsp. lemon juice
½ tsp. salt
2 Tbsp. butter
2 Tbsp. flour
¼ tsp. pepper
½ tsp. Dijon mustard
1 tsp. instant chicken bouillon

½ cup heavy cream or
   half & half
½ cup shredded Swiss cheese
1 lb. frozen shrimp, cleaned
   and cooked, or ¾ lb. fresh
   whole shrimp, cooked
1 Tbsp. snipped parsley
3 lemon slices

Arrange the fish in a large, shallow baking dish or pan. Combine the sherry and lemon juice, pour over the fish and sprinkle with salt. Bake uncovered at 350° for 15 minutes; drain the broth and reserve. Return the fish to the oven, bake until it flakes, about 10 minutes. While the fish bakes, add enough water to the reserved broth to measure 1 cup. Melt the butter in a saucepan over low heat. Stir in the flour, pepper, mustard and chicken bouillon. Cook over low heat, stirring until the mixture is smooth and bubbly. Remove from the heat, stir in the reserved broth and the cream and heat to boiling, stirring constantly. Boil, stirring, for 1 minute. Add the cheese and shrimp, reserving several shrimp for garnish. Heat over low heat, stirring constantly, until the cheese melts. Alternate layers of fish and sauce in a large chafing dish, finishing with the sauce. Sprinkle with the parsley, garnish with the lemon slices and reserved shrimp. Serve over a low flame.

Note: This dish can be placed in an ovenproof casserole and kept in a 250° oven for up to 1 hour. Garnish just before serving.

Beth DiPasquale
Help Desk

## Stuffed Red Snapper

1 (4- to 5-lb.) red snapper
Salt and pepper
Butter, softened
1 cup chopped onions
1 clove garlic, minced
4 cups dry bread crumbs

1 cup minced cucumber
½ cup chopped toasted
   almonds
1 tsp. dried thyme
Dry sherry

Have your fish dealer bone the red snapper and prepare it for stuffing. Rub the inside with salt, pepper and butter. Sauté the onions and garlic in more butter until soft and then combine with the bread crumbs, cucumber and almonds. Season with salt, pepper and the thyme and moisten with the sherry. Stuff the fish and secure it with toothpicks. Sprinkle the outside with salt and pepper. Set in a well-greased casserole and bake at 350° for 40 to 45 minutes or until the fish flakes easily when tested with a fork. While cooking, baste with the pan juices.

## California Seafood Stew

¾ cup plus 1½ Tbsp. finely chopped fresh shallots
6 Tbsp. olive oil
1 lb. red snapper or cod filets, poached, drained and cut into 1" cubes
1 lb. shrimp, drained, peeled and deveined
1 lb. small white scallops, drained
¼ lb. canned cherrystone clams, drained and chopped (reserve juice)

5 cloves garlic, finely chopped
1½ cups California white wine
3 cups water
1 cup tomato puree
½ cup chopped canned tomatoes
1 bay leaf
Pinch of saffron
Dash of Tabasco sauce
Pinch of thyme leaves
Salt and pepper to taste
Freshly chopped parsley

Sauté the 1½ Tbsp. shallots in 3 Tbsp. oil, being careful not to brown. Add the red snapper or cod, shrimp and scallops and cook for 5 minutes. Add the clams and bring to a boil. Strain and reserve the juices; set the juices and stew aside. Sauté the garlic and ¾ cup shallots in 3 Tbsp. oil, being careful not to brown. Add the wine and reduce by half. Add the remaining ingredients (including the reserved canned clam juice and the stew juices) except the parsley and simmer over medium heat for 20 minutes. Add the seafood, season to taste and bring to a boil. Place in a serving dish and top with parsley.

*Serves 10.*

John H. Wolfsheimer
Executive Chef
San Francisco Food Services

### Dick's Favorite Seafood Stew

1 green pepper, cubed
1 onion, cubed
1 green onion, chopped
3 Tbsp. butter
6 large shrimp
6 scallops
1 (8-oz.) can chopped
   clams

½ cup crabmeat
2½ cups whole milk, heated
½ tsp. thyme
¼ tsp. tarragon
¾ tsp. salt
⅛ tsp. white pepper

Sauté the green pepper and the onions in the butter for 1 minute. Add the shrimp and cook for 1 minute. Add the scallops and cook for 1 minute more. Add the clams and their juice and the crabmeat. Add the milk and seasonings. Heat over low heat to blend, about 10 minutes. Do not boil. Serve hot with French rolls and butter. Crisp bacon bits and a little freshly chopped parsley make a nice garnish.

Beth DiPasquale
Help Desk

### Cioppino

3 cloves garlic, finely chopped
2 medium onions, coarsely
   chopped
⅓ cup olive oil
½ lb. shrimp
½ lb. deep sea scallops
1 whole cracked Dungeness
   crab (leg and body
   meat only)
24 cherrystone clams

1 cup dry white wine
½ cup tomato puree
2 tomatoes, peeled and
   chopped
1 bay leaf
Pinch of saffron
Dash of Tabasco sauce
Pinch of thyme leaves
Salt and pepper to taste
1 Tbsp. chopped fresh parsley

In a large pot, sauté the garlic and onions in the olive oil until lightly browned. Add the shrimp, scallops, crab and clams. (The crab legs and clams can be used with the shell; they should, however, be washed prior to use.) Cook all the fish for about 2 minutes, stirring occasionally. Then add 1½ cups water, the wine, tomato puree, tomatoes and bay leaf. Soak and dilute the saffron in 2 Tbsp. water for 2 minutes, then add to the stew. Add the Tabasco sauce, thyme and salt and pepper to taste. Cover the pot and simmer slowly for 15 to 20 minutes. When the fish is cooked, remove from the kettle with a slotted spoon or skimmer and place in a deep serving dish; keep warm. Let the cooking juices reduce by cooking them an additional 10 to 15 minutes. Pour the juices over the fish and sprinkle the top with the parsley. Serve piping hot. Serve with toasted French sourdough bread which has been rubbed with fresh garlic and saturated with melted butter.

*Serves 4.*

John H. Wolfsheimer
Executive Chef
San Francisco Food Services

## Jambalaya

*¼ cup oil*
*1 large onion, sliced*
*2 cloves garlic, chopped*
*1 large green pepper, sliced*
*1 (8-oz.) can peeled tomatoes,*
  *sliced (reserve juice)*
*24 large prawns*
*Salt and pepper to taste*

**Rice:**
*¼ cup oil*
*½ small onion, chopped*
*1 clove garlic, chopped*
*1 cup rice*
*1½ cups chicken stock*
*½ cup frozen peas, thawed*

Heat the oil in a pan, add the onion and garlic and cook until tender. Add the green pepper and cook until it is tender. Add the tomatoes and their juice and simmer for approximately 15 minutes. Add the prawns and simmer for approximately 15 minutes more. Season with salt and pepper and serve over the rice.

**Rice:** Heat the oil in a pan, add the onion and garlic and cook to a clear glaze. Add the rice and mix well. Add the chicken stock and bring to a boil, then bake at 450° to 500° for 20 minutes or until the rice has absorbed all the liquid. Remove from the oven and mix in the peas. Let stand for 5 minutes, then serve.

Rolf Conrad
Executive Chef
Denver Food Services

## Seafood Newburg

¾ lb. King Crab legs, cut into
   1" pieces
18 large shrimp, peeled and
   deveined
½ cup sliced mushrooms
¼ cup plus 2 Tbsp. butter
½ cup dry sherry wine

⅓ cup chopped onions
¾ cup flour
4 cups half & half
¼ cup lobster base
Salt and white pepper to taste
⅛ tsp. ground thyme
⅛ tsp. Spanish paprika

Sauté the seafood and mushrooms in 2 Tbsp. butter until done, add half the wine and set aside. Sauté the onions in the remaining butter until limp but not brown. Add the flour to make a roux; let cool. Add the half & half, stirring constantly, bring to a boil and simmer for 20 minutes. Add the lobster base and seasonings, then the remaining wine. Pour the sauce over the seafood and serve.

Note: If lobster base is unavailable, a high quality shrimp or lobster bisque may be used, adding heavy cream to desired consistency.

Serves 6.

Rold Conrad
Executive Chef
Denver Food Services

## Seafood Redondo Beach

½ lb. medium shrimp, cooked,
   cleaned and deveined
½ lb. crabmeat, cut into
   1" pieces
½ lb. scallops, cooked
½ cup butter
⅓ cup white wine
½ cup sliced fresh
   mushrooms
¼ cup diced celery
¼ cup diced onions

½ large green pepper, cut
   into ½" strips
1 (8-oz.) can diced tomatoes
White pepper
Salt to taste
Bay leaf
Garlic
Aromat
Oregano
Chopped parsley

Sauté the shrimp, crabmeat and scallops lightly in half the butter, then swish with the wine. Remove from the pan and keep warm. Add the remaining butter and sauté the mushrooms, celery, onions and green pepper. Add the tomatoes and their liquid and season to taste with white pepper, salt, bay leaf, garlic, Aromat, oregano and chopped parsley; simmer just until done. Add the seafood and combine carefully, reheat and serve. Good with rice.

W. Reichmuth
Executive Chef
Chicago Food Services

☞ *Unexpected company . . . no rolls? Cut the crusts from bread slices, spread with butter, roll and fasten with toothpicks. Broil until toasted, turning as necessary.*

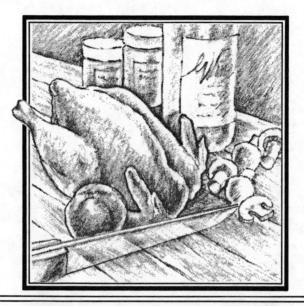

# POULTRY

## Breast of Chicken Paprikash

8 boneless chicken breasts
Salt and pepper

**Paprika Sauce:**
2 Tbsp. butter
1 onion, finely chopped
1 Tbsp. flour
1 cup chicken stock

¼ cup dry white wine
2 Tbsp. Hungarian paprika
½ tsp. salt
⅛ tsp. pepper
Pinch of ground thyme
Pinch of ground bay leaf
1 cup cream

Rinse the chicken breasts and pat dry. Place on a sheet pan and sprinkle with salt and pepper. Bake at 350° for 20 to 25 minutes. Remove from the oven and place on a heated serving platter. Top with **Paprika Sauce** and serve immediately.

**Paprika Sauce:** Melt the butter in a saucepan and add the onion; sauté until tender but not brown. Add the flour and mix well. Slowly add the chicken stock, wine and seasonings. Cook, stirring, until the mixture thickens. Reduce the heat and simmer for 5 to 10 minutes. Add the cream and heat, but do not boil.

Serves 8.

John H. Wolfsheimer
Executive Chef
San Francisco Food Services

## Chicken Tremendous

1 pkg. onion soup mix
½ to ¾ cup uncooked rice
Salt and pepper to taste

1 can cream of chicken soup,
    diluted with 1 can water
4 chicken breasts

Mix together the first 4 ingredients and pour into a greased casserole dish. Arrange the chicken pieces over the rice and bake at 350° for 1 hour or until the chicken is tender. Gently stir up the bottom occasionally and add more liquid, if necessary.

Lillian Warren

### Chicken Breasts Piquant

3 split chicken breasts, boned
¾ cup rosé wine
¼ cup soy sauce
¼ cup salad oil
2 Tbsp. water

1 clove garlic, minced
1 tsp. ginger
¼ tsp. oregano
1 Tbsp. brown sugar

Arrange the chicken in a baking dish. Combine the remaining ingredients and pour over the chicken. Cover and bake at 375° for 1½ hours. Serve with rice.

Sally Keenan
Inflight Services

### Grilled Chicken Breasts Hawaiian

4 chicken breasts, boned
½ cup soy sauce
½ cup pineapple juice
2 Tbsp. lemon juice
1 clove garlic, minced

½ cup finely chopped
  macadamia nuts
1 (3-oz.) can deviled ham
1 tsp. grated onion
¼ cup melted butter

Place the chicken breasts in a marinating dish. Combine the soy sauce, pineapple juice, lemon juice and garlic; pour over the chicken. Let stand at room temperature for 2 hours. Line a firebox with 14" heavy-duty Kaiser Quilted Foil; let the coals burn down until covered with gray ashes. Combine the macadamia nuts, ham and onion. Spoon onto the chicken breasts, roll up and secure with skewers. Brush with the butter and arrange on a large sheet of foil. Grill 4" above the coals for 35 to 40 minutes, turning often and basting with the butter.

Serves 4.

John H. Wolfsheimer
Executive Chef
San Francisco Food Services

## Chicken Cacciatore

¼ cup all-purpose flour
Salt and pepper to taste
4 (5-oz.) chicken breasts or
  legs
¼ cup olive or cooking oil
½ cup chopped onions
¼ chopped celery
¼ cup chopped green peppers
2 cloves garlic, minced

1 (16-oz.) can tomatoes,
  chopped
1 (8-oz.) can tomato sauce
1 (3-oz.) can sliced
  mushrooms, drained
½ tsp. dried basil, crushed
½ tsp. dried rosemary,
  crushed
¼ cup white wine

Mix together the flour and ½ tsp. salt. Dredge the chicken in the flour and brown in the oil; remove the chicken. In the same skillet cook the onions, celery, green peppers and garlic until tender but not brown. Return the chicken to the skillet. Combine the tomatoes, tomato sauce, mushrooms, salt and pepper to taste, the basil, rosemary and wine and pour over the chicken. Cover and bake at 350° until the chicken is tender. Remove the chicken to a warm serving dish and ladle the sauce over the top. Serve with rice and green peas.

Serves 4.

Erich Dorfhuber
Executive Chef
Portland Food Services

## Delicious Chicken

3 Tbsp. milk
3 Tbsp. melted butter
¼ cup prepared mustard
½ cup honey

1 tsp. curry powder
1 tsp. salt
4 chicken breasts or 6 thighs

Mix all the ingredients together except the chicken. Roll the chicken in the mixture. Bake at 350° for 1 hour and 15 minutes, basting often.

Janis Sisley

## Baked Chicken Breasts Supreme

2 Tbsp. butter or margarine
2 Tbsp. salad oil
6 large chicken breast halves,
　boned and skinned
1 (10½-oz.) can condensed
　cream of chicken soup
½ cup light cream

½ cup dry sherry
1 tsp. tarragon leaves
1 tsp. Worcestershire sauce
¼ tsp. chervil leaves
¼ tsp. garlic powder
1 (6-oz.) can sliced
　mushrooms, drained

Place the butter and oil in a 13½" x 9" baking dish and heat in a 350° oven until the butter is melted. Place the chicken in the baking dish, turning to coat with the butter. Bake uncovered for 1 hour. Heat the soup, cream and sherry, stirring occasionally. Combine the remaining ingredients, pour over the chicken, cover tightly and cook for 15 to 20 minutes more.

Serves 6.

Vera Cook
Reservations

## Chicken Hawaiian

⅓ cup salad oil or shortening
2 whole chicken breasts
2 whole chicken legs
½ cup flour
1 tsp. salt
¼ tsp. pepper
1 (20-oz.) can sliced pineapple
1 cup sugar

2 Tbsp. cornstarch
¾ cup cider vinegar
1 Tbsp. soy sauce
¼ tsp. ginger
1 chicken bouillon cube
1 large green pepper,
　sliced in ¼" circles
Cooked rice

Heat the oil in a large skillet. Coat the chicken with the flour, place in the skillet and brown on all sides. Set the chicken in a casserole dish, sprinkle with the salt and pepper. Drain the pineapple. Add water to the syrup to make 1¼ cups. In a saucepan combine the syrup, sugar, cornstarch, vinegar, soy sauce, ginger and bouillon cube. Bring to a boil and boil for 2 minutes. Pour the sauce over the chicken and bake uncovered at 350° for 30 minutes. Add the pineapple and green pepper to the casserole and bake for 30 minutes more or until the chicken is tender. Serve over rice.

*Serves 4.*

Janis Sisley

## Chicken 'N Rice Casserole

*1 ¼ cups raw rice*
*1 can cream of mushroom*
*    soup, undiluted*
*1 can cream of celery soup,*
*    undiluted*
*1 can cream of chicken soup,*
*    undiluted*
*¼ cup melted butter or*
*    margarine*

*¼ cup sherry or white wine*
*10 pieces chicken (legs, thighs,*
*    breasts)*
*½ cup slivered blanched*
*    almonds*
*⅓ cup grated Parmesan*
*    cheese*

Sprinkle the rice over the bottom of a lightly greased, 3-quart baking dish. In a bowl combine the soups, butter and sherry; spread half the soup mixture over the rice. Place the chicken pieces, skin side up, in a single layer over the soup, then spread the remaining soup mixture over the chicken. Sprinkle with the almonds and cheese. Cover and bake at 275° for 2½ hours. Increase the temperature to 400°, uncover the chicken and bake for 20 minutes more to brown.

Gladys Tyo
Reservations

## Chicken Delight

*1 whole chicken*
*Oil*
*½ cup chopped green peppers*
*½ cup chopped onions*
*½ cup chopped mushrooms*

*Chopped, precooked sausage*
*    to taste*
*¼ cup white wine*
*Garlic salt to taste*
*Pepper*
*2 Tbsp. melted butter*

Debone the chicken, cut into bite-size strips and sauté in oil until lightly browned. Bake at 450° for 8 minutes. Remove and add the remaining ingredients. Return to the oven and bake for 5 to 8 minutes more.

Dottie Martin

## Broiled, Deviled Spring Chicken

1 (2½- to 3-lb.) spring chicken
Salt and white pepper to taste
½ cup melted butter
1 Tbsp. dry mustard
4 Tbsp. dry white wine
Tabasco sauce to taste
1 cup white bread crumbs
1 Tbsp. finely chopped parsley
Garlic powder or chopped
    garlic to taste

1 Tbsp. finely chopped
    shallots or onion
½ cup tomato sauce
½ cup thick brown sauce or
    beef broth
Pepper to taste
Worcestershire sauce to taste
Cayenne pepper to taste

Cut the chicken in half lengthwise, along the middle of the back, pound out flat and remove as many bones as possible from the inside. Season lightly with salt and white pepper, then baste with ¼ cup butter and bake uncovered at 400° for 10 to 15 minutes or until nicely browned. Remove from the oven, brush with a light paste of the mustard, 1 Tbsp. wine and Tabasco sauce to taste; then sprinkle over a mixture of the crumbs, parsley and garlic. Press with the flat side of a knife to make the crumbs adhere to the paste, then sprinkle the remaining butter over and broil until golden brown. When ready to serve, make a sauce by cooking the shallots or onion and 3 Tbsp. wine together for a few minutes; then add the tomato and brown sauce and cook for 5 minutes. Season to taste with salt and pepper, Worcestershire sauce and cayenne pepper. Pour the sauce over the chicken and serve.

Hans Jantzen
Executive Chef
New York Food Services

## Capital Chicken

¼ cup butter
1 Tbsp. cooking oil
1 fryer chicken, cut into parts
½ lb. fresh mushrooms, sliced
1 Tbsp. flour
1 can cream of chicken soup
1 cup dry white wine

½ cup heavy cream
1 tsp. salt
¼ tsp. tarragon
¼ tsp. pepper
1 (15-oz.) can artichoke hearts
6 green onions, chopped
2 Tbsp. parsley

In a large skillet, melt the butter and oil over medium heat. Add the chicken and cook for 10 minutes or until brown. Remove the chicken and place in a baking pan. In the same skillet, sauté the mushrooms until tender; stir in the flour, soup, wine and 1 cup water. Simmer for 10 minutes or until the sauce thickens, then stir in the cream, salt, tarragon and pepper. Pour the sauce over the chicken and bake at 350° for 1 hour. Add the artichokes, onions and parsley the final 5 minutes of baking.

Ron Kearney

## Lemon Chicken Broil

1 medium chicken, cut up
1 Tbsp. butter
½ tsp. salt

Pinch of ground pepper
2 Tbsp. water
2 Tbsp. lemon or lime juice

Bake the chicken at 350° for 30 minutes. Melt the butter in a skillet, add the remaining ingredients and bring to a boil over medium heat. Reduce the heat to warm. Baste the chicken with the mixture twice on each side and bake for 30 minutes more.

*Makes 4 to 6 servings.*

Farough

## Poulet Marengo

6 slices bacon, cut
 into 1" pieces
2 broiler-fryers or 4 lbs. chicken
 breasts
½ cup sifted all-purpose flour
2 tsp. salt
¼ tsp. pepper
1 cup chopped onions

1 clove garlic, minced
1 (3- to 4-oz.) can whole
 mushrooms
2 (1-lb.) cans tomatoes
¼ cup chopped parsley
A few drops of Tabasco sauce
2 slices white bread
Parsley

Fry the bacon until almost crisp, drain on a paper towel and set aside. Leave the drippings in the pan. Wash and dry the chicken pieces and shake in a paper bag filled with the flour, salt and pepper, reserving the leftover flour mixture. Brown the chicken, a few pieces at a time, in the bacon drippings. Arrange in a shallow baking dish. Sauté the onions and garlic until soft in the remaining bacon drippings. Stir in the reserved flour mixture. Drain the mushrooms, reserving the liquid. Stir the mushroom liquid, tomatoes, parsley and Tabasco sauce into the frying pan. Heat to boiling, stirring constantly. Spoon the sauce over the chicken and cover. (The casserole can be assembled up to this point, then chilled. Remove from the refrigerator and let stand at room temperature for 30 minutes before baking.) Bake at 350° for 1 hour and 20 minutes or until the chicken is tender. Trim the crusts from the bread. Cut into 1½" cubes. Spread in a single layer in a shallow baking pan and toast at 350° for 10 minutes or until golden; set aside. Uncover the chicken, sprinkle with the bacon pieces and mushrooms. Bake for 10 minutes more or until the bacon is crisp. Just before serving, sprinkle the croutons over the top of the chicken and garnish with parsley.

Janis Sisley

## Roasted Chicken with Browned Potatoes

2 (2- to 2½-lb.) broiler-fryers,
 quartered
1 large green pepper, cut
 into 1" strips
2 lbs. new potatoes, peeled
1 clove garlic, crushed

⅓ cup salad or olive oil
1 tsp. dried oregano leaves
1½ tsp. salt
¼ tsp. pepper
½ tsp. paprika

Wipe the chicken with damp paper towels. In a large, shallow baking dish, arrange a single layer of the chicken, green pepper and potatoes. Combine the garlic, oil and oregano and drizzle over the chicken and vegetables. Sprinkle all around with the salt, pepper and paprika. Bake uncovered, basting frequently, at 375° for 1 hour or until tender. Increase the temperature to 400° and bake for 15 minutes more to brown. Arrange on a warm platter and serve.

Fran Christensen
Tour Desk

## Chicken with Artichokes

¼ cup butter
1 Tbsp. cooking oil
1 chicken broiler-fryer, cut
   into parts
½ lb. fresh mushrooms, sliced
1 Tbsp. flour
1 (11-oz.) can cream of chicken
   soup
1 cup dry white wine

½ cup cream
1 tsp. salt
¼ tsp. tarragon
¼ tsp. pepper
1 (15-oz.) can artichoke
   hearts, drained
6 green onions with tops,
   chopped
2 Tbsp. chopped parsley

In a large skillet, melt the butter in the oil over medium heat. Add the chicken and cook, turning as needed, for 10 minutes or until the chicken is browned on all sides. Remove and place in a baking pan or casserole. In the same pan, sauté the mushrooms for about 5 minutes or until tender. Stir in the flour. Add the soup, wine and 1 cup water and simmer, stirring occasionally, for about 10 minutes or until the sauce thickens. Stir in the cream, salt, tarragon and pepper and pour over the chicken. Bake uncovered at 350° for 1 hour. Remove and mix in the artichoke hearts, green onions and parsley. Bake for 5 minutes more or until the chicken is fork-tender.

Serves 4.

Karen Fudge
Regional Sales

## Almond Chicken

1 (3½-lb.) broiler-fryer, cut up
Flour
1 tsp. celery salt
1 tsp. paprika
1 tsp. salt
½ tsp. curry powder
½ tsp. oregano
½ tsp. pepper

¼ cup plus 2 Tbsp. melted
butter
¾ cup sliced almonds
1½ cups half & half
½ cup sour cream
3 Tbsp. fine dry bread crumbs
blended with 1 Tbsp.
melted butter

Coat the chicken pieces with flour. Blend the spices with the butter and use to coat the chicken pieces. Arrange the chicken in a single layer in a baking dish. Sprinkle evenly with the almonds. Pour the half & half over the chicken. Bake covered at 350° for 45 minutes. Uncover, spoon about ½ cup sauce from the pan into the sour cream and stir well. Pour evenly over the chicken. Sprinkle with the buttered crumbs and bake uncovered for about 15 minutes more or until tender.

Serves 6.

Gail Workman
Reservations

## Lemon Chicken

½ cup flour
1¼ tsp. salt
1 tsp. tarragon leaves
1 whole chicken, cut up
½ cup butter

⅓ cup lemon juice
1 tsp. minced onion
⅛ tsp. pepper
1 clove garlic, crushed

Combine the flour, 1 tsp. salt and tarragon in a paper bag. Add the chicken and shake until coated. Melt the butter in a 13" x 9" x 2" pan. Coat the chicken in the butter and leave in the pan. Bake at 375° for 30 minutes, basting twice with the pan drippings. Combine the remaining ingredients, pour over the chicken and bake for 30 minutes more, basting twice with the lemon and pan drippings.

Eileen Bohach
Reservations

### Raspberry Glazed Chicken

1 (3- to 4-lb.) roasting chicken
Cooking oil
¼ cup red raspberry jelly
1 Tbsp. lemon juice
1 Tbsp. butter

1½ tsp. cornstarch
Dash of ground cinnamon
¼ tsp. salt
1 Tbsp. vinegar

Place the chicken, breast side up, on a rack in a shallow roasting pan. Rub the skin with oil. Insert a meat thermometer in the center of the inside thigh muscle, not touching the bone. Roast uncovered at 375° until the thermometer registers 185°, about 1½ to 2 hours. Combine and heat the jelly, lemon juice and butter until the jelly melts. Combine the cornstarch, cinnamon and salt, blend in the vinegar and stir into the jelly mixture. Cook and stir until thick and bubbly. Baste the chicken frequently with the sauce while roasting for 15 minutes more.

Makes 4 servings.

Dottie Martin

### Chicken Broccoli Casserole

2 pkg. frozen chopped
   broccoli
3 cups cubed, cooked chicken
2 cans cream of chicken soup
1 cup mayonnaise

1 tsp. lemon juice
½ tsp. curry powder (optional)
1 cup shredded cheese
2 Tbsp. melted butter
¾ cup bread crumbs

Cook the broccoli according to the package directions; drain. In a greased, 9" x 13" baking pan, layer the broccoli and chicken. Combine the soup, mayonnaise, lemon juice and curry powder and pour over the broccoli and chicken; sprinkle with the cheese. Combine the butter and crumbs; sprinkle over the casserole and bake at 350° for 25 to 30 minutes.

Rick Sanders
Nola Sears
Reservations

## Chicken Fredericka

1½ cups diced, cooked
  chicken
1 pkg. frozen baby peas
½ cup whole cashew nuts
½ cup slivered almonds
½ cup garbanzo beans
1 cup sliced pitted olives
¾ cup chopped green onions
2 green peppers, chopped
2 red peppers, chopped
1 cup yogurt

1 cup mayonnaise
2 garlic cloves, diced
2 Tbsp. olive oil
1 Tbsp. lemon juice
1 tsp. cumin
⅛ tsp. turmeric
1 tsp. parsley
½ tsp. dill
¼ cup sunflower seeds
Salt and pepper
12 cherry tomatoes

Combine all the ingredients except the cherry tomatoes and spoon into a casserole dish. Cut the cherry tomatoes in half and add to the casserole. Bake at 350° for 30 to 40 minutes or until heated through.

*Note: Crab may be substituted for the chicken.*

Jan Crabb

## Chicken 'N Cheese in Wine Sauce

1 cut up or whole chicken
¾ to 1 cup sherry
2½ cups milk

1 medium pkg. Velveeta
  cheese
3 medium slices cheddar
  cheese

Boil the chicken. When cooked, remove the skin and pour ¼ to ½ cup sherry over; set aside. In a saucepan bring the milk to a boil, stir in the Velveeta cheese until melted, add the cheddar cheese and ½ cup sherry. Remove the chicken from the bones and shred the meat into medium pieces. Stir the chicken into the cheese sauce. Bake at 350° for 30 minutes. Serve over rice, noodles or toast.

*The cheese sauce is also good for fondue.*

Veronica Joyce
Reservations

## Fruit-Stuffed Chicken Breasts

¾ cup butter
1 cup diced apples
½ cup coarsely chopped nuts
½ cup white raisins
1 (1¼-lb.) can crushed
   pineapple
1 cup soft bread crumbs,
   toasted
1 tsp. salt
1 tsp. ground cinnamon
½ tsp. ground nutmeg
¼ tsp. ground cloves
¼ tsp. ground ginger
6 whole chicken breasts,
   boned

**Fruit Sauce:**
1 Tbsp. sugar
1 Tbsp. cornstarch
⅛ tsp. salt
½ tsp. ground cinnamon
¼ tsp. ground nutmeg
⅛ tsp. ground ginger
1 cup orange juice
Reserved pineapple and syrup
¼ cup white raisins
1 Tbsp. butter
Slivered peel of 1 orange
Sections of 1 orange

Melt ½ cup butter in a skillet, add the apples and nuts and cook for 10 minutes; remove from the heat. Add the raisins, ½ cup drained pineapple (reserve the remaining pineapple and the syrup for the sauce), bread crumbs, ½ tsp. salt, cinnamon, nutmeg, cloves and ginger and mix well. Sprinkle the insides of the chicken breasts with the remaining salt. Place ⅓ cup stuffing on the inside of each breast. Fold over the sides and fasten with skewers or string. Place the remaining ¼ cup butter in a foil-lined, 9" x 13" baking pan. Set the pan in a 350° oven for about 5 minutes or until the butter melts. Place the breasts, skin side down, in the melted butter. Return to the oven and bake for 25 minutes. Turn the chicken over and bake for 20 minutes more. Serve with the **Fruit Sauce**.

**Fruit Sauce:** Combine the sugar, cornstarch, salt, cinnamon, nutmeg and ginger and blend well. Stir in the orange juice, the reserved pineapple and syrup, raisins, butter and orange peel. Cook and stir over medium heat until the sauce comes to a boil and thickens. Add the orange sections and heat through. Pour over the stuffed chicken breasts.

Jackie Partlow

☞ For plump and delicious raisins, soak them overnight in orange juice or sherry, then drain before using.

## Chicken Cordon Bleu

2 whole chicken breasts,
  boned (divide in half along
  the bone)
½ tsp. thyme
⅛ tsp. nutmeg
¼ tsp. rosemary

½ cup butter, melted
4 thin slices boiled ham
4 thin slices Swiss cheese
½ cup flour (approx.)
¼ cup dry white wine

Flatten the chicken breasts. Blend the seasonings into the butter and brush the chicken with the mixture. Place 1 ham slice and 1 cheese slice on each chicken piece, roll the chicken around the filling and fasten with a toothpick or tie with a string. Roll each chicken piece in flour, place on a lightly greased baking pan and dribble the remaining seasoned butter mixture over all. Bake uncovered at 375° for 30 minutes. Remove from the oven, turn the pieces over, add 1 cup water and the wine and return to the oven for 30 minutes or until the chicken tests done when pierced with a fork. Transfer to a hot platter, remove the strings or toothpicks. Mix 1 Tbsp. flour with a small amount of water and stir into the pan broth, cook until thickened. Pour the sauce over the chicken on the platter.

Dottie Martin

## Crusty Chicken Wrap-Ups

8 chicken drumsticks
¼ cup margarine
½ cup bottled barbeque sauce
  with onions
1 (8-oz.) pkg. refrigerator
  crescent dinner rolls

1 egg, beaten
2 tsp. Italian seasoning
2 tsp. grated Parmesan cheese
2 tsp. sesame seed

Wash the chicken and dry on paper towels. If desired, remove the skins. Heat the margarine and barbeque sauce, add and sauté the chicken, turning until lightly browned. Cook covered over medium heat, turning occasionally, for 25 minutes or until tender. Remove the chicken from the pan; let cool for about 5 minutes. Unroll the crescents and separate into triangles. Using one-half the egg, brush each triangle lightly, then sprinkle lightly with the Italian seasoning and cheese.

Place one drumstick on the long side of each triangle, bring the sides up over the chicken and press together with your fingers. Twist the end of the crescent around the bone. Arrange seam side down on an ungreased cookie sheet. Brush the tops with the remainder of the egg; sprinkle with the sesame seed. Bake at 375° for 15 to 20 minutes or until golden. Serve warm or cold.

*Makes 8 servings.*

Annemarie Fleming
Reservations

## Ken's Company Chicken

6 chicken thighs
2 tsp. butter
1 chicken bouillon cube
1 cup heavy cream
3 Tbsp. flour
¼ tsp. salt
Dash of pepper
¼ tsp. paprika

¼ cup dry white wine
1 (6-oz.) can button
    mushrooms, drained
6 brown-and-serve pork
    sausages
6 Pepperidge Farm frozen
    unbaked pastry shells

Brown the chicken thighs in the butter. Dissolve the bouillon cube in ½ cup water and pour over the chicken; simmer for 20 to 30 minutes. In a separate saucepan, combine the cream, flour, salt, pepper and paprika. Drain the broth from the chicken and add enough water to make 1 cup, stir into the cream and cook over medium heat until thick. Add the wine and mushrooms and cook until the sauce thickens again. Brown the sausage. Bone the chicken and place a sausage roll in each thigh. Roll out the pastry shells into 6" x 6" squares. Place 1 sausage-stuffed thigh in each square, spoon 2 Tbsp. cream sauce and 1 mushroom over each piece. Fold up the corners of the pastry and pinch shut. Bake, folded side down, in glass dish at 400° for 30 minutes. Reheat the remaining sauce and serve in a gravy boat to pour over individual chicken servings.

*Serves 6.*

Ken Christensen
Operations Planning

## Holiday Chicken with Champagne

4 whole chicken breasts
1 inexpensive bottle
  champagne
1 lb. mushrooms
1 cup butter

½ lb. Monterey Jack cheese
1 bottle plain pearl onions
2 cups heavy cream
4 egg yolks, beaten
Salt and pepper

Bone, skin and halve the chicken breasts, reserving some fat. Make 3 shallow cuts lengthwise in each breast, place in a shallow pan and cover with the champagne. Marinate in the refrigerator for 2 hours. Meanwhile, slice the mushrooms and sauté in ½ cup butter until tender. Wrap the mushrooms in foil and set in a 200° oven. Remove the breasts, reserving the champagne. Cut the cheese into long, thin strips and stuff in the cuts in the breasts. Sauté the breasts and onions in ½ cup butter until done. Remove the breasts and onions, wrap in foil and set in the oven with the mushrooms. Leave all the drippings in the pan and add the reserved champagne. Cook over medium heat until the liquid is reduced to 1 cup. Skim off any fat and stir in the cream and egg yolks. Reduce the heat to low and stir constantly until the sauce thickens. Add salt and pepper to taste. Divide the mushrooms over the chicken breasts and onions, then cover with the sauce and serve.

Dottie Martin

## Chicken 'N Swiss Extraordinaire

3 whole broiler-fryer breasts,
  skinned and boned
1 tsp. MSG
½ cup flour
¼ cup oil
1 Tbsp. butter

½ lb. mushrooms, sliced
⅓ cup dry white wine
1 tsp. salt
¼ tsp. pepper
6 slices Swiss cheese
6 thick slices French bread

Sprinkle the chicken with the MSG and roll in the flour. Pour the oil in a skillet and set over medium heat. When the oil is hot, add the chicken and brown on all sides. Reduce the heat, cover and cook for about 15 minutes or until the chicken is tender. Remove from the pan and set aside. Place the butter and mushrooms in the skillet and sauté over low heat for about 3 minutes. Pour in the wine, stirring to loosen all the browned bits, and add the salt and pepper. Return the chicken to the pan and simmer until the sauce is slightly thickened. Place the cheese on the bread slices and toast at 200° in the oven. Layer the chicken over the toasted cheese bread and spoon the mushroom sauce over. Serve.

Ruth Vantine
Reservations

## Sesame Chicken

¼ cup plus 2 Tbsp. flour
½ tsp. salt
¼ tsp. freshly ground black
  pepper
2 (12-oz.) chicken breasts,
  split and boned
2 eggs
¼ cup milk
3 Tbsp. sesame seeds

Vegetable oil

**Light Supreme Sauce:**
3 Tbsp. butter
2 Tbsp. flour
1½ cups chicken broth
Salt and pepper to taste
1 egg yolk

Combine 2 Tbsp. flour with the salt and pepper in a clean paper or plastic bag. Add the chicken and shake to coat. Beat the eggs with the milk. Combine the remaining flour and the sesame seeds. Dip each breast in the egg mixture, then roll in the sesame seed mixture to coat. Fry in deep oil for 15 minutes or until golden and tender. Drain on crumpled paper towels. Serve with the **Light Supreme Sauce**.

**Light Supreme Sauce:** Melt the butter in a saucepan. Stir in the flour to make a smooth paste. Gradually add the chicken broth and cook and stir over medium heat to make a smooth sauce. Season with salt and pepper. Beat the egg yolk and then gradually add to the sauce. Cook over low heat, whisking, just until the sauce is thickened and smooth. If desired, season the sauce with ground pepper.

Serves 4.

Shirley Schurman
Reservations

### Fried Chicken Bits

4 chicken breasts
½ cup flour
3 eggs
Dash of baking powder

Garlic
Salt and pepper to taste
Oil

Debone the chicken and cut into strips. Combine the remaining ingredients except the oil, mix well, add the chicken and toss. Allow to set for a while. Fry in 2" oil for about 5 minutes. This dish is good served with a white sauce and topped with almonds.

Dottie Martin

### Chicken Stroganoff

2 large, whole chicken breasts,
   boned and skinned (to equal
   1¼ lbs. boned meat)
2 Tbsp. flour
Salt and freshly ground
   black pepper
¼ cup butter
1 Tbsp. plus 1 tsp. minced
   shallots

¾ lb. fresh mushrooms,
   thinly sliced
½ cup dry white wine
1 Tbsp. paprika
2 cups sour cream
1½ tsp. Worcestershire sauce
⅜ tsp. Bovril (no substitutes)

Julienne the chicken meat into 3" x ¼" strips. Combine the flour, ½ tsp. salt and ¼ tsp. pepper in a clean paper or plastic bag. Add the chicken and shake to coat. In a skillet, sauté the chicken in the butter over medium-high heat until golden and tender. Remove to a serving platter; keep warm. Add the shallots, mushrooms and wine to the skillet and cook, stirring until the liquid disappears. Reduce the heat to low, stir in the paprika, sour cream, Worcestershire sauce and Bovril. Season generously with more salt and pepper and heat through. Pour the sauce over the chicken and serve.

Makes 6 servings.

Shirley Schurman
Reservations

## Chicken Breasts Eugenie

8 (6-oz.) boneless chicken
   breasts
Salt and pepper to taste
¼ cup butter
¼ cup margarine
¼ lb. mushrooms, pieces and
   stems, sliced
¼ lb. cured ham, cut into
   8 thin slices

**Supreme Sauce:**
2 Tbsp. butter
1 Tbsp. diced onion
¼ cup all-purpose flour
1½ cups hot chicken stock
¼ cup dry white wine
¼ cup heavy cream

Season the chicken with salt and pepper. Heat the butter and margarine until hot but not brown. Add the chicken and sauté on both sides until browned; remove and set aside. Add the mushrooms and sauté; set aside. Broil each slice of ham on both sides. Place the ham on a plate, top with the chicken, then the mushrooms; pour the **Supreme Sauce** over and serve.

**Supreme Sauce:** Melt the butter, add the onion and sauté for a few minutes. Add the flour and mix well; cook slowly, stirring every minute or so until light pale and then cool. Add the chicken stock and stir until completely smooth. In a separate pan, reduce the wine by one-half, add to the stock and cook slowly for approximately 15 minutes. Add the heavy cream, bring to a boil and strain.

Emile LeBoulluec
Executive Chef
Boston Food Services

## Mexican Chicken and Rice

2½ to 3 lbs. chicken parts
   (thighs, legs, breasts)
1 (28-oz.) can whole tomatoes
1 medium onion, chopped
1½ tsp. salt
1½ to 2 tsp. chili powder
⅛ tsp. instant minced garlic

⅛ tsp. pepper
Dash of cayenne pepper
2 chicken bouillon cubes
2½ cups boiling water
1 cup uncooked regular rice
1 (8-oz.) can whole kernel corn
1 (8-oz.) can kidney beans

Arrange the chicken in a baking pan. Combine the tomatoes and their liquid, the onion, spices and bouillon dissolved in the water; pour over the chicken. Cover and bake at 350° for 30 minutes. Stir in the rice, the corn and its liquid, the beans and their liquid and bake until the chicken and rice are tender and the vegetables are hot, about 30 to 40 minutes more.

Carol Koch
Reservations

## Chicken Enchiladas

2 cans cream of chicken soup
1 (8-oz.) carton sour cream
1 small can diced Ortega chilies
¾ lb. cheddar cheese, grated

¾ lb. Monterey Jack cheese,
  grated
1½ lbs. cooked chicken
1 pkg. flour tortillas

Mix together the soup, sour cream, chilies and half the cheeses. Divide the mixture in half and add the chicken to one half. Fill the tortillas with the chicken mixture. Spread the bottom of a pan with half the remaining soup mixture, lay the filled tortillas over and pour the rest of the filling on top. Sprinkle the remaining cheese over the enchiladas. Bake at 350° for 20 to 30 minutes or until the cheese melts.

Eileen Bohach
Reservations

## Chicken Tortilla Casserole

4 chicken breasts,
  cooked and boned
12 corn tortillas
1 can cream of chicken soup
1 can cream of mushroom
  soup
1 cup milk

1 (8-oz.) can tomato sauce
1 to 1½ (7-oz.) cans Ortega
  green chili salsa
1 onion, chopped
1 Tbsp. chicken broth
1 lb. cheddar cheese, grated

Cut the chicken into large pieces and the tortillas into 1" strips or squares. Mix together the soups, milk, tomato sauce, salsa and onion. Set the chicken broth in a greased, large, shallow baking dish. Place a layer of tortillas on the bottom, then a layer of the chicken bits, then a layer of the soup mixture. Continue layering until all the ingredients are used, ending with the soup mixture. Top with the cheese. Let the casserole stand for 24 hours in the refrigerator (*important*). Bake at 300° for 1½ hours.

Yvonne Erickson
Reservations

## Mexican-Style Chicken Kiev

4 (12-oz.) chicken breasts,
    halved, skinned and boned
1 large can whole green chilies
¼ lb. Monterey Jack cheese
    (approx.)
½ cup fine dry bread crumbs
¼ cup grated Parmesan
    cheese

1 tsp. chili powder
½ tsp. garlic salt
¼ tsp. ground cumin
¼ tsp. black pepper
½ cup butter, melted
¼ cup plus 2 Tbsp. spicy
    tomato sauce

Pound the chicken between wax paper until ¼" thick. Slit the green chilies in half lengthwise and remove the seeds. Cut the Jack cheese into ½" x 1½" fingers and stuff the chilies. Combine the bread crumbs, Parmesan cheese, chili powder, garlic salt, cumin and pepper. Roll the chicken around the chilies and dip in the melted butter; drain briefly, then roll in the crumb mixture. Place the bundles, seam side down, without the sides touching, in a 13" x 9" baking dish. Drizzle the remaining melted butter over all. Cover and chill for at least 4 hours or overnight. To serve, uncover and bake at 400° for 20 minutes or until the chicken is cooked through. Cover with the tomato sauce.

*Serves 8.*

Gail Workman
Reservations

## Chicken Mexicana

6 boneless chicken breasts
1 tsp. garlic salt
¼ tsp. pepper
½ tsp. paprika
¼ cup butter or margarine,
  melted

1 (6-oz.) pkg. tortilla chips,
  crumbled
2 cans enchilada sauce
1 cup shredded cheddar
  cheese
1 cup chopped green onions
1 can sliced black olives

Arrange the chicken breasts in a single layer in a shallow pan. Season with the garlic salt, pepper and paprika. Pour the butter over and bake uncovered at 375° for 1 hour. Sprinkle the chips over the chicken. Add the enchilada sauce and top with the cheese, onions and olives. Bake for 15 minutes or until the cheese melts.

*Makes 6 servings.*

Clark E. Luther
Senior Vice President
Flight Operations

## Chicken Sauté Matador

4 (4-oz.) boneless chicken
  breasts, cut into ¾" x ¾"
  pieces
2 Tbsp. melted butter
½ tsp. salt
⅛ tsp. white pepper
⅓ cup dry white wine
⅓ cup heavy cream

¼ tsp. crushed rosemary
  leaves
¼ cup ½" x ½" strips red
  pimentos
2 avocados, peeled
  and seeded
Chopped parsley

Sauté the chicken in the butter until golden brown. Season with the salt and pepper, remove from the pan and keep warm. Deglaze the pan with the wine until reduced by one-half. Add the cream, and the rosemary in a spice bag; simmer until slightly thickened. Remove the spice bag, add the chicken and pimentos and heat through. Fill each avocado with ½ cup chicken, sprinkle with parsley and serve with rice and carrots.

*Serves 4.*

Duri Arquisch
Executive Chef
Salt Lake City Food Services

## Breast of Chicken Teriyaki

½ cup soy sauce
½ cup sugar
⅓ cup sake
8 boneless chicken breasts
2 tsp. finely grated fresh
  ginger
¼ cup diagonally sliced fresh
  pea pods
⅓ cup julienne of green pepper

⅓ cup Chinese black
  mushrooms
⅓ cup thinly sliced onions
⅓ cup sliced celery
½ cup julienne of carrots
⅓ cup sliced water chestnuts
⅓ cup bamboo shoots
2 Tbsp. peanut or vegetable oil
1 tsp. cornstarch

In a medium saucepan, combine the soy sauce, sugar, sake and ⅓ cup water and heat, stirring constantly, until the sugar is completely dissolved. Rinse the chicken breasts and pat dry. Place on a sheet pan and brush with the soy sauce mixture; set the remaining sauce aside. Bake at 350° for approximately 30 minutes. When the chicken is almost done, stir fry the vegetables in the oil for 2 minutes over high heat, then remove from the heat. Dilute the cornstarch in ¼ cup water, add to the vegetables and stir until the mixture thickens. Reheat the soy sauce mixture and add ½ cup to the vegetables; toss until well coated. Remove the cooked chicken to a heated serving platter, top each breast with the reserved soy sauce mixture and garnish with the vegetables.

*Serves 8.*

Willi Niederer
Executive Chef
San Francisco Food Services

## Chicken Oriental

1 can cream of mushroom
   soup
1 can pineapple chunks,
   undrained
1 Tbsp. soy sauce
2 cups cooked white chicken
   meat

1 cup diagonally sliced celery
1 cup sliced green onions
1 large green pepper, cut into
   squares
½ cup sliced radishes
½ cup sliced water chestnuts
Cooked rice

In a round, 1½-quart copper casserole, combine the soup, pineapple and soy sauce, Add the remaining ingredients except the rice. Cook over low heat for 10 minutes, stirring gently occasionally. Serve with rice and additional soy sauce.

Mike Dearing
Reservations

## Chicken and Cashews

1 lb. chicken breasts, cubed
   into bite-size pieces
1 egg white
2 tsp. cornstarch
¼ cup plus 2 Tbsp. oil
2 slices ginger

1 Tbsp. wine
1 tsp. sugar
3 Tbsp. soy sauce
1 bunch green onions,
   finely chopped
1 cup cashew nuts

Mix the chicken, egg white, and 1 tsp. cornstarch together in a medium bowl. Heat the oil to 350° and sauté the ginger and chicken until the chicken turns white; remove the ginger. Combine the wine, sugar, soy sauce, 1 tsp. cornstarch and 1 Tbsp. water. Stir into the chicken. When the sauce thickens, add the onions and nuts, stir and serve. Rice is an excellent side dish.

Sue Crane
Reservations

### Sweet and Sour Chicken

½ cup plus 2 Tbsp. soy sauce
  (approx.)
¼ cup brown sugar
½ tsp. garlic powder
¼ tsp. onion powder

1 tsp. Dijon mustard
36 chicken wings or 12 to
  18 drumsticks
Paprika
Parsley

Combine the first 5 ingredients in a pan. Add the chicken and marinate for 2 hours or overnight. Bake at 350° for 1 hour, basting frequently. Dash with paprika the final 10 to 15 minutes of baking. Garnish with parsley and serve.

Dottie Martin

### Chicken for the Greek Gods

10 pieces chicken
Juice of 1 lemon
Garlic salt
Pepper
Poultry seasoning
½ cup butter or margarine

2 onions, sliced
Dash of nutmeg
1 cup rosé wine
2 cups chicken broth
2 cups plain yogurt
3 Tbsp. flour

Rub the chicken pieces with the lemon juice, garlic salt, pepper and poultry seasoning. Melt the butter in a large skillet, add the chicken and brown. Place the onion slices underneath the browned chicken and cook for 5 minutes. Sprinkle the chicken with nutmeg, add the wine and 1 cup chicken broth, bring to a boil, then reduce the heat. Combine the yogurt and flour. Heat the remaining broth and stir into the yogurt. Stir thoroughly to eliminate lumps. Gradually add the yogurt mixture to the chicken, mixing well. Place a skillet lid slightly ajar and cook for 1 hour or until tender.

*An exquisite banquet dish!*

*Serves 6 to 8.*

Sarina Ames, Sr.
Reservations

## Coq au Vin

8 (4-oz.) boneless chicken
  breasts
4 (5-oz.) boneless chicken legs,
  halved
Salt and pepper to taste
¼ cup butter
¼ cup margarine
2 Tbsp. brandy
1¼ cups burgundy wine

4 cups semi-heavy demi-glace
2 bay leaves
¼ tsp. thyme
2 medium cloves garlic,
  chopped
10 oz. lean salt pork,
  cut in lardons
24 tiny whole onions
½ lb. mushrooms, pieces and
  stems

Season the chicken with salt and pepper. Heat the butter and margarine until hot but not brown; add the chicken and sauté on both sides until golden brown. Remove the fat from the pan and reserve; deglaze the chicken with the brandy and flame. Remove the chicken and set aside. Pour the burgundy into the casserole and reduce by half. Add the demi-glace, bay leaves, thyme and garlic and bring to a boil; add the chicken and cook for 15 to 20 minutes. Remove from the stove and marinate the chicken in the sauce overnight. Prior to serving, remove the chicken, simmer the sauce until reduced by one-fifth; return the chicken to it and heat until hot. Meanwhile, cook the pork in water until done, then sauté until browned and drain on paper. Sauté the onions and mushrooms in the reserved chicken fat until golden brown and then drain the fat. Add the pork and vegetables to the chicken and serve.

Emile LeBoulluec
Executive Chef
Boston Food Services

## Chicken Hunter Style

1 (1- to 1¾-lb.) chicken, cut up
Salt and pepper
1½ Tbsp. butter
1 Tbsp. olive oil
3 shallots or ¼ onion, chopped
¼ lb. mushrooms, sliced

½ cup sauterne or other
  white wine
1 tomato, peeled and chopped
Chopped parsley
Buttered noodles

Disjoint the chicken and season with salt and pepper. Heat the butter and oil in a skillet, add the chicken, skin side down, and sauté. When the chicken is golden brown on both sides, add the shallots and mushrooms and simmer. Do not brown the vegetables. Then add the wine and simmer for 10 minutes. Remove and arrange the chicken on a platter. Let the sauce reduce by one-half, season as desired and add the parsley. Pour the sauce over the chicken and serve with buttered noodles.

Hans Jantzen
Executive Chef
New York Food Services

## Chicken Canary Islands

1 large chicken, cut into
   8 pieces
Salt and white pepper to taste
Pinch of paprika
2 Tbsp. oil
¼ cup plus 2 Tbsp. butter
1 shallot, chopped
¼ cup brandy

¾ cup Madeira wine
¼ cup demi-glace
½ cup light cream sauce
1 cup heavy cream
4 bananas, peeled and cut
   lengthwise
Pinch of flour

Season the chicken with salt, pepper and paprika. Heat the oil with half the butter in a heavy skillet; when the butter foams, add the chicken and brown to a light golden color on all sides. Add the shallot, cover and simmer slowly for approximately 15 minutes. Drain the grease, add the brandy and flame. Add the Madeira, demi-glace, cream sauce and cream and simmer for 15 minutes more. Remove the chicken to a serving dish, adjust the seasoning, if necessary, and strain the sauce over the chicken. Roll the bananas in the flour and sauté in the remaining butter; serve with the chicken.

Serves 4.

Raoul F. Delbol
Executive Chef
Los Angeles Food Services

### Chicken Paprikash

1 (2½- to 3-lb.) broiler-fryer,
  cut-up
2 Tbsp. cooking oil, heated
Salt and pepper
2 medium onions, chopped
1 Tbsp. paprika

¼ cup dry white wine
¼ cup condensed chicken
  broth
½ cup sour cream
Biscuits, noodles or rice

In 12" skillet, brown the chicken pieces in the oil, season with salt and pepper, remove and set aside. Add the onions to the skillet and cook until tender, but not brown. Stir in the paprika and return the chicken to the skillet, turning once to coat. Add the wine and broth, bring to a boil, reduce the heat, cover and simmer for 30 to 35 minutes or until tender. Place the chicken on a serving platter and keep warm. Boil the skillet drippings until reduced to ½ cup, stir in the sour cream, heat through but do not boil. Pour the sauce over the chicken. Serve over small baking powder biscuits, noodles or rice.

Fran Christensen
Reservations

### Chicken Sauté Hunter Style

In France they call it Poulet Sauté Chasseur; in Italy, Pollo Alla Cacciatore; in Germany, Hunchen Nach Jagerat. But in any language, **Chicken Sauté Hunter Style** is a universal dish enjoyed by epicureans the world over.

1 (2½-lb.) chicken, cut into
  8 pieces
Salt and pepper to taste
Flour
2 Tbsp. butter
2 Tbsp. oil
2 Tbsp. finely chopped onion
Pinch of finely chopped garlic
1 cup canned mushroom slices
  (reserve liquid)

¼ cup dry white wine
1 cup diced canned or fresh
  tomatoes
1 Tbsp. beef base or 2
  bouillon cubes
Oregano
Cornstarch
1 Tbsp. finely chopped parsley

Season the chicken with salt and pepper and pass lightly through flour. Cook in a saucepan with the butter and oil until golden; remove the chicken and set aside. Reduce the heat to low, add the onion and garlic and smother for a few minutes. Add the mushrooms, wine, tomatoes and beef base and return the chicken to the pan. Add enough liquid from the mushrooms and water to cover the chicken. Season to taste with salt, pepper and oregano. Bring to a boil, reduce the heat, cover and simmer until the chicken is cooked. To thicken the sauce, if necessary, dilute some cornstarch with a little white wine, add to the sauce and bring to a boil. Just before serving, top with the parsley and serve with rice, buttered noodles or mashed potatoes.

Paul Steuri
Executive Chef
Omaha Food Services

### Chicken Sauté Cacciatore

1 (3-lb.) frying chicken, cut up
3 Tbsp. oil
3 to 4 Tbsp. butter
Salt and pepper
½ lb. mushrooms, sliced
¼ cup chopped onions
½ cup dry white wine
1 Tbsp. flour
1 cup boiling chicken stock
2 Tbsp. brandy
4 ripe tomatoes, peeled,
   seeded, drained and
   chopped
1 Tbsp. chopped parsley
1 tsp. dried or 1 Tbsp. fresh
   tarragon
Parsley sprigs

Dry the chicken thoroughly. Heat the oil and half the butter in a large, heavy frying pan over medium-high heat. Brown the chicken a few pieces at a time, removing when done. When all are browned, return the thighs and drumsticks to the pan. Cover tightly and simmer for 10 minutes. Add the breasts and wings and simmer for 10 minutes more. Transfer the chicken to a warm platter. Add salt and pepper to taste. Sauté the mushrooms in the remaining butter in a covered pan for 7 to 8 minutes. Remove from the heat, set aside. Drain most of the fat from the chicken pan, add the onions and sauté until browned. Pour in the wine, increase the heat and cook until the wine evaporates. Add the flour, cook for 1 minute, then add the stock and cook until it thickens. Heat the brandy in a ladle over medium heat, ignite and add to the stock. Stir in the tomatoes, herbs and more salt and pepper and simmer for 10 minutes. Add the chicken and the mushrooms and warm through. Turn out on a warm platter, garnish with parsley and serve with a rice pilaf.

David Rieman
Passenger Service

## Braised Chicken with Peanuts

½ cup peanut oil
3 lbs. chicken, cut into pieces
2 large onions, chopped
2 cups chicken stock
½ cup chunky peanut butter

½ cup tomato paste
Salt and pepper to taste
Pinch of cayenne pepper
½ to ¾ cup coarsely chopped
   roasted peanuts

Heat the oil in a large casserole. Add the chicken and sauté to a dark, golden color. Add the onions and stir until the onions are clear; keep hot. Mix the stock, peanut butter and tomato paste together, blend well and pour over the chicken. Season with the salt and peppers, cover and cook slowly until tender. Remove to a serving dish, garnish with peanuts and serve. Good with rice.

Serves 4.

Raoul F. Delbol
Executive Chef
Los Angeles Food Services

## Twelve Boy Curry

¼ cup plus 2 Tbsp. butter
1 cup minced onions
1 cup chopped celery
4 to 5 cloves garlic, minced
½ cup flour
1 to 2 Tbsp. curry powder
   or to taste
1 tsp. dry mustard
½ tsp. salt

¼ tsp. pepper
1 tsp. paprika
Dash of cayenne pepper
1¼ cups strong beef stock
1 cup light cream
3 Tbsp. catsup
1 (3-lb.) chicken, cooked
   and diced
Hot buttered rice

Melt the butter in a large skillet. Add the onions, celery and garlic and cook over medium heat until the onions are soft. Combine all the seasonings and add to the onion mixture, stirring over low heat until blended. Slowly add the beef stock and cream, stirring until smooth. Add the catsup, cook for 2 minutes and then add the chicken; continue cooking until the mixture boils. Remove from the heat, let stand for about 1 hour, then reheat. (You can make this the day before, allowing all the flavors to blend, and reheat before serving.) Serve over hot, buttered rice with any or all of the following condiments: chutney, raisins, crushed pineapple, shredded coconut, chopped peanuts, chopped, hard-cooked eggs, chopped black olives, chopped green peppers and chopped onions.

*Marianne Shute*

## Pineapple Chicken with Sweet and Sour Sauce

*1¼ lbs. white chicken meat, sliced*
*Peanut oil*
*2 slices pineapple, cubed*
*2 cups sliced water chestnuts*
*2 medium green peppers, diced ¾" x ¾"*
*2 cups sliced bamboo shoots*
*2 cups ¾" x ¾" sliced celery*

*Salt and pepper to taste*

**Sweet and Sour Sauce:**
*1 cup white vinegar*
*1 cup pineapple juice*
*1 cup brown sugar*
*½ tsp. Worcestershire sauce*
*2 Tbsp. catsup*
*3 Tbsp. cornstarch*

Sauté the chicken lightly in peanut oil; do not brown. Add the remaining ingredients and combine with the **Sweet and Sour Sauce.** Heat through.

**Sweet and Sour Sauce:** Combine all the ingredients except the cornstarch and simmer for 30 minutes. Combine the cornstarch with ½ cup water and add to the sauce; thicken to desired consistency.

*Serves 8.*

John H. Wolfsheimer
Executive Chef
San Francisco Food Services

### Chicken Sonoma

1 broiler or roasting chicken
Salt and pepper
1 bay leaf
1 medium onion, peeled and
   quartered
2 stalks celery with leaves,
   coarsely chopped
3 Tbsp. olive oil or butter
¼ lb. minced salt pork
½ cup pearl onions
3 shallots, minced
1 clove garlic, minced

2 Tbsp. flour
1 Tbsp. brandy
1 cup Marsala wine
2 Tbsp. minced parsley
1 tsp. fresh chervil or marjoram
⅛ tsp. ground bay leaf
½ tsp. thyme
½ cup diced potatoes
½ cup green peas
½ cup diced carrots
½ cup button mushrooms

Place the chicken in a large pot. Cover with water, add salt and pepper, the bay leaf, onion and celery and cook for approximately 30 minutes. Remove the chicken from the stock and allow to cool. Remove the skin and meat from the bones. Dice the meat, measure 1½ to 2 cups chicken (the remaining chicken can be used in other cooking) and set aside. Heat the olive oil or butter in a large skillet. Add the pork and lightly brown. Add the pearl onions, shallots and garlic and lightly sauté. Add the diced chicken and brown. Using a slotted spoon, remove the ingredients from the skillet and set aside. Add the flour to the drippings, stir well and lightly brown. Slowly add the brandy, wine, parsley, chervil, bay leaf, thyme, 1 tsp. salt and pepper to taste and stir until the mixture begins to thicken. Add the chicken mixture, potatoes, green peas and carrots and cover. Simmer for approximately 30 minutes. Add the mushrooms during the final 5 minutes of cooking.

Serves 4 to 5.

Dick Ferris
Chairman and Chief Executive Officer
United Airlines, Inc.

☞ Freshen nuts by heating them in the oven at 350° for 5 minutes.

## Turkey Parmigiana

1 (1- to 1½-lb.) boneless
   turkey breast
½ cup wheat germ
¼ cup grated Parmesan
   cheese
1 egg
½ tsp. salt
¼ tsp. pepper

¼ cup oil
1 (8-oz.) can tomato sauce
½ tsp. crushed oregano
¼ tsp. crushed thyme
¾ cup grated Monterey Jack
   cheese
Minced parsley

Cut the turkey breast into 4 steaks and pound to ¼" thickness between wax paper. Combine the wheat germ and Parmesan cheese. Beat the egg with 1½ tsp. water and the salt and pepper. Dip the turkey into the egg mixture, then into the wheat germ mixture. Heat the oil in a large skillet, add the turkey and cook over medium heat until browned, about 3 minutes per side. Combine the tomato sauce with the oregano and thyme; pour over the turkey, reduce the heat, cover and simmer for 10 to 12 minutes. Sprinkle with the Jack cheese and parsley just before serving.

Serves 4.

Percy Wood
Vice Chairman of the Board
United Airlines, Inc.

## Cornish Hens and Dressing in Wine Sauce

6 slices bacon
1 cup finely chopped onions
1 cup chopped green peppers
3 cups white bread cubes
1 cup chopped walnuts
3 tsp. salt

1½ tsp. thyme
1 tsp. sage
6 Cornish game hens
½ cup butter, melted
½ cup white wine
1 clove garlic, crushed

Fry the bacon in a skillet, remove and crumble, reserving 3 Tbsp. of the drippings. Sauté the onions and green peppers in the bacon drippings. Stir in the bacon, bread cubes, walnuts, 1½ tsp. salt, thyme and ½ tsp. sage. Stuff the hens and place in a roaster pan. Combine the remaining ingredients and pour in the roaster around the hens. Bake at 400° for 1 hour, basting occasionally with the sauce. Turn off the heat and cool the hens in the sauce for 30 minutes before serving.

*6 servings.*

Fran Christensen
Tour Desk

### Roast Cornish Game Hens

*6 (1-lb.) Rock Cornish hens*
*Salt and pepper*
*6 Tbsp. butter or oil*
*1 medium onion, chopped*
*1 stalk celery, chopped*
*3 cups cooked rice, chilled*
*¼ cup raisins*
*¼ cup walnut pieces*
*2 Tbsp. chopped parsley*
*1½ tsp. grated orange rind*
*Curry powder to taste*

**Cumberland Sauce:**
*Grated rind and juice of*
*  1 orange*
*Grated rind and juice of*
*  1 lemon*
*½ cup red currant or*
*  blackberry jelly*
*½ cup red wine*
*1½ Tbsp. cornstarch*
*½ cup cold water*
*½ tsp. dry mustard*
*⅛ tsp. ground ginger*

Rinse and dry the hens, season inside and out with salt and pepper and set aside. Melt 3 Tbsp. butter in a heavy saucepan over moderate heat, add the onion and celery and sauté just until brown. Pour in the rice and sauté until the grains are well coated with butter. Remove from the heat and stir in the raisins, walnut pieces, parsley, orange rind, more salt and pepper and the curry powder. Fill the cavities of the hens with the stuffing and skewer closed. Tie the legs close to the body and tuck the wings behind the backs. Arrange on a rack in a shallow roasting pan and brush with 3 Tbsp. melted butter. Roast at 375° for 50 to 60 minutes or until the birds are tender. After 20 minutes, baste occasionally with the **Cumberland Sauce**. When tender, remove the trussing strings and serve the birds with the remaining **Cumberland Sauce**.

**Cumberland Sauce:** Combine the grated rinds, jelly and wine in a saucepan and bring to a boil. Mix the cornstarch with the cold water and stir into the wine sauce. Bring to a boil, stirring constantly. Remove from the heat, add the orange and lemon juices and seasonings.

*This sauce is also excellent with ham, pork and chicken.*

*Makes 2 cups.*

Lillian Warren

## Cornish Hens with Apricots and Brandy Sauce

2 Rock Cornish hens
½ tsp. salt
¼ tsp. pepper
2½ cups seasoned bread
   stuffing mix

¼ cup butter, melted
½ cup apricot brandy
2 apricots, peeled and
   halved
¼ cup parsley

Wash the hens with lightly salted water and pat dry. Season the hens inside and out with the salt and pepper. Prepare the stuffing mix according to the package directions. Stuff the hens with the stuffing. Place the hens on a rack in a shallow pan, breast side up. Fold the wings behind the back, tie the legs to the tail and skewer the neck skin. Baste with some melted butter. Add the brandy to the remaining butter. Roast uncovered at 350° for 1 hour, basting often with the butter and brandy. Increase the heat to 400° for 10 minutes more to brown the hens. To serve, place the hens on a platter and pour the remaining sauce from the roasting pan over. Garnish with the apricots and parsley.

☞ *Before peeling oranges, cover them with boiling water and let stand for 5 minutes. The bitter white membrane can then be removed more easily.*

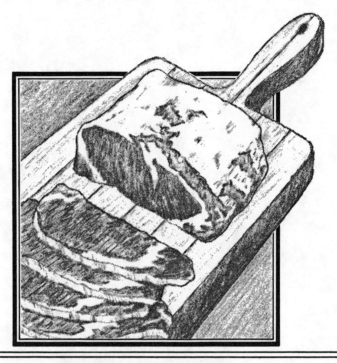

# MEAT

## Lamb Chops with Rice and Onions

4 lamb chops
Flour
Salt and pepper
3 Tbsp. olive or vegetable oil
1 cup uncooked rice
2 cloves garlic, minced
½ cup dry sherry

½ tsp. curry powder
1 tsp. marjoram
½ cup freshly chopped or
  2 Tbsp. dried parlsey
2 bouillon cubes dissolved in
  2 cups boiling water
4 large onions, halved

Coat the meat with the flour, salt and pepper and brown in the oil heated in a skillet. Remove the meat from the skillet, add the rice and garlic and cook until the rice changes color and texture. Push the rice around in sections and lay the meat over the rice. In a separate pan combine the sherry and herbs; heat through. Pour the hot broth over the rice and meat. Lay the onion halves over the top, cover and bake at 325° for approximately 45 minutes. Check for moisture and, if necessary, add 2 to 3 Tbsp. water. Taste for salt. The liquid should all cook away, leaving fluffy rice and delectable, tender onions.

Nette Mitter
Group Desk

## Lamb Chops Marinated in Wine Sauce

⅓ cup Girard's original salad
  dressing
¼ cup burgundy wine
¼ tsp. pepper
⅛ tsp. Spice Island fine herbs

2 to 3 cloves garlic,
  minced or crushed
¼ tsp. finely crushed mint
  flakes
8 lamb chops

Mix together all the ingredients except the lamb chops. Place the lamb chops in a long casserole dish and pour the marinade over. Cover and marinate for 6 to 8 hours. Barbeque for 7 minutes on each side over medium coals, basting with the sauce while cooking.

Note: To substitute chicken, use vermouth or white wine instead of red wine and use poultry seasoning instead of mint flakes.

Barry Gardiner
Reservations

## Lamb Shanks and Pot Roast, Lombard·Style

Cooking oil
2 to 3 lamb shanks
1 large piece round bone
    pot roast or boned chuck
Garlic salt
Pepper

Flour
1 (12-oz.) can V-8 juice
2 bay leaves
1 onion, chopped
Lawry's Pinch of Herbs

Place a thin layer of cooking oil in a large, deep pan (an electric fry pan is ideal). Preheat to 350°. Season the meat, both the lamb and beef, with garlic salt and pepper; dip in flour, coating it well. Brown the meat on both sides and remove from the pan. Reduce the heat to 225° to 250°. Pour the V-8 juice into the pan, add ¾ cup water, the bay leaves and half the onion. Return the beef to the pan and season with the herbs and one-quarter of the onion. Layer the lamb shanks over the beef and add the remainder of the onion. Cover and cook for at least 3 hours. Check periodically to drain excessive liquid, if necessary.

Note: Vegetables may be added during the cooking if the pan is large enough. The juices may be used as a form of gravy when the meal is served.

Serves 6.

Ed Beamish
Senior Vice President
Corporate Planning

## Stuffed Crown Roast of Lamb

1 crown roast of lamb
Chopped onions
Diced celery
Crushed garlic
½ cup all-purpose flour
3 cups beef broth
1 bay leaf
½ cup sauterne wine

**Stuffing:**
½ lb. pork sausage
1 large onion, finely chopped
3 stalks celery, finely chopped
¼ lb. fresh mushrooms
½ loaf Italian or French bread
1 Tbsp. chopped parsley
1 egg
¼ tsp. crushed rosemary
Salt and pepper

Fill the center of the crown roast with the stuffing and cover the stuffing with foil. Place the onions, celery and garlic around the meat and roast at 375° for approximately 1 hour. When done, remove the roast from the pan and set aside in a warm place. Place the roasting pan over low heat and sauté the onions and celery until golden brown, remove and place around the meat; cover the meat with foil and return to the warm place. Add the flour to the roasting pan and allow it to brown, stirring constantly; add the broth and bay leaf and cook for 1 hour. Add the wine, allow to come to a boil and strain. When ready to serve, pour the sauce over the lamb and vegetables.

**Stuffing:** Sauté the sausage and pour off the fat. Add the onion, celery and mushrooms and sauté. Break the bread into small pieces and mix with the sausage and vegetables. Add the remaining ingredients and mix well.

*Note: Have your butcher prepare racks of lamb for the crown roast.*

Hans Jantzen
Executive Chef
New York Food Services

### Savory Roast Lamb

1 (5½-lb.) leg of lamb, boned,
   rolled and trimmed of fat
1 tsp. salt
½ clove garlic, minced or
   crushed
¼ tsp. pepper

¼ bay leaf, crushed
¼ tsp. ginger
¼ tsp. thyme
¼ tsp. sage
¼ tsp. marjoram
1 Tbsp. olive oil

Wipe the lamb with a damp cloth. Cut ¼" gashes on the top surface of the lamb. Combine the remaining ingredients except the olive oil. Rub the herbs well into the meat so that all the gashes are completely filled. Coat the roast with the olive oil. Sear at 500° for 15 minutes. Reduce the heat to 350° and roast for 2 hours or until tender.

Eileen Bohach
Reservations

## Indonesian Lamb Roast

⅓ cup finely chopped celery
⅓ cup finely chopped onions
1 clove garlic, minced
¾ cup olive oil
¼ cup vinegar
2 tsp. A-1 sauce
3 Tbsp. curry powder
2 dashes of Tabasco sauce

3 Tbsp. honey
1 tsp. oregano
2 bay leaves
½ cup prepared mustard
Juice and grated zest of
    1 large lemon
6 lamb chops or 1 rack of lamb,
    trimmed of fat

Sauté the celery, onions and garlic in the oil until the onions are transparent. Stir in the remaining ingredients except the lamb and simmer for a few minutes. Chill. Marinate the lamb in this mixture for 3 to 4 hours in the refrigerator, turning several times. Drain the marinade. Wrap the bones with foil, leaving the meat portions exposed. Arrange in a greased, shallow baking pan. Brush the meat with the marinade and bake at 400° for 20 minutes or more, depending upon the thickness of the meat and desired doneness. Turn the meat once during the baking period and baste frequently. During the last few minutes of cooking, the meat may be placed under the broiler to further brown, if desired. Serve the remaining hot marinade as a sauce for the meat.

*Makes 6 servings.*

Trader Vic's
Seattle, Washington

## Orange-Glazed Lamb Shanks

1 Tbsp. salad oil
4 (¾- to 1-lb.) lamb shanks
1 tsp. curry powder
¼ tsp. ground ginger
1 tsp. grated lemon peel
1 tsp. salt

½ tsp. oregano
2 cloves garlic, minced
1 cup dry white wine
1 cup orange juice
1 Tbsp. minced parsley

Heat the oil in a large frying pan, add the shanks and brown. Transfer to an oven casserole. Combine the seasonings and sprinkle over the meat. Pour in the wine and orange juice. Cover and bake at 350° for 2 hours or until tender. Garnish with the parsley.

## Irish Lamb Stew

2 lbs. boneless lamb breast
  and shoulder meat, diced
  into 1" cubes
1 lb. potatoes, peeled and
  diced into 1" cubes
1 lb. onions, diced
1 lb. white cabbage, diced
3 medium carrots, diced
2 quarts chicken stock
1 clove garlic, finely chopped

1 bay leaf
¼ tsp. thyme leaf
Salt and pepper to taste
2 cups white wine
1 Tbsp. chopped parsley
1 cup medium cream
2 to 3 Tbsp. cornstarch
¼ cup butter
Dash of Maggi seasoning

Combine all the ingredients except the cream, cornstarch, butter and Maggi seasoning in a large pot. Bring to a boil, cover, reduce the heat and simmer for 1½ hours or until the meat is tender. Drain all the juices into a separate pot. Combine the cream and cornstarch and add to the juices; cook to desired consistency. Adjust the seasoning by adding the butter and Maggi seasoning to the sauce. Pour the sauce over the meat and vegetables; mix lightly and serve the stew piping hot.

Serves 8.

John H. Wolfsheimer
Executive Chef
San Francisco Food Services

## Ham and Cheese Pie

½ cup chopped, cooked ham
½ cup grated Swiss cheese
2 Tbsp. Parmesan cheese
1 (7") pie crust
2 eggs

1 cup cream
Salt and pepper
Dash of nutmeg
Dash of Maggi seasoning

Combine the ham and cheeses and place in the pie crust. Combine all the remaining ingredients and pour over. Bake at 350° for 50 to 70 minutes.

Hans Jantzen
Executive Chef
New York Food Services

### Stuffed Ham Roll au Gratin

¼ lb. mushrooms, sliced
2 Tbsp. butter
¼ lb. turkey, cooked and diced
4 (3-oz.) slices ham
¼ cup plus 1 Tbsp. grated
   cheese
Canned celery hearts

**Sauce:**
2 Tbsp. butter
¼ cup flour
1½ cups chicken stock, chilled
½ cup cream
Salt and pepper to taste

Sauté the mushrooms in the butter until cooked. Add the turkey and enough sauce to bind together the mushrooms and turkey. Roll the ham slices around this mixture, place on a dish and cover with the sauce. Sprinkle the cheese over and serve with the celery hearts.

**Sauce:** Melt the butter in a pan and add the flour; cook to a dry, sandy texture. Add the chicken stock, bring to a boil and simmer for 30 minutes. Add the cream, season with salt and pepper and strain.

Serves 4.

Rolf Conrad
Executive Chef
Denver Food Services

### Broccoli Wrapped in Swiss Cheese and Ham

2 Tbsp. flour
2 Tbsp. butter
1 Tbsp. minced onion
2 tsp. horseradish
2 tsp. Worcestershire sauce
2 tsp. mustard
Salt and pepper to taste
1 egg yolk

1 cup pineapple juice
½ cup milk
8 slices ham
8 slices Swiss cheese
8 stalks broccoli,
   partially cooked
Pineapple slices or crab apples

Combine the first 7 ingredients in a small pan. Stir together the egg yolk and pineapple juice and add to the sauce. Add the milk. Bring the sauce to a boil over medium-high heat, reduce the heat to low and simmer for 10 minutes. Wrap the ham and then the cheese around each broccoli stalk, secure with toothpicks and arrange in a baking dish. Spoon the sauce over the vegetables and bake at 350° for 20 minutes. Garnish with pineapples or crab apples. Serve 1 to 2 stalks per person.

*If preferred, can be served as an accompaniment to an entrée.*

Annemarie Fleming
Reservations

## Savory Scottish Sausage

*You will need enough of the following ingredients, except the sausage, to make two layers of whatever size casserole dish you prefer to use:*

Tomatoes, sliced
Potatoes, raw and sliced
Onions, chopped and sautéed

Cheese, grated
Sausage

Arrange the ingredients in an ungreased casserole in this order: first layer, tomatoes; second layer, potatoes; third layer, onions; fourth layer, cheese; fifth layer, sausage. Repeat the first 4 layers. Cover the dish and bake at 350° for 1½ hours.

*British sausages are seasoned differently than those made in the United States. Tastes especially good with Italian sweet sausage.*

Mike Dearing
Reservations

## Polish Sausage with Apples and Red Cabbage

2 Tbsp. vegetable oil
1 Tbsp. butter
2 medium onions, thinly sliced
1 head red cabbage, finely
  shredded
4 tart apples, peeled and
  sliced

2½ lbs. Kielbasa sausage
1 bay leaf
¼ cup red wine vinegar
½ cup stock or water
½ tsp. salt
½ tsp. pepper

Heat the oil and butter in a large pot, add the onions and sauté for about 5 minutes or until tender. Add the cabbage and apples, stirring well. Place the sausage and bay leaf in the center of the pot and cover completely with the vegetables. Pour in the liquid and seasonings. Cover the pot and simmer for 30 to 40 minutes. Remove the sausage and cut into serving pieces. Arrange the vegetables on a warm serving platter and top with the sausage pieces.

Fran Christensen
Tour Desk

## Bali Hai Pork Pieces

1½ lbs. pork, trimmed and cut
   into bite-size pieces
1 (12-oz.) can beer
½ cup orange marmalade
¼ cup sugar
½ cup soy sauce

1 clove garlic, crushed
16 large mushrooms
8 pearl onions, peeled and
   blanched
1 large green pepper, cut
   into wedges

Place the pork in a deep bowl. Combine the next 5 ingredients and pour over the pork. Refrigerate for 8 hours, stirring frequently. One hour before cooking, add the vegetables to the marinade. Alternate the pork and vegetables on skewers and cook over a medium-hot charcoal fire, basting frequently with the marinade.

Janis Sisley

## Easy Pork Chops

Pork chops
1 large onion, thinly sliced
1 lemon, thinly sliced

Brown sugar
Catsup

Place the pork chops in a casserole or baking dish. Place 1 onion slice on each pork chop, then 1 lemon slice on the onion. Put 1 heaping Tbsp. catsup and 1 heaping Tbsp. brown sugar on the lemon. Cover and bake at 350° for 45 minutes to 1 hour. Uncover and cook for 15 to 30 minutes more.

Susan Warren
Reservations

## Mandarin Pork à L'Orange

4 to 6 pork chops
1 can cheddar cheese soup
Wine

1 can Mandarin oranges
Chives

Brown the pork quickly in a skillet over medium-high heat. Combine the soup and enough wine to make a sauce. Arrange the pork chops in a baking dish, pour the sauce over and stir in the oranges and chives. Bake at 350° for 55 to 60 minutes.

Rick Sanders
Reservations

## Barbequed Double Pork Chops

2 cups soy sauce
½ cup plus 1 Tbsp. packed
   brown sugar
1 Tbsp. dark molasses
1 tsp. salt
12 pork chops

**Red Sauce:**
1 Tbsp. dry mustard
½ cup plus 1 Tbsp. packed
   brown sugar
1¾ cups catsup
1½ cups chili sauce

Combine the soy sauce, 1 cup water, the brown sugar, molasses and salt. Put the chops in a pan, pour the marinade over and refrigerate for 12 hours. Remove the pork chops from the marinade, place on a very hot broiler until grill marks are clearly visible on one side of the chop. Place in a baking pan, cover tightly and bake at 375° until tender, about 1 hour. When the chops are tender, remove from the oven, dip in the **Red Sauce** and return to the pan. Bake at 350° for 20 minutes or until lightly glazed.

**Red Sauce:** Combine the mustard, sugar and ¼ cup plus 2 Tbsp. water, stirring until smooth. Pour into a heavy saucepan, add the catsup and chili sauce and bring to a boil. Reduce the heat and simmer for 1 hour.

Serves 6.

Walter J. Schmuki
Sous Chef
Denver Food Services

## Pork Tenderloin Ziganne

3 pork tenderloins, defatted
1 tsp. salt
Pinch of thyme
½ tsp. curry powder
2 Tbsp. flour
2 Tbsp. butter
½ medium onion, finely
  chopped
1 clove garlic, finely chopped
1 (8-oz.) can imported
  chanterelle mushrooms, cut
  into ½" pieces

⅓ cup white wine
1 cup heavy cream
1 tsp. cornstarch
Pinch of MSG
Pinch of spiced salt (optional)
6 half-cling peaches
½ cup chopped Major Gray's
  chutney
½ tsp. chopped parsley

Cut the tenderloins diagonally into 6 equal pieces and flatten to thin medallions; season with a mix of the salt, thyme and curry powder and dredge in the flour; set aside. Heat 1 Tbsp. butter in a skillet, add the onion and garlic and smother for 5 minutes. Then add the mushrooms, sauté and set the vegetables aside. Heat the remaining butter in a larger skillet over high heat, add the medallions and cook for approximately 3 minutes on each side until a golden color, being careful not to burn the butter, and place the pork on a serving dish. Put the wine in the large skillet, cook for a few minutes over high heat, add the cream and bring to a boil. Dilute the cornstarch in a small amount of water and blend into the sauce. Add the MSG and spiced salt and strain into a small saucepan; keep warm. Reheat the mushroom garnish and spoon over the pork. Fill the peach cavitities with the chutney, place beside the medallions and bake at 350° for a few minutes. Just before serving, pour the sauce over the meat and sprinkle with the chopped parsley. Egg noodles and your favorite vegetable will compliment this Bohemian dish.

Oswald M. Gnigler
Executive Chef
Las Vegas Food Services

☞ Cool ham in the pan drippings to maintain its flavor and juiciness.

## Pork Tenderloin Piccata

12 (3-oz.) boneless, center-cut
  pork loin chops
Salt and pepper
1½ cups flour

2 eggs, beaten
2½ cups grated Parmesan
  cheese
Butter

Have your butcher flatten the pork chops to ½" thickness. Season with salt and pepper, coat with the flour, dip in the eggs and roll in the Parmesan cheese. Sauté slowly in butter until the meat is golden brown and well done. Serve with a paprika sauce.

Erich Dorfhuber
Executive Chef
Portland Food Services

## Stuffed, Baked Pork Chops

6 (1" thick) pork chops
1 Tbsp. chopped onion
½ cup diced mushrooms
1 Tbsp. butter
½ tsp. chopped tarragon
  leaves
Salt and pepper to taste

¼ cup diced bread cubes
1 tsp. chopped parsley
¼ tsp. MSG
Flour
½ cup white wine
Dash of lemon juice
1 can chicken stock (approx.)

Ask your butcher to make pockets in the pork chops. Sauté the onion and mushrooms in the butter, add the tarragon and salt and pepper. Remove from the heat, blend in the bread, parsley and MSG. (If the stuffing is too dry, moisten with chicken stock.) Stuff the pork chops and seal with toothpicks. Dredge in flour and brown on both sides, place in a pan and pour the lemon juice and chicken stock over. Cover and bake at 375° for 20 to 30 minutes.

Erich Dorfhuber
Executive Chef
Portland Food Services

## Hawaiian Open Double-Cut Pork Chop Plantation

6 (8-oz.) center-cut, lean pork
   chops (with ribs on)
Salt and ground black pepper
Pinch of garlic salt
½ cup rice flour
3 Tbsp. oil
4 beef bouillon cubes

1½ cups pineapple juice,
   heated
6 slices pineapple, halved
¼ cup dark brown sugar
½ cup chopped macadamia
   nuts
1 large sprig parsley

Season the pork chops with the salt, pepper and garlic salt and dredge in the flour. Heat the oil in a heavy skillet, add and fry the chops to a golden brown on both sides and transfer all to a baking dish. Dissolve the bouillon cubes in the pineapple juice and pour over the pork chops. Bake at 325° for 30 minutes; remove from the oven. Overlap the pineapple slices over the chops. Mix the brown sugar and nuts together, sprinkle over the pineapple and return the dish to the oven to bake for 20 minutes more, basting the chops every 10 minutes. Garnish the dish with parsley and serve.

Serves 6.

George J. Mendreshora
Executive Chef
Honolulu Food Services

## Pork and Chicken Chop Suey, Canton Style

½ cup olive oil
1 lb. raw pork loin, cut into
   long, thin strips
4 cups chicken stock
3 medium onions, sliced
3 stalks celery, thinly sliced
3 cups bean sprouts
2 cups sliced fresh or canned
   mushrooms
⅔ cup soy sauce
2 Tbsp. brown sugar

1 ginger root, peeled and finely
   chopped
1 cup sliced water chestnuts
1 lb. cooked chicken meat,
   cut into long, thin strips
Chinese noodles or steamed
   rice
Chopped parsley
Cooked lean ham, cut into
   long, thin slices

Heat the oil in a deep saucepan; when it begins to bubble and smoke, remove to medium heat. Add the pork and brown but keep the pork tender, not hard. Add the chicken stock, cover and simmer slowly for 15 minutes. Then add the onions, celery, bean sprouts, mushrooms, soy sauce, sugar, ginger and water chestnuts. Simmer for 10 to 15 minutes more, then add the chicken meat, turning from time to time with a wooden spoon. Serve with Chinese noodles, heated in the oven, or steamed rice. Garnish with chopped parsley and a few julienne of cooked lean ham.

*Serves 8.*

Emile LeBoulluec
Executive Chef
Boston Food Services

## Sweet and Sour Pork Chops

*6 (¾" thick) lean pork chops*
*2 cups ½" thick onion slices*
*2½ cups ½" thick apple slices*
*½ cup sugar*

*1½ cups catsup*
*3 Tbsp. vinegar*
*¾ tsp. salt*
*Pepper*

Brown the pork chops quickly in a hot skillet. Layer the chops in a casserole with the onions and apples. Combine the remaining ingredients and pour over the chops. Bake at 350° for 1½ hours. Good served with Venetian rice.

Fran Christensen
Tour Desk

## Spareribs with Ginger and Apricot Sauce

*2½ lbs. spareribs*
*⅓ cup soy sauce*
*1 tsp. chopped ginger*
*1 clove garlic, crushed*

*2 Tbsp. brown sugar*
*3 Tbsp. bourbon*
*1 cup apricot-pineapple jam*

Parboil the spareribs in boiling water for 5 minutes, drain well and cut into serving pieces. Combine the remaining ingredients. Place the ribs in a shallow baking dish and pour the sauce over them. Marinate for at least 1 hour. Bake at 350° for 1 hour or until done, basting occasionally. The meat should be dark brown and moist when done.

*Serve with plenty of napkins!*

## Spareribs Cantonese

Dash of pepper
½ cup soy sauce
½ Tbsp. garlic powder
1 cup orange marmalade

½ Tbsp. ground ginger
3 to 4 lbs. spareribs
Lemon slices

Mix together the pepper, soy sauce, garlic powder, marmalade and ginger and ¾ cup water. Set aside. Bake the ribs in a shallow pan, meat side down, at 450° for 30 minutes. Drain all excessive fat, turn meat side up and roast at 375° for 1 hour. Pour the orange sauce over the ribs, roast for 30 minutes or until tender, basting occasionally with the sauce. Serve with lemon slices.

Serves 5.

Mike Dearing
Reservations

## Chinese Sweet and Sour Spareribs

1 cup vinegar
2 Tbsp. granulated sugar
2 Tbsp. Worcestershire
    sauce
½ cup catsup
1 tsp. salt

1 tsp. dry mustard
1 tsp. paprika
⅛ tsp. pepper
1 clove garlic, minced
1 (2-lb.) rack spareribs

In a saucepan, combine the vinegar, sugar, Worcestershire sauce, catsup, salt, mustard, paprika, pepper and garlic. Cover and simmer for 15 minutes. Meanwhile, place the spareribs, rounded side up, on a wire rack or trivet in a large baking pan. Bake at 500° for 10 to 15 minutes. Then reduce the heat to 325°, pour the sauce over and continue baking, covered or uncovered, for 1 to 1½ hours or until the spareribs are very tender, brushing frequently on both sides with the sweet and sour sauce.

Makes 4 to 5 servings.

Brandon Taylor
Group Desk

## Barbequed Korean Kal Bi
### (Short Ribs)

2 lbs. short ribs
¼ cup plus 1 Tbsp. sliced leeks
2 tsp. garlic puree
1 tsp. sliced fresh ginger

2 Tbsp. sugar
¼ cup plus 1 Tbsp. soy sauce
1½ Tbsp. sesame oil

Make small incisions on the meat, combine the remaining ingredients and marinate the meat in the marinade for 2 hours. Barbeque to taste.

Helmut W. Kopleck
Executive Chef
Philadelphia Food Services

## Carbonnade of Beef à la Flamande

1½ lbs. short rib meat
Salt and pepper
Fat, lard or oil
1½ cups sliced onions
3 cups beer

2 to 3 Tbsp. beef stock
3 Tbsp. canned brown gravy
1 Tbsp. brown sugar
Freshly chopped parsley
Cooked spaetzle or noodles

Cut the meat into thick, serving-size portions. Season well with salt and pepper and brown on both sides in sizzling hot fat, lard or oil. Remove the carbonnades from the sauté pan and fry the onions in the same fat until golden. Remove and place with the carbonnades in alternating layers in an ovenproof casserole. Dilute the pan juices with the beer and beef stock. Thicken with the brown gravy and brown sugar. Stir and cook for a few moments making sure that all of the pan drippings are scraped away from the bottom of the pan. Pass this sauce through a strainer directly into the casserole. Bring to a boil on top of the range, cover tightly with a lid and bake at 325° for 2½ hours. When finished, heap the meat and onions into a serving dish, cover with the sauce, sprinkle freshly chopped parsley over and serve with homemade spaetzle or noodles. A full-bodied red wine is an excellent accompaniment.

Rolf Conrad
Executive Chef
Denver Food Services

# Braised Short Ribs of Beef with Horseradish Sauce

6 (½-lb.) boneless, defatted
   beef short ribs
½ tsp. salt
¼ tsp. black pepper
½ tsp. onion salt
1 tsp. garlic salt
¼ cup plus 2 Tbsp. margarine
1 bay leaf
½ cup tomato puree

**Horseradish Sauce:**
2 Tbsp. butter

⅓ cup flour
3 cups reserved pan juices
1 tsp. salt
½ tsp. pepper
¼ tsp. celery seed
⅛ tsp. rosemary
⅛ tsp. cloves
⅛ tsp. garlic powder
2 Tbsp. Worcestershire sauce
¼ cup tomato paste
¼ cup preparted horseradish

Season the short ribs with the salt, pepper, onion and garlic salt. Sauté in the margarine until golden brown on all sides. Place in a deep kettle; add 6 cups water, the bay leaf and tomato puree. Cover the kettle and simmer slowly for 2½ hours or until the meat is fork-tender. (Add water as needed to keep the ribs covered.) Remove the ribs to a heated serving platter and drain 3 cups of the pan juices for the sauce. Serve the ribs with the **Horseradish Sauce.**

**Horseradish Sauce:** Melt the butter in a large saucepan over low heat. Add the flour to make a roux. Add the pan juices and seasoning. Bring to a boil, stirring frequently, until the sauce is thick and smooth. Add the Worcestershire sauce, tomato paste and horseradish.

Serves 6.

John H. Wolfsheimer
Executive Chef
San Francisco Food Services

☞ Soften lumpy brown sugar by placing it in a dish with an apple slice in the microwave. Cook for 15 seconds or until soft.

# Baked, Barbequed Spareribs

4 lbs. country-style spareribs
1 large onion, thinly sliced
1 lemon, thinly sliced
1 cup catsup
⅓ cup Worcestershire sauce

1 tsp. salt
2 dashes of Tabasco sauce
2 cups water
10 to 12 Tbsp. brown sugar,
  or to taste

Cut up the ribs, if necessary, and place in a baking pan. On each piece of meat place 1 onion slice and then 1 lemon slice. Bake uncovered at 450° for 30 minutes. While the meat is baking, combine the remaining ingredients, place in a saucepan and cook until boiling. When the ribs have baked for 30 minutes, pour the sauce over the meat, reduce the heat to 350° and bake until tender, about 1 hour. Baste the meat every 15 minutes or so. Do not cover the meat while cooking.

Susan Warren
Reservations

# Beef in Mustard Sauce

3 lbs. top sirloin
1 Tbsp. salad oil
1 Spanish onion, minced
1 clove garlic, minced
2 stalks celery, minced
½ cup dry red wine
¼ cup brandy

1 cup tomato sauce
1 cup beef stock
¼ tsp. ground coriander
Salt and pepper to taste
1 Tbsp. cornstarch
¼ cup light cream
¼ cup Dijon mustard

Cut the beef into 1" x 1" x ⅛" strips. (Be accurate with the ⅛" measure.) Heat the oil in a heavy pan and sauté the beef until it loses its red color. Add the onion, garlic and celery, cover and simmer for 5 minutes. Add the wine, brandy, tomato sauce, beef stock, coriander and salt and pepper. When the sauce boils, dissolve the cornstarch in 2 tsp. cold water and slowly stir into the pan. Simmer very slowly until the meat is tender, about 1 to 1½ hours. Remove from the heat. Stir in the cream and mustard, adjust the seasoning and serve.

Serves 6.

David Rieman
Passenger Service

## Sukiyaki

*Sukiyaki is a late entry to the Japanese menu. It did not appear until the 1860s when westerners came to Japan. Prior to that time, beef was not a popular item with the Japanese. Sukiyaki really came into vogue after the Meiji period (1868-1912). It is an easy dish to make and not only tastes good, but is also a lot of fun to prepare and serve.*

*1 piece of suet*
*1 to 2 Tbsp. sugar*
*¼ to ¾ cup soy sauce*
*¼ to ¾ cup sake*
*2 lbs. well-marbled sirloin,*
*  very thinly sliced (approx.)*
*1 yellow onion, cut into*
*  ¼" slices*

*6 scallions, cut diagonally*
*  into 1½" slices*
*Bamboo shoots*
*Chinese cabbage, cut into*
*  ½" slices*
*Mushrooms, cut into*
*  thick slices*
*2 cakes tofu*
*8 oz. Japanese noodles*

Melt the suet in an electric skillet or a frying pan. Sprinkle the sugar into the pan. Add ½ cup water, the soy sauce and sake. Keep the heat medium-high (350° on an electric skillet). Add the beef and then the remaining ingredients, cooking in sequence.

*Note: It helps to precook the noodles before adding them to the skillet.*

Monte Lazarus
Senior Vice President
External Affairs

## Pepper Steak

*1½ lbs. sirloin steak, cut*
*  into ⅛" strips*
*1 Tbsp. paprika*
*2 cloves garlic, crushed*
*2 Tbsp. butter or margarine*
*1 cup sliced green onions*
*  with tops*
*2 green peppers, cut into strips*

*2 green peppers, cut into strips*
*2 large fresh tomatoes,*
*  diced*
*1 cup beef broth*
*2 Tbsp. cornstarch*
*2 Tbsp. soy sauce*
*3 cups hot cooked rice*

Sprinkle the steak with the paprika and allow to stand while chopping or preparing the other ingredients. Cook the steak and garlic in the butter until the meat is browned. Add the onions and green peppers and continue cooking until the vegetables are wilted. Add the tomatoes and broth, cover and simmer for about 15 minutes. Blend the cornstarch and soy sauce with ¼ cup water. Stir into the meat and cook until thickened. Serve over beds of fluffy rice.

*Serves 6.*

JoAnn Olanyk
Reservations

## Minced Beef à la Deutsch

*1 lb. tenderloin tips, minced*
*Salt and pepper to taste*
*Garlic salt to taste*
*½ cup butter*
*1 medium onion, diced*
*1 medium green pepper,*
  *diced*

*1 cup sliced fresh mushrooms*
*½ cup brown beef gravy*
*1 tsp. chopped chives*
*2 Tbsp. catsup*
*1 tsp. Maggi seasoning*

The beef should be minced into fairly large pieces, with no fat or sinews. Season the beef with salt, pepper and garlic salt. Sauté quickly in ¼ cup butter in a skillet over very high heat so that the meat stays rare. In a separate frying pan, sauté the onion, green pepper and mushrooms in the remaining butter. Combine the meat and vegetables, then add the beef gravy, chives, catsup and Maggi seasoning. Blend together with a spoon and bring to a boil. Serve over toast or noodles or in a pastry shell.

*Serves 5.*

John H. Wolfsheimer
Executive Chef
San Francisco Food Services

# Beef Wellington

3 Tbsp. butter
4 lbs. beef tenderloin
Flour
2 cups chopped mushrooms
2 tsp. chopped chives
Dash of cognac
¼ can liver pâté
Ground pepper to taste
½ lb. puff dough
2 egg yolks, beaten

**Brandy Sauce:**
¼ cup plus 2 Tbsp. unsalted
   butter
¼ cup plus 2 Tbsp. dark
   brown sugar
Grated rind of ½ lemon
Squeeze of lemon juice
2 to 3 Tbsp. brandy or to taste

Melt the butter in a large, heavy skillet. Dust the meat with flour and brown quickly on all sides. Remove the meat and set aside in a warm place. Sauté the mushrooms in the same pan in which beef was browned, adding more butter, if necessary. Add the chives and cognac. Remove from the stove and blend in the liver pâté. Cool slightly. Split the meat lengthwise through the center. Spread the mushroom and liver pâté mixture on the center of the filet. Sprinkle with pepper. On a floured board, roll the pastry out thin and large enough to completely wrap the dough around the meat, placing any overlapping dough on the underside of the meat. Secure the ends by wrapping them under the roll as much as possible and set on a greased cooking sheet. Brush the pastry entirely with the egg yolks. Bake at 350° for 30 to 40 minutes. Remove from the pan and let stand for about 15 minutes before serving. Serve with **Brandy Sauce**.

**Brandy Sauce:** Cream the butter and gradually beat in the sugar with the lemon rind and juice. When soft and light, beat in enough brandy, a little at a time, to flavor the butter well. Place in a small bowl and chill before serving.

Note: Rum or cognac can be substituted for the brandy.

Lillian Warren

# Beef Filets in Flaky Pastry

1 Tbsp. butter
6 (3- to 4-oz.) beef filets,
    trimmed
¼ cup plus 2 Tbsp. Madeira or
    sherry
½ lb. mushrooms, minced
1 (10-oz.) pkg. frozen patty
    shells, thawed
Salt

**Bearnaise Cream Sauce:**
2 Tbsp. minced onion
1 Tbsp. wine vinegar
¼ tsp. tarragon
¼ lb. small mushrooms
¼ cup butter
¼ cup heavy cream
2 egg yolks

Melt the butter in a wide skillet over the highest heat and sear the steaks on both sides until browned. Pour in 2 Tbsp. Madeira, transfer the steaks to another container and thoroughly chill. Add the remaining Madeira and the mushrooms to the skillet and cook over medium heat, stirring, until all the liquid has evaporated. Chill. Roll out the 6 pastries, one at a time, on a lightly floured board to make a circle about 8" in diameter. Put one-sixth of the mushroom mixture in the center of each pastry, set one of the cold steaks on top, salt lightly, fold the pastry over the steaks to enclose and place folded side down on a rimmed baking sheet. Repeat for each steak. Cover the steaks and refrigerate as long as overnight. Bake on the lowest rack in the oven at 425° for 10 minutes. Then move to the highest rack and bake for 8 to 10 minutes more, until lightly browned. Serve at once with the **Bearnaise Cream Sauce**.

**Bearnaise Cream Sauce:** In a small saucepan, combine the onion, vinegar and tarragon. Boil over medium heat, stirring until the liquid is evaporated. Slice or quarter the mushrooms if larger than 1" and add the mushrooms and butter to the pan and cook until the mushrooms are lightly browned. Just before serving, pour in the cream and bring to a boil. Stir some of the hot mixture into the egg yolks, then return to the saucepan and cook briefly, stirring until slightly thickened.

Note: This is a great "do ahead" dish. If necessary, the sauce can be reheated by gently stirring over hot, not simmering water.

Beverly Hannah
Wife of Captain Jim Hannah
Manager of Flight Operations

## Bali Miki

2 Tbsp. chopped scallions
1 Tbsp. chopped onion
½ clove garlic, chopped
¼ cup plus 2 Tbsp. butter
1 Tbsp. curry powder
1 tsp. fresh ginger
2 Tbsp. chili sauce
1 Tbsp. soy sauce
1 canned tomato, finely
  chopped

Juice of 1 lemon
1 cup beef gravy
3 lbs. beef tenderloin, cut into
  12 (4-oz.) slices
Steamed wild rice (optional)
Sliced water chestnuts
  (optional)
Bean sprouts (optional)
Wild or black mushrooms
  (optional)

Sauté the scallions, onion and garlic in the butter for 1 minute. Add the curry powder, ginger, chili sauce, soy sauce, tomato, lemon juice and gravy. Cook the mixture for approximately 2 minutes, then correct the seasoning, if necessary; set aside and keep warm. Broil the tenderloin over charcoal for 1½ minutes each side. Arrange the beef over rice (if rice is not used, place the beef directly on a platter), top with the sauce and garnish with the water chestnuts, bean sprouts and mushrooms. Can be served as an entrée or as hors d'oeuvres.

Emile LeBoulluec
Executive Chef
Boston Food Services

## Beef Sauté Stroganoff

*Chefs may not pass out their hard-earned knowledge to customers, but they usually will to other chefs. And while I worked as a Sauce Cook at the Hotel Plaza in Brussels, several talented chefs, who had worked in many parts of the world, taught me a number of foreign dishes. This one was served to the late Tzar of Russia.*

Salt and pepper to taste
2 lbs. beef tenderloin, sliced
  into 3" x ½" strips
½ cup sweet butter
2 cups finely chopped white
  onions

2 cloves garlic, very finely
  chopped
¼ cup tomato paste
1 cup beef stock or bouillon
1 cup heavy cream

Sprinkle salt and pepper over the beef slices. Melt the butter and, when foaming hot, add and sauté the beef over medium heat for approximately 2 minutes, turning the slices often. Add the onions and simmer for 5 minutes. Gently mix in the garlic and tomato paste and add the beef stock and cream. Simmer uncovered until the sauce thickens. Remove the beef slices to a serving dish. Strain the sauce and pour over the beef. Serve piping hot with wild rice or boiled potatoes; a good chilled California rosé will be just right.

*Note: If desired, sherry wine or sautéed, sliced mushrooms can be added to the sauce.*

Raoul F. Delbol
Executive Chef
Los Angeles Food Services

## Broiled Top Round of Beef, Southern Style

*1 cup cooking oil*
*1 cup 86-proof bourbon*
*  whiskey*
*½ tsp. Lawry's seasoned*
*  pepper*
*1 Tbsp. seasoned salt*

*1 tsp. unseasoned meat*
*  tenderizer*
*1 (4-lb.) prime or choice*
*  top round, 2" thick*
*2 Tbsp. flour*
*2 Tbsp. Marsala wine*
*2 Tbsp. dry vermouth*

Combine the first 5 ingredients in a shallow baking pan, add the meat and turn in the mixture. Marinate covered at room temperature for 4 hours, turning the meat every 30 minutes. Just before cooking the meat, combine the remaining ingredients in a small saucepan and blend with the remaining marinade. Stir and cook over low heat until the sauce is slightly thickened, then simmer for approximately ½ hour, stirring occasionally. To cook the meat, place over charcoal or under the broiler, 3½" to 4" from the heat, and broil each side 12 minutes, turning once. Slice the meat very thin and serve with the sauce at the side.

W. Reichmuth
Executive Chef
Chicago Food Services

## Beef Roulades

1 (2-lb.) round steak, trimmed
   and sliced ¼" thick
Salt and pepper
Prepared mustard
¼ to ½ cup finely chopped
   onions

3 Kosher-style dill pickles,
   cut into thin carrot strips
3 Tbsp. oil
¼ lb. fresh mushrooms, sliced
¾ cup dry red wine
1 cup beef broth
2 Tbsp. cornstarch

Cut the steak into 4" x 4" squares. Season each piece with salt and pepper, spread with mustard and sprinkle the onions over. Add the pickle strips and roll up; fasten with a toothpick. Brown the meat in the oil. Add the mushrooms, wine and broth. Cover and cook for 1¼ hours, adding water, if necessary. Remove the toothpicks and transfer the meat to an ovenproof serving dish. Dissolve the cornstarch in 2 Tbsp. water and add to the juice. Stir until thickened and pour the gravy over the roulades. Serve with Duchesse potatoes.

Note: More pickles can be used as desired.

Serves 6.

Yvonne Erickson
Reservations

## Braised Brochette of Beef with Burgundy Wine Sauce

3 lbs. bottom round, cut into
   1" cubes
Salt and pepper
2 Tbsp. oil
½ cup plus 2 Tbsp. butter
½ cup chopped shallots
2 Tbsp. chopped carrots
2 Tbsp. flour

¼ cup tomato paste
3 cloves garlic, minced
1 tsp. thyme
2 bay leaves
2 cups burgundy wine
4 cups beef stock
Cooked rice
18 mushroom caps

Sprinkle the beef with salt and pepper. In a heavy, 12" skillet, heat the oil over low heat until it splatters. Add the beef and cook, turning frequently, until brown on all sides. With tongs, transfer the meat to a platter. Then heat ¼ cup plus 2 Tbsp. butter, add the shallots and carrots and sauté for 3 to 4 minutes over moderate heat. Add the beef and sprinkle in the flour, stirring with a spoon. Add the tomato paste, garlic, thyme and bay leaves. Add the wine and simmer slowly until the wine is reduced by half. Add the beef stock and mix thoroughly. Transfer to a casserole dish, cover and simmer over low heat for 1 to 1½ hours. When done, make a bed of rice on a serving dish and place the mushroom caps on top. Remove the meat from the pan with a slotted spoon and place on the mushrooms. Strain the sauce with a medium strainer, adjust the seasoning and pour over the beef.

*Serves 6.*

Rolf Conrad
Executive Chef
Denver Food Services

## Steak Diane

3 Tbsp. butter
4 minute steaks, pounded to
⅜" thickness
2 shallots or scallions,
very finely chopped
2 Tbsp. brandy or ¼ cup
Marsala

1 Tbsp. Worcestershire sauce
½ cup **Espagnola Sauce** (see index)
2 to 3 Tbsp. tomato sauce
1 Tbsp. chopped parsley

Heat half the butter in a large frying pan or chafing dish until hot and foamy. Immediately add the steaks and fry quickly on each side until brown. Add the shallots or scallions, pour the brandy or Marsala into the pan, ignite and let the flames burn out. Add the Worcestershire sauce, then the **Espagnola Sauce** and tomato sauce. Simmer for 1 to 2 minutes or until thoroughly blended; add the remaining butter, in small pieces, then add the parsley. Shake the pan to blend the butter into the sauce without boiling, remove from the heat and serve at once.

Randall Greseth
International Sales

## Steak Hong Kong

4 (6- to 8-oz.) rib steaks, cut
  ½" thick
Pepper
¼ cup plus 2 Tbsp. brandy
1 Tbsp. soy sauce
1 tsp. Worcestershire sauce
1½ tsp. Dijon mustard

1 Tbsp. steak sauce
1 Tbsp. chili sauce
1 tsp. beef stock base
½ cup water
Salt to taste
2 Tbsp. butter

Sprinkle the steaks with pepper and 2 Tbsp. brandy and set aside for 15 minutes. Grill the steaks in a greased skillet over high heat for 3 minutes on each side for rare meat. Remove from the pan and keep warm. Pour the remaining brandy into the skillet and ignite. When the flames subside, stir in the remaining ingredients except the butter. Cook and stir over high heat until the sauce thickens. Swirl in the butter. Return the steaks to the skillet and baste with the sauce.

Jackie Partlow

## Easy Forget-It Brisket

4 to 6 yellow onions
1 (3- to 4-lb.) fresh brisket
½ cup catsup
¼ cup vinegar

¼ cup oil
1 Tbsp. sugar
1 tsp. water

Slice the onions and spread half over the bottom of a Dutch oven. Add the meat and cover with the remaining onions. Combine the remaining ingredients and pour over the meat. Cover and bake at 275° for 4 to 5 hours.

*Go shopping or whatever. The longer it cooks, the better it is. It is good sliced thin and served over noodles or mashed potatoes with the sauce. Good also with green beans and cole slaw. Great served cold the next day.*

Mikele McKnight
Reservations

# New England Boiled Dinner

3 quarts cold water
2 lbs. beef brisket,
  well trimmed of fat
1 lb. lean smoked bacon
1 ½ tsp. salt
½ tsp. crushed white pepper
3 fresh carrots, peeled
1 fresh celery heart

2 stalks leeks
2 medium onions
1 bay leaf
3 whole cloves
3 all-beef wieners
6 cross-cut beef marrow bones
Chopped parsley or chives

Put the water in a 6-quart cooking pot, add the beef brisket and bacon; bring to a boil and skim well. Add the salt and pepper and simmer for 1 hour. Add all the vegetables and spices and cook for 30 minutes more. Add the wieners and marrow bones and simmer for 5 minutes more. Remove the meat and vegetables; strain the juices and set aside. Cut the beef and bacon into bite-size pieces, cut the wieners in half. Put equal amounts of meat and vegetables in warm soup dishes. Boil the beef stock and pour over the meat and vegetables. Sprinkle with chopped parsley or chives.

Bruno Good
Executive Chef
Seattle Food Services

# Sauerbraten with Red Cabbage

1 cup cider vinegar
1 cup burgundy
2 onions, sliced
1 carrot, sliced
1 stalk celery, chopped
2 whole allspice cloves
4 whole cloves
1 Tbsp. salt
1 ½ tsp. pepper
1 (4-lb.) rump or boned chuck
  pot roast
4 Tbsp. all-purpose flour
1 ⅓ cups salad oil, heated

⅓ cup cold water
1 Tbsp. sugar
¼ cup crushed gingersnaps

**Red Cabbage:**
1 medium head red cabbage
1 Tbsp. salt
2 Tbsp. butter or margarine
½ cup cider vinegar
½ cup sugar
2 tart red cooking apples
1 Tbsp. all-purpose flour

In a large bowl, mix together the vinegar, wine, onions, carrot, celery, allspice, cloves, salt and pepper. Wipe the meat with damp paper towels. Place in the marinade and refrigerate covered for 2 days, turning occasionally. Remove the meat and reserve the marinade. Dry the meat on paper towels. Coat with 2 Tbsp. flour. Heat the oil in a Dutch oven over medium heat, add and brown the meat all over for about 20 minutes, turning with a wooden spoon. Add the marinade, bring to a boil, reduce the heat and simmer covered for 2½ to 3 hours or until tender. When the meat is fork-tender, remove from the Dutch oven. Press the liquid and vegetables through a coarse sieve and skim off the fat. Measure 3½ cups liquid, adding water if necessary, and return to the Dutch oven. Mix 2 Tbsp. flour with the cold water and sugar. Stir into the liquid and bring to a boil, stirring frequently. Stir in the gingersnaps. Return the meat to the Dutch oven, spoon the gravy over and simmer covered for 20 minutes. Remove the meat and thinly slice. Place with the cabbage on a hot platter, pour the gravy over and serve.

**Red Cabbage:** Discard the outer leaves of the cabbage, cut into quarters and remove the core. Shred and measure 10 cups. In a large skillet, combine with the salt, butter, vinegar, sugar and ½ cup water. Cook covered over medium heat for 15 minutes, stirring occasionally. Core but do not pare the apples and thinly slice. Stir into the cabbage and cook for 10 minutes more. Stir in the flour and cook and stir until the cabbage is tender and crisp.

*Serves 6 to 8.*

Karen Fudge
Regional Sales

## Marinated Beef Roast, German Style
### (Sauerbraten)

1 (4-lb.) beef rump or
 round roast
Salt and pepper
1 large onion, sliced
2 stalks celery, diced
1 carrot, sliced

3 bay leaves
1 tsp. pickling spices
¾ cup red wine vinegar
1½ cups burgundy (approx.)
3 Tbsp. fat
½ cup sour cream

Rub the meat well with salt and pepper and place in an earthenware dish with the onion, celery, carrot, bay leaves and pickling spices. Combine the vinegar and ¼ cup water and pour over the meat. Pour over enough wine to cover the meat (approximately 1 cup) and add 1 tsp. salt. Cover the dish and refrigerate for approximately 48 hours. When ready to cook, thoroughly sear the meat on all sides in the fat in a cast iron skillet. Remove from the skillet, place in a Dutch oven and, if desired, add the onion, celery and carrot taken from the brine. Bake at 300° for 2½ to 3 hours or until tender. Remove the meat from the pot, slice and place on a deep platter. Strain the sauce and add the sour cream and ½ cup wine. Simmer for 2 to 3 minutes, season to taste, pour over the beef and serve.

*Note: The meat can marinate for as long as 5 to 6 days, if desired.*

Hans Jantzen
Executive Chef
New York Food Services

## Roast Sirloin of Beef with Mushroom Sauce

*1 (4½ - to 5½-lb.) trimmed
   shell loin of beef
Oil
Salt and pepper to taste
½ bay leaf, crumbled*

**Mushroom Sauce:**
*½ lb. mushrooms, sliced
2 Tbsp. butter
Salt and pepper to taste
⅓ cup red wine*

One hour before roasting, rub the beef with oil and then rub with salt and pepper and the bay leaf. Let stand. Roast at 400° for 45 minutes. Remove the meat to a serving dish, defat the gravy and use in the sauce. Pour the **Mushroom Sauce** over the meat and serve.

**Mushroom Sauce:** Simmer the mushrooms with the butter, salt and pepper for 5 minutes; add the wine and reduce by one-half. Add the gravy from the roast, boil for approximately 2 minutes and serve.

*Serves 8.*

Hans Jantzen
Executive Chef
New York Food Services

## Pot Roast with Sour Cream Gravy

2 Tbsp. flour
2 tsp. salt
¼ tsp. pepper
2½ lbs. beef chuck pot roast
1 Tbsp. shortening
1 Tbsp. vinegar
1 tsp. dill weed
5 small potatoes, pared
5 carrots, quartered

1 lb. zucchini, quartered

**Sour Cream Gravy:**
Meat drippings
1 Tbsp. flour
Water
Salt and pepper
1 cup sour cream
1 tsp. dill weed

Mix together the flour, 1 tsp. salt and the pepper; coat the meat with this mixture. Melt the shortening in a large skillet or Dutch oven and brown the meat. Add ¼ cup water and the vinegar. Sprinkle the dill weed over the meat. Cover tightly and simmer for about 3 hours or until the meat is tender. One hour before the end of cooking time, add the potatoes and carrots; season with ½ tsp. salt. Twenty minutes before the end of cooking time, add the zucchini, season with ½ tsp. salt. Remove the meat and vegetables to a warm platter and serve with the **Sour Cream Gravy**.

**Sour Cream Gravy:** After the meat and vegetables have been removed from the pan, pour the meat drippings into a bowl, leaving the brown particles in the pan. Return 1 Tbsp. drippings to the pan and blend in the flour. Cook over low heat, stirring until the mixture is smooth and bubbly; remove from the heat. Add water to the reserved drippings to measure 1 cup liquid and stir into the flour mixture. Heat to boiling, stirring constantly; boil and stir for 1 minute. Season with salt and pepper, stir in the sour cream and dill weed and heat through. *Makes 2 cups.*

*Serves 4 to 6.*

Glen Burmark
Apollo Systems

☞ *To remove food odors from woodenware, soak the dish for several minutes in a mix of hot water and household ammonia.*

## Larded Beef à la Mode with Red Wine Sauce

5 lbs. beef rump
¼ lb. fresh larding pork,
   cut into ½" strips
½ cup beef fat or vegetable
   oil, heated
1 large onion, sliced
2 carrots, diced
½ cup flour

2 cups claret wine
2 cups tomato sauce
10 whole black peppercorns
1 small bunch of parsley
1 bay leaf
Salt and pepper to taste
Cooked vegetables

Lard the inside of the beef with the pork, truss firmly and place in an earthenware pot with the fat or oil. Add the onion and carrots and fry briskly. Then add the flour and stir until the flour is golden brown. Cover with water and the wine and tomato sauce, then add the peppercorns, parsley and bay leaf; cover and simmer for 2½ to 3 hours. When done, remove the meat, skim the fat, strain, reduce the sauce to a proper consistency and season with salt and pepper. Pour the sauce over the meat and garnish with cooked vegetables such as carrots, glazed, tiny whole onions, peas and potatoes.

Hans Jantzen
Executive Chef
New York Food Services

## Company Stew

2 lbs. stew meat
1 can tomato sauce diluted
   with 1 can burgundy or
   other red wine
¼ cup uncooked tapioca

Salt and pepper to taste
Chopped celery
Chopped carrots
Chopped potatoes
Chopped onions

Combine the meat, tomato sauce and wine, tapioca, salt and pepper. Bake covered at 300° for 3 hours. Add vegetables as desired to the meat, cover and bake for 2 to 3 hours more.

Sally Keenan
Inflight Services

## Joe Booker Stew

6 oz. lean salt pork, diced
½ lb. onions, sliced
2 lbs. beef chuck, cubed
¼ cup flour
4 cups beef stock
⅛ tsp. thyme
Salt

Ground black pepper
¾ lb. potatoes, diced into
    ½" chunks
¾ lb. carrots, sliced into
    ½" chunks
½ lb. white rutabagas, diced

In a heavy skillet, fry the pork over moderate heat until crisp. Remove the pork bits and discard. Add the onions and cook until golden brown; remove with a slotted spoon and set aside. Dust the beef cubes with the flour, brown in the remaining fat and set aside with the onions. Pour 1 cup beef stock into the skillet and bring to a boil, stirring constantly, scraping in the brown particles that cling to the bottom and sides of the pan. Return the onions and beef to the skillet. Add the remaining stock and the seasonings and bring to a boil. Reduce the heat, cover tightly and simmer for 1 hour. Stir in the potatoes, carrots and rutabagas. Recover and simmer for 30 minutes more. Serve.

Serves 6.

Rolf Conrad
Executive Chef
Denver Food Services

## Braised Beef Bourguignonne

1 bay leaf
½ tsp. pickling spices (whole)
Nutmeg
1 parsley sprig
2 lbs. lean stewing beef, cut
    into 1" cubes
Salt and pepper to taste
½ cup butter
2 large onions, minced

2 cloves garlic, chopped
2 cups burgundy wine
½ cup tomato puree
3 cups canned beef gravy
24 pearl onions
24 mushroom buttons
Dash of Maggi seasoning
Chopped chives

Place the first 4 ingredients in a cheesecloth bag to make a bouquet garni; set aside. Season the beef cubes with salt and pepper. Melt ¼ cup butter in a frying pan and sauté the meat until browned on all sides. Place the onions and garlic in a separate braising pan and sauté with the remaining butter until golden brown. Add the beef. Deglaze with the wine, simmer for 3 minutes and add the tomato puree, beef gravy and bouquet garni. Let simmer slowly in the oven, uncovered, until the beef is done. Remove the bouquet garni. Add the pearl onions, mushroom buttons, Maggi seasoning and chopped chives a few minutes before serving.

*Serves 6.*

John H. Wolfsheimer
Executive Chef
San Francisco Food Services

## East Indian Curry

*½ cup butter, melted*
*3 medium cloves garlic, minced*
*2 scallions with tops, diced*
*¼ tsp. ginger*
*3 Tbsp. curry powder*
*3 whole cloves*
*Piece of cinnamon bark*
*3 bouillon cubes or meat stock*
*Diced meat, chicken or lamb*

*1 (6-oz.) pkg. precooked*
*  frozen shrimp, thawed*
*Hot rice*
*Chutney*
*Chopped peanuts*
*Chopped tomatoes*
*Chopped onions*
*Freshly shredded coconut*

Melt the butter in a skillet and add the garlic and scallions. Cook until soft, but not brown. Stir in the ginger, curry powder, cloves, cinnamon bark and bouillon cubes or meat stock. Add the meat, chicken or lamb and the shrimp. Cook uncovered over low heat until slightly thickened, about 45 to 60 minutes. Serve over rice with chutney, peanuts, tomatoes, onions and coconut on the side.

*Serves 5 to 6.*

John L. Cowan
Senior Vice President
Finance

## Gourmet Calves Liver

1 cup butter
4 red onions, chopped
1 cup sliced mushrooms

½ cup red wine
1 ½ lbs. calves liver

Melt the butter in a heavy skillet over medium heat. Add the onions and mushrooms and sauté until tender. Pour in the wine, stirring well. Add the liver, cover and simmer until cooked to taste.

Ann Atwood
Reservations

## Zucchini Beef Pie

½ lb. lean ground beef
½ cup diced green peppers
1 tsp. finely chopped parsley
½ tsp. minced onion
½ tsp. garlic salt
1 tsp. oregano
1 tsp. salt
1 (9") pie crust pastry

½ cup dry whole wheat bread
 crumbs
½ cup grated Parmesan
 cheese
3 medium zucchini, sliced
2 tomatoes, peeled and sliced
2 Tbsp. salad oil
¾ cup grated cheddar cheese

Sauté the ground beef, green peppers, parsley, onion, garlic salt, oregano and salt together until the meat is brown and crumbly. Set aside. Line a 9" pie pan with the pastry. Combine the bread crumbs and Parmesan cheese. Place half the zucchini on the bottom of the crust, top with half the meat mixture, then half the bread crumbs, then half the sliced tomatoes. Sprinkle with the oil and repeat the layers. Top with the cheddar cheese and bake at 350° for 50 to 55 minutes.

Serves 6.

Norma Magoon
Reservations

### Zucchini Lasagna

1 lb. ground beef
⅓ cup chopped onions
1 (15-oz.) can tomato sauce
½ tsp. salt
½ tsp. oregano
¼ tsp. basil
⅛ tsp. pepper

4 medium zucchini
2 cups cottage cheese
1 egg
4 Tbsp. all-purpose flour
6 oz. mozzarella cheese,
    shredded

Brown the ground beef and onions until the onions are tender, about 10 minutes. Spoon off the fat. Add the tomato sauce, salt, oregano, basil and pepper. Heat to boiling, reduce the heat to low and simmer for 5 minutes to blend the flavors. Slice the zucchini lengthwise into ¼" slices. In a small bowl, combine the cottage cheese with the egg and mix well. In the bottom of a 10" x 7" baking dish, arrange half the zucchini in a layer and sprinkle with 2 Tbsp. flour. Top with half the cottage cheese mixture, half the mozzarella, and half the meat mixture. Repeat the layers. Bake at 375° for 40 minutes. Let stand for 10 minutes before serving.

Norma Magoon
Reservations

### Garden Patch Stew

1½ lbs. hamburger
4 to 5 stalks celery, diced
½ medium onion, diced
Dash of pepper
¼ tsp. chili powder
1 (28-oz.) can tomatoes, diced

1 (10¾-oz.) can beef broth
1 (15-oz.) can light red kidney
    beans
1 (15-oz.) can tomato sauce
½ medium head cabbage, cut
    into bite-size pieces

Brown the first 3 ingredients in a large, heavy kettle. Add the remaining ingredients, bring to a boil and boil for 20 minutes. The stew is better if simmered for 1 to 2 hours more.

If a larger quantity is desired, add another can each of beef broth and tomato sauce.

Norma Magoon
Reservations

## Old Fashioned Meat Loaf

2½ lbs. ground sirloin or
  ground round (can use half
  sirloin and half ground
  round)
⅔ cup V-8 or tomato juice
2 eggs
2 cups crushed Team cereal
  flakes

1 Tbsp. salt
2 tsp. minced garlic
Freshly ground pepper to taste
3 Tbsp. minced onion
3 strips bacon, cut in half
  crosswise

In a large bowl, combine the meat and V-8 juice. Add the eggs and
Team flakes, working the mixture to evenly distribute the flakes. Add
the spices and onion and, when the mixture is thoroughly blended,
shape into a large loaf, placing the bacon on top. Set in a baking pan
and bake uncovered at 350° for 1¾ hours. Let stand for 5 minutes or
so before serving.

Note: This meat loaf freezes very well. If you plan to freeze it, shorten
the cooking time by about 20 minutes. After defrosting, bake at 350° to
complete the cooking.

Makes 6 to 8 portions.

D. M. Buckmaster
Retired Senior Vice President
Personnel Headquarters

## Meatballs in Spaghetti Sauce

1 large onion, chopped
Olive oil
1 (29-oz.) can tomato puree
2 (6-oz.) cans tomato paste
Pinch of oregano
1½ lbs. lean ground beef
½ cup Progresso brand
  Italian-style bread crumbs

¾ cup grated Parmesan
  or Romano cheese (fresh
  is best)
4 extra large eggs
1 large clove garlic, minced
Salt and pepper to taste

Brown the onion in a small amount of olive oil in a large pot. Add the tomato puree and an equal amount of water and the tomato paste. Season with oregano, if desired. Simmer until thickened, about 2½ hours. Meanwhile, combine all the remaining ingredients and mix well. Form into large meatballs to retain moisture (if you make them too small, they dry out). Do not brown first. Add to the sauce the final 45 minutes of cooking time. Serve over spaghetti.

Joan Gay Phildius
Wife of Keith Phildius
Regional Sales Manager

## Walnut Meat Loaf

*1 egg, beaten*
*⅓ cup milk*
*2 lbs. ground beef*
*2 Tbsp. finely minced onion*
*1½ tsp. Worcestershire sauce*
*⅛ tsp. pepper*
*1½ tsp. salt*
*½ cup tomato catsup*
*Orange slices*
*Toasted walnuts*

**Stuffing:**
*3 cups soft bread crumbs*
*2 Tbsp. minced onion*
*1 tsp. salt*
*⅛ tsp. pepper*
*1½ cups chopped celery*
*¼ tsp. poultry seasoning*
*½ cup milk, water or stock*
*1 cup coarsely chopped walnuts*

Mix together the egg and milk and combine with the next 5 ingredients. Flatten out on wax paper in a rectangular shape ¾" thick. Combine the stuffing ingredients. Shape the stuffing into a roll on top of the meat and close to the lengthwise side. Roll so that the meat completely covers the stuffing. Remove the wax paper and place the meat roll in a shallow baking pan. Mix the catsup with ¼ cup water and pour over the meat roll. Bake at 375° for 1 hour. Garnish with orange slices and toasted walnuts.

Annemarie Fleming
Reservations

☞ *Try baking meat loaf in individual greased muffin pans. It bakes faster, and in attractive individual servings.*

## Company Casserole

½ medium onion, diced
1 Tbsp. oil
1½ lbs. ground beef
1 tsp. salt
¼ tsp. pepper
2 (8-oz.) cans tomato sauce

¼ cup sour cream
1 cup cottage cheese
1 (8-oz.) pkg. cream cheese
¼ cup chopped green peppers
⅓ cup sliced green onions
½ lb. egg noodles

In a large skillet, fry the onion in the oil. Add the ground beef, salt and pepper, brown and drain. Stir in the tomato sauce and set aside. Mix together the sour cream, cheeses, green peppers and green onions. Cook and drain the noodles. Place a very small amount of the meat mixture on the bottom of a casserole and cover with a layer of noodles. Spread the cheese mixture over the noodles and add a final layer of noodles. Cover with the meat mixture and bake at 350° for 30 to 40 minutes.

Janet Vitcovich
Reservations

## Grilled Salisbury Steak

2 lbs. chopped lean ground
   chuck or round
1 Tbsp. chopped shallots
1 tsp. chopped parsley
½ tsp. chopped chives
1 egg

½ cup light cream or
   half & half
½ large green pepper,
   chopped
Bread crumbs (optional)
Dash of Maggi seasoning
Salt and pepper to taste

Mix together all the ingredients, knead well and form into 6 (5½-oz.) patties. Cook in a well-greased frying pan until lightly browned on each side, then bake at 375° for approximately 10 minutes.

Serves 6.

Hans Jantzen
Executive Chef
New York Food Services

## Pepperoni

5 lbs. ground beef
1 Tbsp. plus 2 tsp. tender
  quick salt
1 Tbsp. plus 2 tsp. mustard
  seed
1 Tbsp. plus 2 tsp. coarse
  black pepper

2 tsp. hickory smoke salt
1 Tbsp. plus 1 tsp. garlic salt
1½ tsp. crushed red pepper
1 tsp. fennel seed, lightly
  crushed
1½ tsp. anise seed, lightly
  crushed

First day, mix all the ingredients together well, cover and refrigerate.
Second day, stir well, cover and refrigerate. Third day, stir again. Form
into 5 rolls about 12" long and 3" around. Place on a rack in a broiler
pan. Bake on the bottom rack of the oven at 140° for 8 hours. Turn
every 2 hours.

Fran Christensen
Tour Desk

## Homemade Poor People's Salami

5 lbs. ground beef
2½ tsp. whole or ground
  black pepper
2½ tsp. Morton's Smoke
  Flavored Sugar Cure

1 Tbsp. plus 2 tsp. Morton's
  Tender Quick Salt
2½ tsp. mustard seeds
2½ tsp. garlic salt

First day, mix all the ingredients together well, cover and refrigerate.
Second and third days, remix well once. Fourth day, remix well and
shape into rolls. Bake at 175° for 10 hours on a broiler pan so that the
grease can drain, turning once. Can be frozen for later use.

Note: Use the least expensive ground beef available.

Paul Steuri
Executive Chef
Omaha Food Services

## Chiles Rellenos Bake

1 lb. ground beef
½ cup chopped onions
1 tsp. salt
¼ tsp. pepper
2 (4-oz.) cans green chilies,
   halved and seeded

1½ cups shredded sharp
   cheddar or Jack cheese
4 eggs, beaten
1½ cups milk
¼ cup flour
Hot pepper sauce

In a skillet, brown the ground beef and onions; drain off the fat. Sprinkle the meat with ½ tsp. salt and the pepper. Place half the chilies in a 10" x 6" x 1½" baking dish. Sprinkle with the cheese and top with the meat. Arrange the remaining chilies over the meat. Combine the eggs, milk, flour, ½ tsp. salt, several dashes of hot pepper sauce and a dash of black pepper. Beat until smooth and pour over the chili mixture. Bake at 350° for 45 to 50 minutes or until a knife inserted in the center comes out clean. Cool for 5 minutes and cut into squares. May be served alone or with enchilada sauce.

Serves 6.

Janet Vitcovich
Reservations

## Glen's Chili

2 lbs. hamburger
3 to 4 Tbsp. chili powder
1 tsp. red pepper flakes
1 tsp. cumin
1 tsp. oregano
3 cups coarsely chopped
   onions
Oil

1 (16-oz.) can tomato paste
4 cups beef stock or 2 cans
   beef broth soup
1 (16-oz.) can kidney beans
1 (30-oz.) can chili beans
1 green pepper, cut into small
   squares (optional)

Brown the hamburger, add the chili powder, red pepper flakes, cumin and oregano and mix well. Transfer the meat to a large pot. Sauté the onions separately in a little oil. Add the onions and the remaining ingredients to the meat. Mix well and cook for at least 2 hours.

Glen Burmark
Apollo Systems

## Fort Still Mexican Food

*3 lbs. ground beef*
*3 (10¼-oz.) cans enchilada*
  *sauce*
*2 (6-oz.) cans tomato sauce*
*2 (4-oz.) cans chopped green*
  *chilies*
*4 cloves garlic, minced*
*Salt and pepper to taste*
*1 (12-oz.) pkg. corn tortillas*
*Oil*
*Chopped onions (optional)*

*Grated cheddar cheese*
  *(optional)*
*Grated Monterey Jack cheese*
  *(optional)*
*Chopped lettuce (optional)*
*Sliced olives (optional)*
*Chopped tomatoes (optional)*
*Sliced avocados or guacamole*
  *(optional)*
*Sour cream (optional)*

Combine the ground beef, enchilada and tomato sauces, chilies, garlic, salt and pepper and approximately 6 cups water in a large pan and simmer for at least 4 hours. Shortly before serving, fry the tortillas in 1" hot oil for approximately 5 seconds on each side and drain on paper towels. To serve, arrange the tortillas, sauce and the remaining ingredients as desired in serving dishes on a counter. Invite guests to serve themselves.

Molly Sumption
Apollo Systems

## Taco Pie

*1 lb. lean ground beef*
*½ medium onion, chopped*
*1 (8-oz.) can tomato sauce*
*1 (1¼-oz.) pkg. taco seasoning*
  *mix*
*⅓ cup sliced pitted ripe*
  *olives (optional)*
*1 (8-oz.) can refrigerated*
  *crescent rolls*

*1½ to 2 cups corn chips,*
  *crushed*
*1 cup sour cream*
*1 cup shredded cheddar*
  *cheese*
*Shredded lettuce*
*Tomato slices*
*1 avocado, peeled and sliced*

In a large frying pan, brown the ground beef and onion; drain the fat. Stir in the tomato sauce, taco seasoning mix and olives. Separate the crescent dough into 8 triangles. Place the triangles in an ungreased, 9" or 10" pie pan, pressing up the sides to form a crust. Sprinkle 1 cup corn chips over the bottom of the crust. Spoon the meat mixture over the crust and corn chips. Spread the sour cream over the meat mixture; cover with the cheese. Sprinkle on the remaining corn chips. Bake at 375° for 20 to 25 minutes until the crust is golden brown. Serve in wedges topped with shredded lettuce and tomato and avocado slices.

Arlene McEachern
Public Affairs

### Piccata of Veal Zingara

8 (2-oz.) scallopini of veal
Salt and pepper to taste
2 Tbsp. flour
2 eggs, beaten
¼ cup grated Parmesan
 cheese
½ cup butter
1 medium onion, chopped
⅓ to ½ cup sliced mushrooms

½ clove garlic, crushed
½ cup white wine
2 medium fresh tomatoes,
 diced
¼ tsp. oregano leaves
Pinch of rosemary
1½ oz. julienne of ham
1½ oz. julienne of beef tongue
½ tsp. Maggi seasoning

Have the butcher cut 8 (2-oz.) pieces of milk-fed veal from the top of the round. Pound them very thin to break down the fibers and season them with salt and pepper. Dip into the flour, then into the eggs and finally into the Parmesan cheese. Sauté the veal in ¼ cup hot butter in a skillet until the cutlets are golden brown on both sides. Remove from the skillet and keep warm. Add the remaining butter to the skillet with the cooking juices and sauté the onion, mushrooms and garlic until lightly browned. Pour in the wine, then add the tomatoes, oregano and rosemary and simmer for 10 minutes. Add the ham and tongue. Adjust the seasoning, if necessary, with more salt and pepper and the Maggi seasoning. Place the meat on a preheated platter and place the warm scallopini on top. Serve piping hot.

Serves 4.

Randy Ko
Assistant to the Chairman of the Board
United Airlines

## Sliced Veal, Swiss Style

2 Tbsp. butter
3 Tbsp. chopped onion
2 lbs. veal top round, ¼" thick,
　cut into 1" strips
Cooking oil
¼ lb. fresh mushrooms, sliced

1 Tbsp. flour
½ cup dry white wine
½ cup heavy cream
½ tsp. lemon juice
Salt and pepper to taste
Chopped parsley or chives

Heat the butter in a saucepan and gently sauté the onion just until wilted. In a heavy skillet, brown the veal strips, one-third at a time, in a little cooking oil; add the mushrooms and sauté for 2 minutes. Place the meat and mushrooms in the saucepan, sprinkle with the flour and stir. Gradually add the wine and cream and heat through, but do not boil. Stir until smooth and slightly thickened. Add the lemon juice, adjust the seasoning and sprinkle with parsley or chives. This can be served with hash browned potatoes, noodles, rice or mashed potatoes.

Serves 6.

Bruno Good
Executive Chef
Seattle Food Services

## Veal Oscar

4 veal cutlets, pounded
　very thin
2 Tbsp. fresh lemon juice
Pepper to taste
Flour seasoned with salt and
　pepper
Butter

16 spears fresh asparagus,
　cooked
4 crab legs, cooked and
　shelled
1 cup **Hollandaise Sauce**
　(see index)

Sprinkle the cutlets with the lemon juice and pepper on both sides; dust with seasoned flour. Heat the butter in a large skillet. Sauté the cutlets over medium-high heat for 4 minutes on each side or until lightly browned. Remove to a warm platter. On each cutlet place 4 asparagus spears and 1 crab leg. Cover with **Hollandaise Sauce.** Serve.

Jackie Partlow

## Filet of Veal Financière

2¼ lbs. veal tenderloin,
   trimmed of fat and sinews
   and cut into 2-oz. scallopinis
¾ cup butter
1½ cups chopped onions
1 clove garlic, finely chopped
Salt and pepper to taste
2 Tbsp. Hungarian paprika
½ cup flour

1½ cups dry white wine
2 cups brown beef stock
1 bay leaf
½ cup sour cream
1 tsp. Maggi seasoning
1 tsp. chopped fresh chives
½ cup Belgian carrot tips, boiled
1 (5-oz.) can mushroom stems
¼ cup quartered ripe olives

Sauté the meat in the butter until browned. Add the onions, garlic, salt and pepper and cook for 8 minutes. Add the paprika and flour and make a roux. Bake at 375° for 10 minutes, stirring occasionally. Deglaze with the wine and stock, add the bay leaf and simmer slowly until the meat is tender; do not overcook. When ready to serve, combine the sour cream, Maggi seasoning and chives and bring just to the boiling point; the sauce will curdle if boiled. Pour the sauce over the meat, garnish with the carrots, mushrooms and olives.

Serves 6.

John H. Wolfsheimer
Executive Chef
San Francisco Food Services

## Veal Scallopini with Shrimp and Oysters, Monterey

1½ lbs. veal, cut into 12 (2-oz.)
   scallopinis
Salt and pepper
Oregano
Flour
¾ cup butter
1 tsp. chopped shallots
⅓ cup sliced fresh
   mushrooms
1 lb. bay shrimp, shelled and
   deveined

18 blue point oysters, shelled
⅔ cup California brandy,
   heated
1½ cups heavy cream
2 egg yolks
3 Tbsp. sliced ripe olives
½ cup sliced artichoke bottoms
¼ cup plus 1 Tbsp. grated
   Parmesan cheese

Season the veal with salt, pepper and oregano and dredge in flour. Melt half the butter in a hot, heavy skillet, add the veal and sauté for 3 minutes on each side. Arrange in a single layer in a baking dish and keep warm. Melt the remaining butter in the skillet, add the shallots, mushrooms and shrimp and gently sauté for 2 minutes. Add the oysters and cook for 2 minutes more. Pour in the brandy, ignite and shake the pan until the flames go out. Add 1 ¼ cups cream and bring to a boil. Whip the egg yolks in the remaining cream, add to the sauce and cook, stirring until thickened. Remove the pan from the heat, add the olives and artichokes and season with salt and pepper. Pour the sauce over the veal, sprinkle the Parmesan cheese over and set under a hot broiler for a few seconds or until the cheese is browned. Serve immediately.

*Serves 6.*

W. Reichmuth
Executive Chef
Chicago Food Services

## Veal Cutlets Saltimbocca
### (Vitello alla Saltimbocca)

4 (4-oz.) veal cutlets, flattened
    to about ¼" thickness
Sage
Salt and pepper to taste
4 thin slices Swiss cheese
4 thin slices cooked lean ham
Flour

1 egg, beaten
3 Tbsp. butter
2 Tbsp. oil
**Rice Pilaf** (see index)
Juice of ¼ lemon
¼ cup browned butter
Chopped parsley

Season the center of each cutlet with sage, salt and pepper. Place on each a slice of cheese, then a slice of ham and fasten with a toothpick. Pass lightly through flour and then through the egg. Heat the 3 Tbsp. butter and the oil, add the cutlets and sauté to a golden brown on both sides (ham side first) or until tender. Serve on a bed of **Rice Pilaf**. Sprinkle with the lemon juice and top with the brown butter and parsley.

Paul Steuri
Executive Chef
Omaha Food Services

## Veal Zürichoise

1½ lbs. veal, cut into strips
1 cup clarified butter
2 tsp. flour
1 Tbsp. chopped shallots
½ lb. fresh mushrooms, sliced

1 cup white wine
2 cups heavy cream
Salt and pepper to taste
Chopped parsley

Sauté the veal in the butter until lightly browned; sprinkle with the flour to absorb the butter and remove from the pan. In the same pan, sauté the shallots and mushrooms, then add the wine and bring to a boil. Add the cream and boil until the liquid is reduced by half. Add the veal to the sauce. Season with salt and pepper and sprinkle with chopped parsley.

Lyell E. Cook
Manager
Detroit Food Services

## Veal Cordon Bleu

8 thinly sliced veal cutlets
   (from the top round of
   leg veal)
½ cup sherry
½ lb. Swiss cheese, grated
Salt and pepper to taste
Nutmeg to taste
½ cup chopped white
   bread crumbs
1 Tbsp. freshly chopped parsley

4 (1-oz.) slices Canadian
   bacon or cooked ham
2 eggs
2 Tbsp. milk
1 cup flour
2 cups regular bread crumbs
Butter
4 lemon wedges
Paprika to taste

Pound the cutlets to ¼" thickness so that they are approximately 6" x 3½"; set aside. Warm the sherry in a saucepan, add the cheese and stir constantly until it melts. Add salt, pepper and nutmeg to taste. Then add the white bread crumbs and parsley. Remove from the heat and cool. Place 1 slice Canadian bacon or ham on each cutlet and one-fourth of the cheese mixture on top of the ham, preferably in a small, long patty form. Cover each with the remaining cutlets. Intermash both ends of the veal cutlets with a knife to make a sealed edge. Season the outside with salt. Beat the eggs with the milk. Dip each cutlet first into the flour, then the egg wash and then the regular bread crumbs. Fry the cutlets in fresh butter over a brisk fire until golden brown on both sides. Place in a shallow pan and bake at 400° for 15 minutes. Garnish with the lemon wedges, and, if desired, more chopped parsley. Sprinkle with paprika and serve immediately.

*Note: If desired, brown sauce or tomato sauce can be added during baking.*

*Serves 4.*

John H. Wolfsheimer
Executive Chef
San Francisco Food Services

## Minced Veal, Swiss Style

*1 lb. top round leg of veal,
  completely deveined and
  trimmed of fat
Salt and pepper to taste
¼ cup plus 2 Tbsp. butter
1 Tbsp. flour
¾ cup dry white wine
1 cup beef consommé*

*1 Tbsp. chopped shallots
2 Tbsp. chopped onion
24 small whole mushroom
  bottoms
1 small bay leaf
½ tsp. chopped chives
Dash of Maggi seasoning*

Mince the meat into fine, thin pieces and season with salt and pepper in a skillet with half the butter until lightly browned. Dust with the flour; cook for 5 minutes, stirring constantly. Deglaze with the wine and consommé and set aside. In a separate skillet, sauté the shallots, onion and mushrooms in the remaining butter until golden brown. Combine with the meat. Add the bay leaf and simmer for 20 minutes. Add the chives and Maggi seasoning.

*Note: If the sauce is too thin, add a little cornstarch.*

John H. Wolfsheimer
Executive Chef
San Francisco Food Services

## Braised Veal Shanks, Osso Buco, Kalbshaxe

4 (1-lb.) veal shanks
Salt to taste
12 peppercorns, crushed
2 Tbsp. flour
½ cup butter
1 Tbsp. salad oil
2 medium onions, chopped
2 small cloves garlic,
   finely chopped
½ cup 1" square pieces celery
1 cup 1" long pieces fresh
   carrots
2 cups dry white wine

2 cups chicken stock
½ cup tomto puree
1 large bay leaf
½ tsp. MSG
1 Maggi bouillon cube
1½ Tbsp. cornstarch
½ cup canned mushroom
   caps
½ cup frozen carrot tips,
   cooked
½ cup canned pearl onions
1 oz. brandy
1 Tbsp. chopped fresh parsley

Preseason the veal shanks with salt and the peppercorns, then dust with the flour on all sides. In a roasting pan, melt the butter and oil, and, when hot, brown the meat on both sides. Remove the meat, add the chopped onions, garlic, celery and carrots to the pan and lightly brown. Deglaze with the wine and chicken stock. Add the tomato puree, bay leaf, MSG, bouillon cube and bring to a boil; then return the browned veal shanks to the roasting pan and bake uncovered at 400°, occasionally turning the meat in the pan. When the veal shanks are cooked and tender, remove the meat and place in a serving dish; keep warm. Strain the sauce, adjust the seasoning and, if necessary, thicken with the cornstarch diluted in water; do not make the sauce too thick. Add the mushroom caps, carrot tips, pearl onions and brandy to the sauce. Bring to a boil, then pour over the meat, sprinkle with chopped parsley and serve hot. Serve with noodles, tagliarinis, potato salad or mashed potatoes. Beer or a rosé or chablis wine are nice with the dish.

Serves 4.

John H. Wolfsheimer
Executive Chef
San Francisco Food Services

☞ Clarify butter easily by heating in the microwave until it bubbles. Pour off the clear liquid for use and discard the residue.

## Veal Scallopini Sauté, North Beach

1 ½ lbs. veal, cut into 8 (3-oz.)
   scallopinis
Salt and pepper to taste
Garlic salt to taste
2 Tbsp. flour
¼ cup plus 1 Tbsp. grated
   Parmesan cheese
½ cup butter

1 cup sliced fresh mushrooms
3 Tbsp. chopped onion
1 cup sliced green peppers
½ cup dry white wine
¼ cup sherry wine
3 beef bouillon cubes
Dash of Maggi seasoning
2 tsp. chopped parsley

Pound the veal with a meat cleaver so that the pieces are flat and season with salt, pepper and garlic salt. Mix the flour with the Parmesan cheese. Dredge the scallopini in the flour, then sauté in a skillet in ¼ cup butter until the cutlets are golden brown; remove from the skillet and keep hot. Add the remaining butter and sauté the mushrooms, onion and green peppers, stirring constantly; deglaze with the wines and add the bouillon cubes. When the bouillon cubes melt, add the scallopini, cover the pan and bake at 375° for 8 minutes. Remove and dress the meat on a serving platter, add the Maggi seasoning and adjust the seasonings, if necessary. Pour the sauce over the meat and sprinkle the parsley over. Serve piping hot, 2 pieces of meat per person. Chianti, burgundy, Beaujolais or a dry white wine are good with this dish.

Serves 4.

John H. Wolfsheimer
Executive Chef
San Francisco Food Services

## Ossi Buchi Esterhazy

6 center-cut veal hind shanks,
   cut 1 ½" thick
Salt and pepper
¾ cup flour (approx.)
Oil
1 cup finely diced carrots
1 cup finely diced celery
1 cup finely diced onions

1 cup finely diced leeks
1 cup finely diced turnips
1 cup dry white wine
5 cups boiling brown veal or
   beef stock
1 cup peeled, diced tomatoes
1 Tbsp. cornstarch
¼ cup Madeira wine

Sprinkle the veal shanks with salt and pepper, dip in flour and brown well on all sides in an greased skillet. In a large pot or Dutch oven, sauté the carrots, celery, onions, leeks and turnips in a little oil over medium heat until browned. Sprinkle ½ cup flour over the vegetables and mix well. Add the wine and then the stock. Stir until the mixture comes to a boil, adjust the seasoning and add the veal shanks. Simmer uncovered for 45 minutes or until the meat becomes loose around the center bone. Add the tomatoes, cover and cook at 375° for 1 to 2 hours or until tender. If the sauce appears too thin, thicken it with the cornstarch and Madeira. This dish can be served with saffron rice, noodles or mashed potatoes.

*Serves 6.*

Bruno Good
Executive Chef
Seattle Food Services

## Veal Côtelette Liègoise

6 center-cut veal cutlets
Salt and pepper
1 Tbsp. flour
¼ cup salad oil
1 cup butter

6 pineapple slices
18 dark grapes
1 cup white wine
1 Tbsp. cornstarch
2 Tbsp. sherry

Season the cutlets on both sides with salt and pepper, then turn in the flour and shake off the excess. Heat the oil in a skillet, add and lightly brown the cutlets on both sides. Drain off the oil, add the butter to the pan and simmer for 3 minutes. Fill the center of each pineapple ring with 3 grapes. Heat on hot plates and arrange the cutlets around. Add the wine to the pan in which the veal was cooked and let it reduce by half, carefully dissolving the meat juices in the pan. Dissolve the cornstarch in the sherry and add to the white wine. Bring this mixture to a boil, season to taste with salt and pepper and pour over the veal cotelettes.

*Serves 6.*

John H. Wolfsheimer
Executive Chef
San Francisco Food Services

# EGGS & CHEESE

# Baked Eggs with Bercy Sauce

6 eggs
6 slices ham or Canadian
  bacon, broiled
6 slices bread, toasted

**Bercy Sauce:**
½ small onion, chopped
2 Tbsp. chopped mushrooms
¼ cup butter, melted

1 cup milk
¼ cup white wine
½ can Aunt Penney's
  Hollandaise sauce
1 Tbsp. flour
2 Tbsp. Parmesan cheese
1 tsp. chives
Salt and pepper to taste

Boil the eggs for 7 minutes until hard-cooked. Peel and cut with an egg slicer. Place 1 ham or bacon slice on top of each slice of toast. Place the eggs on top of the ham. Press lightly from the top so the slices fan out. Cover with the **Bercy Sauce** and bake at 350° for 3 to 5 minutes. Serve hot.

**Bercy Sauce:** Sauté the onion and mushrooms in the butter. Add the milk, wine and Hollandaise sauce. Stir often and boil for several minutes, then add the remaining ingredients. The sauce should be of a fairly thick consistency, but if too thick, add a little water.

Serves 6.

John H. Wolfsheimer
Executive Chef
San Francisco Food Services

☞ To restore frozen eggs, place them in boiling water and let sit until the water is cooled.

## Baked Eggs with Sausage

1 can refrigerator biscuits
1¼ cups Ragu or other Italian
   cooking sauce
1 cup shredded mozzarella
   cheese

5 eggs
2 Tbsp. cream
5 sausage links, cooked
   (approx.)

Press 2 biscuits into a 5" circle, pinching a rim along the edge. Repeat with 8 more biscuits to form 4 more shells. Spoon ¼ cup Ragu sauce into each and sprinkle one-half the cheese over the shells. Bake at 350° for 20 minutes. Mix the eggs with the cream and scramble; spoon into the shells. Top each with 1 or more sausages. Sprinkle the remaining cheese over the shells and bake until the cheese melts.

*Serves 5.*

Annemarie Fleming
Reservations

## Poached Eggs Florentine

¾ cup white vinegar
12 large eggs

**Sautéed Spinach:**
1 Tbsp. margarine
¼ cup diced onions
⅛ tsp. garlic powder
¼ cup diced ham or Canadian
   bacon
1 (12- to 16-oz.) pkg. frozen
   spinach, cooked, thoroughly
   drained and chopped
Salt to taste
Pinch of white pepper

Pinch of nutmeg

**Mornay Sauce:**
3 Tbsp. butter
3 Tbsp. margarine
¾ cup all-purpose flour
1 chicken bouillon cube
2½ cups milk, heated
½ cup half & half
¾ cup plus ½ Tbsp. grated
   Parmesan cheese
¾ cup plus ½ Tbsp. grated
   cheddar cheese
Salt and pepper to taste

In a 2-quart pot, boil the vinegar with 2 cups water. Break the eggs individually into a small bowl so that the egg yolks do not break. Drop 6 eggs, one at a time, into the boiling water and simmer for 5 minutes. (The eggs may be removed from the water earlier or cooked longer, if desired.) Remove the eggs from the vinegar water and put in a bowl of warm water; repeat the procedure with the remaining eggs. For each serving, arrange some **Sautéed Spinach** on a plate, put 2 poached eggs on top and cover with some **Mornay Sauce**.

**Sautéed Spinach:** Melt the margarine in a saucepan, add the onions, garlic powder and ham; sauté until the onions are limp but not brown. Add the spinach and seasonings and heat through. Serve warm.

**Mornay Sauce:** Melt the butter and margarine in a saucepan. Stir in the flour and cook the roux over low heat for about 10 minutes, stirring occasionally. Do not brown. Cool the roux. Dissolve the bouillon cube in the milk, add to the roux and stir well with a wire whip until the sauce is smooth. Bring to a boil and simmer slowly for about 20 minutes. Heat the half & half, add the cheeses and stir until the cheeses melt. Add to the cream sauce and bring to a boil, stirring constantly. Remove from the heat, season with salt and pepper and keep warm. If the sauce appears too thick, add more heated milk.

*Serves 6.*

Erich Dorfhuber
Executive Chef
Portland Food Services

## 8" x 12" Pan Breakfast

2 lbs. link sausage
8 slices bread
1 cup grated cheese
4 eggs

2½ cups milk
¾ tsp. dry mustard
1 tsp. salt

Brown the sausage, drain and cut into bite-size pieces. Set aside to cool. Remove the crusts from the bread and cut into cubes. Place one-half the sausage on the bottom of a greased baking pan, layer one-half the bread and then one-half the cheese over. Repeat the layers. Beat the remaining ingredients together and pour over the sausage mixture. Refrigerate for 8 hours. Bake at 325° for 1 hour.

Effie Johnston
Reservations

## Bacon and Eggs Crescent Sandwich

½ lb. bacon, fried, drained
  and crumbled
3 oz. Swiss or cheddar cheese,
  shredded
¼ cup finely chopped celery
4 eggs, hard-cooked and chopped

3 Tbsp. plus 2 tsp. mayonnaise
1 Tbsp. prepared mustard
1 (8-oz.) pkg. crescent dinner
  rolls
1 Tbsp. plus 1 tsp. sesame
  seeds

In a medium bowl, combine the bacon, cheese, celery, eggs, 3 Tbsp. mayonnaise and the mustard. Mix well. Separate the dough into 4 rectangles; firmly press perforations to seal. Cut each rectangle in half and press or roll each to a 4" square. Spoon about ¼ cup of the mixture into the center of each square. Pull the 4 corners of each square to the top of the filling; pinch the edges to seal. Place seam side down on an ungreased cookie sheet. Flatten each slightly. Brush each with ¼ tsp. mayonnaise and sprinkle each with the sesame seeds. Bake at 375° for 12 to 18 minutes or until golden brown. Serve immediately.

Makes 8 sandwiches.

Annemarie Fleming
Reservations

## Un Pan Kocha

2 cups milk
1 cup heavy cream
1 cup flour
¼ tsp. salt

4 eggs
7 slices bacon, cooked until
  not quite crisp and cut into
  1" pieces

In a blender, blend the milk, cream, flour and salt. Add the eggs and blend lightly. Pour the batter into a well-greased, 9" x 14" baking pan that has been dusted with flour. Cut the bacon strips into 1" pieces, drop into the batter and dunk under the surface. Bake at 400° for 30 to 35 minutes. Serve warm with a strawberry or raspberry sauce and butter, if desired.

Lucille Anderson
Reservations

## Cheddary Creamed Eggs

2 Tbsp. butter
2 Tbsp. flour
1½ cups milk
2 tsp. parsley
1 tsp. prepared mustard

¼ tsp. seasoned salt
⅓ cup shredded cheddar
   cheese
8 eggs, hard-cooked and sliced
Biscuits, muffins or toast

In a medium saucepan over medium heat, melt the butter. Blend in the flour and cook, stirring constantly, over medium-high heat until smooth and bubbly. Stir in the milk all at once, cook and stir until the mixture thickens and boils. Remove from the heat. Stir in the parsley, mustard, salt and cheese and cook until the cheese melts. Add the eggs. Cook over low heat, just until thoroughly heated. To serve, spoon over biscuits, muffins or toast.

Annemarie Fleming
Reservations

## Eggs Baked in English Muffins

4 large English muffins,
   unseparated
2 Tbsp. soft butter

4 eggs
4 tsp. cream or milk
4 Tbsp. grated cheese

Cut the center from each muffin almost to the bottom with a 3" cookie cutter and work the circles out. Spread the centers and the cutout portion with the butter and place on a baking sheet. Break an egg into each muffin "cup" and put 1 tsp. cream and 1 Tbsp. cheese on each egg. Bake at 350° for about 15 minutes or until the eggs are soft-set. Serve the cutout portion with each egg.

Ruth Vantine
Reservations

☞ Sprinkle a dash of cornstarch or flour over the melted butter in which eggs will be fried to keep them from splattering.

## Quiche Lorraine #1

½ lb. Swiss cheese, grated
1 Tbsp. flour
6 slices bacon, diced
½ cup finely diced onions
1(10") pie shell, partially baked

3 eggs
1 cup half & half
Dash of salt
Dash of ground white pepper

Combine the cheese and flour; set aside. Fry the bacon crisp, drain the fat and place the bacon on a paper towel. Sauté the onions in the bacon fat (do not brown) and place the onions and bacon on the bottom of the pie shell. Cover the onions and bacon with the cheese and flour. Beat the eggs, half & half and salt and pepper together and pour over the cheese. Bake at 325° for 35 to 40 minutes. Serve warm.

Emile LeBoulluec
Executive Chef
Boston Food Services

## Quiche Lorraine #2

3 eggs, lightly beaten
1 cup light cream
5 slices bacon, crisply cooked
    and crumbled
3 Tbsp. Grey Poupon Dijon
    mustard

¼ cup finely minced onions
1 cup grated Swiss cheese
¼ tsp. salt
⅛ tsp. pepper
1 (9") unbaked pie shell

Combine all the ingredients except the pie shell and pour into the pie shell. Bake at 375° for 35 to 40 minutes or until a knife inserted in the center comes out clean. The secret to the taste of this quiche is the Grey Poupon mustard.

Note: This quiche may be baked in a shallow dish without the pie shell, if desired.

Al Brown
Communications Network

## Quiche Lorraine #3

**Crust:**
2 cups flour
1 cup butter
1 tsp. salt

**Filling:**
¼ lb. bacon, diced and sautéed

¼ lb. Gruyère cheese, grated
¼ lb. Swiss cheese, grated
1½ cups cream
3 medium eggs, whipped
Pinch of salt
2 Tbsp. butter

To make the crust, blend together the flour, butter and salt until the dough flakes; form into a ring and pour ¼ cup water into the center. Slowly fold the flour and water together as little as possible because the longer the dough is mixed, the tougher the pie crust will be. Roll out and place in a 9" pie pan. Then combine all the filling ingredients, pour into the pie shell and bake at 375° for 30 to 35 minutes. Allow to cool before cutting.

Hans Jantzen
Executive Chef
New York Food Services

## Quiche Lorraine à la Suisse

1 tsp. butter
1 medium onion, finely
  chopped
1 pint fresh mushrooms, diced
¼ lb. bacon, cut into fine strips
1 (8") pie crust, chilled for
  30 minutes
¼ lb. Swiss cheese, diced

4 eggs
1½ cups half & half
1 tsp. cornstarch
Pinch of pepper
Dash of nutmeg
¼ cup grated Parmesan
  cheese
Cheese slices (optional)

Heat the butter in a skillet, add the onion and sauté for a few minutes. Add the mushrooms and sauté for 3 to 4 minutes more; put in a strainer to drain. Clean the skillet, return to the heat and sauté the bacon to remove the fat but not to crisp the bacon and place in the strainer with the other ingredients. Prick the pie crust with a fork, evenly place the Swiss cheese in it and top with the ingredients from the strainer. Combine the remaining ingredients except the cheese slices and pour into the pie shell. If desired, top with cheese slices for a nice pattern when baked. Bake at 375° to 400° for 20 to 30 minutes or until the pie is lightly puffed and golden brown.

*Note: The ingredients may be varied as desired. For example, the bacon can be omitted and replaced with increased amounts of the cheeses for a delicious cheese pie.*

Oswald M. Gnigler
Executive Chef
Las Vegas Food Services

## Seafood Quiche

6 slices lean bacon, diced
½ cup finely diced onions
2 oz. baby shrimp,
   well drained
1 (10") pie shell, partially baked
6 oz. imported Swiss cheese,
   grated
1½ tsp. all-purpose flour

3 eggs
1 cup half & half
½ tsp. salt
Pinch of ground white pepper
Pinch of ground cayenne
   pepper
Pinch of ground nutmeg

Fry the bacon crisp and remove to a paper towel. Sauté but do not brown the onions in the bacon fat and drain the fat. Distribute the shrimp, onions and bacon on the bottom of the pie shell. Combine the cheese and flour and place on top of the shrimp mixture. Beat the eggs and the cream together, add the salt, peppers and nutmeg and pour over the cheese. Bake at 325° for 35 to 40 minutes, until the top is golden brown. Serve warm with a well-chilled, dry California white wine.

*Serves 8.*

George J. Mendreshora
Executive Chef
Honolulu Food Services

## Roquefort Cheese Soufflé

6 eggs
½ cup heavy cream
1 tsp. Worcestershire sauce
Dash of liquid red pepper

¼ tsp. pepper
Pinch of salt
¼ lb. Roquefort or blue cheese
11 oz. cream cheese

Place the eggs, cream, Worcestershire sauce, red pepper, pepper and salt in a electric blender and whirl until smooth. Break the Roquefort cheese into pieces and add, piece by piece, to the mixture in the blender while the motor is running. Cut the cream cheese into pieces and add to the blender. When all the cheese has been added, whirl the mixture at high speed for 5 seconds. Pour the soufflé mixture into a greased, 5-cup soufflé dish. Bake at 375° for 45 minutes for a soft, liquidy center or 50 minutes for a firm soufflé. Serve immediately.

*Note: The soufflé can be prepared and poured into the soufflé dish, then covered and held for 1 to 2 hours at room temperature. If holding longer or if the kitchen is hot, refrigerate, then allow an extra 5 to 10 minutes baking time.*

Serves 6.

Jan Rowley
Supervisor
Reservations

## Cheese Soufflé

⅓ cup margarine
⅓ cup flour
1½ cups milk
1 tsp. salt
Dash of cayenne

2 cups shredded Cracker
  Barrel sharp natural cheddar
  cheese
6 egg yolks, lightly beaten
6 egg whites

Melt the margarine over medium heat and stir in the flour. Cook, stirring constantly, for 5 minutes. Slowly stir in the milk and seasonings. Cook, stirring, until thick and bubbly. Add the cheese and stir until melted. Remove from the heat, gradually add the egg yolks and cool. Beat the egg whites until stiff and fold into the cooled cheese sauce; pour into a 2-quart soufflé dish or casserole. With the tip of a spoon, make a slight indentation or "track" around the top of the soufflé 1" from the edge. Bake at 300° for 1 hour and 15 minutes. Serve immediately.

Karen Fudge
Regional Sales

# PASTA & RICE

## Best Yet Complete Spaghetti

2 (1-lb. 12-oz.) cans tomato
  puree
3 (8-oz.) cans tomato sauce
½ cup dry red wine
1 Tbsp. salt
1 Tbsp. sugar
¼ tsp. pepper
½ tsp. cayenne
1 tsp. dry rosemary
1 tsp. oregano leaves

4 cloves garlic, minced or
  pressed
1 medium onion, coarsely
  chopped
2 lbs. lean, boneless pork
  shoulder, cut into 1" cubes
¼ lb. mushrooms, sliced
1 lb. spaghetti or vermicelli
Grated Parmesan or Romano
  cheese

In a 6- to 8-quart kettle, blend together the tomato puree, tomato sauce, wine, salt, sugar, pepper, cayenne, rosemary, oregano, garlic, onion and pork. Bring to a boil; reduce the heat, cover and simmer for 1½ hours or until the pork is fork-tender. (For a thicker sauce, remove the lid the last 30 minutes.) Add the mushrooms and simmer uncovered for 10 minutes more. Skim, discarding the excess fat. Cook the spaghetti and drain; toss with grated cheese to taste. Ladle the sauce over the spaghetti and serve.

*Freeze any remaining sauce for another meal.*

*Serves 6 to 8.*

Sue Martin
Reservations

## Million Dollar Spaghetti

1 (7-oz.) pkg. thin spaghetti
1½ lbs. ground beef
½ lb. sausage meat
3 Tbsp. butter
2 (8-oz.) cans tomato sauce
Salt and pepper to taste

1 (8-oz.) pkg. cream cheese
½ lb. cottage cheese
¼ cup sour cream
⅓ cup chopped scallions
1 Tbsp. minced green pepper

Cook the spaghetti and drain. Sauté the beef and sausage in 1 Tbsp. butter until browned. Add the tomato sauce and salt and pepper. Remove from the heat. Combine the cheeses, sour cream, scallions and green pepper. Spread one-half the spaghetti into a square, 2-quart casserole and cover with the cheese mixture. Add the remaining spaghetti. Melt 2 Tbsp. butter and pour over the spaghetti. Spread the tomato and meat sauce over the top. Chill. Remove from the refrigerator 20 minutes before baking. Bake at 350° for 45 minutes or until hot and bubbly. Serve with a green salad and French bread.

Annemarie Fleming
Reservations

## Brother Bobbie's Sketti

2 lbs. lean hamburger
2 cloves fresh garlic, minced
Braum's O'Boy Oberto
  German smoked sausage
1 (12-oz.) can tomato paste
1 (29-oz.) can tomato sauce
1 to 2 Tbsp. Salsa Ranchero or
  DeGelatino Freso
  taco sauce

1 Tbsp. whole thyme
2 tsp. whole oregano
1 tsp. garlic salt
½ lb. small fresh mushrooms
Butter
1 can whole black pitted olives
Cooked spaghetti or noodles

Brown the hamburger with the garlic. Slice the sausage into ¼" chunks and brown separately. Pour the tomato paste and sauce and the taco sauce into a large pot and add the meats and juices. Bring to a rolling boil and stir in the spices. Cook for about 1 hour, stirring occasionally. Sauté the mushrooms in a little butter and pour into the sauce along with the olives. Cook for 10 minutes more. Toss the sauce and noodles together and serve.

Jean McColman
Inflight Services

## Carbonara

1 lb. bacon
1 clove garlic, crushed
1 lb. thin spaghetti
2 eggs, beaten

1 lb. fresh Parmesan cheese,
  grated
3 small tomatoes, chopped
1 small can sliced black olives
Medium parsley sprigs

Cut the bacon into 1" squares and fry with the garlic. Remove the bacon, reserve ¼ to ½ cup of the bacon drippings and keep hot. Cook the spaghetti al dente and toss with the beaten eggs, Parmesan cheese (added a little at a time) and the hot bacon drippings. The hot drippings help to cook the egg and melt the cheese. After the cheese is melted and thoroughly mixed with the egg, combine the bacon, tomatoes, olives and parsley and toss with the pasta. Serve with a salad and crusty kaiser rolls.

*Note: Have all the ingredients ready before final assembly as the spaghetti will cool off rapidly.*

Cindy Trumble
Secretary
Regional Office

## Spaghetti Pie

6 oz. spaghetti (3¼ cups cooked)
2 Tbsp. butter or margarine
⅓ cup grated Parmesan cheese
2 eggs, well beaten
1 lb. ground beef or bulk pork sausage, or ½ lb. of each
½ cup chopped onions

¼ cup chopped green peppers
1 (8-oz.) can tomatoes, cut up
1 (6-oz.) can tomato paste
1 tsp. sugar
1 tsp. dried oregano
½ tsp. garlic salt
1 cup cottage cheese
½ cup shredded mozzarella cheese

Cook the spaghetti according to the package directions and drain. Stir the butter or margarine into the hot spaghetti. Stir in the Parmesan cheese and eggs. Form the spaghetti mixture into a crust in a greased, 10" pie plate. In a skillet, cook the ground beef and/or pork sausage, onions and green peppers until the vegetables are tender and the meat is browned. Drain off the excess fat. Stir in the tomatoes and their juice, tomato paste, sugar, oregano and garlic salt. Heat through. Spread the cottage cheese over the bottom of the spaghetti crust. Fill the pie with the tomato mixture. Bake uncovered at 350° for 20 minutes. Sprinkle the mozzarella cheese on top. Bake for 5 minutes more or until the cheese melts.

*Serves 6.*

Annemarie Fleming
Reservations

### Fresh Pasta and Garlic Sauce

1 lb. hot or mild Italian sausage
3 garlic cloves, minced or
    crushed
Chopped fresh parsley
1 (24-oz.) can whole tomatoes,
    undrained
1 (8-oz.) can tomato sauce

¾ tsp. oregano
½ tsp. basil
Pinch of rosemary
Salt and white pepper to taste
1½ lbs. spinach fettuccini or
    other fresh pasta
⅓ cup grated Romano cheese

In a large, deep-dish skillet, fry the sausage until almost done, remove and set aside. Drain all but 2 Tbsp. of the drippings from the skillet and return to the heat. Sauté the garlic and parsley in the drippings until the garlic is cooked but not browned. Add the tomatoes and their liquid, the tomato sauce and spices. Simmer for 20 to 30 minutes, breaking up the tomatoes. Add the sausage to the sauce and continue to simmer while preparing the pasta. Cook the pasta in salted water for about 10 minutes. Drain and transfer to a large mixing/serving bowl. Add the sauce and cheese. Toss and serve immediately with toasted French or Italian bread and a small salad.

Note: For a variation, omit the sausage, prepare the sauce and add to it ½ to ¾ lb. cooked crabmeat. Cook only until the crab is heated or it will become tough.

Ron Carlson
Regional Manager
Reservations and Ticket Offices

### Chicken or Turkey Tetrazzini

½ lb. macaroni or spaghetti
½ to ¾ lb. fresh mushrooms,
    sliced
Butter
½ cup slivered blanched
    almonds
3 Tbsp. chicken fat or butter
2 Tbsp. flour

2 cups chicken broth
Salt and pepper to taste
1 cup heavy cream
3 Tbsp. dry white wine
2 to 3 cups shredded chicken
    or turkey
Grated Parmesan cheese

Cook the pasta according to the package directions; drain. Sauté the mushrooms in a little butter until tender and stir into the pasta with the almonds. Over medium heat, melt the chicken fat or butter and stir in the flour to make a roux. Cook for 3 to 5 minutes, stirring constantly. Gradually stir in the chicken broth and salt and pepper. Cook, stirring constantly until the sauce thickens; remove from the heat and add the cream and wine. Stir half the sauce into the chicken or turkey and the remainder into the pasta. Mound the pasta in a greased baking dish, make a hole in the center and pour the chicken or turkey into it. Sprinkle with the Parmesan cheese and bake at 375° until lightly browned.

*Serves 8 to 10.*

Cindy Trumble
Regional
Vice President's Office

## Barbara's Fettuccini

1 (12-oz.) pkg. fettuccini
   noodles
¼ cup butter
1 cup heavy cream
1 cup sour cream

1 small container Kraft
   Parmesan cheese
3 to 4 green onions, chopped
Garlic salt
Pepper

Cook the noodles and drain. Melt the butter in the same pan, add the noodles and toss with the remaining ingredients. Heat through, over medium-low heat. Be careful not to burn, and do not let the mixture boil or it will curdle. Serve hot.

Rick Sanders
Reservations

### Pasta E Fagioli

¼ cup olive oil, heated
1 cup chopped onions
1 clove garlic, crushed
3 mild Italian sausages,
  skinned
3 oz. ham, cubed
1 large can Italian plum
  tomatoes
1 tsp. salt
¼ tsp. pepper

½ tsp. dried oregano leaves
2 Tbsp. chopped fresh parsley
1 can beef bouillon, undiluted
½ cup burgundy or other dry
  red wine (optional)
3½ to 4 oz. shell macaroni
1 (1-lb.) can kidney beans,
  undrained
⅓ cup grated Parmesan
  cheese

In the heated oil, sauté the onions and garlic until translucent, about 5 minutes. Remove and set aside. In the same skillet, brown and crumble the sausages, add the ham and brown briefly. Drain the tomatoes, pouring the juice into a large kettle. Cut the tomatoes into medium-small pieces and add to the kettle. Add the onions, sausages, ham, salt, pepper, oregano, parsley, bouillon and wine. Simmer covered for 30 minutes. Meanwhile, cook the macaroni al dente, then add to the tomato mixture. Add the beans and simmer for 5 minutes. Serve in individual bowls topped with Parmesan cheese and more freshly chopped parsley. Good with Italian or French narrow-loaf bread, green salad and red wine.

Serves 6.

Bobbie Sylvain
Passenger Service

☞ Add 1 teaspoon water when beating egg yolks. They will beat better and can be combined with hot mixtures more easily.

## Greek-Style Macaroni Bake

¾ lb. ground beef
½ cup chopped onions
1 (6-oz.) can tomato paste
½ tsp. salt
¼ tsp. ground cinnamon
½ cup mayonnaise
¼ cup flour

2 cups milk
2 eggs
⅓ cup grated Parmesan
  cheese
¼ tsp. ground nutmeg
½ lb. elbow macaroni, cooked
  and drained

Brown the ground beef and onions, drain the fat. Stir in the next 3 ingredients and set aside. Combine the mayonnaise and flour, gradually stir in the milk and cook, stirring over medium heat until thick (do not boil). Beat together the eggs, Parmesan cheese and nutmeg and gradually stir into the sauce. Add the macaroni. Spoon half the macaroni mixture into a 2-quart baking dish, cover with the meat mixture and top with the remaining macaroni. Bake at 325° for 45 minutes.

Carol Koch
Reservations

## Manicotti Cheese Bake

½ lb. ground beef
½ cup minced onions
¼ cup chopped green peppers
3 (6-oz.) cans tomato paste
½ tsp. salt
½ tsp. pepper
1 tsp. sugar

1½ tsp. Italian seasoning
  (oregano, garlic, onion)
8 to 9 manicotti shells
2 cups ricotta cheese
1 to 1½ cups shredded
  mozzarella cheese

Sauté the meat, onions and green peppers; drain off the fat. Add the tomato paste, salt, pepper, sugar, Italian seasoning and 2 cups water. Simmer for 15 minutes. Parboil the manicotti shells in salted water for 4 minutes. Drain on paper towels. Combine the ricotta and mozzarella cheese and use to fill the shells. Place the filled shells in a baking dish, cover with the meat sauce and bake at 350° for 20 to 30 minutes.

Serves 4.

Glen Burmark
Apollo Systems

## Tortellini Florentine

1 (10-oz.) pkg. frozen chopped
  spinach
¼ cup butter (approx.)
¼ cup finely chopped onions
½ tsp. minced garlic
½ tsp. salt
⅛ tsp. freshly ground pepper
⅛ tsp. nutmeg
1 lb. frozen tortellini, cooked
  and drained
1 cup smoked ham, cut into
  thin strips

Parmesan cheese
Chopped pistachio nuts

**Mornay Sauce:**
3 Tbsp. butter
3 Tbsp. all-purpose flour
2 cups milk, scalded
½ tsp. salt
⅛ tsp. pepper
½ cup grated Gruyère cheese
1 egg yolk

In a saucepan, place ½ cup water and the spinach. Bring to a full boil over high heat, separating the spinach with a fork. Cover, reduce the heat and simmer for 5 minutes or until tender; drain well. Heat 2 Tbsp. butter in a saucepan and sauté the onions and garlic until glossy. Add the spinach and seasonings and mix well. Spread the spinach evenly over the bottom of a greased, large, shallow baking dish. Place the tortellini on top of the spinach, top with the ham strips and pour the **Mornay Sauce** over. Sprinkle with Parmesan cheese and dot with the remaining butter. Bake at 450° for 15 to 20 minutes or until the top bubbles. Sprinkle with pistachio nuts and serve.

**Mornay Sauce:** Melt 2 Tbsp. butter in a saucepan, stir in the flour and cook over low flame without coloring for 3 minutes, stirring constantly. Add the milk, stir until smooth and simmer for 15 minutes. Add the salt, pepper and cheese and stir until the cheese melts. Beat the egg yolk lightly and mix half the sauce into it. Return the mixture to the pan and stir in the remaining butter.

Serves 6.

Rolf Conrad
Executive Chef
Denver Food Services

## Lasagna

2 Tbsp. olive oil
3 Tbsp. vegetable oil
¾ lb. top round, ground
½ lb. Italian sausage,
  skinned and sliced
2 onions, finely chopped
2 cloves garlic, minced
5 tomatoes, peeled and
  coarsely chopped, or 1
  (1-lb. 13-oz.) can Italian
  tomatoes
2 (8-oz.) cans tomato sauce
3 Tbsp. sugar

1 Tbsp. salt
1 Tbsp. fresh or 1 tsp. dried
  oregano
1 Tbsp. chopped fresh or
  1 tsp. dried basil
1¾ cups grated Parmesan
  cheese
¼ tsp. freshly ground pepper
½ lb. lasagna noodles
1 lb. mozzarella cheese,
  grated
1 lb. ricotta cheese

Heat the 2 Tbsp. olive and 2 Tbsp. vegetable oil in a heavy saucepan. Add the beef and sausage and sauté until browned. Add the onions and garlic and sauté for 3 minutes more. Add the tomatoes, tomato sauce, sugar, salt, oregano, basil, ½ cup Parmesan cheese and pepper. Mix well, bring to a boil over medium heat, reduce the heat to low and simmer slowly for 2 hours, stirring occasionally. When the sauce is almost done, fill a large kettle with water, add a generous pinch of salt and 1 Tbsp. vegetable oil. Bring the water to a boil and add the lasagna noodles, two at a time. Let the water come to a boil again after each addition. Simmer for 15 minutes, then drain and rinse with hot water. In the bottom of a greased, 13" x 9" x 2" baking dish, put a thin layer of sauce, then a layer of noodles and then a layer of 1 cup Parmesan combined with the mozzarella and ricotta cheeses. Repeat these layers twice, ending with a third layer of sauce and sprinkle with ¼ cup Parmesan cheese. Bake at 350° for 40 minutes and let stand for about 15 minutes before serving.

*If you are serving 4 persons, bake the lasagna in 2 smaller pans and freeze one for a busy day.*

*Serves 8.*

Annemarie Fleming
Reservations

## Vegetable Noodles

¼ cup mixed vegetables
1 egg, lightly beaten
¼ tsp. salt

2 cups flour
Melted butter

Cook the vegetables until soft; drain, press dry and strain through a fine sieve. Add the egg, salt and flour to the vegetables and knead to a smooth dough. Cover the dough and let stand for 30 minutes or more. Roll out very thin, let stand and, when no longer sticky, cut into ⅓"-wide noodles. Drop into boiling, salted water. Boil for 10 to 20 minutes or until tender; drain, pour melted butter over and serve.

Sue Heavilon
Reservations

## Taglereni

1 large onion, chopped
2 Tbsp. chopped green pepper
2 cloves garlic, chopped
2 Tbsp. olive oil
1 lb. lean ground beef
3 cans tomato sauce
1 can whole kernel corn,
    drained
2 cans mushrooms, drained

2 Tbsp. sugar
1 tsp. oregano
1 large bay leaf
1 Tbsp. salt
2 Tbsp. Worcestershire sauce
5⅓ oz. twisted egg noodles
1 large can ripe olives,
    drained (optional)
1 lb. sharp cheese, grated

Cook the onion, green pepper and garlic in the olive oil in a large skillet until tender. Add the ground beef and cook until brown. Add the tomato sauce, corn, mushrooms and seasonings. Simmer for 1 hour, stirring frequently. Meanwhile, cook the noodles according to the package directions. Combine the noodles with the meat mixture and add the ripe olives. Place in a large casserole, alternating layers of meat and cheese, ending with the cheese. Bake at 325° for 1 hour.

*This recipe is better assembled the day before, refrigerated and then baked for 1 hour before serving.*

JoAnn Olanyk
Reservations

## Paella

¼ cup olive oil
1 cup lean pork cubes
1 large yellow onion, peeled
   and minced
1 clove garlic, peeled and
   crushed
½ cup diced red bell peppers
½ cup diced green bell peppers
¼ lb. ham, diced
2 cups cooked, skinned and
   diced chicken meat
½ cup hot Italian sausage or
   Spanish chorizo

1½ cups uncooked rice
2¾ cups chicken broth
2 tsp. salt
Dash of freshly ground pepper
¼ tsp. powdered saffron
¼ cup tomato paste
1 (1-lb. 13-oz.) can tomatoes
¾ lb. raw shrimp, shelled
   and deveined
18 clams in the shell,
   prepared for cooking
1 cup cooked green peas
   (approx.)

Heat the oil in a large skillet. Brown the pork cubes in the oil, remove from the pan and set aside. Over moderate heat in the same pan, stir fry the onion, garlic, red and green peppers, ham and chicken meat. Add the pork cubes, blend and set aside. Pierce the casing of the sausage with a fork in several places. Place in boiling water and cook for 5 to 10 minutes to drain the fat. Remove from the water and cut into ½" slices. Place the rice in the bottom of a paella pan or Dutch oven. Add the chicken broth. Bring to a boil, add the salt, pepper, saffron, tomato paste and tomatoes and stir until well blended. Remove from the heat. Add the meat and vegetable mixtures and stir to combine the ingredients. *Do not stir again or the rice will become mushy.* Place the shrimp and clams around the mixture. Cover and bake at 350° for 30 minutes. Sprinkle with the peas and serve.

*Serves 12.*

Jim Hartigan
President
United Airlines

☞ *Add a teaspoon of vinegar or lemon juice to the water in which rice is cooked to keep it light, separated and fluffy.*

## Rice Pilaf

¼ cup finely chopped onions
¼ cup butter
¼ cup oil
1 cup uncooked white rice

2 cups chicken broth or
   consommé, heated to boiling
¼ medium bay leaf
Salt to taste

Smother the onions in the butter and oil in a casserole dish for 2 minutes (do not brown) and then mix in the rice. Stir in the chicken broth until the mixture boils, cover the pan and bake at 350° for 18 to 20 minutes. Do not overcook. Add salt to taste, if desired.

Paul Steuri
Executive Chef
Omaha Food Services

# VEGETABLES

## Asparagus with Almond Mushroom Sauce

1 lb. fresh asparagus
2 Tbsp. butter
¾ cup sliced mushrooms
2 Tbsp. flour
½ tsp. salt
⅛ tsp. pepper

⅛ tsp. dry mustard
1 cup milk
2 Tbsp. cooking sherry
½ cup toasted blanched
  almonds
½ cup grated sharp cheese

Cook the asparagus until crisp-tender, drain and set aside. Melt the butter, add the mushrooms and sauté. Add the flour and seasonings and blend well. Gradually stir in the milk and cook until thickened. Add the cooking sherry. Put the asparagus in a greased, 1½-quart baking dish, pour the sauce over and sprinkle with the almonds and cheese. Place under a broiler and broil until the cheese melts. Serve at once.

*Makes 4 servings.*

Virginia Hansen

## Beans in Sour Cream

1 lb. green beans
½ cup sour cream
Salt
Pepper
Nutmeg

½ tsp. caraway or dill seeds
  (optional)
4 Tbsp. butter
¾ cup coarse fresh
  bread crumbs

Trim the beans, slice crosswise into 1" pieces and cook in boiling, salted water for 5 minutes. Drain thoroughly. Combine the sour cream with salt, pepper and nutmeg to taste. Add the seeds. Toss the beans in this dressing until thoroughly coated. Use 1 tsp. of the butter to grease a casserole. Melt the remaining butter and toss the bread crumbs in it. Put the beans in the casserole, top with the bread crumbs and bake at 350° for 15 to 20 minutes or until the topping is crisp and brown.

Marianne Shute

## Asparagus Soufflé

Grated Parmesan cheese
1 lb. frozen asparagus, cooked
   and drained
6 egg yolks

Dash of nutmeg
Salt and pepper to taste
7 egg whites

Dust a greased, 2-quart soufflé dish with Parmesan cheese and set aside. Puree the asparagus in a food processor with a metal blade, then push through a fine metal sieve and place in a bowl. Beat the egg yolks into the asparagus puree; when blended, add the nutmeg and salt and pepper. Beat the egg whites in a large copper bowl with a balloon whip until stiff but not dry. Stir a small amount into the asparagus mixture to lighten it and fold in the remaining egg whites by hand. Pour into the soufflé dish, gently smooth out the top, set on the lowest rack of the oven and bake at 325° for approximately 40 minutes. The soufflé is done when it has browned on the top, is fully risen and starts to pull away from the sides of the dish. Serve immediately with Hollandaise sauce on the side, if desired.

Note: Broccoli may be substituted for the asparagus. This soufflé will not have a runny center because the batter is too heavy to cook well at the high heat required to produce that effect.

Serves 6.

Jerry F. Boyer
Executive Chef
Newark Food Services

## Calico Beans

½ lb. ground beef
½ lb. bacon, cut into pieces
1 large onion, chopped
½ cup catsup
2 tsp. salt
2 tsp. prepared mustard
1 Tbsp. plus 1 tsp. white
   vinegar

¾ cup brown sugar
1 (30-oz.) can pork and beans
1 (15-oz.) can garbanzo beans
1 (15-oz.) can kidney beans
1 pkg. frozen lima beans,
   thawed

Cook the ground beef, bacon and onion in a skillet. Stir in the catsup, salt, mustard and vinegar. Combine the remaining ingredients in a 3-quart casserole. Stir in the meat mixture, cover and bake at 350° for 40 minutes. Garnish with bacon strips if desired.

*This is a delicious change from ordinary baked beans.*

Fran Christensen
Tour Desk

## Green Beans in Sabayon Sauce

*1½ lbs. green beans*
*Salt*
*2 egg yolks*

*2 Tbsp. dry white wine*
*1 Tbsp. sugar*
*1 Tbsp. white wine vinegar*

Trim and wash the beans. Cook in boiling, salted water until tender, about 4 to 6 minutes. Drain in a colander and transfer to a shallow serving dish. Cover and keep warm in a 250° oven. Set the remaining ingredients in the top of a double boiler over simmering water. Stir gently with a fork. Whisk until thick and frothy. Pour the sabayon over the beans and serve at once.

## Sweet and Sour Beans

*1 lb. lean ground beef*
*1 large can B & M oven-baked*
*  or other beans*
*1 large can red kidney beans*

*2 small cans crushed*
*  pineapple*
*½ bottle catsup*
*3 Tbsp. brown sugar*
*1 tsp. mustard*

Brown the ground beef and drain off the fat. Stir in the remaining ingredients and place in a casserole dish. Bake at 325° for 45 minutes.

## Beets with Orange

1 lb. beets, cooked
2 Tbsp. butter

1 Tbsp. marmalade
Juice of ½ orange

Peel and dice the beets. Combine the remaining ingredients in a saucepan. Heat until the butter melts, add the beets and simmer gently for about 10 minutes, stirring occasionally. Serve warm.

## Broccoli Casserole

2 pkg. frozen chopped
  broccoli
2 cups cooked rice
2 cups grated sharp cheddar
  cheese

1 can cream of mushroom
  soup
1 cup milk
Salt and pepper to taste
Cracker crumbs

Thaw the broccoli and combine with the remaining ingredients except the crumbs. Pour into a casserole dish, sprinkle the crumbs on top and bake at 325° for 45 minutes. Serve warm.

Deborah Gile
Inflight Services

## Marinated Broccoli

3 bunches fresh broccoli
1 cup cider vinegar
1 Tbsp. sugar
1 Tbsp. dill weed
1 Tbsp. MSG

1 tsp. salt
1 tsp. pepper
1 tsp. garlic salt
1½ cups vegetable oil

Cut the broccoli into small florets and put in a bowl. Combine the remaining ingredients, pour over the broccoli, cover and refrigerate for 24 hours, basting occasionally. Drain and serve.

Note: For added color, add cherry tomatoes just before serving.

Karen McKay
Sales

### Herbed Brussel Sprouts

1 ¼ lbs. brussel sprouts
1 tsp. mustard
1 tsp. Worcestershire sauce
1 tsp. sugar
1 tsp. salt
½ tsp. dry basil
¼ tsp. thyme leaves

¼ tsp. pepper
¼ cup red wine vinegar
1 cup salad oil
2 cups cherry tomatoes
½ cup thinly sliced green
    onions

Cut the brussel sprouts in half and cook in lightly salted water until crisp-tender, about 7 minutes. Transfer the sprouts to a bowl and add the mustard, Worcestershire sauce, sugar, salt, basil, thyme and pepper. Add the vinegar and salad oil and shake or stir to blend. Cover and chill for 4 hours. Before serving, stir in the cherry tomatoes and green onions.

Dottie Martin

### Cantonese Cabbage

2 Tbsp. butter
8 cups finely shredded
    cabbage
1 clove garlic, minced
½ cup sour cream

1 Tbsp. sugar
2 Tbsp. vinegar
1 tsp. salt
¼ tsp. caraway seeds (optional)

Heat the butter in a large saucepan, add the cabbage, garlic and ¼ cup water. Cover tightly and steam over low heat for 10 to 12 minutes. Combine the next 4 ingredients and stir into the cabbage. Heat through, but do not boil. Sprinkle with the caraway seeds.

Serves 6.

Marianne Shute

## Cabbage Stir-Fry

1 small head green cabbage,
  shredded
1 Tbsp. cooking oil
2 green onions, chopped
1 clove garlic, crushed
½ tsp. salt

½ tsp. sugar
½ cup minced ham
2 Tbsp. coriander and/or
  2 Tbsp. parsley
Pepper to taste

Cook the cabbage in the oil over medium-high heat for 2 minutes, stirring constantly. Add the remaining ingredients and toss. Cook for about 3 minutes.

*Note: Increase the cooking time by 2 minutes if using a Teflon pan.*

Dorothy Stitt
Reservations

## Carrot Casserole

2 lbs. carrots
2 Tbsp. butter
1 small onion, grated
½ green pepper, chopped
Salt and pepper

6 to 8 oz. sharp cheddar
  cheese, grated
Pepperidge Farm or other
  bread crumbs

Chop and cook the carrots. Mash thoroughly with the butter and put into a greased, 1½-quart casserole. Add the onion, green pepper and salt and pepper. Sprinkle the cheese over and top with bread crumbs. Bake at 375° for 20 minutes.

*Serves 8.*

Annemarie Fleming
Reservations

## Carrots Paysanne

1 lb. small carrots
¼ cup plus 1 Tbsp. butter
2 slices lean bacon, diced
1 large onion, thinly sliced
¾ cup chicken stock or water

1 tsp. sugar
¼ cup heavy cream
Salt
Parsley

Clean the carrots and blanch in boiling, salted water for 5 minutes. Drain in a colander. Melt the butter in a wide, shallow pan over low heat, add the bacon and onion and cook just until soft and beginning to change color. Add the carrots and enough stock or water to barely cover the vegetables, cover and cook over moderate heat until tender. Remove the carrots with a slotted spoon, set aside and keep hot. Boil the remaining liquid over high heat until reduced to a few Tbsp. Add the sugar, cream and salt to taste. Simmer uncovered until slightly thickened. Pour the sauce over the carrots and sprinkle with parsley.

Marianne Shute

## Hawaiian Carrots

½ cup pineapple juice
½ cup carrot stock
1 Tbsp. cornstarch
½ tsp. salt
⅛ tsp. pepper

1 Tbsp. butter
2 cups cooked, sliced carrots
½ cup drained pineapple
   chunks

In a saucepan, combine the juice and stock, stir in the cornstarch and bring to a boil, stirring constantly. Add the remaining ingredients and serve hot.

Fran Christensen
Tour Desk

## Offbeat Carrots

½ cup mayonnaise
2 Tbsp. horseradish
2 Tbsp. grated onion
½ tsp. salt

¼ tsp. pepper
6 carrots, sliced and cooked
   until tender
½ cup buttered crumbs

Combine the first 5 ingredients, stir in the carrots and place in a 1-quart casserole. Top with the buttered crumbs and bake at 350° until lightly browned.

Serves 4.

JoAnn Olanyk
Reservations

## Cauliflower Polonaise

1 head cauliflower
2 eggs, hard-cooked
¼ cup butter
¾ cup dry bread crumbs

2 Tbsp. chopped parsley
Salt and pepper
Lemon juice

Trim the thick outer leaves and stalk from the cauliflower and wash thoroughly. Cook whole in boiling, salted water for 10 to 15 minutes or until tender. Drain in a colander and keep warm. Rub the cooked egg yolks through a sieve and finely chop the whites. Melt the butter in a skillet, add the crumbs and sauté until crisp. Remove from the heat, add the parsley and season to taste with salt, pepper and lemon juice. Place the whole cauliflower in a warm serving dish, sprinkle evenly with the bread crumbs and garnish in an attractive pattern with the chopped yolks and whites.

## Cauliflower Steamed in Wine

1 (1-lb.) head cauliflower
1 cup dry white wine
3 Tbsp. olive oil
2½ Tbsp. fresh lemon juice

¾ Tbsp. salt
1 clove garlic, minced
¼ tsp. freshly ground pepper

Remove and discard the leaves from the cauliflower. Detach the florets and cut into 2" pieces. Soak in cold water for 30 minutes and place stem side down in a single snug layer in a dish. Mix together the remaining ingredients in a small bowl until the salt is dissolved. Pour over the cauliflower, cover and bake at 400° until tender, about 35 to 40 minutes. Let the cauliflower stand for 5 minutes before serving.

Serves 4.

Fran Christensen
Tour Desk

☞ Add a little milk to the water in which cauliflower is steamed to keep the vegetable white.

## Corn Soufflé

1 Tbsp. butter
2 Tbsp. flour
1 cup milk
2 eggs, separated

½ tsp. salt
Pepper to taste
2 cups canned creamed or
  whole corn

Melt the butter, add the flour and milk gradually, then the seasonings and bring to a boil, stirring constantly. Beat the egg yolks, combine with the corn and stir into the milk mixture. Beat the egg whites until stiff and fold into the corn. Turn into a greased casserole and cook at 350° for 25 to 30 minutes.

Note: Chopped green peppers can be added along with the corn, if desired.

Pat Logue
Reservations

## Cranberry Puff

12 oz. cranberries
1 small apple
1 small carrot
1 Tbsp. plus 1 tsp. sugar
¼ cup orange juice

1 tsp. coconut
1 Tbsp. cream sauce
1 tsp. bread crumbs
2 egg whites
3 egg yolks

Grind the cranberries, apple and carrot through a fine meat grinder. Add 1 Tbsp. sugar, the orange juice and coconut and cook very slowly for 20 to 30 minutes. Remove from the heat and add the cream sauce and bread crumbs. Gently whip the egg whites with the remaining sugar, fold into the fruit mixture and add the egg yolks. Place in a greased, 6-cup muffin dish and bake at 350° for 35 minutes or until done. Good with turkey with sage and apple dressing.

Serves 6.

Rolf Conrad
Executive Chef
Denver Food Services

## Eggplant Parmesan

1 large eggplant
3 eggs, beaten
1 cup dry bread crumbs
¾ cup salad or olive oil
½ cup grated Parmesan
  cheese
2 tsp. dried oregano

½ lb. mozzarella cheese,
  cut into slices
Deep-fried onions (optional)
Garlic powder (optional)
Seasoned pepper (optional)
Ground beef (optional)
3 (8-oz.) cans tomato sauce

Cut the eggplant into ¼" slices and dip each piece into the eggs, then into the crumbs. Sauté in the oil until golden brown on both sides. Place a layer of eggplant in a 2-quart casserole dish, sprinkle with the Parmesan cheese, oregano and some mozzarella cheese, the optional ingredients and some tomato sauce. Repeat until all the eggplant is used. Top the last layer with the remaining tomato sauce and several slices of mozzarella cheese. Bake uncovered at 350° for 30 minutes or until the sauce is bubbly and the cheese melted.

Joseph Byerwalter
Senior Vice President & General Manager
Division Headquarters-San Francisco

## Wilted Lettuce

2 slices bacon
⅔ cup milk
2½ Tbsp. vinegar
Leaf lettuce

Finely chopped green onions
Salt
Sugar

Fry the bacon until crisp, remove from the pan and add the milk and vinegar to the bacon drippings. Crumble the bacon and stir it into the milk, bringing it to a full boil. Wash the lettuce and tear the leaves into a bowl, add the green onions and sprinkle with salt and sugar to taste. Pour the hot salad dressing over the salad. Set the pan upside-down over the salad bowl to hold in the heat and wilt the lettuce. Serve warm.

Lillian Warren

## Mushrooms Parmesan

5 Tbsp. butter or margarine
1 lb. mushrooms, sliced
3 Tbsp. flour
¾ cup milk
¾ cup cream
½ tsp. salt
¼ tsp. pepper
¼ tsp. nutmeg
¼ cup bread crumbs
½ cup grated Parmesan
cheese

In a heavy pan, melt 2 Tbsp. butter, add the mushrooms, cover and cook over low heat until wilted. In a saucepan, blend 3 Tbsp. butter with the flour. Add the milk, cream, salt, pepper and nutmeg; cook over low heat, stirring until thickened. Place the mushrooms in a casserole and pour the sauce over. Sprinkle with the crumbs and cheese. Brown under the broiler for a few minutes.

Fran Christensen
Tour Desk

## Mushrooms and Sour Cream

1 lb. small to medium fresh
mushrooms
3 Tbsp. butter
1 medium onion, sliced
½ tsp. salt
Dash of pepper
¼ tsp. crushed dried tarragon
1 Tbsp. sherry
½ cup sour cream
Parsley

Clean the mushrooms; set aside. Heat the butter in a frying pan and sauté the onion until limp. Add the mushrooms, sprinkle with the salt, pepper and tarragon and cook over medium-high heat, stirring until the onion and mushrooms are lightly browned and the liquid nearly evaporated. Reduce the heat to low and add the sherry and sour cream. Stir over low heat until just heated through; do not allow to boil. Adjust the seasoning with more salt or pepper, if needed. Sprinkle with parsley and serve.

Pat Shea

## Creamed Mushrooms and Ham

1 cup small mushroom
bottoms
¼ cup plus 2 Tbsp. butter
2 Tbsp. chopped onion
1 cup diced smoked ham
1 Tbsp. flour
⅓ cup white wine
1 cup chicken consommé
1 bay leaf
Salt and pepper
Dash of Maggi seasoning
¼ cup cream
1 tsp. chopped parsley
4 puff pastry shells

Wash the mushrooms. Melt the butter and sauté the mushrooms, onion and ham together, stirring frequently. Lower the heat, add the flour and mix well, stirring constantly for 2 minutes. Add the wine and chicken consommé, bay leaf and salt and pepper to taste. Let simmer for at least 10 minutes. Remove the bay leaf. Add the Maggi seasoning, cream and parsley and serve in the puff pastry shells.

*Note: Puff pastry shells can be purchased in a fine pastry shop.*

*Serves 4.*

John H. Wolfsheimer
Executive Chef
San Francisco Food Services

## "Mashed" Potatoes

4 cups mashed potatoes
3 cups cream-style cottage
   cheese, sieved
¾ cup sour cream
1½ Tbsp. grated onion

2½ tsp. salt
½ tsp. pepper
Butter
Toasted almonds

Combine all the ingredients except the butter and almonds in a baking dish. Dot with butter. Bake at 350° for 30 minutes or more. Just before serving, sprinkle almonds over and set under the broiler for a few minutes.

*Best potatoes you've ever eaten.*

*Serves 10 to 12.*

Sally Keenan
Supervisor
Inflight Services

## French-Fried Potato Puffs

Oil
2 cups mashed potatoes
2 eggs, well beaten
4 slices bacon, crisply cooked
   and crumbled

1 cup sifted flour
2 tsp. baking powder
1 tsp. salt

Fill an electric frying pan with about 1½" oil and heat to 380°. Combine the potatoes, eggs and bacon. Sift together the flour, baking powder and salt and stir into the potato mixture; blend well. Drop by spoonfuls into the hot oil and fry for 3 to 5 minutes. Drain on paper towels.

*Serves 6.*

Ken Christensen
Operations Planning

## Deluxe Potato Casserole

6 to 9 potatoes, cooked
¼ cup plus 2 Tbsp. butter
1 can cream of chicken soup
2 cups sour cream

½ cup chopped green onions
1½ to 2 cups shredded
   cheddar cheese
Crushed corn flakes

Cube the potatoes and place in a casserole dish. Heat ¼ cup butter with the chicken soup, blend in the sour cream, onions and cheese. Pour over the potatoes. Melt the remaining butter and combine with enough corn flakes to sprinkle over the top of the casserole. Bake at 350° for about 45 minutes.

Janet Vitcovich
Reservations

## Party Potatoes

6 potatoes, boiled, peeled,
   shredded and refrigerated
   overnight
1 bunch green onions,
   chopped

1 cup grated sharp cheese
Salt and pepper
2 to 3 cups sour cream
Milk
Poppy seeds

Mix together all the ingredients except the milk and poppy seeds. Pour in milk, a little at a time, until the mixture is of the consistency of mashed potatoes. Bake at 350° for 30 minutes. Sprinkle poppy seeds on top and serve.

Susan Warren
Reservations

## Scalloped Potatoes

1 ½ lbs. potatoes (6 large)
2 Tbsp. chopped onion
2 cloves garlic, chopped
2 Tbsp. butter or margarine
1 ½ Tbsp. flour
1 cup chicken bouillon

1 cup milk
½ tsp. salt
Pinch of white pepper
¾ cup grated Parmesan or
other cheese (approx.)

Peel and slice the potatoes. Place in a saucepan, cover with water and boil until tender; drain. In a frying pan over medium heat, sauté the onion and garlic in the butter until golden brown. Add the flour, stir for 1 minute, then add the chicken bouillon, milk, salt, pepper and ½ cup cheese, stirring constantly until of a smooth consistency. Add the potatoes to the sauce and place the mixture in a shallow, ovenproof serving dish. Sprinkle with a little more cheese. Bake at 325° until the potatoes are golden brown, about 20 minutes.

Serves 4 to 6.

Walter J. Schmuki
Sous Chef
Denver Food Services

## Potato Breakfast Casserole

4 medium potatoes
8 slices bacon, diced
¼ cup minced green onions
1 cup shredded Swiss cheese
½ cup cream-style cottage
cheese

5 eggs, beaten
½ tsp. salt
4 drops of Tabasco sauce
Parsley

Cook the potatoes in boiling, salted water until tender; peel and dice to make 2½ cups. Fry the bacon and drain. Lightly brown the potatoes and green onions in a small amount of bacon drippings. Combine with the cheeses, eggs and seasonings. Turn into a greased, shallow baking dish. Bake at 400° for 15 minutes. Reduce the heat to 350° and bake for 15 minutes more or until set. Garnish with parsley.

Janet Vitcovich
Reservations

### Sweet Potato Soufflé

3 (2-oz.) cans sweet potatoes
   or yams
½ cup melted butter
6 eggs, separated
¾ cup sugar

½ cup milk
1 Tbsp. lemon rind
1 tsp. ginger
½ tsp. salt

Drain, mash and beat the potatoes at medium speed. Beat in the melted butter; add the egg yolks, then the remaining ingredients except the egg whites. Beat the egg whites and fold into the potato mixture. Pour into a greased, 2-quart casserole or soufflé dish. Bake at 325° for 1 hour. Serve immediately.

Fran Christensen
Tour Desk

### Baked, Stuffed Tomatoes

6 tomatoes, unpeeled
6 slices bacon, cooked and
   crumbled
¼ cup chopped celery
1 small onion, finely chopped

1 cup soft bread crumbs
½ tsp. salt
¼ cup grated cheese
Butter

Cut a slice from the top of each of the tomatoes. Scoop out the centers and mix the pulp with the bacon, celery, onion, bread crumbs and salt. Fill the tomatoes with the stuffing, place on a greased baking dish or in greased muffin cups and sprinkle the cheese over. Dot with butter. Bake at 350° for approximately 30 minutes.

Fran Christensen
Tour Desk

☞ To shorten the cooking time for baked potatoes, soak them first either in salted water for 20 minutes or hot water for 15 minutes.

## Bread-Stuffed Tomatoes

8 tomatoes
1 cup chopped onions
½ cup chopped celery with
  leaves
¼ cup butter
1 Tbsp. parsley flakes

1 clove garlic, crushed
Salt
Pepper
½ Tbsp. basil
5 cups bread cubes

Slice off the tops of the tomatoes, scoop out the centers and reserve; turn the tomatoes upside-down to drain. Sauté the onions and celery in the butter until soft. Chop the tomato centers and add to the onion mixture with the parsley, garlic, salt, pepper and basil. Cook until the mixture thickens, about 15 minutes; stir in the bread cubes. Place the tomatoes in muffin tins, fill the shells with the bread mixture and bake at 350° for 30 minutes.

David Rieman
Passenger Service

## Magic Yams

1 (16-oz.) can sliced cling
  peaches
1 Tbsp. cornstarch
⅓ cup liquid brown sugar

1 (8-oz.) can whole berry
  cranberry sauce
½ tsp. cinnamon
2 Tbsp. butter
2 (17-oz.) cans yams, drained

Drain the peaches, reserving the juice. Dissolve the cornstarch in ¼ cup juice and set aside. In an 11" skillet, heat the remaining juice, sugar, cranberry sauce, cinnamon and butter. When the butter melts, add the cornstarch mixture. Stir over medium heat until the mixture thickens. Add the yams, cover the skillet and cook for 10 minutes. Stir in the peaches and cook for 5 minutes more or until heated through. Serve as a vegetable dish or over ice cream as a sauce.

Cranberry jelly can be substituted for the cranberry sauce.

Effie Johnston
Reservations

## Yams Richard

3 lbs. yams
¼ tsp. nutmeg
¼ tsp. cinnamon
¼ cup butter, melted

½ cup light cream
⅓ cup chopped pecans
⅓ cup seedless raisins
16 marshmallows

Boil the yams until tender; peel and mash. Stir in the next 6 ingredients, mixing thoroughly. Place in a greased, 2-quart casserole, cover with the marshmallows and bake at 350° for 25 to 30 minutes.

*Serves 6.*

Vera Cross
Payroll

## Zucchini Casserole

1 small can Ortega chilies,
    seeded
Sliced zucchini
Grated sharp cheese
2 eggs

⅔ cup Bisquick
Dash of salt
Dash of pepper
Pinch of oregano
1⅔ cups milk

Chop the chilies and spread over the bottom of a greased, 9" x 12" dish. Cover with a layer of zucchini, then a layer of cheese. Repeat the layers. Combine the remaining ingredients. Stir and pour over the chilies. Let the casserole stand for 30 minutes to 2 hours and then bake at 350° for 1 hour or until set.

Gladys Tyo
Reservations

☞ *Add ½ teaspoon sugar when cooking corn, peas or carrots to help bring out the flavor.*

## Zucchini Cheese Bake

1 large zucchini
1 small can evaporated milk
2 Tbsp. butter
2 Tbsp. flour
½ cup grated American cheese

3 Tbsp. slivered blanched
   almonds
2 Tbsp. melted butter
1 cup soft bread crumbs
Parsley

Slice or cut the zucchini into cubes and cook in a small amount of salted, boiling water for 5 minutes; drain and reserve the liquid. Add enough evaporated milk to the reserved liquid to make 1 cup. Place the zucchini in a greased casserole. Melt the butter in a small saucepan and stir in the flour. Add the milk gradually and cook, stirring constantly, until thickened. Stir in the cheese and cook over low heat until melted. Add the almonds and pour over the zucchini. Toss 2 Tbsp. melted butter with the bread crumbs and sprinkle over the zucchini. Bake at 350° for 30 to 35 minutes or until the crumbs turn golden brown. Garnish with parsley.

Sue Heavilon
Reservations

## Zucchini-Stuffing Casserole

4 medium zucchini, sliced
   ½" thick
¾ cup shredded carrots
½ cup chopped onions
¼ cup plus 2 Tbsp. butter

2¼ cups Lady Pepperidge
   Farm Herbal Stuffing mix
1 can cream of chicken soup
½ cup sour cream

Cook the zucchini in boiling, salted water until tender; drain and set aside. In a saucepan, sauté the carrots and onions in ¼ cup butter. Remove from the heat, stir in 1½ cups stuffing, the soup and sour cream. Gently stir in the zucchini and spoon the mixture into a 1½-quart casserole dish. Melt the remaining butter and mix with the remaining stuffing. Sprinkle on top of the casserole. Bake at 350° for 40 minutes.

Cindy Hibbert
Apollo Help Desk

## Vegetable Royal

1 cup sliced carrots
1 cup diced broccoli
1 cup sliced celery
½ cup sliced fresh or canned
  mushrooms
1 cup sliced zucchini
¼ cup thinly diced red bell
  peppers
Salt and pepper
2 Tbsp. butter or margarine
3 Tbsp. all-purpose flour

2½ cups milk, heated
4 cups shredded American
  cheese
½ tsp. Worcestershire sauce
8 oz. Rigatoni pasta, cooked,
  drained and rinsed with cold
  water (approx. 3½ cups
  cooked)
2 tsp. paprika (approx.)
1 Tbsp. chopped parsley

Blanch the vegetables, season to taste with salt and pepper and set aside. Heat the butter or margarine until the foam subsides; do not brown. Blend in the flour and cook over very low heat without browning for 1 minute, stirring constantly. Add the milk, stir until smooth, bring to a boil and simmer for 10 minutes, stirring frequently. Slowly add the cheese over low heat. Stir until melted and smooth, add 1 tsp. salt, ⅛ tsp. ground pepper and the Worcestershire sauce and remove from the heat. Mix the Rigatoni with 2 cups cheese sauce and place in a greased, 2-quart, heat-proof dish, forming a well in the center. Place the vegetables in the center and top with the remaining cheese sauce. Sprinkle paprika over and bake at 350° for 30 minutes or until bubbling hot. Sprinkle with parsley and serve.

*Note: If desired, the mushrooms, zucchini and bell peppers may be sautéed in additional margarine.*

*Serves 6 to 8.*

Rolf Conrad
Executive Chef
Denver Food Services

## Vegetable Medley

4 cups sliced zucchini
2 cups sliced fresh mushrooms
1 stalk celery, sliced
1 small onion, chopped
¼ cup butter
½ tsp. thyme leaves

2 medium tomatoes, chopped,
  or 1 pint cherry tomatoes
½ tsp. salt
¼ cup grated Parmesan
  cheese

In a large skillet, combine the zucchini, mushrooms, celery and onion with the butter and thyme. Cover and cook over medium-high heat until tender, stirring occasionally. Add the tomatoes, salt and Parmesan cheese; cook for 1 to 2 minutes more or until the cheese melts. Serve hot or cold.

Yvonne Erickson
Reservations

# SALADS

## Shrimp and Crab Surprise Salad

1 large loaf sandwich bread
Butter
1 onion, finely chopped
4 eggs, hard-cooked and chopped
2 small cans shrimp or an
  equal amount of fresh shrimp

1 can crab or an equal amount
  of fresh crab
1 cup chopped celery
3 cups Best Foods mayonnaise

Cut the crusts from the bread; butter lightly and cut into 1" cubes. Add the onion and eggs. Refrigerate overnight. In the morning, mix in the remaining ingredients. Cover and refrigerate for 3 to 4 hours more before serving.

Susan Warren
Reservations

## Crabmeat Ravigote

1½ cups mayonnaise
1 Tbsp. chopped onion
1 tsp. chopped capers
1 medium dill pickle, chopped
2 eggs, hard-cooked and chopped
½ tsp. chopped chives
½ tsp. chopped parsley
Juice of 1 lemon
Dash of Worcestershire sauce

Lettuce leaves
3 Tbsp. chopped celery
2 oz. Alaskan or Dungeness
  crabmeat
Pimento strips
Parsley sprigs
Olives
Lemon wedges

Mix the first 9 ingredients together to make a Ravigote sauce. Line a dish or cup with lettuce. Add the celery, top with the crabmeat and cover with a generous amount of the sauce. Garnish with pimento, parsley, olives and lemon wedges.

Serves 8.

John H. Wolfsheimer
Executive Chef
San Francisco Food Services

## Alaskan Crabmeat on Tomato Remoulade

3 medium tomatoes
1 lb. frozen Alaskan
  crabmeat, legs and body
1 cup diced celery hearts
Salt and pepper to taste
Juice of 1 lemon
Dash of Worcestershire sauce
¾ cup mayonnaise
Pimento strips
Lettuce leaves
Olives
Lemon wedges
Parsley sprigs

**Remoulade Sauce:**
1 cup mayonnaise
1 tsp. chopped chives
1 small dill pickle, finely
  chopped
1 egg, hard-cooked and
  chopped
Dash of Maggi seasoning
Salt and pepper to taste
½ oz. gelatin powder
¼ cup hot water

Remove the cores from the tomatoes and discard. Scald the tomatoes in boiling water for a few seconds, then remove the skins and slice the tomatoes into pieces approximately ⅜" thick. Defrost the crab and drain off the excess juices. Mix in the celery and season with salt and pepper, the lemon juice and Worcestershire sauce. Add the mayonnaise and mix well. Divide the crabmeat mixture evenly on top of the tomato slices, rounding the top. Set in the refrigerator and chill well. When ready to serve, glaze the crabmeat on the tomatoes with the **Remoulade Sauce** and return to the refrigerator for 10 minutes. Decorate the top of each portion with a cross of red pimento strips and serve on a plate on a leaf of lettuce, with some ripe olives, a lemon wedge and a parsley sprig.

**Remoulade Sauce:** To the mayonnaise add the chives, dill pickle and egg. Season with a dash of Maggi seasoning, salt and pepper and mix well. Dissolve the gelatin powder in the hot water, add to the sauce and mix well.

Serves 8.

John H. Wolfsheimer
Executive Chef
San Francisco Food Services

☞ *Pickle juice can be used to stretch salad dressing, and it adds a nice flavor, too.*

## Shrimp Salad

1 lb. bay shrimp
½ cup diced fresh pineapple
⅓ cup diced green peppers
⅓ cup diced celery

¼ cup sliced water chestnuts
Dash of lemon juice
Dash of salt and pepper
Mayonnaise

Place the shrimp, pineapple, green peppers, celery, water chestnuts and lemon juice in a bowl. Season with salt and pepper. Mix together well and add enough mayonnaise to bind the ingredients together.

Serves 5.

Rolf Conrad
Executive Chef
Denver Food Services

## Seafood Tomato Aspic

1 (8-oz.) can Hunts tomato
  sauce
1 pkg. lemon jello
⅓ cup sweet pickle juice
1 cup finely chopped celery

½ cup finely chopped onions
⅓ cup finely chopped green
  peppers
½ cup crab or shrimp

Heat the tomato sauce and dissolve the jello in it. Add the pickle juice and ⅔ cup water, then stir in the vegetables and seafood. Chill until set.

Pat Dehlinger
Reservations

## Hot Seafood Salad

2 cups cooked macaroni
  sea shells
1 can water-packed tuna
1 can crab
1 jar chopped pimentos
2 eggs, hard-cooked

1 pint Miracle Whip
1 green pepper, diced
2 to 3 large stalks celery,
  diced
1 medium onion, diced
Lettuce or baked tart shells

Mix together all the ingredients except the lettuce or tart shells. Store in the refrigerator overnight. Bring to room temperature for several hours before heating. Heat at 500° for 15 to 20 minutes. Serve on lettuce leaves or prebaked tart shells. Good with hot rolls such as brown-and-serve or Parker House types.

Jan Boynton
Reservations

## Chinese Chicken Salad

2 boneless chicken breasts
⅓ cup dry sherry
1 cup soy sauce
1 slice fresh ginger
1 clove garlic, crushed
1 whole green onion
1 cup salad oil
1½ cups rice sticks
2 heads iceberg lettuce,
   shredded
6 green onions, diagonally
   sliced

Chopped fresh coriander
   leaves
2 Tbsp. sesame seeds, toasted
½ cup chopped cashews

**Dressing:**
3 Tbsp. salad oil
½ tsp. MSG
1 tsp. salt
2 Tbsp. sesame oil

Cook the chicken breasts for 45 minutes in a saucepan with the sherry, soy sauce, ginger, garlic and whole onion. Remove the chicken from the broth, place on a cookie sheet and bake at approximately 275° for 15 minutes; shred and set aside. Heat the oil in a 2-quart pan and drop in the rice sticks, one at a time, which will puff up immediately. Turn, remove, drain on a paper towel and break up into small pieces. When ready to serve, mix together the chicken, rice sticks, lettuce, sliced onions, coriander, sesame seeds and cashews in a large serving bowl. Combine the dressing ingredients and pour over.

Serves 8 to 10.

Helmut W. Kopleck
Executive Chef
Philadelphia Food Services

## California Chicken Salad

1½ cups shredded, cooked
   chicken
1 cup sliced ripe olives
⅓ cup green pepper strips
¼ cup chopped red onions
2 to 3 Tbsp. pimento strips
4 cups shredded lettuce
1 avocado, cut into crescents
Lettuce leaves.

**Dressing:**
⅓ cup salad oil
¼ cup red wine vinegar
¼ cup lemon juice
1 Tbsp. sugar
1 tsp. salt
½ tsp. pepper
¼ tsp. minced fresh garlic

Combine the first 6 ingredients, cover and chill. Then combine the dressing ingredients in a jar, shake well and refrigerate. Just before serving add the avocado to the salad. Shake the dressing, pour it over the salad and toss lightly. Serve over lettuce leaves.

Fran Christensen
Tour Desk

## Fruited Chicken Salad

3 cups diced chicken
1 cup diced celery
1 cup fresh or canned and
   drained Mandarin orange
   sections
1 (9-oz.) can pineapple tidbits,
   drained

½ cup toasted slivered
   almonds
2 Tbsp. salad oil
2 Tbsp. orange juice
2 Tbsp. vinegar
½ tsp. salt
½ cup mayonnaise
Lettuce

Combine the first 5 ingredients and set aside. Blend together the salad oil, orange juice, vinegar and salt. Combine with the chicken mixture and chill for 1 hour. Drain, add the mayonnaise and toss. Serve on a bed of lettuce.

Rick Sanders
Reservations

## Hot Chicken Salad

4 slices bread
3 cups diced chicken
2 cups diced celery
2 Tbsp. minced onion
Salt and pepper
1 (4-oz.) can mushrooms

2 cans cream of chicken soup
5 eggs, hard-cooked
¾ cup mayonnaise
2 tsp. lemon juice
Chopped almonds
Crushed potato chips

Remove the crusts from the bread and cut the bread into cubes. Combine with all the remaining ingredients except the potato chips. Top the salad with potato chips and bake at 350° for 45 minutes.

Arlene McEachern
Public Affairs

## Taco Salad

2 lbs. ground beef
1 pkg. taco flavoring mix
2 cans garbanzo beans,
   drained, or 1 can garbanzo
   beans and 1 can kidney
   beans
4 avocados, chopped
2 cans chopped black olives
6 tomatoes, chopped

Shredded lettuce
½ lb. cheddar cheese, grated
½ pkg. Doritos, crushed

**Dressing:**
¾ pkg. Hidden Valley Ranch
   dressing mix
1½ to 2 cups buttermilk
1 to 2 cups mayonnaise

Brown the meat and stir in the taco flavoring mix. Add the beans, avocados, olives and tomatoes; toss well. Pour the dressing over the salad and toss again. Pile the salad into 1 large bowl or individual bowls lined with shredded lettuce. Sprinkle with the cheese and crushed Doritos and serve with the remaining Doritos. To prepare the dressing, combine all the ingredients and shake well.

Rick Sanders
Janet Wanink
Reservations

### Corn and Cabbage Slaw

1 (12-oz.) can whole
   kernel corn
1 tsp. mustard seed
1 tsp. dry mustard
½ tsp. salt
¼ tsp. pepper
⅔ cup cider vinegar
2 Tbsp. salad oil

¼ cup packed light
   brown sugar
½ cup chopped onions
1 (4-oz.) jar pimentos,
   drained and sliced
¼ cup chopped green peppers
2 cups shredded green
   cabbage

Drain the liquid from the corn into a small saucepan. Stir in the mustard seed, mustard, salt, pepper, vinegar, oil and brown sugar; bring to a full boil. Combine the corn, onions, pimentos and green peppers in a medium bowl. Pour the hot liquid over the corn mixture, tossing lightly until well mixed. Refrigerate covered for 30 minutes. Fold in the cabbage. Refrigerate covered for several hours or overnight. Before serving, toss several times to mix well.

Makes about 4 cups.

Karen Fudge
Regional Sales

### Cole Slaw

1¼ lbs. white cabbage,
   shredded
¼ lb. carrots, shredded
1 cup mayonnaise
1 cup sour cream

1 tsp. salt
¼ tsp. white ground pepper
1 Tbsp. cider vinegar
½ cup sugar
2 tsp. fresh lemon juice

Combine all the ingredients and season to taste. To allow the flavors to blend well, refrigerate for 5 hours before serving.

Makes 12 (3-oz.) portions.

Rolf Conrad
Executive Chef
Denver Food Services

## Hot Sweet and Sour Cabbage Salad

4 slices bacon
½ tsp. salt
1 heaping tsp. sugar

3 Tbsp. vinegar
1 small head red cabbage,
  shredded

Fry the bacon slices until crisp, remove from the pan and crumble. Add the salt, sugar and vinegar to the bacon drippings. Sprinkle in the crumbled bacon and heat through. Stir well and pour the sauce over the shredded cabbage. Serve immediately while hot.

Lillian Warren

## Marinated Carrots

5 cups cooked carrots
½ onion, chopped
½ green pepper, chopped
1 can tomato soup
½ cup salad oil

1 cup sugar
¾ cup vinegar
1 tsp. mustard
1 Tbsp. Worcestershire sauce
1 tsp. salt

Combine all the ingredients and chill for at least 12 hours before serving.

Tim Walker
Reservations

## Hot Green Bean and Bacon Salad

2 lbs. fresh green beans
3 slices raw bacon, diced
1 onion, minced

½ cup vinegar
Dash of pepper

Wash and string the beans; cut diagonally and cook in salted water until tender. Drain and keep hot. Fry the bacon until crisp, add the onion, stir for a minute and add the vinegar, letting it boil up once. Pour the sauce over the beans, sprinkle with pepper and serve hot.

Serves 6.

Ruth Vantine
Teleticketing

## Three Bean Salad

2 cans wax beans
2 cans green beans
2 cans kidney beans
1 large bell pepper, chopped
1 large onion, chopped

**Dressing:**
⅓ cup salad oil
¾ cup sugar
⅔ cup vinegar
1 tsp. salt
½ tsp. pepper

Combine together the wax, green and kidney beans and the pepper and onion. Mix well. Combine the dressing ingredients, shake well and pour over the salad. Chill for several hours or overnight before serving.

*Note: This salad is good for several days. You may add a little hot pepper for a tangier taste.*

Lillian Warren

## Hot German Potato Salad

1 cup chopped onions
¾ cup diced celery
⅓ cup bacon drippings
2 tsp. salt
1 tsp. sugar
⅛ tsp. pepper
⅔ cup water

½ cup cider vinegar
6 cups diced, cooked potatoes,
    kept warm
2 Tbsp. mayonnaise
6 slices bacon, crisply cooked
    and crumbled

Sauté the onions and celery in the bacon drippings for 5 minutes or until the onions are tender. Add the next 5 ingredients, bring to a boil and boil for 2 minutes. Stir in the potatoes, mayonnaise and bacon; toss lightly. Serve hot.

*Serves 6 to 8.*

Janis Sisley

☞ *To remove the core from head lettuce, firmly rap the head, core side down, on a cutting board. The core should pull right out, and you can then separate the leaves by pouring cold water into the center of the head.*

### Spinach Salad St. Louis

1 head spinach
½ head iceberg or romaine
   lettuce
2 Tbsp. sugar
Salt to taste
1 tsp. dry mustard
1 tsp. onion juice
¼ cup cider vinegar

½ cup salad oil
1 Tbsp. poppy seeds
6 slices bacon, cooked and
   diced
¾ cup small curd cottage
   cheese
3 eggs, hard-cooked and
   chopped

Tear the greens into bite-size pieces and chill. In a jar, combine the sugar, salt, mustard, onion juice, vinegar, oil and poppy seeds, shake well and chill. Pour the dressing over the greens and toss, add the bacon, spoon the cottage cheese over and toss again. Garnish with the chopped eggs.

Note: I always double the dressing because there never seems to be enough.

Serves 6 to 8.

Ray Stokes
Retired Supervisor
Reservations

### 24-Hour Head Lettuce Salad

1 large head lettuce
¼ cup finely chopped onions
¼ cup thinly diced celery
1 (6-oz.) can water chestnuts,
   sliced
1 pkg. frozen peas, unthawed
2 cups mayonnaise

Parmesan cheese
1 Tbsp. sugar
¾ lb. bacon, fried and
   crumbled
4 tomatoes, cut into wedges
2 eggs, hard-cooked and sliced
Parsley

Shred the lettuce into a fine layer in a 9" x 12" pan, then add layers of onions, celery, and water chestnuts. Sprinkle the peas over, frost with the mayonnaise and sprinkle with the cheese and sugar. Cover and refrigerate overnight. Garnish with the bacon, tomatoes, eggs and parsley.

*Serves 12.*

Brandon Taylor
Kristi Severson
Reservations
Loretta Kirby
Ticket Office

## Spinach Salad

*Chopped spinach leaves*
*Shredded iceberg lettuce*
*Chopped green onions*
*Bacon, fried and crumbled*
*Sliced mushrooms*

**Dressing:**
*⅔ cup salad oil*

*¼ cup wine vinegar with garlic*
*2 Tbsp. white wine*
*2 Tbsp. soy sauce*
*½ tsp. salt*
*Pepper to taste*
*1 tsp. sugar*
*½ tsp. curry powder*
*1 tsp. dry mustard*

Combine all the salad ingredients, toss well, pour the dressing over, toss again and serve. To prepare the dressing, combine all the ingredients in a bottle, cover tightly and shake well.

*Note: Hard-cooked eggs, garbanzo beans and avocados may also be added to the salad.*

Mary Montgomery
Reservations

## Mediterranean Salad

*1 (10-oz.) pkg. frozen Italian*
*green beans*
*2 Tbsp. butter or margarine*
*3 slices bread, cubed*
*1 (12-oz.) can whole kernel*
*corn, drained*

*½ cup mayonnaise*
*2 Tbsp. pimentos, drained*
*and chopped*
*1 Tbsp. dried basil leaves,*
*crushed*
*¼ tsp. salt*

Cook the beans according to the package directions; drain and cool. In a skillet, melt the butter, add the bread cubes and sauté over medium-high heat until crisp, turning occasionally. Combine the beans, corn, mayonnaise, pimentos, basil and salt; chill. Before serving, add the toasted bread cubes to the mixture and toss.

*Serves 8.*

Mikele McKnight
Reservations

## Greek Salad

1½ lbs. feta cheese, cut into
   ½" x ¾" cubes
16 to 20 Greek olives
4 fresh tomatoes, cut into
   large pieces
4 cucumbers, cut into large
   pieces
4 red onions, sliced

4 green peppers, diced into
   large squares

**Dressing:**
1 cup oil
¼ cup red wine vinegar
1 tsp. salt
¼ tsp. freshly ground or Java
   pepper

Combine all the salad ingredients and pour the dressing over; serve. To prepare the dressing, combine all the ingredients, shake well and chill.

*Note: You may substitute Monterey Jack for the feta cheese and large, pitted black olives for the Greek olives.*

Susan Warren
Reservations

## Gazpacho Salad

2 medium cucumbers, peeled
   and thinly sliced
2 tsp. salt
⅔ cup olive oil
⅓ cup wine vinegar
1 clove garlic, crushed
1 tsp. basil
½ tsp. freshly ground pepper
10 medium mushrooms,
   sliced

4 green onions, thinly sliced
½ cup minced parsley
3 large tomatoes, peeled and
   chopped
1 medium green pepper,
   chopped
½ lb. Swiss or Monterey Jack
   cheese, sliced into thin strips
4 eggs, hard-cooked and
   thinly sliced

Place the cucumber slices in a bowl and sprinkle with 1 tsp. salt; let stand for 30 minutes. In a large bowl combine the olive oil, vinegar, garlic, basil, 1 tsp. salt and the pepper; add the mushrooms and green onions. Drain the cucumber slices, pat dry and add to the bowl of mushrooms. Gently mix in the parsley. Add a layer of tomatoes and a layer of green pepper. Cover the bowl and chill for at least 4 hours. Just before serving, add the cheese. Toss the salad gently and garnish with the hard-cooked eggs.

Jackie Partlow

## Marinated Vegetable Salad

1 (20-oz.) pkg. frozen
   California-blend vegetables
   (carrots, cauliflower and
   sliced broccoli)
3 stalks celery, sliced into
   ¼" chunks
½ cup sliced pimento-stuffed
   olives
1 small can whole pitted
   ripe olives

1 medium can mushroom
   pieces and stems, drained
3 to 4 green onions, chopped
3 tomatoes, cut into 8 wedges

**Dressing:**
1 pkg. Hidden Valley Ranch
   dressing (original recipe)
⅔ cup oil
¼ cup vinegar

Bring the frozen vegetables to a boil in a small amount of cold, salted water; boil for 2 minutes. Add the remaining vegetables and toss lightly. Pour the dressing over the vegetables and chill for 24 hours or more, tossing 2 or 3 times.

**Dressing:** Combine all the ingredients; let stand for about 20 minutes.

Adelaide Haferbecker
Food Services

## Banana and Peanut Salad

3 bananas, chilled
1 cup salted Spanish peanuts

**Dressing:**
1 Tbsp. vinegar

½ cup water
2 Tbsp. flour
½ cup sugar
1 rounded Tbsp. butter
2 egg yolks, beaten

In a chilled serving bowl, make a layer of the bananas, a layer of the nuts, and then a layer of the chilled dressing. Continue layering until all the ingredients are used up. Chill before serving.

**Dressing:** Mix the first 4 ingredients together well, add the butter and cook over low heat until the sauce begins to thicken. Pour the egg yolks into the mixture and continue cooking until thick and creamy. Chill well.

Carole Hirose
Training

## Spiced Fruit Compote

2 (29-oz.) cans cling peach
   halves
2 (3") cinnamon sticks
½ tsp. ground allspice
⅛ tsp. ground ginger
⅛ tsp. ground nutmeg

2 (29-oz.) cans pear halves,
   drained
1 (17-oz.) can figs, drained
½ cup brandy
3 medium bananas

Drain the syrup from the peach halves into a 1-quart saucepan, stir in the cinnamon sticks, allspice, ginger and nutmeg, set over medium heat and heat to boiling. Reduce the heat to low, cover and simmer for 10 minutes, stirring occasionally. Remove the saucepan from the heat; cool. In a large bowl, combine the drained peaches, pears, figs and brandy; pour the peach syrup mixture over the fruit. With a large rubber spatula, gently toss the mixture to mix well; cover and refrigerate overnight. Just before serving slice the bananas into 1" chunks and stir gently into the fruit mixture.

*Serves 12.*

Karen Fudge
Regional Sales

## Watergate Salad

1 box pistachio pudding
1 large carton Cool Whip
1 large can crushed
   pineapple, drained

1½ cups small marshmallows
1 cup crushed walnuts

Prepare the pudding according to the package directions. When the pudding sets, mix in the remaining ingredients. Cover and chill overnight.

*Serves 10 or more.*

Loretta Kirby
Ticket Office

## Fruit Salad

2 eggs
¼ cup vinegar
¼ cup sugar
1 cup heavy cream, whipped
1 can fruit cocktail,
   well drained

1 can pineapple chunks,
   well drained
2 oranges, diced and soaked
   in sugar
3 bananas, sliced
1 cup grapes
2 cups cut marshmallows

Cook the eggs, vinegar and sugar in a double boiler, beating until thick and smooth. Cool. Fold the whipped cream into the egg custard. Fold in all the fruit and the marshmallows and refrigerate for at least 8 hours before serving.

Pat Dehlinger
Reservations

## Beet Jello Salad

1 cup beet juice
1 cup sweet pickle juice
1 large pkg. raspberry jello
2 cans shredded beets
1 large can crushed pineapple

**Dressing:**
1 cup sour cream
1 cup finely chopped celery
1 cup finely chopped green
   peppers
1 cup chopped green onions

Boil the beet and pickle juices, add the jello and chill until partially set. Then fold in the beets and pineapple, pour into a mold and chill until the jello sets. Just before serving, combine the dressing ingredients and mix well; unmold the jello, top with the dressing and serve.

Arlene McEachern
Public Affairs

# Cranberry Ring Salad

2 cups cranberries
1½ cups cold water
1 cup sugar
1 Tbsp. unflavored gelatin
Dash of salt

½ cup chopped nuts
¾ cup diced celery
Lettuce
Mayonnaise

Wash the cranberries and cook until tender in 1 cup cold water. Stir in the sugar and cook for 5 minutes. Soften the gelatin in ½ cup cold water until it dissolves. Add the cranberries and salt. Chill until the mixture starts to thicken. Add the nuts and celery, mixing thoroughly. Pour into an oiled ring mold and chill until firm. Unmold and place on a large salad plate lined with lettuce leaves. Top with mayonnaise, if desired.

Note: You may wish to fill the center with shrimp or garnish the salad with pineapple rings, filled with cream cheese and topped with grapes or maraschino cherries.

Ruth Vantine
Reservations

# Broccoli Molded Salad

1 (3-oz.) pkg. lemon jello
1 cup boiling water
1½ Tbsp. vinegar
½ cup mayonnaise
Dash of salt and pepper

1 pkg. frozen broccoli,
  cooked and chopped
½ cup chopped celery
1 Tbsp. grated onion
¾ cup small-curd cottage
  cheese

Dissolve the jello in the boiling water, stir in the vinegar, mayonnaise, salt and pepper. Pour the mixture into a freezer tray and partially freeze for about 15 minutes or until frozen to 1" around the edge. Turn into a bowl and beat until fluffy. Fold in the broccoli, celery, onion and cottage cheese. Pour into a mold and chill until firm.

Effie Johnston

## Apricot Nectar Salad

2 pkg. orange jello
1½ cups hot water
2½ cups apricot nectar
2 small cans Mandarin oranges
1½ cups small marshmallows

Frosting:
½ cup sugar
2 Tbsp. flour
1 egg
Dash of salt
1 cup apricot nectar
1 cup heavy cream or 1 pkg.
   Dream Whip

Dissolve the jello in the hot water, add the apricot nectar, oranges and marshmallows. Pour into a mold and refrigerate. When the jello sets, spread the frosting over and serve.

**Frosting:** In a saucepan, combine the sugar, flour, egg, salt and nectar. Cook until thickened and cool thoroughly. Whip the cream and fold it into the cooled custard.

Arlene McEachern
Government Affairs

## Festive Frozen Fruit Salad

1 (3-oz.) pkg. cream cheese
¼ cup mayonnaise
½ cup lemon juice
⅔ cup heavy cream, whipped
   and chilled
½ cup sugar

Dash of salt
½ cup seedless raisins
¼ cup sliced candied cherries
¾ cup drained crushed
   pineapple

Soften the cream cheese and thoroughly blend with the mayonnaise and lemon juice. Gently fold in the whipped cream, then fold in the remaining ingredients. Combine gently but thoroughly. Turn into a 9" x 9" pan that has been sprayed with Pam. Freeze until firm, at least 4 hours.

Serves 9.

Julie Jacobson
Reservations

## Golden Delight

1 (13½-oz.) can crushed
   pineapple
2 pkg. lemon jello
2 cups boiling water
2 cups cold water
3 bananas, sliced

½ pkg. miniature
   marshmallows
1 egg
½ cup sugar
2 heaping Tbsp. cornstarch
1 cup heavy cream, whipped
Nuts or grated cheese

Drain the pineapple, reserve the juice and add enough water to make 1 cup. Dissolve the jello in 2 cups boiling water, then stir in 2 cups cold water. Chill until it reaches the soft jello stage. Add the pineapple, bananas and marshmallows. Chill until firm. Beat together the egg, sugar and cornstarch, add the reserved juice and cook in a double boiler until thick. Cool and fold in the whipped cream; spread over the jello. Garnish with nuts or grated cheese.

Makes about 18 servings.

Connie Brown
Reservations

## Avocado Salad

1 cup crushed pineapple and
   juice
Boiling water
1 pkg. lime jello
3 Tbsp. mayonnaise

¼ cup cream, whipped
1 Tbsp. lemon juice
1 avocado, mashed and
   salted to taste

Drain the juice from the pineapple and add enough boiling water to make 1 cup. Heat the pineapple juice to boiling and stir in the lime jello and pineapple. Refrigerate. When the jello is almost set, combine the remaining ingredients and gently fold into the jello. Refrigerate until firm.

Lillian Warren

## Pineapple and Cottage Cheese Salad

1 pkg. lime or lemon jello
1 cup hot water
½ cup cottage cheese

½ cup mayonnaise
1 small can crushed pineapple, drained

Dissolve the jello in the hot water. Refrigerate until partially congealed. Meanwhile, combine the cottage cheese and mayonnaise and beat until smooth. Fold into the partly congealed jello and add the pineapple. Mix well, pour into a mold and chill until set.

Lillian Warren

## Lime Fruit Salad

1 pkg. lime jello
1 cup applesauce, heated
Juice of 1 orange

⅔ cup 7-Up
Canned pear halves

Dissolve the jello in the applesauce and add the orange juice and 7-Up. Pour over pear halves. Refrigerate until set.

Percy Wood
Vice Chairman of the Board
United Airlines, Inc.

## Summer Fruit

1 (3-oz.) pkg. raspberry jello
1¼ cups boiling water
1 (8-oz.) carton raspberry
  yogurt

¼ cup honey
1 pint fresh or frozen
  raspberries

Combine the jello and water and stir until the jello is dissolved. Beat in the yogurt and honey. Chill until partially set. Whip the jello until light and fluffy, about 1 to 2 minutes. Fold the berries into the jello and re-chill.

Yvonne Erickson
Reservations

## Molded Pear Salad

1 (29-oz.) can pears
1 (3-oz.) pkg. lime jello
1 (8-oz.) pkg. cream cheese,
  softened

1 cup heavy cream, whipped
Maraschino cherries

Drain the pears, reserving 1 cup of the juice. Heat the juice and dissolve the jello in it. Gradually stir the jello into the cream cheese and chill the mixture until it stiffens slightly. Blend in the whipped cream and pears, pour into a mold and chill until firm. Unmold and garnish with maraschino cherry halves.

Barbara Sharpe
District Sales

## Waldorf Crown Salad

2 (3-oz.) pkg. strawberry
  flavored gelatin
2 cups boiling water
1½ cups cold water
1 cup chopped apples
½ cup thinly sliced celery
¼ cup chopped walnuts
Lettuce

**Fluffy Dressing:**
1 cup sour cream
½ cup salad dressing or
  mayonnaise
1½ cups Kraft miniature
  marshmallows

Dissolve the gelatin in the boiling water, stir in the cold water and chill until partially set. Fold in the apples, celery and walnuts, pour into a 4½-cup ring mold and chill until firm. Unmold, surround with lettuce and fill the center with the **Fluffy Dressing**.

**Fluffy Dressing:** Combine the sour cream and salad dressing; mix well. Fold in the marshmallows.

Serves 6 to 8.

Annemarie Fleming
Reservations

## Blueberry Fruit Salad

1 pkg. unflavored gelatin
Juice of 1 lemon
¼ tsp. salt
¼ tsp. ginger
¼ cup honey
½ cup canned and drained
   crushed pineapple
1 cup canned and drained
   sliced peaches

1 cup canned and drained
   sliced pears
1 cup fresh or frozen
   blueberries
1 cup syrup from the
   canned fruits
1 cup heavy cream, whipped
⅔ cup mayonnaise
Greens

Soften the gelatin in ⅓ cup water. Place over low heat and stir until the gelatin dissolves. Add the lemon juice, salt, ginger, honey, pineapple, peaches, pears, blueberries and syrup from the canned fruits. Chill until slightly thickened. Fold in the whipped cream and mayonnaise. Pour into 2 (1-quart) refrigerator trays and freeze until firm. Serve on greens.

Makes 8 servings.

Ruth Vantine
Reservations

## Ray's Special French Dressing

1 cup salad oil
½ cup white vinegar
1 can tomato soup
½ tsp. Worcestershire sauce
2 Tbsp. sugar

1 tsp. salt
1 tsp. dry mustard
½ tsp. pepper
½ tsp. paprika
1 clove garlic, pressed

Combine and shake all the ingredients well. Store in a cool place. Serve on a tossed green salad.

Ray Stokes
Retired Supervisor
Reservations

### Javanese Dressing

2 cups olive oil
¾ cup red wine vinegar
1 tsp. Spanish paprika
½ tsp. onion salt
¼ tsp. garlic powder
1½ tsp. Maggi seasoning

2 tsp. freshly chopped parsley
1 tsp. salt
2 tsp. prepared mustard
¼ tsp. MSG
1 tsp. tomato paste

Mix all the ingredients together well and chill before serving.

Rolf Conrad
Executive Chef
Denver Food Services

### Stone Jug Salad Dressing

½ cup sugar
1 cup vinegar
1 cup oil
½ tsp. paprika

1½ cups catsup
2 cloves garlic, crushed
1 tsp. salt

Boil the sugar and vinegar together for 1 minute in a saucepan, then add the remaining ingredients. Mix well in a blender. This is a strong French dressing, especially good for use as a shrimp dip.

Makes 1 quart.

John and Sid Reed
Reservations

### Oregano Salad Dressing

¾ cup vinegar
1 Tbsp. salt
1 Tbsp. sugar
1 tsp. oregano

2 tsp. pepper
1½ Tbsp. sweet basil
2 garlic cloves, split
¾ cup salad oil

Combine all the ingredients except the oil and marinate for 24 hours. Strain the mixture, add the oil and shake well. Serve over salad greens.

*Makes 1½ cups.*

David Rieman
Passenger Service

## Sweet and Sour Sesame Seed Dressing

¼ cup sesame seeds
1⅓ cups salad oil
⅔ cup tarragon vinegar
2 tsp. salt
1 tsp. dry mustard

½ tsp. garlic powder
½ tsp. black pepper
¼ cup sugar
¼ cup grated Parmesan
   cheese

Toast the sesame seeds on an ungreased cookie sheet at 275° for 10 to 15 minutes or until light brown; set aside to cool. Combine the oil, vinegar, salt, mustard, garlic powder, pepper and sugar in a glass jar. Shake the dressing until well blended. Add the toasted sesame seeds and cheese; shake. Chill until ready to serve.

## Winter Salad Dressing

12 slices bacon
½ cup plus 1 Tbsp. vinegar
3 egg yolks
1 Tbsp. flour

¼ cup plus 2 Tbsp. sour cream
½ tsp. salt
3 Tbsp. sugar

Cook the bacon, drain and reserve ¼ cup plus 2 Tbsp. bacon drippings. Stir the vinegar into the bacon drippings and cool. Add 1 Tbsp. water to the egg yolks and blend in the flour. Pour the egg mixture into a saucepan. Cut the bacon into bite-size pieces and add to the egg mixture. Stir in the bacon grease and vinegar. Cook over medium heat, stirring constantly, until the mixture thickens. Add the sour cream, salt and sugar and bring to a boil. Pour over lettuce and serve at once.

Marianne Shute

## Russian Dressing

2 cups mayonnaise
2 Tbsp. chili sauce
3 drops of Worcestershire
  sauce

1 ½ drops of Tabasco sauce
3 Tbsp. vinegar
3 Tbsp. Russian caviar
2 Tbsp. chopped fine relish

Combine all the ingredients and mix well.

Hans Jantzen
Executive Chef
New York Food Services

## Catalina Dressing

1 cup mayonnaise
¼ cup honey
¼ cup heavy cream

2 Tbsp. lemon juice
¾ cup catsup
½ onion, grated

Mix all the ingredients together well and use with green salad. To use with fruit salad, omit the onion.

Emile LeBoulluec
Executive Chef
Boston Food Services

## Dill Dressing/Dip

⅔ cup sour cream
⅔ cup mayonnaise
1 Tbsp. minced dried onion

1 Tbsp. parsley flakes
1 heaping tsp. dill weed
1 tsp. Beau Monde seasoning

Blend all the ingredients together. Serve as a salad dressing or vegetable dip.

Carole Hirose
Training

☞ Try mustard dressing on tomato salads instead of oil and vinegar as the acid in vinegar tends to eat the tomatoes.

## Sweet and Sour Bacon Dressing

4 slices bacon
2 Tbsp. chopped onion
3 Tbsp. sugar

3 Tbsp. white vinegar
1 ⅓ cups homemade
  mayonnaise

Fry the bacon, crumble and set aside. Sauté the onion in the bacon drippings until tender. Add the sugar, vinegar and ½ cup water. Bring to a boil and cool completely. Combine the vinegar mixture with the mayonnaise and beat until smooth. Mix in the bacon and chill. Good for potato salad.

Makes 1 pint.

David Rieman
Passenger Service

## Sesame Seed Dressing

½ cup sesame seeds
1 Tbsp. butter
½ cup freshly grated
  Parmesan cheese
½ cup mayonnaise
1 cup sour cream

1 Tbsp. tarragon vinegar
1 Tbsp. sugar
½ cup chopped green peppers
2 Tbsp. minced onion
¾ tsp. salt
½ tsp. garlic salt

Sauté the sesame seeds in the butter until brown. Cool and add the cheese. Combine the remaining ingredients and add the cooled sesame mixture to it.

Note: If the seed and cheese mixture is stored separately from the cream mixture, this dressing will keep for at least a week in the refrigerator.

Sue McCaffray
Reservations

## Roquefort Dressing #1

2 cups mayonnaise
1½ cups sour cream
1½ cups finely crumbled
   Roquefort cheese
¼ cup finely grated onions

Dash of garlic powder or
   ½ clove fresh garlic, crushed
   with salt to a paste
Salt and white pepper to taste
Tabasco sauce to taste

Combine all the ingredients well and refrigerate for 24 hours before serving.

Paul Steuri
Executive Chef
Omaha Food Services

## Roquefort Dressing #2

1 tsp. salt
½ tsp. white pepper
1 tsp. Dijon mustard
1 Tbsp. white wine vinegar

2 Tbsp. olive oil
1½ tsp. grated horseradish
2 Tbsp. Roquefort cheese
1 Tbsp. sour cream

In a wooden salad bowl, thoroughly mix together the salt, pepper and mustard, add the vinegar and mix well. Add the oil slowly, then the horseradish; finally add the cheese, in lumps, and the sour cream. Mix until smooth and serve immediately.

Note: This dressing should not be refrigerated.

Makes ½ cup.

Raoul F. Delbol
Executive Chef
Los Angeles Food Services

## Caesar Dressing

2 cups mayonnaise
1 tsp. Worcestershire sauce
1 Tbsp. finely chopped
   anchovies

1 clove garlic, finely chopped
2 eggs, hard-cooked and
   finely chopped
Salt and pepper to taste

Blend all ingredients together and season to taste.

*Makes 8 to 10 portions.*

Rolf Conrad
Executive Chef
Denver Food Services

## Green Goddess Dressing

2 cups mayonnaise
1 cup sour cream
2 Tbsp. lemon juice
1 ¼ tsp. salt
¼ tsp. crushed peppercorns
1 ½ cloves garlic, minced
¼ cup plus 2 Tbsp. finely
   chopped anchovies

¼ cup finely chopped
   pearl onions
¼ cup tarragon vinegar
   (approx.)
¼ cup red wine vinegar
   (approx.)

Mix the mayonnaise, sour cream and lemon juice together and add the salt, peppercorns and garlic. Mix in the anchovies and onions. Add the vinegars to taste and blend well.

Emile LeBoulluec
Executive Chef
Boston Food Services

## Celery Seed Fruit Dressing

½ cup sugar
1 tsp. dry mustard
1 tsp. salt
½ tsp. grated onion

5 Tbsp. white vinegar
1 cup salad oil
1 Tbsp. celery seed

Combine the sugar, mustard, salt, onion and 2 Tbsp. vinegar. Slowly add the salad oil, beating constantly. Add the remaining vinegar and the celery seed. Continue beating until the dressing is thick. Serve with fruit compote.

Barbara Sharpe
District Sales

## Orange Dressing

1 cup mayonnaise
1 cup sour cream
2 Tbsp. sugar
½ cup ground sweet orange
  marmalade

Grated peel of 1 small orange
Juice of 1 small orange
Juice of 1 small lemon

Combine the mayonnaise and sour cream. Add the remaining ingredients, one by one. Chill until ready to serve and serve over fruit.

Ray Stokes
Retired Supervisor
Reservations

## Rum Lime Sauce

⅔ cup sugar
¼ cup plus 2 Tbsp. lime juice

½ cup white rum

Bring the sugar to a boil with ⅓ cup water. Simmer for 5 minutes; cool. Stir in the juice and rum. Serve over fresh fruit or melon balls.

Fran Christensen
Tour Desk

## Poppy Seed Dressing

¾ cup sugar
1 tsp. dry mustard
1 tsp. salt
⅓ cup cider vinegar

1 Tbsp. onion juice
1 cup salad oil
1½ Tbsp. poppy seeds

Combine the first 5 ingredients. Slowly drizzle in the oil while beating constantly with a rotary beater or wire whisk. Beat until the mixture is smooth and thick. Stir in the poppy seeds. This dressing is good for both fruit and green salads.

Carole Hirose
Training

## Luscious Fruit Salad Dressing

1 Tbsp. flour
⅓ cup sugar
1 egg, lightly beaten
1½ Tbsp. lemon juice

¼ cup orange juice
½ cup pineapple juice
½ cup heavy cream

Combine the flour and sugar in the top of a double boiler. Stir in the egg. Cook, stirring over the hot water until the sauce thickens. Chill, add the juices. Whip the cream and fold it in. Serve over your favorite fruit salad.

Makes 1½ cups.

Ken Christensen
Operations Planning

## Honey Lime Dressing

1 egg
1 cup mayonnaise
1 cup oil
2 Tbsp. vinegar
¼ tsp. dry mustard
⅛ tsp. sugar

½ tsp. salt
2 Tbsp. honey
Juice of 2 limes
Juice of 1 lemon
Dash of green food color

Whip the egg, then whip in the mayonnaise, add the oil and vinegar and blend in the remaining ingredients in order. Refrigerate until ready to use.

Hans Jantzen
Executive Chef
New York Food Services

☞ When preparing oil and vinegar dressings, combine the vinegar and seasonings first, and the grains will dissolve.

# SOUPS

# Fresh Seafood Bisque

¼ lb. raw shrimp
10 steamer clams (approx.)
2 medium onions
4 Tbsp. butter
¼ lb. scallops, quartered
1 lb. red snapper, chopped
½ cup white wine
3 cloves garlic, minced
2 Tbsp. flour

¾ cup milk
1 (6-oz.) can tomato paste
Minced parsley
Rosemary
Thyme
Basil
Freshly ground white pepper
Salt
¼ lb. crabmeat

In boiling water, cook the shrimp for about 3 minutes; reserve the water. Shell the shrimp and devein; set aside. Using about 3 Tbsp. of the reserved water, steam the clams in a pot until they open. Set the clams aside; reserve all the water. In a medium pot, sauté 1 onion in 1 Tbsp. melted butter over medium-high heat. Add the scallops, snapper and wine. Cook covered over medium-low heat until the fish begins to break down. In a large pot over medium heat, sauté the other onion and the garlic in 3 Tbsp. melted butter. Make a roux by adding the flour and constantly scraping the sides and the bottom of the pot with a wooden spoon. Cook for about 3 minutes; the heat should be high, but the butter must not burn. Add the milk in thirds, allowing it to thicken and boil after each addition, stirring constantly. Stir in the tomato paste, a heaping tablespoon at a time. Water down with the reserved shrimp and clam water until of desired consistency. The broth should be full-bodied. Season to taste with parsley, rosemary, thyme, basil, white pepper and salt. Add the shrimp, the clams in their shells and the crabmeat. Pour the contents of the medium pot into the larger pot. Simmer covered for about 1 hour.

*Serves 4.*

Susan Brentzel
Reservations

☞ *Too much salt in the soup? Add a pinch of brown sugar.*

## Lobster Bisque

1 cup oil
1 (3-lb.) lobster, cut into
   8 pieces
½ cup brandy or cognac
1 cup finely chopped onions
4 cloves garlic, chopped
½ cup white flour
1 cup dry white wine
2 quarts **Fish Stock** (see index)
1 Tbsp. salt

½ tsp. ground white pepper
4 tomatoes, peeled, seeded
   and diced
¼ cup tomato paste
1 bay leaf
1 thyme leaf
⅓ tsp. cayenne pepper
1 cup heavy cream
½ cup sweet butter

Heat the oil in a deep, thick-bottomed saucepan. When very hot, add the lobster and sauté quickly over high heat for 10 minutes, turning the pieces so they turn a nice red color. Add the brandy and flame, add the onions and simmer over low heat for 5 minutes, add the garlic and simmer for 2 minutes. Sprinkle in the flour, stirring constantly, and simmer for 3 minutes. Stir in the remaining ingredients except the cayenne pepper, heavy cream and butter. Mix well and bring to a boil; lower the heat and simmer covered for approximately 50 minutes. Remove the lobster and strain the liquid, forcing the vegetables through a fine sieve. Cook uncovered for about 15 minutes, until the liquid is reduced to 1½ quarts. Blend in the pepper and cream, then gradually stir in the butter in dots and check the seasoning. Dice the lobster meat and serve with the bisque or with rice.

Serves 6.

Raoul F. Delbol
Executive Chef
Los Angeles Food Services

## Bratten's Clam Chowder

¾ lb. clams or 2 (6½-oz.) cans
   minced clams
1 cup finely chopped onions
1 cup finely diced celery
2 cups finely diced potatoes
¾ cup butter or margarine

¾ cup flour
4 cups half & half
1½ tsp. salt
Dash of pepper
½ tsp. sugar

Drain the juice from the clams and combine with the vegetables in a medium saucepan. Add enough water to barely cover and simmer covered over medium heat until the potatoes are tender, about 20 minutes. In the meantime, melt the butter, blend in the flour and cook, stirring, for 1 to 2 minutes. Add the half & half, cook and whisk until smooth and thick. Add the vegetables and undrained clams and heat through. Season to taste with the salt, pepper and sugar.

*Serves 8.*

Nola Sears
Reservations

## Lobster Shrimp Chowder

¼ cup chopped celery
2 Tbsp. chopped green onion
  with tops
2 Tbsp. butter
1 can frozen condensed cream
  of shrimp soup
1 can cream of mushroom
  soup

1 soup can milk
1 cup light cream
1 (5-oz.) can lobster or an
  equal amount of fresh
  lobster
¼ cup dry sherry
1 Tbsp. snipped fresh parsley

Sauté the celery and onion in the butter until tender. Add the soups, milk and cream and heat until the shrimp soup thaws, stirring occasionally. Stir in the remaining ingredients and heat through.

## Jim's Crab and Asparagus Soup

1 (6- to 8-oz.) King crab
  and 5 to 6 claws
¼ cup chopped green onions
½ tsp. curry powder
1 Tbsp. butter or margarine

2 (10¾-oz.) cans cream
  of asparagus soup
2 cups half & half
2 Tbsp. sherry

Cut the crab into bite-size pieces and set aside. Sauté the green onions and curry powder in the butter. Combine with the soup, stir in the half & half and crab and heat through. Stir in the sherry.

Dorothy Stitt
Reservations

## Martha Washington Crab Soup

1 Tbsp. butter
1½ Tbsp. flour
3 eggs, hard-cooked
Grated rind of 1 lemon
Salt and pepper
4 cups milk

1 cup canned or frozen
  crabmeat
⅓ cup heavy cream
½ cup sherry
Worcestershire sauce

Combine the butter, flour, eggs, lemon rind and salt and pepper to taste. In a saucepan, bring the milk to a boil and slowly pour it over the egg mixture, stirring constantly. Add the crabmeat, transfer the mixture to a pot and cook gently for 5 minutes. Stir in the cream and bring the soup to a slow boil. Remove from the heat before it reaches a full boil, stir in the sherry and a dash of Worcestershire sauce.

Note: Do not use cooking sherry in the recipe as it does not have the right flavor.

Serves 6.

Phyllis Lindblad
Reservations

## Fish Stock

1 Tbsp. oil
1 onion, chopped
1 small carrot, sliced
1 clove garlic, chopped
1 tsp. salt
6 peppercorns

3 lbs. sole or turbot fish bones
¾ cup dry white wine
3 quarts water
1 bay leaf
1 thyme leaf
½ cup mushroom trimmings

Heat the oil in a skillet, add the onion and carrot and simmer for 10 minutes. Add the garlic, salt, peppercorns, fish bones and wine and simmer for 3 minutes more. Add the remaining ingredients and simmer uncovered for 1 hour. Strain through a fine cheesecloth.

Makes 2 quarts.

Raoul F. Delbol
Executive Chef
Los Angeles Food Services

## Bay Scallop Chowder

3 medium potatoes, diced
1 small carrot, chopped
1 stalk celery, chopped
1 medium onion, chopped
2 cups chicken stock
½ tsp. salt
¼ tsp. freshly ground pepper
½ bay leaf
½ tsp. crumbled thyme

½ lb. fresh mushrooms,
   sliced
1½ Tbsp. butter
1 lb. fresh bay scallops
½ cup dry white wine
1 cup heavy cream
1 egg yolk, lightly beaten
2 Tbsp. chopped parsley
Paprika

Place the potatoes, carrot, celery and onion in a large pot, cover with the chicken stock and bring to a boil. Add the salt, pepper, bay leaf and thyme. Simmer covered until the vegetables are tender. Remove the bay leaf and transfer the mixture to a blender; blend until smooth. Meanwhile, sauté the mushrooms in the butter. Add the scallops and wine, cook for 1 minute. Stir in the cream mixed with the egg yolk. Combine this mixture with the pureed vegetables and broth. Heat through and serve with a sprinkling of the parsley and paprika.

Susan Warren
Reservations

## Sicilian Meat Ball Soup

1 egg, slightly beaten
1 lb. ground chuck
½ cup soft white bread crumbs
2 Tbsp. freshly chopped
   parsley
2 Tbsp. Parmesan cheese
½ clove garlic, crushed

½ tsp. salt
⅛ tsp. pepper
2 Tbsp. red wine (optional)
3 cans condensed beef
   bouillon
1 (8-oz.) pkg. ribbon noodles

To the beaten egg, add the ground chuck, bread crumbs, parsley, Parmesan cheese, garlic salt, pepper and wine; shape into 36 balls (1 rounded tsp. per ball) and set aside. In a large kettle, bring the beef bouillon plus enough water to make 9 cups liquid to a boil. Add the meatballs, simmer for 5 minutes. Using a slotted spoon, remove the meatballs and set aside. Return the soup to a boil, add the noodles and cook for about 10 minutes, stirring occasionally. Return the meatballs to the soup and simmer for about 5 minutes. Ladle into bowls and, if desired, sprinkle with additional Parmesan cheese and parsley.

*Serves 8.*

Bobbie Sylvain
Passenger Service

## Beef Bouillon or Stock

4 lbs. shank or shin beef
2 large beef bones
3 beef marrow bones
5 quarts cold water
1 Tbsp. salt
4 peppercorns, crushed
4 whole peppercorns
6 white onions, each peeled
   and studded with 1 clove

2 large leeks, each cut
   into 3 pieces
2 stalks celery with leaves,
   each cut into 3 pieces
3 carrots, each peeled and cut
   into 3 pieces
4 sprigs parsley
2 small bay leaves

Place the beef and bones in a very large kettle and add the water (cold water gathers the flavors.) Bring to a boil, then reduce the heat until the water simmers and skim the foam from the surface. Stir in the remaining ingredients and simmer uncovered, stirring frequently and skimming the foam until it stops floating to the surface. Cook for approximately 5 hours, until reduced by at least 1 quart and strain the stock. Refrigerate overnight, then remove and discard the crust of fat on the top. Freeze and/or refrigerate as desired.

*Note: Butchers will usually give away beef bones.*

*Makes 2½ quarts.*

Raoul F. Delbol
Executive Chef
Los Angeles Food Services

### Bloody Mary Soup

2 cups tomato juice
2 cups vegetable cocktail
   juice
¼ cup plus 1 Tbsp. vodka
1 Tbsp. sugar

2 tsp. Worcestershire sauce
1 tsp. salt
½ tsp. freshly ground pepper
3 drops of hot red pepper
   sauce

Combine all the ingredients in a saucepan and heat to boiling, stirring occasionally. Serve hot.

Fran Christensen
Tour Desk

### Creamed Tomato Bisque

½ cup butter or margarine
1 cup chopped celery
1 cup chopped onions
½ cup chopped carrots
⅓ cup all-purpose flour
2 (1-lb. 12-oz.) cans whole
   tomatoes, drained and
   chopped
2 tsp. sugar

1 tsp. basil
1 tsp. marjoram
1 bay leaf
4 cups chicken broth
2 cups heavy cream
½ tsp. paprika
½ tsp. curry powder
¼ tsp. white pepper
Salt to taste

Melt the butter or margarine in a large saucepan. Add the celery, onions and carrots and sauté until tender. Stir in the flour and cook for 2 minutes, stirring constantly. Add the tomatoes, sugar, basil, marjoram, bay leaf and chicken broth. Cover and simmer for 30 minutes, stirring occasionally. Discard the bay leaf. Puree the mixture in thirds in a blender. Add the cream, paprika, curry powder and pepper, stir to blend. Add salt to taste. Serve hot or cold.

Note: This soup may be refrigerated for several days or frozen.

Serves 8.

Annemarie Fleming
Reservations

## French Onion Soup

6 large onions, thinly sliced
½ cup butter
2 cups condensed beef broth
1 soup can water

1 soup can dry white wine
4 slices French bread
4 slices Swiss cheese

Sauté the onions in the butter until lightly browned. Add the broth, water and wine and simmer until the onions are tender. Spoon the soup into 4 earthenware bowls. Top each with a slice of bread and a slice of cheese. Set under the broiler until the cheese melts.

Serves 4.

Norm Groesbeck
Reservations

## Mushroom Soup Supreme

½ lb. mushrooms
2 Tbsp. butter or margarine
2 tsp. lemon juice
1 Tbsp. all-purpose flour
½ tsp. salt

2 envelopes or 2 tsp. instant
    chicken broth
2 egg yolks
1 tsp. sherry

Wash the mushrooms, trim off the stem ends and cut through the caps to make tissue-thin slices. Sauté, stirring often, in the butter or margarine in a medium saucepan for 2 minutes; sprinkle with the lemon juice, tossing lightly to mix. Blend in the flour and salt, stir in 4 cups water and the chicken broth and cook, stirring constantly, until the mixture bubbles, about 3 minutes. Thoroughly beat the egg yolks with the sherry in a small bowl; blend in about ½ cup of the hot mushroom mixture, then stir back into the remaining mixture in the saucepan. Heat, stirring constantly for about 1 minute. Ladle the soup into heated cups or bowls. Serve plain or with crackers.

Serves 6.

Ruth Vantine
Reservations

## Puree of Leek and Potato Soup

4 leeks
2½ Tbsp. butter
1 onion, peeled and diced
5 potatoes, peeled and cut
   into ½" squares
3½ cups hot water

2 tsp. salt
Pinch of white ground pepper
3 cups milk, heated
3 egg yolks (optional)
¾ cup cream (optional)

Remove the green tops and roots from the leeks. Clean the leeks well and dice into ⅓" pieces. (There should be about 1½ cups.) Melt 1½ Tbsp. butter in a large, thick-bottomed pot. Add the leeks and onion, cover and cook slowly for a few minutes until the vegetables are soft but not brown, stirring occasionally with a wooden spoon. Add the potatoes, water, salt and pepper and cook until the potatoes are very soft. Remove the pan from the heat, force the mixture through a sieve or food mill. Bring the soup back to a boil, stirring constantly to prevent scorching. Add the milk and 1 Tbsp. butter. Season to taste.

Note: For a richer soup, beat the egg yolks lightly with the cream. Gradually stir 1 cup of the hot soup into this mixture and return the mixture to the pot, stirring briskly. Bring the soup just to the boiling point, stirring constantly, but do not boil.

Rolf Conrad
Executive Chef
Denver Food Services

## Russian Borscht

1 large head cabbage, chopped
2 (10½-oz.) cans beef bouillon
1 (10½-oz.) can water
2 cans whole red beets,
   chopped

2 medium onions, chopped
½ cup wine vinegar
2 cups sour cream

Boil the cabbage in 1 quart water until tender. Add the beef bouillon and can of water. Add the beets and onions and simmer for 30 minutes. Stir in the vinegar. Serve with dollops of sour cream.

## Broccoli Soup

¼ lb. onions
¼ lb. leeks
½ lb. broccoli
Oil

¼ cup flour
4 cups chicken stock
¼ bay leaf
Salt and pepper

Dice all the vegetables and sauté in oil until tender. Add the flour and cook to a sandy texture. Add the chicken stock and bay leaf; simmer for about 1 hour. Pass through a strainer, making sure that all the ingredients are forced through the sieve. Season with salt and pepper.

Rolf Conrad
Executive Chef
Denver Food Services

## Spinach Soup

2 medium onions, finely diced
2 tsp. butter
½ cup diced bacon
3 Tbsp. flour
2 cups chicken broth, heated

½ cup cooked, chopped
  spinach
Salt and pepper to taste
Nutmeg to taste
½ cup milk or cream
White bread croutons

Sauté the onions in the butter until transparent, add the bacon and sauté for approximately 4 minutes more. Stir in the flour, add the broth and bring to a soft boil. Add the spinach and seasonings and finish with the milk or cream. Adjust the seasoning, if necessary, and serve with the croutons.

Lyell E. Cook
Manager
Detroit Food Services

## Cream of Cauliflower Soup

1 (20-oz.) pkg. frozen
   cauliflower
2 cans cream of celery soup

2 cups milk
4 oz. cheddar cheese, grated

Cook the cauliflower as directed on the package, reserve 1 cup for garnish. Combine the soup and milk in a bowl and pour into the undrained cauliflower; add the cheese. Bring to a boil. Cool and puree in a blender. Return to a saucepan, add the reserved cauliflower and heat through.

Serves 6.

Debbie Erickson
Reservations

☞ To remove excess grease from soups and gravies, drop several ice cubes into the pot. The grease will cling to the cubes and can be easily removed.

# SAUCES
# &
# RELISHES

## Bearnaise Sauce

3 Tbsp. wine vinegar
6 peppercorns
½ bay leaf
1 blade of mace
1 slice onion
2 egg yolks
½ cup butter
Salt

1 tsp. meat glaze
1 tsp. tarragon
1 tsp. chervil
1 tsp. chopped parsley
Pinch of chopped chives or a
little grated onion
Pepper

Put the vinegar, peppercorns, bay leaf, mace and onion in a pan; bring to a boil and boil until reduced to 1 Tbsp. Set aside. Place the yolks in a small bowl with ½ Tbsp. butter and a pinch of salt and beat until thick. Strain in the vinegar mixture and set the bowl in a pan of boiling water; turn off the heat and whisk vigorously until it begins to thicken. Add the remaining butter, softened, in small pieces, beating well after each addition. Add the meat glaze, herbs and chives or grated onion and season with pepper. The finished sauce should have the consistency of whipped cream.

*Makes ¾ cup, enough for 4 steaks.*

Jackie Partlow

## Mornay Sauce

3 Tbsp. butter
2 Tbsp. flour
2 cups milk

Salt and pepper to taste
½ cup grated cheese
Pinch of dry mustard

Melt the butter in a saucepan, remove from the heat and stir in the flour. Pour in 1 cup milk and blend until smooth with a whisk or wooden spoon. Add the remaining milk, season lightly with salt and pepper and bring to a boil, stirring constantly. Simmer for 2 minutes, remove from the heat and gradually stir in the cheese and dry mustard.

*Makes 2 cups.*

## Bordelaise Sauce

2 shallots or scallions,
   finely chopped
1 cup Bordeaux wine
1 small sprig of thyme or
   1 pinch of dried thyme
1 small bay leaf

1 cup **Espagnola Sauce**,
   preferably made with white
   bone stock (see index)
Bone stock, chilled
1 tsp. arrowroot, mixed to a
   paste with 1 Tbsp. stock
1 to 2 marrow bones or
   1½ Tbsp. butter

Put the shallots, wine and herbs in a pan, simmer until reduced by about one-third, then add to the prepared **Espagnola Sauce**. Bring to a boil and simmer for 6 to 7 minutes, skimming well. Add a little cold bone stock to help in the skimming. When the flavor is strong and good, thicken, if necessary, with the arrowroot paste. Strain into a clean pot and keep warm. With a knife dipped in hot water, scoop the marrow from the bone and cut into small cubes. Poach for 6 to 7 minutes in simmering water, drain carefully on paper towels and add to the sauce just before serving. If marrow is not available, cut the butter into small pieces and briskly stir it into the sauce just before serving. Serve with broiled or roast beef.

Makes 1 cup.

## Provençale Sauce

½ cup diced onions
Pinch of crushed fresh garlic
1 Tbsp. olive oil
1 bay leaf
Pinch of thyme

1 cup diced ripe California
   tomatoes
2 Tbsp. imported Parmesan
   cheese

Sauté the onions and garlic in the olive oil until lightly browned; add the bay leaf, thyme and tomatoes. Simmer for 20 minutes, add the Parmesan cheese and serve with fish, meat, chicken or eggs.

Hans Jantzen
Executive Chef
New York Food Services

## Hollandaise Sauce

¼ cup white wine vinegar
6 peppercorns
1 blade of mace
1 slice onion
1 small bay leaf
3 egg yolks

¾ cup unsalted butter, at
   room temperature
Salt
1 to 2 Tbsp. light cream or milk
Dash of lemon juice
   (optional)

In a small pan, boil the vinegar with the peppercorns, mace, onion and bay leaf until reduced to a scant Tbsp. Set aside. With a wooden spoon, beat the egg yolks in a bowl with ½ Tbsp. butter and a pinch of salt until light and slightly thick. Strain the vinegar into the eggs, set the bowl in a pan of boiling water, turn off the heat and add the remaining butter in small pieces, whisking vigorously. When all the butter has been added and the sauce is thick, add the cream or milk and lemon juice. The sauce should be pleasantly sharp, yet bland, and should have the consistency of heavy cream.

*Note: Hollandaise sauce is often flavored with lemon juice, but this version uses seasoned, reduced vinegar instead to add a mellow touch to the sauce. If you prefer, substitute lemon juice for the vinegar and spices.*

*Makes 1 cup.*

Jackie Partlow

## Elegant Sauce for Ham

1 large can sliced peaches
1 large can sliced pears
1 large can sliced pineapple
¼ cup butter

2½ Tbsp. cornstarch
2½ Tbsp. brown sugar
2 tsp. curry powder or to taste

Drain the juices from the peaches, pears and pineapple and combine to make 2 cups juice. Cook the juice, butter, cornstarch, brown sugar and curry powder until thick. Pour over the fruit and serve hot over ham.

## Sauce Poivrade

½ cup butter
½ cup chopped onions
½ cup chopped celery
½ cup chopped carrots
¼ cup chopped ham
½ tsp. thyme

1 bay leaf
1 cup Madeira wine
1 cup brown stock
1 Tbsp. tomato paste
Freshly ground black pepper

Heat ¼ cup butter in a saucepan. Add the onions, celery, carrots, ham, thyme and bay leaf and fry until the vegetables are lightly browned. Add the wine, reduce to two-thirds, then add the stock and tomato paste; cook slowly for 1 hour. Remove from the heat, strain and add the pepper and ¼ cup softened butter. Serve with meat dishes.

Hans Jantzen
Executive Chef
New York Food Services

## Sauce Café de Paris

1 cup sweet butter, softened
2 Tbsp. beef base
½ tsp. salt
2 Tbsp. dry mustard
½ tsp. MSG
2 Tbsp. finely chopped parsley
1 Tbsp. ground sage

1 clove garlic, finely chopped
¼ tsp. ground thyme
Juice of 1 ½ lemons
½ tsp. Tabasco sauce
1 Tbsp. Worcestershire sauce
¼ tsp. freshly ground pepper

Combine all the ingredients and whip. Serve lukewarm.

Hans Jantzen
Executive Chef
New York Food Services

## Espagnola Sauce

¼ cup plus 2 Tbsp. oil
1 small onion, finely diced
1 carrot, finely diced
1 celery stalk, finely diced
3 Tbsp. flour
1 tsp. tomato paste

2 Tbsp. chopped mushroom
   stalks or 1 mushroom,
   chopped
5 cups well-flavored brown
   stock, chilled
Bouquet garni
Salt
Pepper

In a saucepan, heat the oil and add the diced vegetables. Reduce the heat and cook gently until the vegetables are tender. They will shrink slightly at this point. Stir in the flour and brown it slowly, stirring occasionally with a wire whisk or metal spoon and scraping the flour well from the bottom of the pan. When it is brown, remove from the heat and cool slightly. (The flour should be cooked until dark brown, but do not allow it to burn.) Stir in the tomato paste, mushrooms, 4 cups stock, bouquet garni and seasoning. Bring to a boil, whisking constantly, then reduce the heat, partially cover the pan and cook for 35 to 40 minutes. During this time, skim off any scum that rises to the surface. Add half the remaining stock, bring to a boil again and skim. Simmer for 5 minutes, add the remaining stock, bring to a boil and skim again. (The addition of cold stock accelerates the rising of scum and so helps to clear the sauce.) Cook for 5 minutes more, then strain, pressing the vegetables gently to extract the juice. Clean the pan and return the sauce to it. Partially cover the pan and continue to simmer the sauce until it is very glossy and the consistency of heavy cream. It is now ready to be used alone or as a base for any of a number of sauces.

*Note: When serving broiled steak, a Tbsp. of* **Espagnola Sauce** *added to the gravy or mixed with the juices in the broiler pan makes a delicious accompaniment.*

*Makes 2 cups.*

Marianne Shute

☞ *In a hurry? Add a tablespoon of liquid coffee to a gravy base, and it will brown more quickly without tasting like coffee.*

# Choron Sauce for Poached Salmon

3 Tbsp. wine vinegar
6 peppercorns
½ bay leaf
1 blade of mace
1 slice onion
2 egg yolks
½ cup butter, softened

Salt
1 tsp. meat glaze
2 Tbsp. tomato paste
1 tsp. chopped parsley
Pinch of chopped chives or
    a little grated onion
Pepper

Put the vinegar, peppercorns, bay leaf, mace and onion in a pan; boil until reduced to 1 Tbsp. and set aside. Place the yolks in a small bowl with ½ Tbsp. softened butter and a pinch of salt and beat until thick. Strain in the vinegar mixture, set the bowl in a pan of boiling water, turn off the heat and stir until the mixture begins to thicken. Add the remaining softened butter in small pieces, beating well after each addition. Add the meat glaze, tomato paste, parsley and chives or onion and season with pepper. The finished sauce should have the consistency of whipped cream.

*May also be served over broiled beef steaks.*

*Makes ¾ cup.*

# Teriyaki Sauce #1

1 cup soy sauce
3 (¼") slices fresh ginger
¼ onion, sliced
2 cloves garlic, crushed

¼ tsp. ground black pepper
1 tsp. sugar
¼ tsp. Aji-No-Moto (MSG)

Combine all the ingredients and let stand for approximately 1 hour to blend together. Use as a marinade for meat. Especially good with top sirloin, cut into 3" x 1" pieces which are woven through bamboo skewers, marinated for 45 minutes in the sauce and then drained and broiled. Be especially sure not to overcook the meat when using this sauce.

Hans Jantzen
Executive Chef
New York Food Services

## Teriyaki Sauce #2

1 cup brown sugar
½ cup sugar
2 tsp. salt
½ tsp. black pepper
1 tsp. Lawry's seasoned salt
1 tsp. MSG

¼ cup soy sauce
½ cup cooking sherry
Pinch of crushed ginger
2 cloves garlic, finely chopped
½ tsp. dry mustard

Combine all the ingredients and stir until the sugar is completely dissolved. Let the sauce stand in a container or jar for a couple of days before using, so that all the ingredients blend. Can be served hot over rice or on the side as a meat dip.

*Note: Always store the sauce in the refrigerator as it will keep for weeks, and it can be reused after each marinade. Simply pour it back into the jar. When the sauce becomes too thin, it is time to make up another batch. By doubling this recipe you will get exactly 1 quart.*

Harry G. Irell
Supervisor
Food Services

## Shirley Sauce

24 medium tomatoes, peeled
  and chopped
4 green peppers, chopped
4 onions, peeled and chopped
2 cups chopped celery

2 Tbsp. mustard seed
1 Tbsp. celery seed
2 cups sugar
3 cups vinegar
3½ Tbsp. salt

Combine all the ingredients in a heavy kettle, bring to a boil, reduce the heat and boil slowly for 2 hours or until slightly thickened, stirring occasionally. Pour into jars and seal.

*Makes 3 quarts.*

Jan Taylor
Reservations
Brandon Taylor
Group Desk

### Zucchini Hot Salsa Sauce

3 cups ground onions
3½ cups ground Anaheim
  peppers (about 25)
10 cups ground zucchini
¼ cup plus 1 Tbsp. salt
1 Tbsp. garlic powder
1 Tbsp. cumin
1 cup brown sugar

1 Tbsp. cornstarch
2 tsp. dry mustard
2 cups vinegar
1 Tbsp. crushed red peppers
1 tsp. nutmeg
1 tsp. coarse pepper
1 tsp. turmeric
5 cups ground tomatoes

Combine the onions, peppers and zucchini, add the salt and let sit overnight. The next morning, transfer to a colander and rinse thoroughly. Combine with all the remaining ingredients in a saucepan over medium heat, bring to a boil and boil for 30 minutes. Seal in hot jars.

Note:  10 small red peppers and 2 green peppers may be substituted for the Anaheim and crushed red peppers.

Sarina Ames, Sr.
Reservations

### Barbeque Sauce #1

1 medium onion,
  finely chopped
2 Tbsp. margarine
2 Tbsp. vinegar
¼ cup lemon juice
3 Tbsp. Worcestershire or
  A-1 sauce

2 Tbsp. brown sugar
1 cup catsup
1 cup water
Salt
Pepper
Pinch of red pepper

Brown the onion in the margarine. Add the remaining ingredients. Stir over medium heat until thick and bubbly.

Kathy Morgan
Inflight Services

### Barbeque Sauce #2

1 tsp. salt
¼ tsp. pepper
1 tsp. paprika
1 Tbsp. sugar
1 clove garlic, crushed

½ cup chopped onions
½ cup water
1 cup catsup
¼ cup lemon juice
2 Tbsp. butter

Combine the first 8 ingredients in a saucepan over medium heat. Heat to boiling, reduce the heat and simmer uncovered for 20 minutes. Remove from the heat, add the lemon juice and butter. Blend well.

*Makes about 2½ cups.*

David Rieman
Passenger Service

### Best Barbeque Sauce

1 large can tomato sauce
¼ cup brown sugar
1 tsp. mustard

¼ tsp. salt
Dash of garlic salt or powder

Combine all the ingredients and pour over selected meat; bake or barbeque. Good with ribs or chicken.

Sheldon Best
Regional Vice President
Seattle

### Piquant Marinade for Beef Steaks

1 cup tomato juice
¼ cup olive oil
½ green bell pepper, cored,
    seeded and finely chopped

½ red bell pepper, cored,
    seeded and finely chopped
2 cloves garlic, crushed
1 tsp. chili powder
1 tsp. Worcestershire sauce

Combine all the ingredients in a saucepan, bring to a boil and simmer for 10 minutes. Cool and pour over the steaks. Cover and refrigerate for 2 to 3 hours, turning the meat once or twice. Drain and pat the steaks dry with paper towels before broiling.

### Marinade for Beef

2 cloves garlic, peeled
2 medium onions, thinly sliced
2 medium carrots, thinly sliced
2 stalks celery, thinly sliced

10 to 12 peppercorns
Bouquet garni
3 Tbsp. olive oil
1½ cups burgundy wine

Mince the garlic and combine with the remaining ingredients. Cover and bring to a boil. Simmer for 2 minutes, pour into a bowl and cool.

*Makes enough marinade for a 3- to 4-lb. cut.*

### Meat Marinade

1½ cups salad oil
¾ cup soy sauce
¼ tsp. Worcestershire sauce
2 Tbsp. dry mustard
2½ tsp. salt
1½ tsp. parsley flakes

1 Tbsp. pepper
½ cup vinegar
1 clove garlic, crushed
⅓ cup lemon juice
1 Tbsp. chopped ginger root
  or ¼ to ½ tsp. ground ginger

Blend all the ingredients together in a blender for 30 to 40 seconds. Store covered in the refrigerator until ready to use.

*Makes 3½ cups and keeps for 4 weeks in the refrigerator.*

Julie Jacobson
Reservations

### Spiced Marinade for Lamb

½ tsp. ground ginger
½ tsp. ground turmeric
½ tsp. ground allspice
½ tsp. curry powder

1 clove garlic, crushed
1 tsp. lemon juice
¼ cup plus 2 Tbsp. yogurt or
  sour cream

Combine all the ingredients and brush or toss the meat with the mixture. Refrigerate for 2 to 3 hours before broiling.

## Sauté Marinade for Chicken or Pork

1 tsp. ground caraway
1 tsp. ground coriander
1 clove garlic, minced
1 Tbsp. dark brown sugar

2 Tbsp. soy sauce
1 Tbsp. lemon juice
Salt and pepper to taste

Combine all the ingredients and mix well. Use as a marinade for pork or chicken which are especially good if diced, marinated for 1 to 2 hours, threaded on bamboo skewers and broiled or barbequed.

## Marinade for Game

2 cloves garlic, peeled
2 medium onions, thinly sliced
2 medium carrots, thinly sliced
2 stalks celery, thinly sliced
10 to 12 peppercorns
3 Tbsp. olive oil

1½ cups burgundy wine
3 Tbsp. red wine vinegar
3 strips of lemon rind
8 allspice or juniper berries,
    crushed

Mince the garlic and combine with the remaining ingredients. Cover and bring to a boil. Simmer for 2 minutes, pour into a bowl and cool before using.

*Also good with pork.*

## Fresh Chutney

1 medium tart apple
1 small onion
2 tomatoes, peeled, seeded
    and chopped
1 clove garlic, crushed with
    1 tsp. salt
1 slice canned pimento,
    chopped

3 Tbsp. chopped celery
1 Tbsp. chopped mint
1 Tbsp. grated fresh
    horseradish or 2 Tbsp.
    prepared horseradish
1 Tbsp. sugar
2 Tbsp. wine vinegar

Pare and core the apple and work it through a food mill with the onion. Combine with all the remaining ingredients in a saucepan and cook, stirring, for 2 to 3 minutes. Serve the chutney hot or cold.

## Rhubarb Relish

4 cups finely chopped rhubarb
4 cups finely chopped onions
2 cups white vinegar
1 Tbsp. salt
1 tsp. cinnamon

1 tsp. cloves
¼ tsp. cayenne
½ tsp. paprika
½ tsp. celery salt
½ tsp. steak sauce

Combine all the ingredients. Bring to a boil, reduce the heat and simmer until thick, stirring occasionally. Spoon into canning jars and seal.

*Note: Chop or grind the rhubarb and onions in a meat grinder or blender.*

Pat Logue
Reservations

## Watermelon Relish

1 (20-lb.) watermelon
4 cups sugar
2 cups cider vinegar
2 limes, thinly sliced

½ cup lime juice
1 tsp. whole cloves
2 (1") cinnamon sticks

Cut the watermelon meat into chunks. Place about 1 cup of the chunks at a time in a square of double-thickness cheesecloth and squeeze out the liquid. Remove the seeds and measure the pulp; you should have about 14 cups. Place the pulp in a large kettle. Stir in the sugar and vinegar. Bring to a boil, lower the heat and simmer, stirring often, for 30 minutes. While the pulp is simmering, bring the limes to a boil in 2 changes of water (to remove bitterness); drain. Add the limes, lime juice, cloves and cinnamon to the watermelon and cook, stirring often, for 30 minutes more or until the relish is thick. Ladle into 8 hot, sterilized half-pint jars to within ¼" of the rim. Seal as the manufacturer directs; process in a hot water bath for 20 minutes. Label, date and store in a cool, dry place.

*Makes 8 half-pints.*

Ruth Vantine
Reservations

### Zucchini Relish

10 cups chopped zucchini
4 cups chopped onions
¼ cup plus 1 Tbsp. salt
2½ cups dark vinegar
6 cups sugar
1 tsp. nutmeg
1 tsp. dry mustard

1 tsp. turmeric
1 Tbsp. cornstarch
2 tsp. celery seeds
½ tsp. pepper
1 red pepper, finely chopped
1 green pepper, finely chopped

Combine the first 3 ingredients and let sit overnight. The next morning, drain, then rinse in cool water. Add the remaining ingredients to the vegetables. Mix well and cook for 30 minutes. Seal in jars.

*Makes 6 pints.*

Tethi Poulos
Reservations

### Grandma's Hamburger Goop Relish

1 crate tomatoes (approx. 16 lbs.), peeled and chopped
6 large onions, chopped
6 green peppers, chopped
12 ears corn (optional)

¼ cup plus 2 Tbsp. salt
1 Tbsp. red chili peppers
1 Tbsp. mixed pickling spice
6 cups vinegar (approx.)
6 cups sugar (approx.)

Combine the first 5 ingredients in a saucepan. Place the chili peppers and pickling spice in a spiceball and add to the vegetables. Cook slowly for 3 to 6 hours or until the mixture thickens considerably. Add the vinegar and sugar, alternating, about one cup at a time, until the balance of sweetness to sourness suits you. (Use the 6 cups as a guide only, as each batch is different.) Cook for several more hours, stirring frequently, as the sugar makes the mixture more prone to burn. The mixture will be quite thick and reduced to about one-half of the original volume when done. Seal in canning jars according to the manufacturer's instructions.

*Makes about 12 pints.*

Rick Sanders
Reservations

## Martha's Cabbage and Celery Relish

| | |
|---|---|
| 4 large cabbages | ½ cup dry mustard |
| 3 bunches celery | 9 cups packed brown sugar |
| 8 onions | 1 cup white mustard seed |
| 3 red peppers | Vinegar, chilled |
| Salt | |

Shred the cabbage and cut the celery as for a salad. Finely chop the onions and peppers. Layer the vegetables, salting each layer, and let stand for 24 hours. Drain and rinse out the salt, squeeze out the water and add the dry mustard, brown sugar and mustard seed. Cover with vinegar. Refrigerate for 2 to 3 days before using.

Rick Sanders
Reservations

## Cucumber Relish

| | |
|---|---|
| 6 large cucumbers | 1 Tbsp. mixed spices |
| 1 Tbsp. salt | 1 stick cinnamon |
| 1 cup vinegar | 1 piece ginger |
| 1½ cups sugar | |

Peel and cut the cucumbers lengthwise. Remove the seeds and slice crosswise to ½" thickness. Soak for a few hours in 8 cups water combined with the salt. Combine the vinegar, ½ cup water, the sugar and spices, add the cucumber pieces and boil for 20 to 30 minutes; cool. Store in the refrigerator until ready to serve.

Catherine Lakey
Reservations

## Cranberry Relish

1 lb. fresh cranberries                    3 apples
1 orange                                   1 ½ lbs. sugar

Run the cranberries through a food chopper. Quarter the orange and remove the seeds, but do not peel. Core the apples, quarter and run the orange and apples through the chopper. Combine all the fruit together, add the sugar and mix well. Chill in the refrigerator for at least 3 hours before serving.

Hans Jantzen
Executive Chef
New York Food Services

## Cranberry Sauce

2 cups sugar                              4 cups cranberries

Combine the sugar with 2 cups water in a saucepan and stir until the sugar is dissolved. Heat to boiling and boil for 5 minutes. Add the cranberries, cook until the skins pop, about 5 minutes more, and remove from the heat. Serve the sauce warm or chilled.

Makes 4 cups.

Kathy Morgan
Inflight Services

☞ To eliminate rummaging around for loose spices in soups or sauces, place them in the pan in a metal tea ball. When ready to serve, simply remove the ball and discard its contents.

# BREADS

## Honey Whole Wheat Bread

1 cup milk
¾ cup shortening
½ cup honey
2 tsp. salt
¾ cup warm water
  (105° to 115°)

2 pkg. active dry yeast
3 eggs, slightly beaten
4½ cups unsifted all-purpose
  flour
1½ cups whole wheat flour
1 tsp. soft butter

In a small saucepan, heat the milk until bubbles form around the edge of the pan. Remove from the heat and add the shortening, honey and salt, stirring until the shortening is melted. Let the mixture cool to luke-warm or tepid. Pour the warm water into a large bowl, sprinkle in the yeast and stir until the yeast is dissolved. Stir in the milk mixture and the eggs. Combine the flours, add two-thirds of the flour mixture to the yeast mixture and beat with an electric mixer at low speed until blended. Then beat at medium speed until smooth, about 2 minutes. With a wooden spoon, gradually beat in the remaining flour mixture. Mix by hand, squeezing the dough between your fingers 20 to 30 times to develop gluten. Cover the bowl with wax paper and a towel. Set the dough in a warm place, free from drafts, until the dough rises above the rim of the bowl, about 1 hour. Punch the dough down, beat with a spoon until smooth, about 30 seconds. Lightly grease a 3-quart casserole or heat-proof bowl. Turn the dough into the casserole, patting evenly. Cover and let rise until it doubles in bulk and rises slightly above the casserole, about 40 to 50 minutes. With a sharp knife, cut a 4" cross about ½" deep in the top of the dough. Bake at 375° for 45 to 50 minutes or until the bread is browned and sounds hollow when rapped with your knuckles. Remove to a wire rack, rub the butter over the top. Cut into wedges and serve warm.

Note: To freeze: cool, wrap in foil and freeze. To serve: thaw at room temperature for several hours and reheat at 325° for 30 minutes.

Makes 1 loaf.

Bill Fudge
Manager
Reservations

## Ninety-Minute Whole Wheat Bread

4 yeast cakes
4 cups warm water
1 Tbsp. plus 1 tsp. salt

½ cup sugar
¼ cup melted shortening
7 to 8 cups whole wheat flour

Dissolve the yeast in 1 cup water. Mix in the remaining ingredients, adding the flour to make a soft but not sticky dough. Cut into 4 pieces and let stand for 15 minutes. Using the handle of a butcher knife or any other heavy, mallet-like instrument, pound each piece of dough for 1 minute. Form into 4 loaves and put each loaf in a greased bread pan; let stand for 30 minutes. Bake at 400° for 30 minutes.

Nola Sears
Reservations

## Dilly Bread

1 pkg. active dry yeast
¼ cup warm water
1 cup cottage cheese, at a
    lukewarm temperature
2 Tbsp. sugar
1 Tbsp. instant minced onion

1 Tbsp. butter
2 tsp. dill seed
¼ tsp. soda
1 egg
1 tsp. salt
2¼ cups flour

Soften the yeast in the water and let stand for 5 minutes. Add the cottage cheese. Combine the remaining ingredients except the flour and add to the yeast. Then add the flour and beat well. Let the dough rise until doubled in size, about 1 hour. Knead well, put in an 8" round casserole dish and let rise again. Bake at 350° for 40 to 50 minutes.

Lillian Warren

## Aunt Lulu's Rye Bread

2⅓ cups warm water
2 pkg. active dry yeast
¼ cup molasses
2 tsp. salt

2 Tbsp. shortening
⅓ cup sugar
3 cups rye flour
3 to 4 cups white flour

Combine the water and yeast in a mixing bowl. Stir in the remaining ingredients except the white flour. Add the white flour, a little at a time, until the dough is stiff. Turn onto a floured board and knead to a firm dough. Place in a greased bowl, cover and let stand until it rises. Form the dough into 2 loaves and place in greased pans. Let rise until doubled in bulk, about 1 hour. Bake at 400° for 50 minutes.

Mrs. John Brice
Wife of John Brice, Trainer

## Swedish Rye Bread

1 pkg. active dry yeast
¼ cup warm water (110°)
¼ cup brown sugar
¼ cup light molasses
1 Tbsp. salt
2 Tbsp. shortening
1½ cups hot water

2½ cups stirred medium rye
   flour
3 Tbsp. caraway seeds or
   2 Tbsp. grated orange peel
3½ to 4 cups sifted all-purpose
   flour
Melted butter

Soften the yeast in the warm water. In a large bowl, combine the sugar, molasses, salt and shortening. Add the hot water and stir until the sugar dissolves. Cool to lukewarm. Add the rye flour and beat well. Add the softened yeast and caraway seeds or orange peel; mix well. Stir in enough all-purpose flour to make a moderately stiff dough. Knead on a well-floured surface until smooth and satiny, about 10 minutes. Place the dough in a lightly greased bowl, turning once to grease the surface. Cover, let rise in a warm place until doubled, about 1½ to 2 hours. Punch down and turn out on a lightly floured surface; divide into 2 portions. Shape each half into a small ball, cover and let stand for 10 minutes. Pat the dough into 2 round loaves and place on a greased baking sheet or shape the dough into 2 oblong loaves and place in greased, 8½" x 4½" x 2½" loaf pans. Cover and let rise in a warm place until doubled in bulk. Bake at 375° for about 25 to 30 minutes. For a soft crust, place foil loosely over the top of the loaves for the last 10 minutes. Brush with melted butter and cool on a rack.

*Makes 2 loaves.*

LaVaun Hinton
Sales

## Sourdough Starter

¼ cup milk
2 tsp. salad oil
1 pkg. active dry yeast

2 tsp. sugar
1¼ tsp. salt
2⅓ cups flour

Combine the milk and oil with ½ cup water and bring to a boil; cool. Sprinkle the yeast in ¼ cup warm water, add to the milk mixture, stir in the sugar, salt and flour. Cover and let stand in a warm place for 12 to 18 hours to sour. Keep covered in the refrigerator until used. The starter must be used every 1 to 2 weeks and must not be allowed to warm for more than 2 hours at a time once it has been refrigerated.

Susan Warren
Reservations

## Malco's Sourdough Bread

1 cup **Sourdough Starter**
9½ cups all-purpose flour
   (approx.)
2 cups warm water
2 Tbsp. butter
2 cups warm milk

1 pkg. active dry yeast
¼ cup honey
¼ cup wheat germ
2 Tbsp. sugar
2½ Tbsp. salt
2 Tbsp. soda

The day before, mix together the starter, 2½ cups flour and the water. Cover loosely and let stand overnight. The next morning, melt 1 Tbsp. butter, add to the warm milk and stir in the yeast until dissolved. Add the honey and, when thoroughly mixed, add 2 cups flour and stir in the wheat germ. Sprinkle the sugar, salt and soda over, gently press into the dough and lightly mix. Allow to stand for 30 to 50 minutes until the mixture is bubbly. Add more flour until the dough cannot be stirred. Place on a floured table and knead 100 times or until a silky texture develops. Form into 1-lb. loaves, place in well-greased, 9" x 5" metal pans and allow the loaves to double in size. In a warm room, this will take 2½ to 3 hours. Bake at 400° for 20 minutes. Reduce the temperature to 325° and bake for 20 minutes more. When thoroughly baked, remove the bread from the pans and place on a rack to cool. Butter the top of the loaves with the remaining butter to prevent excess crustiness.

*The starter should be light and bubbly before mixing with the other ingredients. By experimenting, each cook can develop his own recipe.*

Hubert Malco
Pastry Chef
Seattle Food Services

## Quick Hot Dinner Rolls

*¾ cup warm water*
*1 pkg. active dry yeast*

*2½ cups prepared biscuit mix*
*Melted butter or margarine*

Put the water in a large mixing bowl and sprinkle in the yeast. Stir until dissolved. Add the biscuit mix and beat vigorously for 1 minute. Turn onto a floured board and knead 20 times. Let the dough stand for 5 to 10 minutes. Pull off pieces and shape into 2" balls, dip in melted butter or margarine and place in a greased, 9" layer cake pan, letting the balls almost touch. Cover, let rise in a warm place, free from drafts, until doubled in bulk, about 40 minutes. Bake at 400° for 20 minutes or until golden brown.

Linda Rice
Reservations

## Hot Cheese Onion Bread

*2 pkg. active dry yeast*
*⅓ cup very warm water*
*1 (10½-oz.) can condensed*
  *onion soup*

*4 cups biscuit mix*
*⅓ cup grated cheddar cheese*
*1 Tbsp. sesame seeds*

Sprinkle the yeast in the water, stirring until dissolved, and stir in the onion soup. Add the biscuit mix and stir until well blended. Spread in a greased, 9" square pan, sprinkle with the cheese and seeds. Cover and let rise in a warm place for 30 minutes. Bake at 400° for 25 to 35 minutes.

Linda Rice
Reservations

## Pao Doce
### (Sweet Bread)

2 pkg. active dry yeast
1¾ cups plus 3 Tbsp. sugar
½ cup lukewarm potato water
1 cup mashed potatoes
⅛ tsp. ginger

¾ cup milk
2 tsp. salt
8 eggs (approx.)
½ cup melted butter, cooled
8 cups flour

Stir the yeast and 3 Tbsp. sugar into the potato water until dissolved. Blend in the potatoes and ginger and set aside to rise until doubled in bulk. Scald the milk, add the salt and set aside to cool to lukewarm. Beat 6 eggs and gradually add the remaining sugar while continuing to beat; stir in the butter. Combine the yeast and egg mixtures, blending thoroughly. Stir in 2 cups flour, add the milk and heat until blended. Add 2 more cups flour and beat for 5 minutes. Add the remaining flour gradually, kneading when the dough becomes too stiff to beat. Turn out onto a floured board and knead for 10 minutes. Place the dough in an oiled bowl, roll to grease all the sides, cover and let rise until doubled. Divide the dough into 4 portions and shape into round loaves on greased baking sheets or place in greased loaf pans. Allow to rise until doubled. Brush the loaves with additional beaten eggs and bake at 350° for 20 minutes, reduce the heat to 325° and bake for 20 minutes more or until brown.

Makes 4 loaves.

Yvonne Erickson
Reservations

## Portuguese Sweet Bread

2 yeast cakes
2 cups fresh milk, warmed
1 cup mashed potatoes
⅛ tsp. salt
2 cups sugar

1 cup butter
6 eggs
8 cups flour
Beaten egg whites or milk

Dissolve the yeast in a small amount of milk, then mix with the potatoes. Stir the remaining ingredients except the beaten egg whites or milk into the potato mixture and mix well. Cover the dough with a heavy cloth and set in a warm place to rise until doubled in bulk. Pinch the dough off in large sections, shape into rounds and place in greased round or loaf pans. Before baking, brush the loaves with egg whites or milk. Bake at 375° for 45 minutes or until browned.

Sue Crane
Reservations

## Sally Lunn

**Sally Lunn**, *a pride of southern cooks, is named after a young 18th century woman who sold the warm, crumbly bread that bears her name by "crying" it in the streets of England's fashionable spa, Bath. A respectable baker and musician bought her business and wrote a song about her. The song is forgotten, but Sally has a place in the* Oxford English Dictionary, *and hers was a household name in the colonies.*

| | |
|---|---|
| *1 cup milk* | *2 tsp. salt* |
| *½ cup shortening* | *2 pkg. active dry yeast* |
| *4 cups sifted all-purpose flour* | *3 eggs* |
| *⅓ cup sugar* | |

Heat the milk, shortening, and ¼ cup water until very warm, about 120°; the shortening does not need to melt. In a large bowl, blend 1⅓ cups flour, the sugar, salt and yeast. Blend the warm liquids into the flour mixture and beat with an electric mixer at medium speed for about 2 minutes, scraping the sides of the bowl occasionally. Gradually add ⅔ cup of the remaining flour and the eggs and beat at high speed for 2 minutes. Add the remaining flour and mix well; the batter will be thick, but not stiff. Cover and let rise in a warm, draft-free place (about 85°) until doubled in bulk, about 1 hour and 15 minutes. Beat the dough down with a spatula or with an electric mixer set at the lowest speed and turn into a greased, 10" tube or bundt pan. Cover and let rise in a warm, draft-free place until increased in bulk by one-third to one-half, about 30 minutes. Bake at 350° for 40 to 50 minutes. Run a knife around the center and outer edges of the bread and turn onto a plate to cool.

Barb Cantrell
Supervisor

## Hot Roll Monkey Bread

1 pkg. Pillsbury hot roll mix
¾ cup very warm water
    (105° to 115°)
½ tsp. salt

2 eggs
⅓ cup butter or margarine,
    melted
Dill weed (optional)

In a large bowl, dissolve the yeast from the hot roll mix in the warm water; stir in the salt and eggs. Add the hot roll mix, blend well. Cover, let rise in a warm place until light and doubled in size, about 30 to 45 minutes. Using a solid shortening or margarine (not oil), grease a 12-cup, fluted tube pan. On a floured surface, toss the dough until no longer sticky; press or roll the dough into a 15" x 12" rectangle. Using a pastry wheel or sharp knife, cut the dough into 2" to 2½" diamond-shaped pieces. Dip each piece in the butter and layer in the greased pan, overlapping the pieces. Sprinkle each layer with dill weed. Cover, let rise again in a warm place until light and doubled in size, about 20 to 30 minutes. Bake at 400° for 20 to 25 minutes or until a deep golden brown. Cool upright in the pan for 2 minutes, then turn onto a serving plate. Serve warm.

Makes a 10" pull-apart loaf.

Linda Rice
Reservations

## Gooey Rolls

½ cup Crisco
¼ cup plus 2 Tbsp. sugar
½ cup boiling water
1 pkg. active dry yeast
½ cup warm water
1 tsp. salt

3½ cups flour

**Brown Sugar Spread:**
½ cup packed brown sugar
3 Tbsp. melted butter
1 Tbsp. water

Blend the Crisco and sugar and add the boiling water; cool to lukewarm. Soak the yeast in the warm water and add to the cooled sugar mixture. Sift together the salt and flour. Add to the yeast mixture, 1 cup at a time, beating well after each addition. Cover and set in the refrigerator overnight. Roll the dough out and spread evenly with **Brown Sugar Spread**, reserving ¼ cup. Roll up the dough and slice into 24 rolls. Put about ½ tsp. reserved spread in greased muffin tins and set a roll on top. Let the rolls rise until the dough is doubled in size, about 2 hours. Bake at 400° for 20 to 25 minutes.

**Brown Sugar Spread:** Combine all the ingredients and stir over low heat until the sugar dissolves.

*Note: Do not bake the* **Gooey Rolls** *too dark.*

Debbie Erickson
Reservations

## Whole Wheat Croissants

1 pkg. active dry yeast
1 cup warm water
¾ cup evaporated milk
1½ tsp. salt
⅓ cup honey

2 eggs
3 cups whole wheat flour
1¼ cups firm butter
3 cups all-purpose or
    unbleached flour

In a large bowl dissolve the yeast in the water. Add the milk, salt, honey, 1 egg and 2 cups whole wheat flour. Melt and cool ¼ cup butter, stir into the flour mixture and set aside. In another large bowl, stir together the remaining whole wheat flour and the all-purpose or unbleached flour. With a pastry blender or two knives, cut in the 1 cup firm butter until the particles are the size of peas. Pour the yeast batter into the butter/flour mixture and gently stir until the flour is evenly moistened. Cover with plastic wrap and refrigerate for at least 4 hours or up to 4 days. Turn the dough out onto a well-floured board and knead for about 5 minutes. Divide the dough into 4 equal parts. Working with 1 part at a time (keep the remaining dough covered in the refrigerator), roll out on a well-floured board into a 17" circle; the dough will be stiff. Using a sharp knife, cut into 8 equal wedges. For each croissant, loosely roll a wedge toward its point. Shape into crescents and place, point down, 1½" apart on an ungreased baking sheet. Cover with plastic wrap and let rise at room temperature in a draft-free place until almost doubled, about 2 hours. Beat 1 egg with 1 Tbsp. water and brush over the croissants. Bake at 325° for 25 minutes or until lightly browned. Cool thoroughly on racks or serve warm.

Debbie Erickson
Reservations

## Swedish Coffee Bread

2 pkg. active dry yeast
2½ cups lukewarm milk
1 cup sugar
2 eggs
½ tsp. salt

1 cup melted butter
20 cardamon seeds, pounded
8 cups flour
Slivered almonds

Dissolve the yeast in ½ cup milk. Combine the remaining milk, sugar, 1 egg, salt, butter, cardamon seeds and a small amount of flour and beat until smooth. Add the yeast and remaining flour, beating with a wooden spoon until smooth and firm. Sprinkle the dough with a small amount of flour, cover with a clean towel and let rise in warm place until doubled in bulk, about 2 hours. Turn onto a lightly floured board and knead until smooth. Divide the dough into 2 parts and cut each part into 3 equal pieces. Roll with your hands into long ropes and braid. Place the braids on a greased baking sheet, cover and let rise. Beat the remaining egg and lightly brush over the braids. Sprinkle with additional sugar and slivered almonds and bake at 375° for 15 to 20 minutes.

Evelyn Wolf
Reservations

## Christmas Fruit Bread

½ cup sugar
1 tsp. salt
¾ cup shortening (approx.)
1 cup warm milk
½ cup warm water
2 pkg. active dry yeast

4½ cups sifted enriched flour
(approx.)
1½ cups mixed fruit (raisins, citron and candied fruit)
½ cup chopped nuts

Stir the sugar, salt and ½ cup shortening into the milk and set aside. Pour the water into a bowl, sprinkle the yeast over, stir until dissolved and then stir in the milk mixture. Add 2 cups flour, beat thoroughly and cover. Let rise in a warm place, free from drafts, until doubled in bulk, about 30 minutes; stir down. Stir in the fruit and nuts and approximately 2½ cups flour. Turn out on a lightly floured board and knead until smooth and elastic. Place in a greased bowl, brush with shortening and cover. Let rise in a warm place, free from drafts, until doubled in bulk, about 55 minutes. Punch down, form into 1 or 2 round balls, place either on a greased, large baking sheet or in 2 greased bread pans and cover. Let rise in a warm place, free from drafts, until doubled in bulk, about 1 hour. Bake at 400° for 10 minutes, reduce the heat to 350° and bake for 40 minutes more.

Duri Arquisch
Executive Chef
Salt Lake City Food Services

## Irish Soda Bread

4 cups flour
1 Tbsp. sugar
1 ½ tsp. soda
1 tsp. salt

1 tsp. baking powder
¼ cup butter or margarine
1 ½ cups buttermilk

Sift the dry ingredients into a bowl. Cut in the butter until crumbly and add the buttermilk. Stir to make a soft dough. Turn onto a floured board and knead for about 10 minutes to form a smooth ball. Place on a greased baking sheet. Pat down to 1 ¼" thickness. With a sharp knife, score into 4 sections. Bake at 350° for 1 hour.

Fran Christensen
Tour Desk

## Robert Redford's Whole Wheat Quick Bread

2 cups whole wheat flour
1 tsp. baking powder
1 tsp. baking soda
1 tsp. salt
1 large egg
2 cups buttermilk

3 Tbsp. light molasses or
  honey
1 ½ Tbsp. lightly salted butter
  or margarine, melted
½ cup chopped walnuts
½ cup dark seedless raisins

Combine the flour, baking powder, baking soda and salt. In a large bowl, beat the egg and stir in the buttermilk, molasses and butter. Stir in the flour mixture, walnuts and raisins. Pour the batter into a greased, 9" x 5" pan and bake at 400° for 1 hour or until well browned. Remove from the oven and set on a wire rack to cool.

Makes 1 loaf.

Mary Ellen Harpster
Sales

## Corn Spoon Bread

⅔ cup corn meal
¾ tsp. salt
1¼ cups milk, scalded
2 Tbsp. butter
1 (17-oz.) can cream style corn

2 Jalapeño peppers, chopped
    (optional)
¾ tsp. baking powder
3 eggs, separated

Stir the corn meal and salt into the milk, beating well. Cook for a few seconds over low heat, stirring until of the consistency of thick mush. Blend in the butter, corn and peppers, then the baking powder. Beat the egg whites until stiff and add to the corn mixture. Beat the egg yolks until thick and add to the corn mixture. Pour into a greased, 2-quart baking dish. Bake at 375° for 35 minutes until puffy and golden brown or until a knife inserted in the center comes out clean.

Makes 5 to 6 servings.

## Beer Bread

3 cups self-rising flour,
    unsifted
3 Tbsp. sugar

1 (12-oz.) can beer, at room
    temperature
Softened butter

Mix the flour, sugar and beer together and pour into 1 large or 2 small loaf pans. Score the top of the dough and spread it with butter. Bake at 375° for 1 hour, or, if using 2 small loaf pans, bake for about 30 minutes.

JoAnn Olanyk
Fran Christensen
Pat Logue
Reservations

## Gougère

½ cup butter
1 cup sifted flour
½ tsp. salt
Black pepper

4 eggs
1½ cups shredded Swiss
    cheese

Bring the butter and 1 cup water to a boil, add the flour, salt and a generous amount of pepper all at once. Beat over low heat until the mixture leaves the sides of the pan and does not separate. Remove the mixture from the heat and beat with an electric mixer to cool, about 2 minutes.

Add the eggs, one at a time, and beat after each addition until shiny. Stir in the cheese. Drop by heaping teaspoons onto a greased cookie sheet; place an additional ½ tsp. dough on top of each. Bake at 375° for 25 to 30 minutes.

*Looks like a cream puff, tastes like a cheese layer pastry.*

*Makes about 3 dozen.*

## Butter Dips

⅓ cup butter
2¼ cups sifted flour
1 Tbsp. sugar

3½ tsp. baking powder
1½ tsp. salt
1 cup milk

Place the butter in an 13" x 9½" x 2" pan and set in a 450° oven. Remove the pan once the butter melts. Sift the flour, sugar, baking powder and salt together into a bowl. Add the milk, stirring slowly with a fork, until the dough just clings together, about 30 strokes. Turn out onto a well-floured board. Roll over to coat with flour and knead lightly about 10 times. Roll out ½" thick into a 12" x 8" rectangle. With a floured knife, cut the dough in half lengthwise, then crosswise into 16 strips. Dip each strip on both sides in the butter and lay closely together in 2 rows in the pan. Bake at 450° for 15 to 20 minutes or until golden brown. Serve hot.

*Variations:*
   *Add ½ clove, finely minced, to the butter before melting.*
   *Add ½ cup grated sharp American cheese to the dry ingredients.*
   *Add ¼ cup minced chives or parsley to the dry ingredients.*
   *Sprinkle paprika, celery seed or garlic salt over the* **Butter Dips** *before baking.*
   *Sprinkle 2 Tbsp. sugar and ½ tsp. cinnamon over the* **Butter Dips** *before baking.*
   *Sprinkle sesame seeds or poppy seeds over the* **Butter Dips** *before baking.*

*Makes 32 sticks.*

Linda Rice
Reservations

## Date Nut Bread

| | |
|---|---|
| 8 oz. pitted dates | 2 cups flour, sifted |
| 1 tsp. baking soda | 2 tsp. baking powder |
| 1 cup boiling water | 1 tsp. salt |
| ⅔ cup sugar | 1 tsp. vanilla |
| 1 egg, beaten | 1 cup chopped walnuts |

Chop the dates, sprinkle on the baking soda and add the water. Let stand until cool. Add the sugar and egg, mixing well. Sift the flour with the baking powder and salt. Gradually add to the moist ingredients, mixing well. Add the vanilla and walnuts. Place in a loaf pan and bake at 325° until a toothpick inserted in the middle comes out clean.

Ann Atwood
Reservations

## Rhubarb Nut Bread

| | |
|---|---|
| 1½ cups sugar | 1 egg |
| ⅔ cup oil | 1½ cups diced rhubarb |
| 1 tsp. salt | ½ tsp. cinnamon |
| 1 tsp. soda | Chopped walnuts |
| 1 tsp. vanilla | ¼ cup sugar |
| 2½ cups flour | ⅔ tsp. cinnamon |
| 1 cup sour milk | |

In a bowl combine the first 11 ingredients, stirring well to blend. Divide the mixture evenly between 2 greased loaf pans. For the topping, combine the sugar and cinnamon and sprinkle over the batter. Bake at 325° for 1 hour. *Do not overbake.*

*Note: To make sour milk, add 1 Tbsp. lemon juice or vinegar to 1 cup milk.*

Janet Wanink
Reservations

## Carrot Loaf Bread

3 eggs
1½ cups vegetable oil
2 cups sugar
2 cups finely grated raw carrots
1 small can crushed pineapple,
    undrained

1 cup finely chopped nuts
    (optional)
1 Tbsp. vanilla
3 cups flour
3 Tbsp. cinnamon
1 tsp. salt
1 tsp. soda

Combine the eggs, oil and sugar and beat well. Add the carrots, pineapple with its juice, nuts and vanilla and beat until smooth. Sift together the dry ingredients and add to the carrot mixture. Bake in loaf pans at 325° for 45 minutes.

*Makes 3 loaves.*

Jacque Cate
Reservations

## Pearl's Coffee Cake

1 cup butter
2¼ cups sugar
1 cup sour cream
2 eggs
1 tsp. vanilla
Dash of salt

2 cups flour
½ tsp. soda
½ tsp. baking powder
½ tsp. cinnamon
¼ cup sliced almonds

Cream together the butter, 1¼ cups sugar, sour cream, eggs, vanilla and salt. Combine the flour, soda and baking powder and stir into the butter mixture. Spread half of the batter in a bundt pan. Combine 1 scant cup sugar, the cinnamon and almonds and sprinkle half over. Add the remaining batter and top with the rest of the almond mixture. Bake at 350° for 55 minutes.

Rick Sanders
Reservations

## Apricot Nut Bread

2¼ cups flour
2 tsp. baking powder
¼ tsp. salt
¾ cup sugar
1 cup chopped nuts

½ cup chopped dried apricots
1 egg, beaten
½ cup orange juice
¼ cup water
3 Tbsp. melted shortening

Mix together the flour, baking powder, salt and sugar, then add the nuts and apricots. Add the remaining ingredients and stir until the flour is moistened. Pour into a well-greased pan and bake at 325° for 1 hour.

Fran Christensen
Tour Desk

## Peanut Butter Loaf

1¾ cups sifted flour
2 tsp. baking powder
½ tsp. salt
¼ tsp. baking soda
⅓ cup shortening

¾ cup chunky peanut butter
⅔ cup sugar
2 eggs, slightly beaten
1 cup mashed ripe bananas

Sift the first 4 ingredients together. Cream together the shortening and peanut butter. Add the sugar gradually and continue to cream until light and fluffy. Add the eggs and beat well. Stir in the dry ingredients, alternating with the mashed bananas; mix well, but do not beat. Spoon the batter into a well-greased, 8" x 4" x 3" loaf pan and bake at 350° for 1 hour.

## Pumpkin Bread

3½ cups flour
1½ tsp. salt
1 tsp. nutmeg
2 tsp. cinnamon
2 tsp. baking soda

3 cups sugar
1 cup salad oil
4 eggs
2 cups pumpkin
1 cup chopped nuts

Sift the dry ingredients into a large bowl. Combine the oil, eggs, pumpkin, and ⅔ cup water and add the dry ingredients. Stir in the nuts and pour into 2 large, greased and floured loaf pans. Bake at 325° for 1 to 1½ hours.

Rick Sanders
Reservations

## Gumdrop Bread

3 cups flour
1 tsp. salt
3½ tsp. baking powder
¾ cup sugar
1 cup cut-up gumdrops

½ cup chopped nuts
1 egg, beaten
2 Tbsp. melted shortening
1½ cups milk

Combine the dry ingredients, gumdrops and nuts. Add the egg, shortening and milk all at once, stirring just until moistened. Pour into a greased loaf pan and bake at 350° for 1 hour.

*Kids love it!*

Fran Christensen
Tour Desk

## Banana Bread

½ cup shortening
1 cup sugar
2 eggs
3 very ripe bananas, crushed

2 cups sifted flour
1 tsp. salt
1 tsp. soda
¼ cup chopped nuts

Cream the shortening and sugar until light and fluffy. Stir in the eggs and bananas. Sift together the dry ingredients and gently stir into the moist ingredients. Add the nuts and bake in a greased and floured bread pan at 350° for 1 to 1¼ hours.

Geri Shippee
Reservations

## English Muffins

1 pkg. active dry yeast
¼ cup warm water
1⅔ cups milk
3 Tbsp. butter or margarine
1 Tbsp. sugar

1½ tsp. salt
2⅓ cups all-purpose flour
2⅓ cups whole wheat flour
Corn meal

In a large bowl, dissolve the yeast in the warm water. Combine the milk, butter, sugar and salt. Stir the milk mixture into the dissolved yeast. Combine the flours and gradually stir in until the dough is moderately stiff but not firm enough to knead. Beat for 2 minutes, cover and let rise until doubled, approximately 1 hour. Turn the dough onto a well-floured board, roll about ½" thick and cut into 3" rounds, using a floured cutter. Cover and let stand on the floured board. Heat a griddle over medium heat or preheat an electric fryer. Grease the griddle and sprinkle it lightly with corn meal. Carefully transfer the muffins to the pan. Bake over medium heat for 10 to 12 minutes, turn and bake for 15 to 20 minutes on the other side. To serve, split the muffins horizontally with a fork.

Makes about 2 dozen.

Connie Drinkwine
Reservations

## Bran Muffins

1½ cups sugar
½ cup oil
2 eggs
2 cups buttermilk
2⅓ cups flour
½ tsp. salt

2½ tsp. soda
2 cups Kellogg's All Bran
1 cup Nabisco 100% Bran
1 cup raisins, dates and/or nuts
1 cup boiling water

Combine the first 7 ingredients. Stir in the cereals and raisins, dates or nuts. Mix well and beat in the boiling water. Bake at 400° for 15 to 20 minutes in greased muffin tins.

Note: The batter will keep in the refrigerator for about 2 weeks. It need not be cooked all at once, so fix 1 or 2 muffins each morning–it's great!

Dorothy Stitt
Reservations

## Sour Cream Peach Muffins

1 cup chopped peaches
1 egg
1 cup sour cream
¼ cup melted butter, slightly
  cooled

2 cups flour
1 Tbsp. baking powder
¼ tsp. baking soda
¼ tsp. salt
¼ to ½ cup sugar

Blend together the peaches, egg and sour cream; stir in the butter and set aside. Combine the flour, baking powder, baking soda and salt; blend in the sugar. Pour the peach mixture over the flour mixture and stir only to blend. Divide the batter equally into 12 greased muffin cups, filling each about two-thirds full. Bake at 375° for about 35 minutes. Let cool for about 10 minutes before serving.

Fran Christensen
Tour Desk

## Icebox Muffins

2 cups boiling water
2 cups Nabisco 100% Bran
1 cup shortening
2½ to 3 cups white sugar
4 eggs, beaten

1 quart buttermilk
5 cups flour, sifted
1 Tbsp. plus 2 tsp. soda
1 tsp. salt
4 cups Kellogg's All Bran

Pour the water over the Nabisco 100% Bran and cool. Cream together the shortening and sugar. Add the eggs, buttermilk and soaked bran. Add the flour, soda, salt and Kellogg's All Bran and fold in until well moistened. Store in 4 (1-quart) jars in the refrigerator. Will keep for 6 weeks. To bake, pour into greased muffin cups and bake at 400° for 20 minutes.

Note: Sour milk or dried buttermilk can be substituted for the liquid buttermilk.

Makes 7 dozen.

Linda Rice
Reservations

## Apple Muffins

3½ cups flour
3 cups peeled and finely
  chopped apples
2 cups sugar
1 tsp. salt

1 tsp. baking soda
1 tsp. cinnamon
1½ cups vegetable oil
½ cup chopped nuts
1 tsp. vanilla

Thoroughly combine the flour, apples, sugar, salt, soda and cinnamon in a large bowl. Stir in the oil, nuts and vanilla. Fill greased and floured muffin cups one-half to two-thirds full. Bake at 350° for 30 minutes or until a toothpick inserted in the center comes out clean.

Makes 24.

Fran Christensen
Tour Desk

## Stouffer's Pumpkin Muffins

1½ cups flour
2 tsp. baking powder
¾ tsp. salt
½ cup plus 3 tsp. sugar
½ tsp. cinnamon
½ tsp. nutmeg

¼ cup butter
½ cup seeded raisins
1 egg, beaten
½ cup canned pumpkin
½ cup milk

Sift together the flour, baking powder, salt, ½ cup sugar, cinnamon and nutmeg. Cut in the butter and add the raisins. Combine the egg with the pumpkin and milk, add to the flour mixture, stirring only until moistened. Fill greased muffin cups two-thirds full. Sprinkle ¼ tsp. sugar over each muffin. Bake at 400° for 18 to 20 minutes. Serve hot, right from the oven.

Makes 1 dozen.

☞ When cooking muffins, fill one of the cups half-full with water, and the muffins will not scorch.

## Whole Wheat Pancakes

1 cup whole wheat pancake
  mix
½ cup wheat germ
2 Tbsp. nonfat dry milk powder
2 Tbsp. baking powder
½ tsp. salt
2 eggs, beaten

1½ cups milk
1 tsp. vanilla
4 drops of lemon extract
1 banana, chopped
½ cup chopped pecans or
  walnuts

In a mixing bowl, combine the pancake mix, wheat germ, dry milk, baking powder and salt; set aside. Combine the eggs, milk, vanilla and lemon extract and stir into the flour mixture just until moistened. Fold in the banana and nuts. Cook on a hot griddle, using ¼ cup batter for each pancake.

Rick Sanders
Reservations

## Griddle Cakes

1 cup sifted all-purpose flour
2 tsp. double-acting baking
  powder
½ tsp. salt
2 Tbsp. sugar

1 egg
1 cup milk
3 Tbsp. butter or margarine,
  melted

Sift the flour with the baking powder, salt and sugar into a medium bowl. With a rotary beater, beat the egg and add the milk and butter, beating until well combined. Pour into the dry ingredients, stirring only until moistened; the batter will be lumpy. Using ¼ cup batter for each griddle cake, pour the batter into a hot griddle or heavy skillet and cook until bubbles form, flip over and cook the other side.

*Makes 8 (4") griddle cakes.*

Ann Atwood
Reservations

# German Pancake with Orange Sauce

½ cup unsifted flour
½ cup milk
¼ tsp. salt
4 extra large eggs
¼ cup butter

**Orange Sauce:**
½ cup sugar

2 Tbsp. cornstarch
¼ tsp. salt
½ cup orange juice
2 Tbsp. butter
1 tsp. lemon juice
2 oranges, peeled and cut into
   bite-size pieces

Combine the flour, milk and salt; add the eggs, one at a time, whipping with a wire whisk after each addition. Melt the butter in a 10" skillet. Add the batter and cook over moderate heat until the edges are firm enough to loosen with a spatula. Make a criss-cross slash across the top and bake at 425° for 15 minutes or until puffed and golden. Serve with the **Orange Sauce.**

**Orange Sauce:** In a saucepan combine the sugar, cornstarch and salt. Add the orange juice and 1 cup water, bring to a boil and simmer for 3 minutes, stirring constantly, until thick and bubbly. Add the butter, lemon juice and the orange pieces and cook until heated through.

Karen Fudge
Regional Sales Office

# Cottage Cheese Pancakes

2 eggs
⅓ cup cottage cheese
¾ cup sour cream

½ cup sifted flour
½ tsp. baking soda
½ tsp. salt

Place all the ingredients in a bowl and mix well. Or place all the ingredients in a blender, moist ones first, and mix well. Let stand for 10 minutes. Cook on a hot, lightly greased griddle.

Makes 8 to 10 small pancakes.

Sue Crane
Reservations

## German Pancakes

1 cup flour
2 cups milk
1 tsp. salt
3 Tbsp. sugar
6 eggs

6 Tbsp. melted butter
Syrup
Powdered sugar
Lemon juice
Lemon wedges

Combine the flour and 1 cup milk. Stir in the salt and sugar and add the eggs, two at a time, mixing well after each addition. Beat in the remaining milk and 3 Tbsp. butter. Pour ¾ cup batter into a heated, greased frying pan. Bake at 450° for 7 minutes. Remove from the pan, roll up as for a jelly roll and pour some melted butter over the top. Repeat the process until all the batter is used up. Serve with syrup, powdered sugar and lemon juice sprinkled over the top. Garnish with lemon wedges.

Susan Warren
Reservations

## Swedish Pancakes

3 eggs
1 cup milk
1 cup flour
Dash of salt

¼ cup oil
½ cup milk or cream
Sour cream
Powdered sugar

Thoroughly beat the eggs, add the milk and beat again. Add the flour and salt and beat again. Add the oil and milk or cream. Pour 2 Tbsp. batter per cake onto a hot, greased griddle and spread very thin with the back of a spoon. Flip and cook the other side. Roll up and fill the inside with sour cream and sprinkle with powdered sugar. Serve with jam, heated pie filling, syrup or butter and powdered sugar.

Dorothy Stitt
Reservations

## Washington Waffles

½ tsp. baking soda
½ tsp. baking powder
½ tsp. salt
2 cups all-purpose flour

¼ cup sugar
3 eggs, separated
1 cup sour cream
1½ cups buttermilk

Sift together the baking soda, baking powder, salt and flour; set aside. Combine the sugar and egg yolks and beat. Add the sour cream and buttermilk, then add the dry ingredients. Beat the egg whites until peaks form and gently fold into the batter. Pour about ½ to ¾ cup batter on a preheated and lightly greased waffle iron. Cook the waffles to preferred doneness.

*These waffles are delicious topped with fresh berries and whipped cream.*

*Serves 6 to 8.*

## Birchermüesli
### (Swiss Health Specialty)

2 cups Quaker quick-cooking
    oatmeal
2 cups fortified skim or
    whole milk
½ tsp. salt
1 Tbsp. sugar
½ cup currants or seedless
    raisins

Juice of 1 lemon
2 apples, unpeeled
    and shredded
1 banana, halved and
    finely sliced
½ cup finely chopped walnuts
1 orange, peeled and diced

Mix the first 5 ingredients together thoroughly and refrigerate for 4 hours. Combine the remaining ingredients and mix with the oatmeal mixture; refrigerate until ready to serve. Delicious for breakfast or as an afternoon snack.

*Note: Other raw fruits can be added as desired.*

Paul Steuri
Executive Chef
Omaha Food Services

## Breakfast Bars

½ cup butter
1 cup honey
4 eggs, beaten
1 cup oatmeal
1 cup raisins
1 cup wheat germ

1 cup sunflower seeds
1 cup chopped walnuts
1 cup whole wheat flour
½ tsp. salt
2 tsp. sifted baking powder

Blend together the first 2 ingredients. Add the remaining ingredients and mix well. Pour into an ungreased, 9" x 13" pan. Bake at 350° (or 325° if using a glass pan) for 20 to 30 minutes, until golden brown or until a cake tester comes out clean.

A. J. MacLean
Reservations

## Edna's Yorkshire Pudding

1 cup flour
1 cup milk
Pinch of salt

1 egg
Hot fat

Mix the first 4 ingredients together and beat until smooth. Pour into hot fat in a shallow pan. Bake at 375° for 35 to 45 minutes.

Note: For seasoned dumplings, add 1 Tbsp. poultry seasoning to the mixture before baking. May be served with meat or poultry.

Edna Harris
Food Service

☞ To cut marshmallows or sticky fruit easily, rub butter or oil on the scissors.

# Cornbread Stuffing for Turkey

4 cups chopped celery
2 cups minced onions
Chicken or turkey stock
½ cup butter
7 cups toasted and crumbled
   bread
7 cups crumbled fresh
   cornbread

1 Tbsp. salt
2 tsp. ground pepper
2 tsp. sage or poultry
   seasoning
1 cup fresh parsley
5 eggs, beaten

Place the celery and onions in a large saucepan, add stock to cover and the butter. Simmer very slowly for about 1½ hours; cool. Combine the breads, pour in the celery mixture; add the seasonings and eggs and mix thoroughly with your hands until smooth. Stuff the turkey and bake the leftover dressing in a casserole dish.

Various additional ingredients you may add to the dressing:
4 cups whole or chopped oysters
2 cups sliced mushrooms, sautéed
4 cups clams
2 cups chestnuts, pecans, almonds or filberts, roasted and chopped
2 cups whole cranberries, cooked
½ cup bourbon

This recipe makes enough to stuff a 12- to 15-lb. bird and enough to fill an 8" casserole.

Sue Martin
Reservations

☞ To cut fresh bread easily, heat a serrated knife.

# DESSERTS
# &
# SWEETS

## Cheesecake

2½ lbs. curd cheese
1½ cups sugar
7 egg yolks
½ cup butter, melted

Vanilla flavored with mace and
  lemon
½ cup flour
½ cup cornstarch
9 egg whites, stiffly beaten

Rub the cheese through a sieve until fine. Stir in the sugar, yolks and butter. Add the flavored vanilla, flour and cornstarch, mixing well. Fold in the egg whites. Pour into a pan. Bake at 400° for 8 to 10 minutes until light golden brown; reduce the heat to 180° and bake for 1 hour.

Hubert F. Malco
Pastry Chef
Seattle Food Services

## Weehawken Cheesecake

1 lb. creamed cottage cheese,
  whipped
1 lb. cream cheese
1½ cups sugar
4 eggs, slightly beaten
1 tsp. vanilla

Juice of ½ lemon
2 heaping Tbsp. cornstarch
2 heaping Tbsp. flour
½ cup butter, melted
1 pint sour cream

Blend together the cottage cheese and cream cheese, add the sugar and eggs and blend well. Add, in order, the vanilla, lemon juice, cornstarch and flour; mix well. Stir in the butter and add the sour cream. Pour into a well-greased, spring-form pan. Bake at 325° for 1 hour. After baking for 1 hour, turn off the oven and leave the cake in for an additional 2 hours. Do not open the oven. The cake will rise over the top of the pan and then slowly recede.

Hugo Moirano
Senior Vice President & General Manager
Central Division-Chicago

## Raoul's Cheesecake

**Crust:**
2 Tbsp. sugar
¼ cup butter
1 egg
1¼ cups flour

**Filling:**
¼ cup plus 3 Tbsp. sugar
14 oz. cream cheese
3 eggs

**Topping:**
2 Tbsp. sugar
7 oz. sour cream

**Crust:** Mix the sugar and butter together until creamy, add the egg and mix until smooth. Fold in the flour, let rest for approximately 10 minutes, then roll out and line a greased, 9" pie pan with the dough. Bake very lightly at 400° for approximately 10 minutes; set aside to cool.

**Filling:** Mix the sugar and cream cheese together until creamy, then add the eggs and mix until smooth. Pour into the pie shell and bake at 400° for 10 minutes, then reduce the temperature to 350° and bake for 20 minutes more.

**Topping:** Stir the sugar and sour cream together in a mixing bowl until well blended. After the pie is baked, remove from the oven, spread on the topping, return to the oven and bake at 300° for 5 minutes more.

Raoul F. Delbol
Executive Chef
Los Angeles Food Services

## Blueberry-Glazed Cheesecake

2 cups graham cracker crumbs
1¼ cups sugar
½ cup melted butter
2 (8-oz.) pkg. cream cheese

3 eggs, beaten
2 tsp. vanilla
2 cups sour cream
1 can blueberry pie filling

Combine the cracker crumbs, ½ cup sugar and the butter. Mix well and press to form a crust into a 9" pie pan. Work the cream cheese until soft with a spoon; add the eggs, one at a time, beating well after each addition. Add ½ cup sugar and 1 tsp. vanilla, blend and pour into the graham cracker crust. Bake at 375° for 20 minutes. Remove from the oven and let stand for 15 minutes. Combine ¼ cup sugar, 1 tsp. vanilla and the sour cream; stir gently and spread over the cheese filling. Bake at 475° for 10 minutes. When cool, cover with the pie filling. Chill for several hours.

*Makes 8 to 10 servings.*

Connie Brown
Reservations

## Anne's Cheesecake

3 eggs
1 cup sugar
1 tsp. vanilla
2 Tbsp. cornstarch
3 (8-oz.) pkg. cream cheese

2 cups heavy cream

**Crust:**
1 pound cake
1 (9") spring-form cake pan

All the ingredients must be at room temperature. Mix the eggs and sugar together, add the vanilla and cornstarch. Stir in the cream cheese and heavy cream, beating well until the batter thickens. Pour the batter into the **Crust** and bake at 450° for 20 minutes. Reduce the heat to 350° and bake for 35 minutes. Turn off the oven and leave the cake in the oven, with the door open, for 10 minutes. Cool at room temperature for at least 2 hours and then chill in the refrigerator for several hours.

**Crust:** Scrape the top and bottom crusts off the pound cake. Cut the cake into ¼" slices and press the slices into the bottom of the pan until it is completely covered.

*One of the best cheesecakes around!*

Annemarie Fleming
Reservations

☞ *Keep a brand-new powder puff in the flour canister for dusting greased cake pans.*

## Duri's Cheesecake

2 cups cracker meal
¾ cup butter, melted and
   cooled
3 (8-oz.) pkg. cream cheese,
   softened

1 cup sugar
3 eggs
Dash of vanilla extract

Combine the cracker meal with ¼ cup butter, roll out and use to line a 10" pie tin. In a large mixing bowl stir the cream cheese with a wooden spatula until it is smooth and creamy. Slowly add the sugar, then the eggs, one at a time. When smooth, mix in the remaining butter and vanilla extract and pour the filling into the pie shell. Bake at 450° for 18 minutes.

Duri Arquisch
Executive Chef
Salt Lake City Food Services

## Chocolate Rum Cake

1 pkg. chocolate cake mix
2 (3-oz.) pkg. instant chocolate
   pudding
4 eggs
1 cup dark rum (80 proof)

½ cup oil
½ cup slivered almonds
1½ cups milk
2 envelopes Dream Whip

Combine the cake mix, 1 pkg. pudding, the eggs, ½ cup rum, ½ cup water, the oil and almonds in a large bowl. Blend well, then beat at medium speed for 2 minutes. Turn into 2 greased and floured, 9" layer cake pans. Bake at 350° for 30 minutes or until the cake tests done; do not underbake. Cool in the pans for 10 minutes, remove and cool on racks. Split the layers in half. Combine the remaining pudding, rum, the milk and Dream Whip and mix in a bowl; beat at high speed for 4 minutes. Set the 4 cake layers on top of one another, spreading filling between each layer and fully frost the cake with the remaining filling. Garnish with chocolate curls. Chill the cake until serving.

Yvonne Erickson
Reservations

## Chocolate Chip Date Cake

1¼ cups boiling water
1 cup chopped dates
1¾ tsp. baking soda
1 cup sugar
½ cup margarine
2 eggs

1½ cups flour
¼ tsp. salt
1 (12-oz.) pkg. chocolate chips
½ cup brown sugar
½ cup chopped pecans

Pour the water over the dates. Add 1 tsp. baking soda and set aside to cool. Cream the sugar and margarine, add the eggs, beating well, and stir in the cooled date mixture. Add ¾ tsp. baking soda, the flour and salt and mix well. Pour into a greased and floured, 9" x 13" pan. In a separate bowl, combine the chocolate chips, brown sugar and pecans. Sprinkle over the cake and bake at 350° for 45 minutes.

Karen Fudge
Regional Sales

## Dark Chocolate Cake

1 (18½-oz.) pkg. dark
    chocolate devil's food
    cake mix
1 (3¼-oz.) pkg. instant
    chocolate pudding
1 cup sour cream

½ cup cooking oil
½ cup warm water
4 eggs
1½ cups semisweet chocolate
    chips
Confectioners' sugar

In a large bowl, combine all the ingredients except the chocolate chips and sugar and beat for 4 minutes. Fold in the chocolate chips. Bake in a greased and floured, 12-cup bundt pan at 350° for 50 to 60 minutes or until the cake tests done. Cool in the pan for 10 to 15 minutes; turn out on a wire rack or serving plate to complete cooling. Sprinkle with confectioners' sugar, if desired.

Karen Fudge
Regional Sales

☞ When greasing and dusting the pan for chocolate cakes, substitute cocoa for the flour.

## Crazy Cake

3 cups flour
2 cups sugar
¼ cup plus 2 Tbsp. cocoa
1 tsp. salt

¾ cup salad oil
2 Tbsp. vinegar
2 cups cold water

Put the flour, sugar, cocoa and salt in a greased, 9" x 13" cake pan and mix well with a fork. Make 3 wells in the dry ingredients and add the oil and vinegar, putting half the oil in wells in wells 1 and 3, and the vinegar in well 2. Pour the cold water over all, stir well and bake at 350° for 35 to 40 minutes.

Jan Taylor
Reservations

## Mississippi Mud

2 cups flour
2 cups sugar
½ tsp. salt
1 cup margarine
¼ cup cocoa
2 eggs
½ cup buttermilk
1 tsp. soda

1 tsp. vanilla

**Frosting:**
½ cup margarine
1 tsp. vanilla
⅓ cup cocoa
⅓ cup buttermilk
1 box powdered sugar

Sift together the flour, sugar and salt and set aside. Combine the margarine, cocoa and 1 cup water, bring to a boil and pour over the flour. Beat together the remaining ingredients and stir into the flour. Pour into a greased, 18" x 12" jelly-roll pan and bake at 350° for 20 minutes. Frost when cool.

**Frosting:** Combine the margarine, vanilla, cocoa and buttermilk and bring to a boil. Remove from the heat and mix in the sugar.

*Chopped walnuts can be added to the cake and/or the frosting, if desired.*

Cookbook Committee

## Cocoa Cake

3 cups flour, sifted
1½ cups sugar
¼ cup plus 2 Tbsp.
  unsweetened cocoa

2 tsp. baking powder
2 tsp. baking soda
1 cup mayonnaise

Sift the dry ingredients together. Add 2 cups water and the mayonnaise and pour into a cake pan. Bake at 350° for 30 to 40 minutes.

Jim Small
Reservations

## Apple Crumb Cake

6 cups peeled and sliced apples
½ cup sugar
⅓ cup plus 2 Tbsp. flour
¼ tsp. salt
⅛ tsp. nutmeg
⅛ tsp. grated lemon rind

2 tsp. lemon juice
1 (9") unbaked pie crust
½ cup brown sugar
¼ cup butter
¼ tsp. cinnamon

Combine the apples, sugar, 2 Tbsp. flour, the salt, nutmeg, lemon rind and juice and pour into the pie shell. Mix together the ⅓ cup flour, the brown sugar, butter and cinnamon and sprinkle over the pie filling. Cover the pie with foil, tucking it under the rim of the pan. Bake at 425° for 20 minutes. Uncover and bake for 20 to 25 minutes more.

Rick Sanders
Reservations

## Fresh Apple Cake with Rum Sauce

4 cups diced apples
2 cups sugar
½ cup salad oil
1 cup nuts
2 eggs, well beaten
2 tsp. vanilla
2 cups flour
2 tsp. soda
2 tsp. cinnamon

1 tsp. salt

**Rum Sauce:**
1 cup sugar
Dash of salt
2 Tbsp. cornstarch
1½ cups boiling water
1 Tbsp. oil
Rum extract to taste

Mix the apples and sugar together, add the salad oil, nuts, eggs and vanilla, mixing well. Stir in the remaining ingredients and bake in a 9" x 13" pan at 350° for 1 hour. Serve with warm **Rum Sauce.**

**Rum Sauce:** Combine the sugar, salt, cornstarch and water; then stir in the oil and rum extract.

Jacque Cate
Reservations

## Applesauce Cake

1 ½ cups applesauce
1 cup sugar
½ cup Crisco
2 cups flour
½ tsp. salt
1 tsp. cinnamon
½ tsp. allspice

½ tsp. cloves
½ tsp. nutmeg
½ tsp. baking soda
½ tsp. baking powder
1 cup raisins
1 cup citron
1 cup nuts, sprinkled with flour

Warm the applesauce and combine it with the sugar and Crisco. Then sift together the flour, salt, cinnamon, allspice, cloves, nutmeg, baking soda and baking powder. Stir in the raisins, citron and nuts. Bake in a loaf pan at 350° for 1 hour.

Gladys Tyo
Reservations

## Carol's Carrot Cake

2 cups sugar
2 cups flour
1 tsp. salt
2 tsp. cinnamon
2 tsp. soda

4 large or 6 small eggs, beaten
1 ½ cups salad oil
2 cups grated carrots
1 tsp. vanilla

Combine all the dry ingredients, add the eggs, then the oil and the carrots and mix together. Pour into a greased pan and bake at 350° for 30 minutes. Cool and spread with your favorite cream cheese frosting.

Carol Milliman
Reservations

### Carrot Cake

1½ cups corn oil
2 cups sugar
3 eggs
2 cups flour
1½ cups shredded carrots
2 tsp. soda
2 tsp. salt
1 tsp. cinnamon
1 tsp. allspice
1 tsp. vanilla

1 Tbsp. instant clear gel or
   cornstarch
¾ cup chopped nuts

**Cream Cheese Icing:**
¾ cup butter or margarine
1 (8-oz.) pkg. cream cheese
2 cups powdered sugar
½ tsp. vanilla
1 tsp. lemon juice
Chopped nuts

Combine all the cake ingredients in a large bowl and mix well until blended. Pour the batter into a 9" x 13" pan and bake at 350° for 1 hour. After cooling, frost with the **Cream Cheese Icing**.

**Cream Cheese Icing:** Cream together the butter, cream cheese, powdered sugar, vanilla and lemon juice until slightly fluffy. Stir in the nuts.

Walter J. Schmuki
Sous Chef
Denver Food Services

### Orange Carrot Cake

3 cups flour
2 cups sugar
1 cup coconut (optional)
2½ tsp. baking soda
2½ tsp. cinnamon
1 tsp. salt
2 cups shredded carrots
1¼ cups cooking oil
2 tsp. vanilla
1 (11-oz.) can Mandarin
   oranges, undrained
3 eggs

1 tsp. grated orange peel

**Frosting:**
1 (8-oz.) pkg. cream cheese,
   softened
2 Tbsp. butter or margarine,
   melted
1 tsp. vanilla
3 cups powdered sugar
½ to 1 cup chopped nuts
   (optional)

In a large bowl, blend the cake ingredients and beat for 2 minutes at high speed. Pour into a greased, 9" x 13" pan and bake at 350° for 45 to 55 minutes or until a toothpick inserted in the center comes out clean. Cool and frost.

**Frosting:** In a medium bowl blend all ingredients except the nuts, beating until smooth. Spread the frosting over the cake and sprinkle with the nuts.

Kathy Ideta
Communications Field Services

## Pig Pickin' Cake

1 pkg. golden cake mix
4 eggs
¾ cup vegetable oil
1 can Mandarin oranges
   with juice

**Frosting:**
1 (3-oz.) pkg. instant vanilla
   pudding
2 cups milk
1 large can crushed pineapple,
   drained
1 (9-oz.) carton Cool Whip

Combine all the cake ingredients and bake in 2 greased, 9" layer cake pans at 350° for 30 minutes. When cooled, divide each layer in half to make 4 layers and frost the cake. Refrigerate until serving.

**Frosting:** Mix the pudding and milk, beating well. Blend in the pineapple, fold in the Cool Whip and chill until ready to use.

*This cake is best if prepared the day before serving.*

Annemarie Fleming
Reservations

## Orange Walnut Cake

1 pkg. yellow cake mix
2 tsp. grated orange peel
½ cup orange juice
½ cup finely chopped walnuts

**Glaze:**
1 cup sifted powdered sugar
1 to 2 Tbsp. orange juice

Combine the cake mix, orange peel, orange juice and ¾ cup water. Beat, following the cake mix directions. Add the walnuts and pour into a greased and floured, 8" spring-form pan. Bake at 350° for 50 minutes. Cool in the pan on a wire rack for 10 minutes. Loosen the cake around the edges with a knife. Release the spring and remove the side of the pan. Place the cake on a wire rack and cool completely. Remove the cake from the base of the pan and place on a plate. Drizzle the glaze over the cake and down the side.

**Glaze:** Blend the powdered sugar with 1 Tbsp. orange juice until smooth. Gradually add more orange juice until the glaze is thin enough to drizzle.

Ken Christensen
Operations Planning

## Dump Cake

*1 large can crushed pineapple*
*1 can cherry pie filling*
*1 (2-layer) pkg. yellow*
  *cake mix*
*½ cup chopped nuts*
*½ to ¾ cup butter*
*Whipped cream*
*Cherries*

Grease a 9" x 12" cake pan and dump in the pineapple, spreading it evenly over the bottom and into the corners of the pan. Dump in the pie filling and spread around. Dump in the cake mix; spread. Sprinkle the nuts over the top, dot with the butter. Bake at 350° for about 1 hour. Serve with whipped cream and cherries.

*Serves 14 to 20.*

Kathy Morgan
Inflight Services

## Pineapple Caramel Upside-Down Cake

*1 cup all-purpose flour*
*1 tsp. baking powder*
*⅓ tsp. salt*
*3 eggs*
*1 cup sugar*
*½ cup pineapple juice*
*1 tsp. vanilla*
*4 slices canned pineapple*
*½ cup brown sugar*

Sift the flour, baking powder and salt together; set aside. Beat the eggs and sugar together until light, add the pineapple juice and vanilla and gradually fold into the flour mixture. Arrange the pineapple slices in a greased, deep cake pan, sprinkle the brown sugar over and pour in the cake batter. Bake at 325° to 350° for approximately 1 hour. When done, turn upside-down on a plate and serve hot.

Emile LeBoulluec
Executive Chef
Boston Food Services

## Harvey Wallbanger Bundt Cake

1 pkg. yellow cake mix
1 large pkg. instant vanilla
  pudding
4 eggs
1 cup cooking oil

¾ cup orange juice
¼ cup vodka
¼ cup Galliano
Powdered sugar

Combine and beat all the ingredients together for 5 minutes. Pour into a well-greased and lightly floured bundt pan. Bake at 350° for 45 to 50 minutes. Dust with powdered sugar.

Kristi Severson
Reservations

## Dinah Shore's Quick Cake

1 pkg. yellow cake mix
1 pkg. instant vanilla pudding
½ to ¾ cup oil
½ tsp. nutmeg

4 eggs
¼ cup cream sherry or 1 cup
  water
Confectioners' sugar

Combine all the ingredients and mix until well blended. Pour into a greased and floured bundt or angel food cake pan. Bake at 350° for 45 to 50 minutes. Sprinkle confectioners' sugar on the cake before serving.

Kathy Morgan
Inflight Services

### Sherry Wine Cake

1 pkg. Duncan Hines yellow
   cake mix
1 (14-oz.) pkg. instant vanilla
   pudding
4 eggs

¾ cup salad oil
¾ cup Taylor sherry
1 tsp. nutmeg
¼ cup powdered sugar

Combine all the ingredients except the powdered sugar. Beat with an electric mixer for 5 minutes at medium speed. Pour into a greased angel food or bundt pan. Bake at 350° for 50 to 60 minutes. Cool in the pan for 5 minutes, turn out on a cake rack and, when cool, sprinkle with the powdered sugar.

Geri Shippee
Reservations
Kathy Morgan
Inflight Services

### Fudpucker Cake

1 pkg. yellow cake mix
½ cup oil
1 (3½-oz.) pkg. instant vanilla
   pudding
4 eggs
¼ cup vodka
¼ cup apricot brandy

¾ cup apricot nectar

**Frosting:**
1 cup powdered sugar
1 Tbsp. orange juice
1 Tbsp. apricot brandy
1 tsp. vodka

Combine the cake ingredients in a bowl and mix for 4 minutes. Pour into a tube or bundt pan and bake at 350° for 45 to 50 minutes. Cool and drizzle the frosting over the cake.

**Frosting:** Combine all the ingredients, stirring well.

Yvonne Erickson
Reservations

## Red Velvet Cake from the Waldorf Astoria

*This recipe has an interesting history. A friend of the mother of a friend of a friend of my aunt (if you follow me) had the pleasure of dining at the Waldorf Astoria in New York and was served this cake. After returning to Portland, she wrote to the hotel to say how muich she enjoyed the cake and to ask for the recipe. She got it along with a bill for $300 which she took to an attorney who said she would have to pay it. She did pay the bill but said she wanted all her friends to benefit from that, so here is the recipe.*

½ cup shortening
1½ cups sugar
2 eggs
2 Tbsp. cocoa
¼ cup red food coloring
1 tsp. salt
1 tsp. vanilla
1 cup buttermilk
2½ cups sifted cake flour
1½ tsp. baking soda

1½ tsp. vinegar

**Frosting:**
¼ cup plus 1 Tbsp. flour
Dash of salt
1 cup milk
1 cup butter and shortening, combined (can use some margarine)
1 cup sugar
1 tsp. vanilla

Cream the shortening, sugar and eggs. Make a paste with the cocoa and the food coloring and add to the mixture. Mix the salt and vanilla with the buttermilk and add, alternating with the flour, to the creamed mixture. Then combine the soda and vinegar and fold into the batter. Do not beat. Pour into 2 (9") greased and floured layer pans and bake at 350° for 30 minutes or until the cake tests done. Cool and frost.

**Frosting:** Mix the flour, salt and milk until smooth and cook over low heat until thick and pasty, stirring constantly to prevent scorching. Let the paste stand until cold. Cream the butter and shortening with the sugar and vanilla. Stir into the paste and beat until light and fluffy. The longer you beat, the nicer the frosting. Makes enough to frost the tops and sides of 2 layers.

Susan Warren
Reservations

## Poppy Seed Cake

½ cup butter
1 cup sour cream
1 pkg. yellow cake mix
1 pkg. instant vanilla pudding

4 eggs
2 oz. poppy seeds
Powdered sugar

Cream the butter until light and fluffy, add the sour cream and beat the mixture until very fluffy. Add the yellow cake mix, vanilla pudding, eggs and poppy seeds. Blend and beat for 4 minutes. Bake in a bundt or tube pan at 325° for 1 hour. Cool and sprinkle with powdered sugar.

Susan Warren
Reservations

## Walnut Cake

1 (12-oz.) box vanilla wafers
2 cups sugar
1 cup butter
6 eggs, separated

⅓ cup milk
1 cup finely chopped walnuts
1 cup coconut

Finely crush the vanilla wafers and combine with the sugar, butter, egg yolks, milk, walnuts and coconut. Beat the egg whites until stiff peaks form. Fold them into the vanilla wafer mixture and pour the batter into a greased tube pan. Bake at 300° for 90 minutes. Let the cake cool for 2 hours in the pan.

*This freezes very well or can be refrigerated.*

Ed Hoenicke
Vice President & Associate General Counsel
Law Division

## Virgins' Gold Cake

1 cup margarine
1½ lbs. cream cheese
2 cups sugar

6 eggs
2 cups self-rising flour
2 tsp. vanilla

Cream the margarine and cream cheese until smooth; slowly add the sugar, beating until light. Add the eggs, one at a time, beating well after each addition. Stir in the flour and vanilla and beat for 2 minutes. Pour into a greased and floured, 9" cake pan. Bake at 375° for 1 hour.

*Serves 8 to 10.*

Mike Dearing
Reservations

## Rich Chocolate Mousse
### (Crème au Chocolat Glacé)

*3 squares bitter chocolate*
*2 Tbsp. butter*
*4 egg whites*
*¼ tsp. cream of tartar*
*⅓ cup sugar*
*3 egg yolks*
*¼ cup powdered sugar*
*1 Tbsp. rum*

*½ cup chopped pecans*
*(optional)*
*½ cup chopped maraschino*
*cherries (optional)*
*½ cup heavy cream,*
*whipped and chilled*
*(optional)*

Melt the chocolate and butter over hot water. Beat the egg whites with the cream of tartar until soft peaks form. Put the sugar and 3 Tbsp. water in a small saucepan and bring to a boil. Beat the sugar syrup into the egg whites until stiff. Beat the yolks and the powdered sugar. Add the melted chocolate mixture and rum. Fold in just enough to blend. Fold the egg whites into the chocolate mixture until they disappear. Divide the mixture among 4 custard cups or other small serving dishes and refrigerate. Garnish with the pecans, cherries and whipped cream before serving.

Vera M. Cook
Reservations

## Lemon Mousse

*1 quart blueberries*
*1 cup sugar*
*5 eggs, separated*
*Juice of 2 large lemons*

*1 cup heavy cream, stiffly*
*whipped*
*2 tsp. grated lemon zest*

Wash the blueberries and remove the stems; pour the berries into a glass serving bowl and sprinkle with ¼ cup sugar. In the top of a stainless steel or enamel double boiler (do not use aluminum as it affects the flavor and color of the mousse), beat the egg yolks with the remaining sugar until a light lemon color. Add the lemon juice and cook the mixture over simmering water, whisking constantly, until it heavily coats a spoon; do not let it boil. Immediately remove from the heat and cool. Beat the egg whites until they are stiff but not dry and fold them gently into the lemon mixture. Fold in the whipped cream and lemon zest until smooth and well mixed. Chill and, just before serving, cover the berries with the cold mousse.

*Serves 6.*

Karen Fudge
Regional Sales

## Cream Puffs

½ cup butter
1 cup flour
4 eggs

1 small pkg. vanilla pudding
1 cup heavy cream
2 Tbsp. sugar

Combine the butter with 1 cup water and bring to a rolling boil. Stir in the flour all at once. Stir vigorously over low heat until the mixture leaves the sides of the pan and forms a ball, about 1 minute. Remove from the heat and beat in the eggs, one at a time. Continue beating until the mixture is smooth and velvety. Drop from a spoon onto an ungreased cookie sheet. Bake at 400° for 45 to 50 minutes or until dry. Allow to cool. Prepare the pudding according to the package directions. Whip the cream with the sugar and fold into the cooled pudding; set aside. With a sharp knife, slice off the top of the puffs, scoop out the soft, moist dough inside and discard. Then fill the cream puff cavities with the filling, replace the top and refrigerate until serving.

*Makes 8 large or 10 small cream puffs.*

Carole Hirose
Supervisor
Reservations

## Danish Pastry

2 cups flour
1 cup butter
1 tsp. almond flavoring
3 eggs
Toasted almonds

**Powdered Sugar Frosting:**
2 cups powdered sugar
½ cup butter, softened
1 tsp. vanilla

Place 1 cup flour in a bowl and blend in ½ cup butter. Sprinkle in 2 Tbsp. water and mix with a fork. Roll into a ball and divide into 2 equal parts. Pat the dough into 2 (3" x 12") strips and place 3" apart on a cookie sheet. Place the remaining butter and 1 cup water in a saucepan and bring to a boil. Remove from the heat and add the almond flavoring. Immediately stir in the remaining 1 cup flour to keep from lumping. When smooth and thick, add the eggs, one at a time, beating until smooth. Divide in half and spread out evenly over each piece of dough. Bake at 350° for about 55 minutes until the topping is crisp and light brown. Cool and frost with **Powdered Sugar Frosting**. Sprinkle the top with toasted almonds.

**Powdered Sugar Frosting:** Sift the powdered sugar and gradually beat it into the butter. When the frosting is light and fluffy, blend in the vanilla.

Susan Warren
Reservations

## Banana Torte

4 eggs, separated
1 cup sugar
1 cup graham cracker crumbs
½ tsp. baking powder
½ cup chopped pecans
½ cup flaked coconut

½ tsp. vanilla
1 (18-oz.) can ready-to-serve
  vanilla pudding
Lemon juice
2 bananas, sliced
½ cup heavy cream, whipped

Beat the egg yolks with the sugar; add the graham cracker crumbs, baking powder, pecans, coconut and vanilla. In another bowl, beat the egg whites until stiff and fold into the crumb mixture. Pour into 2 greased, 8" cake pans. Bake at 350° for 20 to 25 minutes. Cool. Spread one-half of the pudding on 1 layer. Brush the lemon juice on half the banana slices and place on the pudding. Stack the top layer on, spread the remaining pudding over and refrigerate. Just before serving, garnish with the remaining banana and top with the whipped cream.

*Serves 6 to 8.*

Karen Fudge
Regional Sales

## Fresh Plum Tart

¾ cup milk
3 pkg. yeast
1¼ cups flour (approx.)
1¼ cups sugar

½ tsp. salt
¼ cup plus 1 Tbsp. butter
1 egg
5 lbs. fresh plums

Combine the milk and yeast over low heat and stir until lukewarm. Combine the flour, ¼ cup sugar, the salt and butter and pour onto a board; make a ring and add the egg. Add the yeast mixture and stir with your finger around the inner edge, thoroughly mixing in the flour little by little. If necessary, add more flour so that the dough is smooth, not sticky. Let the dough rest covered in a warm place. Meanwhile, prepare the plums by slitting the sides, removing the seeds and slitting again in quarters, being careful to keep the sections intact. When the dough is ready, roll out and set in a slightly floured, 17" x 11" sheet pan. Place the plums on in a shingle form, overlapping some. Bake on the center rack at 350° for 30 minutes. Sprinkle with the remaining sugar while the tart is still warm.

Helmut W. Kopleck
Executive Chef
Philadelphia Food Services

## Rhubarb Crisp

4 cups rhubarb, cut into
    1" cubes
1 cup sugar
2 Tbsp. cornstarch

1 cup brown sugar
1 cup flour
¾ cup oatmeal
½ cup butter

Place the rhubarb in an ovenproof dish. Combine the sugar, 1 cup water and the cornstarch in a saucepan over medium heat. Bring to a boil, stirring constantly; cool. Combine the remaining ingredients to make a crumbly mixture. Pour the cooled sauce over the rhubarb and sprinkle on the topping. Bake at 350° for 45 minutes to 1 hour or until browned.

Andrea Meyer
Reservations

## Blueberry Cobbler

2 cups blueberries
Juice of ½ lemon
3 Tbsp. butter
1¼ to 1¾ cups sugar
½ cup milk

1 cup flour
½ tsp. salt
1 tsp. baking powder
1 Tbsp. cornstarch
1 cup boiling water

Set the blueberries in a greased, 8" square dish and sprinkle with the lemon juice. Make a batter of the butter, ¾ cup sugar, the milk, flour, ¼ tsp. salt and the baking powder. Pour over the berries. To prepare the topping, mix together the remaining sugar, ¼ tsp. salt and cornstarch. Sprinkle over the batter and pour boiling water over all. Bake at 350° for about 45 minutes.

Nola Sears
Reservations

## Lillian's Blueberry Delight

3 cups fresh or frozen
   blueberries
¾ cup sugar
¼ cup cornstarch
1 cup vanilla wafer crumbs
½ cup butter

1½ cups powdered sugar
2 eggs
½ to ¾ cup finely chopped
   walnuts
1 cup heavy cream
Sugar (optional)

Combine the berries, sugar and cornstarch and cook over medium heat until clear and bubbly. Set aside to cool. Cover the bottom of an 8" x 8" pan with most of the vanilla wafer crumbs, reserving about 2 Tbsp. Combine the butter, powdered sugar and eggs; beat until of whipped cream consistency and spread over the crumbs. Spread the cooled blueberry filling over the butter cream layer and sprinkle on the nuts. Whip the cream and sweeten it to taste. Spread the whipped cream over the nuts and dust with the reserved wafer crumbs. Refrigerate overnight.

Susan Warren
Reservations

## Peaches and Cream

¾ cup flour
1 tsp. baking powder
1 (3¼-oz.) pkg. vanilla
   pudding (not instant)
3 Tbsp. margarine, softened
1 egg

½ cup milk
1 (15- or 21-oz.) can peaches
1 (8-oz.) pkg. cream cheese,
   softened
½ cup plus 1 Tbsp. sugar
1 Tbsp. cinnamon

Combine the first 6 ingredients in a bowl, beat for 2 minutes at medium speed and pour into a greased, 9" pie pan. Drain the can of peaches and reserve 3 Tbsp. of the juice. Place the peaches on top of the batter. Combine the cream cheese, ½ cup sugar and juice in a small bowl; beat for 2 minutes. Spoon over the peaches 1" from the side. Mix 1 Tbsp. sugar and the cinnamon and sprinkle on top. Bake at 350° for 30 to 35 minutes.

Yvonne Erickson
Reservations

## Crème Fraîche

3 cups heavy cream
½ cup sour cream

Fresh strawberries
Brown sugar

Let the heavy cream stand at room temperature for 24 hours. Blend in the sour cream and pour over the strawberries. Sprinkle with brown sugar, if desired.

Kathy Pickering
Reservations

## Deluxe English Trifle

1 box Bisquick
½ cup raspberry jam
⅓ cup sherry
1 (3-oz.) pkg. vanilla pudding

⅓ cup toasted slivered
  almonds
¾ cup heavy cream, chilled
3 Tbsp. confectioners' sugar
Chopped candied cherries

Follow the directions on the back of the Bisquick box for velvet crumb cake. Bake in an 8" square pan; cool. Carefully split the cake to make 2 layers and fill with the raspberry jam. Stack the cake and cut into 9 or 12 pieces. Arrange the pieces in a baking dish and sprinkle with the sherry. Cook the pudding as directed on the package, except increase the milk to 2½ cups. Cool to room temperature. Pour the pudding over the cake and sprinkle with the almonds. Chill for at least 4 hours. In a chilled bowl, beat the cream and confectioners' sugar until stiff, spread on the cake, garnish with cherries and cut into servings.

Makes 9 to 12 servings.

Vera M. Cook
Reservations

## Pistachio Dessert

1 cup flour
3 Tbsp. sugar
½ to ¾ cup nuts (approx.)
½ cup margarine
1 (8-oz.) pkg. cream cheese

⅔ cup powdered sugar
1 (12-oz.) carton Cool Whip
2 (3-oz.) pkg. instant
  pistachio pudding
3 cups milk

Combine the flour, sugar, nuts and margarine and bake in a 9" x 13" pan at 350° for 15 minutes. Cool. Mix together the cream cheese and powdered sugar and fold in half the Cool Whip. Pour over the crust. Prepare the pistachio pudding with the milk and pour over the cream cheese mixture. Spread the remaining Cool Whip over the top and sprinkle with more chopped nuts to taste. Chill until serving.

Kristi Severson
Reservations

## Fluffy Peanut Butter Dessert

1 ½ cups graham cracker
    crumbs
½ cup firmly packed light
    brown sugar
½ cup plus ⅓ cup crunchy
    peanut butter
¼ cup melted butter or
    margarine

¾ cup powdered sugar
1 (8-oz.) pkg. cream cheese
¾ cup sugar
2 cups heavy cream, whipped
1 (4-oz.) can pie sliced apples,
    drained
½ tsp. cinnamon

Combine the graham cracker crumbs, brown sugar, ½ cup peanut butter and the butter; mix until crumbly. In another bowl, combine the powdered sugar and ⅓ cup peanut butter; mix until crumbly. Mash the cream cheese and beat in the sugar gradually until the mixture is soft and creamy. Fold in the whipped cream. Sprinkle two-thirds of the crumb mixture over the bottom of a 9" x 12" pan and press in the crumbs evenly. Spoon half the cheese mixture over the crumbs and carefully spread into an even layer. Spread the apples slices evenly over the cheese; sprinkle with cinnamon. Sprinkle two-thirds of the powdered sugar mixture over the apples. Top with the remaining cheese mixture, spreading evenly over the crumbs. Top with the remaining graham cracker crumbs and powdered sugar mixture. Cover the pan with foil and chill for 24 hours before serving in squares.

Karen Fudge
Regional Sales

## Four-Layer Dessert

1 cup flour
½ cup melted butter or
    margarine
1 cup chopped nuts
1 (8-oz.) pkg. cream cheese
1 cup powdered sugar

1 ½ to 2 large cartons
    Cool Whip
Sliced strawberries
2 pkg. instant vanilla
    pudding
3 cups milk

Mix the flour, butter and ½ cup nuts together and press into a 9" x 13" pan. Bake at 350° for 12 to 13 minutes; cool. Beat together the cream cheese, powdered sugar and 2 cups Cool Whip. Pour over the cooled crust. Add the strawberries. Combine the instant pudding and milk and beat well. Spread over the strawberries. Top with most of a large carton of Cool Whip and garnish with ½ cup chopped nuts. Chill.

*Note: Two pkg. instant lemon pudding can be substituted for the sliced strawberries and vanilla pudding. Chocolate pudding is another especially good variation.*

Arlene McEachern
Public Affairs

## Swedish Chocolate Roll

| | |
|---|---|
| *3 eggs* | **Filling:** |
| *¾ cup sugar* | *½ cup butter* |
| *⅓ cup potato flour* | *½ cup powdered sugar* |
| *2 Tbsp. cocoa* | *2 egg yolks* |
| *2 tsp. baking powder* | *1 tsp. vanilla* |

Beat the eggs and sugar together until white and fluffy. Sift together the flour, cocoa and baking powder, add to the eggs and stir until well blended. Pour the batter into a jelly roll pan lined with buttered wax paper. Bake at 425° for 5 minutes. Turn onto wax paper sprinkled with granulated sugar. Let stand until cold. Spread the cooled cake with the filling and roll up lengthwise. Wrap in wax paper and refrigerate for several hours before serving.

**Filling:** Cream the butter and powdered sugar until fluffy, stir in the egg yolks and vanilla.

Rick Sanders
Reservations

## Berry Blender Ice Cream

| | |
|---|---|
| *1 pint strawberries,* | *2 eggs* |
| *washed and stemmed* | *⅓ cup sugar* |
| *½ cup heavy cream* | *2 tsp. lemon juice* |

Early in the day arrange the berries in a shallow pan or ice cube trays and freeze. A few minutes before serving, remove the berries from the freezer. Put the cream, eggs and sugar in a blender container and whirl for 2 seconds. With the motor on high, drop in the frozen berries, one at a time. Whirl until smooth, stopping the motor, when necessary, to stir the thickened mixture with a rubber spatula. Stir in the lemon juice. Spoon into serving dishes. Serve at once or store in the freezer, removing 15 to 20 minutes before serving to soften slightly.

*You can also make this with other frozen fruits.*

Dorothy Stitt
JoAnn Olanyk
Reservations

### Vanilla Bavarian Cream

*2 pkg. unflavored gelatin*
*½ cup cold water*
*½ cup plus 1 Tbsp. sugar*
*1 Tbsp. cornstarch*
*2 eggs, beaten*

*1½ cups milk, scalded*
*1 cup vanilla ice cream*
*1 tsp. vanilla*
*1 cup heavy cream, whipped*
*Fresh fruit*

Sprinkle the gelatin over the water to soften. Heat to dissolve the gelatin completely. Mix together the sugar and cornstarch, add the eggs and beat for 2 minutes. Slowly add the warm milk, beating constantly. Pour into a 1-quart saucepan. Cook, stirring over medium heat, until the custard coats a spoon. Add the gelatin and ice cream while the custard is hot. Cool until slightly thickened. Add the vanilla, fold in the whipped cream and pour into a 1-quart mold. Chill until set. Unmold carefully and garnish with fresh fruit.

*Serves 6 to 8.*

Tim Walker
Reservations

☞ *To get the greatest volume when whipping cream, chill the cream, bowl and beater together.*

## Toffee Ice Cream Supreme

6 egg yolks
2 cups homogenized milk
1 cup sugar
⅓ tsp. salt
2 cups heavy cream
2 cups half & half
1½ Tbsp. pure vanilla extract
    or the seeds scraped from a
    2½" vanilla bean

**Toffee Crunch:**
4 cups sugar

1 cup hot water
⅓ cup corn syrup
2 cups sweet butter
1 tsp. salt
½ cup finely chopped
    unroasted almonds
1 tsp. pure vanilla extract
4 oz. sweet chocolate, melted
4 oz. lightly toasted nutmeat
    (use almonds, hazelnuts,
    pecans or walnuts)

Combine the egg yolks, milk, sugar and salt and cook in the upper part of a double boiler until the mixture is thick enough to coat a wooden spoon. Remove from the heat, place in a clean bowl and cover with plastic wrap to prevent skin from forming. Set in the refrigerator for at least 4 hours (preferably overnight). Stir in the creams and vanilla and pour the mixture into a sterilized freezer can. (Follow the manufacturer's instructions for operating the ice cream maker.) When half-frozen, add 2 cups **Toffee Crunch** to the vanilla ice cream and freeze.

**Toffee Crunch:** Stir the sugar, water and corn syrup together in a 6-quart saucepan until blended; bring to a full boil and wash down the sides of the pan with a pastry brush dipped in cold water. Boil to 280° on a candy thermometer, then add the butter in small pieces until all is blended. Add the salt and stir until the temperature reaches 315°. Add the nuts and continue stirring until the temperature reaches 320° or slightly below. Immediately remove from the heat and stir in the vanilla extract; pour out onto a greased piece of marble or 2 greased jelly roll pans. While the candy is still quite warm, spread the top side with half the chocolate and cover with half the nutmeat. Turn the candy over and repeat. When cool, break into fine pieces.

*Note: Add* **Toffee Ice Cream Supreme** *to a graham cracker pie shell for* **Deluxe Ice Cream Pie**.

Jerry F. Boyer
Executive Chef
Newark Food Services

### Rice Pudding

1 cup rice
½ cup sugar or to taste
4 cups milk
1 tsp. vanilla
¼ tsp. salt

1 cup heavy cream, whipped
1 (17-oz.) can crushed
  pineapple, drained
1 (8-oz.) jar maraschino
  cherries, halved

Cook the rice and sugar in the milk, bringing to a boil. Reduce the heat, cover and cook until done, stirring occasionally. Add the vanilla and salt and cool. Fold in the whipped cream, pineapple and cherries. Gently combine all the ingredients and serve.

Kathy Morgan
Inflight Services

### Burnt Cream

2 cups milk
4 egg yolks
⅓ cup sugar

1 tsp. vanilla
Sugar for topping

Heat the milk over low heat until bubbles form around the edge of the pan. Beat the egg yolks and sugar together until thick, about 3 minutes. Gradually beat the milk into the egg yolks. Stir in the vanilla and pour into 6 (6-oz.) custard cups. Place the custard cups in a pan filled with about ½" water. Bake at 350° until set, about 45 minutes. Remove the cups from the water and refrigerate until chilled. Sprinkle each custard with about 2 tsp. sugar. Place on the top rack of the oven and broil until the topping is medium brown. Chill before serving.

Dorothy Stitt
Reservations

### Charlie Pie

1 (6-oz.) pkg. instant
  chocolate pudding
3⅔ cups milk
1 prebaked pie shell

1 (6-oz.) pkg. instant vanilla
  pudding
⅓ cup crème de menthe
Whipped cream

Thoroughly mix together the chocolate pudding and 2 cups milk and pour into the pie shell. Combine 1⅔ cups milk, the vanilla pudding and the crème de menthe and pour on top of the chocolate pudding mixture. Refrigerate for about 1 hour. Serve with whipped cream.

Janet Vitcovich
Reservations

## Creamy Lemon Meringue Pie

3 eggs, separated
1 (14-oz.) can Eagle Brand milk
½ cup Real Lemon juice
1 tsp. grated lemon rind

1 graham cracker pie shell
½ tsp. cream of tartar
⅓ cup sugar

In a medium bowl, beat the egg yolks; stir in the milk, lemon juice and rind. Pour into the graham cracker crust. In a small bowl, beat the egg whites with the cream of tartar until foamy. Gradually add the sugar, beating until stiff but not dry. Spread the meringue on top of the pie, carefully sealing the edge of the crust. Bake at 350° for 15 minutes or until golden brown. Cool and chill before serving. Refrigerate the leftovers.

Lynda Brooks
Reservations

## Streusel Cream Peach Pie

4 cups peeled and quartered
  peaches
1 (9") unbaked pie crust
½ cup sugar
½ tsp. nutmeg

1 egg
2 Tbsp. cream
¼ cup packed brown sugar
½ cup flour
¼ cup butter, softened

Arrange the peaches in the pie shell. Sprinkle on the sugar and nutmeg. Beat the egg and cream together and pour over the peaches. Mix the brown sugar, flour and butter until crumbly; sprinkle over the peaches and bake at 425° for 35 to 45 minutes or until browned. Serve while slightly warm.

Ken Christensen
Operations Planning

## Ginger Rum Pumpkin Pie

1½ cups solidly packed
  pumpkin
½ cup packed dark brown
  sugar
¼ cup plus 2 Tbsp. sugar
3 egg yolks, beaten
1 cup sour cream
¼ tsp. salt
⅛ tsp. ground nutmeg

1 (2-oz.) jar crystallized ginger,
  minced
5 Tbsp. Jamaican rum
3 egg whites, at room
  temperature
1 pastry pie shell or graham
  cracker crust
1 cup heavy cream
Crystallized ginger slivers

Combine the pumpkin, brown sugar and ¼ cup sugar in the top of a double boiler. Beat in the egg yolks, sour cream, salt and nutmeg. Cook, stirring occasionally, over simmering water until the mixture thickens, about 5 minutes; remove from the heat. Fold in the minced ginger and 3 Tbsp. rum; cool to lukewarm. Beat the egg whites in a small bowl until foamy. Gradually beat in 2 Tbsp. sugar; beat until stiff. Fold the egg whites into the pumpkin mixture; spoon into the pie shell. Bake at 350° until the filling sets, about 40 to 45 minutes. Cool on a wire rack. Serve at room temperature or refrigerate until cold. Whip the heavy cream in a chilled bowl until soft peaks form; add 2 Tbsp. rum and beat until stiff. Garnish the pie with the whipped cream and ginger slivers.

Susan Warren
Reservations

## Amazing Coconut Pie

2 cups milk
¾ cup sugar
½ cup biscuit mix
4 eggs

¼ cup butter
1½ tsp. vanilla
1 cup coconut

Combine all the ingredients except the coconut in an electric blender. Cover and blend on low speed for 3 minutes. Pour into a greased, 9" pie pan and let stand for 5 minutes. Sprinkle the coconut on top. Bake at 350° for 40 minutes.

Kathy Morgan
Inflight Services

## Lemon Sour Cream Pie

1¼ cups plus 2 Tbsp. sugar
¼ cup cornstarch
Dash of salt
1 cup milk
3 egg yolks, slightly beaten
¼ cup butter
1 tsp. finely shredded lemon
    peel

¼ cup lemon juice
1 cup sour cream
1 (9") prebaked pastry shell
3 egg whites
¼ tsp. cream of tartar
½ tsp. vanilla

In a saucepan, combine 1 cup sugar, the cornstarch and salt; slowly stir in the milk. Cook, stirring until the mixture thickens and bubbles. Blend in a small amount of the hot mixture into the egg yolks, then stir the yolks back into the mixture. Cook, stirring, for 2 minutes more. Add the butter, lemon peel and juice. Fold in the sour cream. Cover the surface with clear plastic wrap or wax paper and cool to room temperature; spoon into the pastry shell. Beat the egg whites with the cream of tartar and vanilla until soft peaks form. Gradually add the remaining sugar, beating to stiff peaks. Spread the meringue over the pie, sealing the edge. Bake at 350° for 12 to 15 minutes or until golden brown; cool.

Serves 8.

Janet Wanink
Reservations

## Black Bottom Pie

2¼ tsp. unflavored gelatin
2 Tbsp. cold water
1⅓ cups milk
⅓ cup plus ¼ cup sugar
2¼ tsp. cornstarch
Pinch of salt
3 egg yolks, slightly beaten
1½ squares unsweetened
    chocolate

¾ tsp. vanilla
Prebaked pastry or graham
    cracker pie shell
3 egg whites
Pinch of cream of tartar
2¼ tsp. white rum
Whipped cream (optional)
Chocolate shavings (optional)

Sprinkle the gelatin on the water and let it soften for 5 minutes. Scald the milk in a double boiler. Combine the ⅓ cup sugar, the cornstarch and salt and add the egg yolks. Slowly stir into the milk. Return to the double boiler. Cook, stirring over hot, not boiling water, until the mixture coats a spoon. Remove from the heat and stir in the gelatin. Melt the chocolate and stir into half the custard. Add the vanilla, beating until smooth. Pour into the pie shell. While the chocolate custard begins to set, beat the egg whites with the cream of tartar until moist peaks form. Gradually add the ¼ cup sugar and beat until stiff. Very carefully fold in the remaining custard and the rum. Pour on top of the chocolate layer. Chill until set. Cover with whipped cream and chocolate shavings before serving, if desired.

Edward E. Carlson
Chairman of the Board
United Airlines, Inc.

## Strawberry Bavarian Pie

1 Tbsp. unflavored gelatin
2 Tbsp. cold water
1 cup strawberry juice
½ cup sugar
1 cup sliced fresh or frozen
   strawberries

2 tsp. lemon juice
¼ cup kirsch
1 cup heavy cream, whipped
1 (9") pastry or graham
   cracker pie shell

Soften the gelatin in the cold water. Bring the strawberry juice and sugar to a boil, add the softened gelatin and cool. When cooled, fold in the strawberries, lemon juice, kirsch and whipped cream. Pour into the pie shell and refrigerate until set. If desired, garnish with more whipped cream, small strawberries and chocolate curls.

Note: Strawberry juice is available in health food stores.

Lyell E. Cook
Manager
Detroit Food Services

## Brandy Alexander Pie

1 pkg. pie crust sticks or
  mix
3 cups miniature
  marshmallows
½ cup milk

¼ cup dark crème de cacao
3 Tbsp. brandy
1½ cups heavy cream,
  whipped and chilled
Chocolate curls

Prepare and bake a pie shell as directed on the package. Cool. Heat the marshmallows and milk over low heat, stirring constantly, just until the marshmallows melt. Chill until thickened and blend in the liquors. In a chilled bowl, beat the cream until stiff. Fold the marshmallow mixture into the whipped cream and pour into the pie shell. Garnish with chocolate curls. Chill for at least 4 hours before serving.

Annemarie Fleming
Reservations

## Paper Bag Apple Pie

10 to 11 apples
1 cup sugar
½ cup plus 2 Tbsp. flour
½ tsp. cinnamon

1 (9") unbaked pie shell
2 Tbsp. lemon juice
½ cup butter or margarine

Pare and core the apples, cut into quarters, rinse in water and place in a large bowl. Combine ½ cup sugar, 2 Tbsp. flour and the cinnamon; sprinkle over the apples and toss to coat well. Spoon into the pie shell. Sprinkle with the lemon juice. Combine the ½ cup sugar, ½ cup flour and butter and sprinkle over the apples. Slip the pie into a large brown paper bag, fold the open end twice and fasten with paper clips. Place on a cookie sheet and bake at 425° for 1 hour. Slit the bag open, remove the pie and cool on a wire rack.

Annemarie Fleming
Reservations

---

☞ Use light or sour cream in place of the liquid in pie crust mixes. Makes a very rich pie crust.

---

## Perfect Pie Crust

4 cups unsifted flour
1 Tbsp. sugar
2 tsp. salt
1¾ cups shortening

½ cup water
1 large egg
1 Tbsp. vinegar

Mix the dry ingredients with a fork and cut in the shortening. Beat together the remaining ingredients; pour over the dry mixture and mix until all is moistened. Divide the dough into 5 portions, shape each portion into a flat, round patty and wrap in wax paper. Chill for at least 30 minutes. Lightly flour both sides of each patty. With a rolling pin and board roll the crusts out separately and press into 9" pie pans.

Makes 5 (9") crusts.

Lou Gardiner
Reservations
Edna Harris
Food Services

## Wheat Germ Brownies

½ cup melted butter
1 Tbsp. refined molasses
2 eggs, slightly beaten
⅞ cup sugar
2 tsp. vanilla

1 cup wheat germ (can be
 toasted)
½ cup powdered milk
½ tsp. baking powder
¼ tsp. salt

Combine the first 5 ingredients, stirring well. Sift in the remaining ingredients and beat 20 strokes; do not overstir. Spread in an 8" x 8" pan completely lined with wax paper. Bake at 350° for 30 minutes, turn out of the pan and immediately remove the paper. Cut into squares while hot.

Susan I. Brentzel
Reservations

## Brownies

2 cups flour
2 cups sugar
½ tsp. salt
1 cup margarine
1 cup shortening
¼ cup cocoa
2 eggs
1 tsp. baking soda
½ cup buttermilk

1 tsp. vanilla

**Frosting:**
½ cup margarine
3 Tbsp. cocoa
¼ cup plus 2 Tbsp. buttermilk
4 cups powdered sugar
½ cup nuts

Combine the flour, sugar and salt. In a saucepan, bring the margarine, shortening and cocoa to a boil. Pour over the flour mixture, stirring well. Add the remaining ingredients, place in a cake pan and bake at 300° until done. Remove from the oven, prick the cake with a fork and, while still warm, spread the frosting on the brownies.

**Frosting:** Bring the margarine, cocoa and buttermilk to a boil. Then add the powdered sugar and nuts. Stir well to combine.

Janis Sisley

## Butterscotch Brownies

¼ cup butter
1 cup brown sugar
1 egg
½ cup flour

1 tsp. baking powder
½ tsp. salt
½ tsp. vanilla
½ cup walnuts

Melt the butter and stir in the sugar and egg. Sift together the flour, baking powder and salt and stir into the sugar mixture. Add the vanilla and walnuts and spread into a greased, 8" x 8" pan. Bake at 350° for 20 to 25 minutes.

Rick Sanders
Reservations

### Glazed Brownies

¾ cup margarine
2 cups sugar
4 eggs
1 tsp. vanilla
1 (1-lb.) can chocolate syrup
1 cup plus 1 Tbsp. sifted flour

½ tsp. baking powder
¼ tsp. salt
½ cup chopped walnuts
 (optional)
¼ cup milk
1 cup semisweet chocolate bits

Beat ½ cup margarine with 1 cup sugar until light and fluffy. Beat in the eggs, two at a time, and the vanilla. Mix well and stir in the chocolate syrup. Lightly measure the flour and combine with the baking powder and salt, stir into the batter and add the nuts. Pour into a well-greased, 15½" x 10½" x 1" jelly roll pan and spread evenly. Bake at 350° for 22 to 25 minutes or until a slight imprint remains when touched lightly with your finger. Remove the pan to a rack and let the brownies cool. Combine the ¼ cup margarine, 1 cup sugar and milk in a saucepan, bring to a boil and boil for 1 minute only. Add the chocolate bits and stir quickly until all are melted. Immediately pour the entire amount on the brownies and spread it evenly (the mixture will harden rapidly). Cut into 2½" x 1" bars.

*Note: The glaze makes a candy-like topping.*

*Makes 5 dozen.*

Bill Speicher
Senior Vice President & General Manager
Eastern Division-New York City

### Angel Bars

Whole graham crackers
1 cup sugar
1 egg
½ cup margarine, melted
¾ cup milk (approx.)
1 cup angel flake coconut
1 cup chopped nuts

1 cup graham cracker crumbs
1 cup crushed pineapple,
 well drained
2 cups powdered sugar
¼ cup margarine
1 tsp. vanilla

Line a 9" x 13" baking pan with whole graham crackers. Combine the sugar, egg, margarine and ½ cup milk in a saucepan over medium-high heat; bring to a boil, stirring constantly. Stir in the coconut, nuts, cracker crumbs and pineapple. Spread the mixture over the whole crackers and cover with more whole crackers. Cool. Combine the powdered sugar, margarine, vanilla and enough milk to make a smooth frosting. Frost the graham crackers and cut into bars.

*These freeze well.*

Kathy Morgan
Inflight Services

## Seven-Layer Cookies

½ cup margarine, melted
1 cup graham cracker crumbs
1 cup coconut
1 (6-oz.) pkg. chocolate chips

1 (6-oz.) pkg. butterscotch
  flavored chips
1½ cups chopped walnuts
1 large can sweetened
  condensed milk

Pour the margarine into a 9" x 13" cake pan. Then add, in layers, the graham cracker crumbs, coconut, chocolate and butterscotch chips and walnuts. Pour the milk over the top and bake at 350° for 30 minutes. Cool and cut into squares.

Jan Taylor
Reservations

## Aunt Martha's Party Squares

½ cup melted butter
¼ cup sugar
¼ cup plus 1 Tbsp. cocoa
1 tsp. vanilla
1 egg, beaten
2 cups crushed graham
  crackers
1 cup fine coconut
1½ cups chopped nuts

2 cups powdered sugar
¼ cup evaporated milk
¼ cup butter
2 Tbsp. Jello instant vanilla
  pudding mix
4 squares semisweet
  chocolate
1 Tbsp. butter

Combine the first 4 ingredients. Add, mixing thoroughly after each addition, the egg, crackers, coconut and nuts. Press into a 9" x 9" pan and chill. Combine the powdered sugar, milk, butter and pudding mix; spread over the cracker mixture and chill again. Melt the semisweet chocolate and butter, stirring to combine. Spread over the pudding mixture and thoroughly chill. Cut into squares and serve.

Rick Sanders
Reservations

## Cheese and Pecan Diamonds

¼ cup plus 1 Tbsp. sweet
   butter
⅓ cup brown sugar
1 cup flour
¼ cup chopped pecans
½ cup sugar

1 (8-oz.) pkg. cream cheese,
   softened
1 egg
2 Tbsp. cream
1 Tbsp. lemon juice
Grated rind of 1 lemon
½ tsp. vanilla

Cream the butter and brown sugar and add the flour and pecans, mixing well. Set aside 1 cup of the mixture for topping and press the remainder into the bottom of a greased, 8" x 8" pan. Bake at 350° for 12 to 15 minutes. Blend the sugar and cream cheese until smooth. Add the remaining ingredients and beat well. Spread over the baked crust and sprinkle with the reserved topping. Return to the oven and bake for 25 minutes more. Cool, then chill and cut into diamonds to serve.

*I sometimes freeze and serve them frozen; they're also good this way.*

Yvonne Erickson
Reservations

## Cream Cheese Cake Bars

1 yellow cake mix
½ cup butter, melted
1 egg
1 (8-oz.) pkg. cream cheese,
   partially softened

2 eggs
1 tsp. vanilla
3½ cups powdered sugar

Combine the cake mix, butter, egg and 1 Tbsp. water; mix well and pat into an ungreased, 9" x 13" pan and set aside. Combine the remaining ingredients and pour over the cake mix. Bake at 350° for 30 minutes. Cool at room temperature for 1 hour and refrigerate for several hours. Cut into squares and serve.

Cindy Hibbert
Apollo Systems

## Raisin Energy Squares

½ cup butter or margarine
¾ cup firmly packed light
   brown sugar
1 egg
1 tsp. vanilla
1 cup rolled oats

½ cup flour
1¼ cups raisins
1 cup chopped walnuts
½ cup carob or semisweet
   chocolate chips
2 Tbsp. wheat germ

Combine the butter, brown sugar, egg and vanilla and beat until well blended. Add the oats and flour, mix well and stir in the raisins, walnuts and carob or chocolate chips. Spread the batter evenly in a greased, 8" x 8" pan and sprinkle with the wheat germ. Bake at 350° for 25 minutes. Cool in the pan on a wire rack before cutting into 2" squares.

Makes 16.

Margaret McCone
Wife of Bob McCone
Regional Sales Promotion Rep.

## Chocolate Mint Bars

⅔ cup butter
3 squares unsweetened
   chocolate
2 cups brown sugar
3 eggs
1 tsp. vanilla
1¼ cups flour
1 tsp. baking powder

¼ tsp. salt

**Frosting:**
2 cups powdered sugar
¼ cup butter
2 tsp. milk
½ tsp. peppermint flavoring

Melt the butter and chocolate in a double boiler. Add the brown sugar, eggs and vanilla. Sift together the flour, baking powder and salt and fold into the chocolate mixture. Spread evenly in a 9" x 13" pan and bake at 350° for 25 to 30 minutes. Cool and chill. Mix the frosting ingredients together well and glaze over the bars.

Nola Sears
Reservations

## Lemon Bars

1 (17-oz.) pkg. lemon cake mix
½ cup butter or margarine,
  softened
3 eggs

1 (13½-oz.) pkg lemon
  frosting mix
1 (8-oz.) pkg. cream cheese,
  softened
Powdered sugar

Combine the cake mix, butter and 1 egg, mixing well. Pat into a greased, 9" x 13" pan. Beat the remaining eggs, the frosting mix and cream cheese with a mixer for 3 to 5 minutes. Pour over the cake mixture and bake at 350° for 30 to 40 minutes. Remove from the oven and immediately sift lots of powdered sugar over. When cool, cut as desired. Store in the refrigerator.

Sally Keenan
Kathy Morgan
Inflight Services

## Butter Tart Bars

1¼ cups all-purpose flour
¼ cup brown sugar
⅓ cup butter
1 cup seedless raisins
2 eggs

½ cup sugar
½ cup dark corn syrup
⅛ tsp. salt
1 tsp. vanilla

Combine ¾ cup flour, the brown sugar and butter to make coarse crumbs. Press into the bottom of an ungreased, 8" pan. Bake at 350° for 12 to 15 minutes. Meanwhile, rinse and drain the raisins. Beat the eggs and sugar, add the raisins, the remaining flour, the syrup, salt and vanilla. Pour over the baked layer, return to the oven and bake for 25 to 30 minutes more or until the topping is golden brown. Cool and cut into bars.

Pat Logue
Reservations

## Forfar Shortbread

6 cups all-purpose flour
¾ cup rice flour or ground rice

2 cups butter
½ cup castor sugar

Combine the flours and rub in the butter; stir in the sugar and turn onto a floured board. With your hands, knead the mixture thoroughly into a smooth dough. Shape into rounds, notching the edges with your forefingers and thumbs. Bake at 350° until golden brown.

Margaret Hamilton
Inflight Services

## Scottish Shortbread

4 cups flour
1 cup cornstarch

2 cups butter
1 cup sugar

Sift the flour and cornstarch together. Work the butter until very soft, then add the sugar, a little at a time, until well blended. Add the flour and cornstarch mixture in small amounts until all is worked in thoroughly. Turn onto a board and knead the dough until it is smooth but not oily. Roll out the dough until it is about ¼" thick. Cut into 2" x 1" fingers. Prick all over with a fork and flute the edges. Bake at 325° to 350° for 30 minutes or until a pale golden color.

*Traditionally shortbread is made in rounds and broken into pieces when served.*

Mike Dearing
Reservations

## Little Gems

3 cups unsifted flour
1 cup sugar
⅛ tsp. salt
1 ½ cups butter, softened

2 egg yolks
1 tsp. vanilla
Strawberry preserves or jam
Pecan halves

Combine the first 3 ingredients and cut in the butter until the mixture resembles corn meal. Beat the egg yolks with the vanilla, add to the flour mixture and blend well. Pinch off small pieces of the dough (approximately ¾ tsp.) and roll into balls. With your finger make a small indentation in the center of each ball and fill with ¼ tsp. strawberry preserves; top with a pecan half. Bake at 325° for 20 to 25 minutes until light brown.

*Makes approximately 9 dozen.*

Lynda Brooks
Reservations

## Diagonaler
### (Norwegian Diagonals)

½ cup butter
¼ cup sugar
1 egg, beaten

¼ tsp. salt
1 ½ cups flour
Tart jelly

Cream the butter and slowly add the sugar, beating until very light. Add the egg, salt and flour. Shape into a smooth dough. Roll two-thirds of the dough into a 5" wide oblong, ⅛" thick. Cut into 2 (2½") strips and lay separately on a greased cookie sheet. Roll out the remaining dough ⅛" thick, the same length as the strips. Cut into 6 long, thin strips. Lay 3 of the strips (2 at the sides and 1 in the center) lengthwise on top of each of the 2 wider strips on the cookie sheet. Use a little water to seal the strips. Fill between the strips with jelly, using different kinds, if desired. Bake at 375° for 12 to 15 minutes. While warm, cut diagonally into slices 1" wide.

Sue Heavilon
Reservations

## Peanut Butter Surprise Cookies

1½ cups all-purpose flour,
  unsifted
½ cup sugar
½ tsp. baking soda
¼ tsp. salt
½ cup vegetable shortening
½ cup chunk or cream style
  peanut butter
¼ cup light corn syrup

1 Tbsp. milk

**Fillings:**
Strawberry or raspberry jam
Peanut butter
Semisweet chocolate, butter-
  scotch or peanut butter
  flavored morsels

In a large mixing bowl, combine the flour, sugar, soda and salt. Cut in the shortening and peanut butter to make moist, even crumbs. Stir in the corn syrup and milk until blended. Roll the dough up inside a sheet of wax paper to form a smooth log 2" in diameter and about 17" long. Twist the ends of the paper to seal and chill for at least 2 hours or as long as 1 week. Cut the chilled roll crosswise into ⅛" slices. Place half the slices about ½" apart on an ungreased baking sheet and top each with a filling of your choice: ½ tsp. strawberry or raspberry jam, ½ tsp. peanut butter, or 5 to 6 semisweet chocolate, butterscotch or peanut butter flavored morsels. Place another slice of dough on top and press down lightly to mold the dough around the filling, lightly pressing the edges with a fork to seal. Bake at 350° for 8 to 10 minutes or until the cookies are light brown. Cool on the baking sheet for about 5 minutes, then remove to a wire rack.

*Makes about 4 dozen.*

Annemarie Fleming
Reservations

## Melanie's Own Chocolate Chip Cookies

½ cup butter
½ cup sugar
¼ cup firmly packed brown
  sugar
1 egg, well beaten
1 cup plus 1 Tbsp. sifted flour

½ tsp. salt
½ tsp. soda
1 (6-oz.) pkg. chocolate chips
½ cup chopped pecans
1 tsp. vanilla

Cream the butter, gradually add the sugars and cream together until light and fluffy. Add the egg and mix thoroughly. Sift the flour once, measure, add the salt and soda and sift again. Add the flour in 2 parts and mix well. Add the chocolate chips, pecans and vanilla and mix thoroughly. Chill the dough for 10 to 15 minutes. Drop from a teaspoon onto a baking sheet, 2" apart. Bake at 375° for 10 to 12 minutes.

Sheila Kent
Apollo Systems

## Famous Amos Chocolate Chip Cookies

2 cups margarine, softened
¾ cup firmly packed brown
  sugar
¾ cup sugar
1 tsp. vanilla
2 medium eggs

4 cups sifted all-purpose flour
¼ tsp. baking soda
½ tsp. salt
2 cups raisins
1 (12-oz.) pkg. chocolate chips

Beat the margarine, sugars, vanilla, 1 tsp. water and the eggs in a large bowl until creamy. By hand stir in the flour, baking soda and salt until well mixed. Stir in the raisins and chocolate chips. Measure large spoonfuls onto a cookie sheet, allowing space for spreading. Bake at 375° for 10 to 12 minutes.

Annemarie Fleming
Reservations

## Fruit Balls

16 marshmallows, finely cut
1 cup finely chopped dates
½ cup finely chopped walnuts

1 tsp. vanilla
½ cup heavy cream, whipped
16 graham cracker wafers,
  finely crushed

Mix together the marshmallows, dates, walnuts and vanilla and fold in the whipped cream. Roll into balls a little bigger than a walnut and coat the balls well with the graham cracker crumbs. Chill in the refrigerator for 2 hours or more.

Pat Logue
Reservations

## Raisin Crispies

¾ cup raisins
½ cup butter
1 tsp. vanilla
1 cup brown sugar
¾ cup flour

½ tsp. salt
½ tsp. soda
½ tsp. cinnamon
1½ cups rolled oats

Rinse and drain the raisins, combine with the butter and ¼ cup water and heat until the butter melts, stirring constantly. Cool, then stir in the vanilla and sugar. Sift together the dry ingredients and blend into the raisin mixture; stir in the oats. Drop onto a greased cookie sheet and bake at 350° for 7 to 8 minutes. Cool for 1 to 2 minutes before removing from the pan.

*Makes about 3½ dozen.*

Julie Jacobson
Reservations

## Persimmon Cookies

2 to 3 very soft persimmons
1 tsp. soda
½ cup butter
1⅓ cups sugar
1 tsp. vanilla
1 egg, well beaten

2 cups flour
1 tsp. cinnamon
½ tsp. nutmeg
½ tsp. salt
1 cup raisins or dates
1 cup chopped walnuts

Scrape out the inside of the persimmons to make 1 cup pulp and stir the soda into the pulp; set aside. Cream together the butter and sugar, add the vanilla and egg, then the persimmon pulp. Sift together the dry ingredients and stir into the persimmon mixture. Fold in the raisins and nuts. Drop onto a greased cookie sheet and bake at 350° for 8 to 10 minutes or until browned.

Ann Atwood
Reservations

## Lebkuchen

1 cup clover, orange-
blossom or other full-
flavored honey
⅔ cup packed dark brown
sugar
1 egg, well beaten
Grated rind of 1 lemon
2 Tbsp. lemon juice
½ cup slivered or finely
chopped almonds
½ cup minced citron
2½ cups all-purpose flour
1 tsp. cinnamon
½ tsp. ground cloves
½ tsp. allspice

½ tsp. mace
½ tsp. freshly grated nutmeg
½ tsp. soda
½ tsp. salt
Blanched almond halves
(optional)
Thin slivers of citron or angelica
(optional)

**Glaze:**
1 egg white
⅔ cup confectioners' sugar
Dash of salt
¼ tsp. vanilla or lemon juice

Preheat the oven to 400°. In a saucepan, heat the honey to just under the boiling point, then cool to lukewarm. Add the sugar, egg, lemon rind and juice. Mix the ½ cup almonds and the citron with ¼ cup flour. Mix the remaining flour with the spices, soda and salt and combine this flour mixture with the honey mixture. Add the nuts and citron and mix together with your hands. Put in a bowl, covered with foil or wax paper and set in the refrigerator for 12 hours or more. Divide the dough into quarters and roll each into a 6" x 4½" rectangle. With a pastry wheel, cut each into 6 (3" x 1½") cookies. Place on a greased cookie sheet, 2" apart, and set in the oven. Reduce the heat immediately to 375° and bake for 15 to 20 minutes or until the cookies test just done. Remove from the oven, spread glaze over each cookie and top with blanched almonds and citron or angelica.

**Glaze:** Beat the egg white until stiff. Fold in the remaining ingredients and mix until of spreading consistency.

*Note: Be sure not to bake the cookies so long that they become hard and dry as they should be chewy and moist.*

Duri Arquisch
Executive Chef
Salt Lake City Food Services

### No-Bake Cookies

2 cups sugar
½ cup butter
½ cup milk
3 cups oatmeal
1 tsp. soda

¼ cup plus 2 Tbsp. cocoa
   or melted chocolate chips
½ cup coconut
½ cup nuts

In a saucepan, combine the sugar, butter and milk; bring to a boil. Stir in the dry ingredients and drop from a teaspoon onto wax paper. Cool until solid.

Andrea Meyer
Reservations

### Almond Cookies

½ cup butter
1 cup chopped almonds
¼ cup sugar

1 tsp. vanilla
1 cup flour
Pinch of salt

Cream the butter, almonds, sugar and vanilla with an electric mixer until well creamed; beat in the flour and salt. Chill the dough overnight. Roll out to about ¼" thickness and cut with a small, round cookie cutter. Bake at 375° for 10 minutes.

Makes about 50 cookies.

Emile LeBoulluec
Executive Chef
Boston Food Services

### Lunch Box Cookies

¾ cup sugar (half white,
   half brown)
2 cups unbleached flour or
   1 cup unbleached and 1 cup
   wheat flour
1 tsp. salt
1 tsp. cinnamon
1 tsp. nutmeg

1 tsp. vanilla
½ cup milk
¾ cup salad oil
2 cups rolled oats
½ cup rolled barley
1 Tbsp. wheat germ
1 cup raisins
1 cup chopped walnuts

Combine all the ingredients, mixing well. Bake on ungreased cookie sheets at 350° for 15 to 20 minutes or until golden brown.

*Keeps well in the freezer. Very nutritious.*

Lucille Anderson
Reservations

## Dutch Anise Drops

1 ½ cups sifted flour
¼ tsp. baking power
½ cup eggs (about 2 to 3)

1 cup sugar
¼ tsp. anise

Sift together the flour and baking powder. Mix together the eggs, sugar and anise, beat until the mixture is thick and mounds softly. Fold in the dry ingredients, one-fourth at a time. Drop by a teaspoon onto a well-greased cookie sheet, about 2" apart. Place in a cool spot (not the refrigerator) for 8 to 10 hours; do not disturb. Bake at 350° for 5 to 6 minutes. Promptly place on racks to cool.

*These cookies have a cake-like texture on the base and are self-frosting on the top.*

Sue Heavilon
Reservations

## Crispy Cookies

½ cup butter
½ cup sugar
1 ½ cups brown sugar
1 egg
½ tsp. vanilla
½ cup coconut (optional)

¼ tsp. salt
1 cup corn flakes
1 cup Rice Krispies
½ cup oatmeal
½ tsp. baking soda
¼ tsp. baking powder

Cream the butter and sugars together. Stir in the remaining ingredients, mixing with your hands, if necessary. Shape into balls, drop onto a greased cookie sheet and bake at 350° for 10 to 15 minutes or until browned.

Jan Taylor
Reservations

## Hamilton Gingerbread

¾ cup butter
¾ cup plus 1½ Tbsp. brown
   sugar
¾ cup treacle
4 cups self-rising flour

2 tsp. powdered ginger
1 tsp. baking soda, dissolved
   in water
Milk

Cream together the butter, sugar and treacle. Sift together the flour and ginger and stir into the treacle mixture with the baking soda and enough milk to make a soft, dropping consistency. Pour into a greased and wax paper-lined, shallow, 10" square cake pan. Bake at 350° for 1½ hours or until firm to the touch. Cool and cut into squares.

*This is truly the old Scottish Hamilton gingerbread.*

Margaret Hamilton
Inflight Services

## Cherry Divinity

3 cups sugar
¾ cup light corn syrup
2 egg whites

3½ Tbsp. cherry flavored
   gelatin
½ cup chopped nuts or mixed
   candied fruit

Combine the sugar, corn syrup and ¾ cup water in a saucepan. Bring to a boil over low heat, stirring occasionally, until a small amount of syrup forms a hard ball in cold water or to a temperature of 252°. Meanwhile, beat the egg whites until stiff but not dry. Add the gelatin, 1 Tbsp. at a time, and continue beating until the mixture stands in soft peaks. When the syrup has reached the hard ball stage, pour in a fine stream over the egg white mixture, beating constantly. Continue beating until the mixture holds its shape and loses its gloss. Add the nuts and quickly pour onto a greased, 9" x 9" pan or drop by teaspoons onto wax paper.

*Makes about 5 dozen pieces.*

Geri Shippee
Reservations

## Divinity

2 cups sugar
½ cup light corn syrup
½ cup water
⅛ tsp. salt

2 egg whites
1 tsp. vanilla
1 tsp. powdered sugar

In a saucepan mix together the first 4 ingredients. Slowly bring to a boil, stirring until the sugar dissolves and the mixture cooks to the hard ball stage (260°). Meanwhile, beat the egg whites until stiff. Gradually pour the hot syrup into the whites, beating constantly. Beat until the candy begins to hold its shape. Beat in the vanilla and powdered sugar (this amount of powdered sugar makes a real improvement in texture). Drop from a teaspoon onto wax paper or pour into a greased pan. Let stand for several hours until firm. Store in an airtight container.

*Makes about 50 pieces.*

Nola Sears
Reservations

## Almond Roca

2 cups butter
2 cups sugar
1 cup chopped almonds

1 large Hershey candy bar
1 large pkg. chocolate chips
Chopped walnuts

In a heavy saucepan, combine the butter and sugar, bring to a boil and boil for 5 minutes. Stir in the almonds and continue to cook, stirring constantly with a wooden spoon, until the mixture reaches the hard crack stage. Pour onto a greased cookie sheet with a lip; cool. Melt the candy bar and chocolate chips in a double boiler. Spread half the mixture over the cooled, hardened candy, then sprinkle on the chopped walnuts. When the chocolate frosting is cool, turn over and frost the other side. Break into pieces.

Arlene McEachern
Public Affairs
Linda House
Food Services

### Peanut Brittle

2 cups sugar
1 cup white Karo syrup
Pinch of salt

1 lb. raw peanuts
1 tsp. butter
1 tsp. soda

Combine the sugar, syrup, salt and peanuts and boil until a light golden brown or to about 290° on a candy thermometer. Remove from the heat and stir in the butter. Add the soda and stir in quickly and immediately. Pour out on a greased cookie sheet; cool and break into pieces. Store in an airtight container.

Geri Shippee
Reservations

### Glass Candy

7 to 12 cups powdered sugar
3½ cups sugar
1 cup hot water

1 cup white syrup
Flavorings
Food color

Sift powdered sugar smoothly into a pan with ½" to 1" sides to make a bed. Be sure the sugar is sifted evenly, otherwise there will be holes in the candy. Boil the next 3 ingredients together, without stirring, to exactly 300° on a candy thermometer. Remove from the heat, add flavoring and color; pour immediately into the bed of powdered sugar. Sprinkle the top with additional powdered sugar. Let the candy cool completely and break or cut with scissors while the candy is still quite warm.

Note: You can buy flavorings such as peppermint, spearmint and cherry at a drug store. Other flavorings such as chocolate and butter rum can be purchased from a grocery store. Use a food color which matches the flavor.

Jean Feely (Retired)
Credit Union
Geri Shippee
Reservations

## Lemon Drops

2 cups sugar
1 cup light corn syrup

½ tsp. oil of lemon
2 drops of yellow food coloring

Combine the sugar, corn syrup and ½ cup water in a heavy, medium saucepan and heat quickly to boiling, stirring constantly. Wrap a fork with damp paper toweling to wipe the sugar crystals from the side of the pan as the mixture cooks. Reduce the heat to medium and cook, without stirring, to 300° on a candy thermometer. (When done, a teaspoon of syrup will separate into threads that are hard and brittle when dropped into cold water.) Remove the saucepan from the heat and stir in the oil of lemon and the food coloring until the mixture stops bubbling. Pour the syrup by spoonfuls into 60 small, fancy metal molds thoroughly coated with vegetable oil. (If desired, the mixture can also be dropped onto greased cookie sheets to form patties.) If the syrup becomes too hard, return the saucepan to a very low heat just until the mixture thins, but not so long that the syrup darkens. Cool the candies in the molds for at least 1 hour. To remove the candies, insert the pointed tip of a small paring knife around the edge of the mold and press to loosen. Store in layers, separated by aluminum foil, in an air-tight container.

Variation: Orange Drops: Increase the yellow food coloring to ¼ tsp., add 2 drops of red food coloring and substitute ½ tsp. oil of orange for the oil of lemon.

Note: Oil of lemon and oil of orange can be purchased in any drug store. The oils can be substituted with 1½ tsp. lemon extract or orange extract, if desired.

Makes 5 dozen or 1½ lbs.

Elaine Musselman
Reservations

## Peanut Butter Fudge

2 cups sugar
⅔ cup evaporated milk
2 Tbsp. margarine

1 Tbsp. vanilla
1 cup peanut butter
½ cup walnuts (optional)

Cook the sugar, milk and margarine to the soft ball stage and add the vanilla, peanut butter and walnuts. Spread in a pan and cool.

Rick Sanders
Reservations

## Maple Fudge

4 cups brown sugar
1 cup milk or cream
⅓ cup corn syrup

1 Tbsp. butter
Chopped nuts
1 tsp. maple flavoring

Boil the first 4 ingredients together for 20 minutes over low heat until a soft ball forms when dropped in cold water. Let the confection cool for 10 minutes, then beat and add the nuts and flavoring.

Pat Logue
Reservations

## Chocolate Fudge

3 cups sugar
1 cup heavy cream
3 Tbsp. white syrup

2 squares bitter chocolate
1 tsp. vanilla
2 Tbsp. butter

Boil together the sugar, cream, syrup and chocolate in a heavy aluminum pan until a soft ball forms when dropped in cold water. Add the vanilla and butter, remove from the heat and cool. When cool, beat or mix on a marble slab until the candy holds its shape.

Nola Sears
Reservations

## Five-Pound Fudge

4 cups sugar
½ cup clear Karo syrup
1 (14-oz.) can evaporated milk

1 cup butter
1 tsp. vanilla
1 cup chopped walnuts

Combine the sugar, syrup, milk, ¼ cup water and the butter in a 4-quart pan. Cook over medium heat until the mixture forms a soft ball in cold water. This will take quite some time, and the mixture should be at a full rolling boil. Once the soft ball has formed, remove the mixture from the heat and add the vanilla. Beat the mixture until thickened and slightly creamy. Stir in the nuts and then spread onto a lightly greased, 9" x 13" pan. Cut the fudge while still warm.

Sue Crane
Reservations

## Peanut Butter Chocolate Candy

⅓ (1-lb.) box graham
  crackers
1½ cups peanut butter

1 cup butter, melted
4 cups powdered sugar
1 (6-oz.) pkg. chocolate chips

Crush the graham crackers and mix with the peanut butter; add the butter and sugar. Press into a 9" x 13" pan. Melt the chocolate chips and spread on the top. Refrigerate for 30 minutes to set.

Jan Taylor
Reservations

## Rocky Road Candy

3 (6-oz.) pkg. semisweet
  chocolate chips
2 cups miniature
  marshmallows

1¼ cups coarsely chopped
  walnuts

Melt the chocolate chips over hot, not boiling water, stirring until smooth. Spread about one-third of the melted chocolate in a foil-lined or greased, 8" x 8" pan. Mix together the marshmallows and walnuts and spread over the chocolate. Pour the remaining chocolate over, mixing lightly until the marshmallows and walnuts are coated. Let set until firm and cut into squares.

Makes 1⅔ lbs.

Karen Fudge
Regional Sales

## Apple Candy

2½ cups unsweetened
   applesauce
4 pkg. Knox gelatin
2 cups sugar
Pinch of salt

1 cup nutmeats
1 tsp. vanilla
¼ tsp. rose extract
Powdered sugar

Combine 1 cup applesauce with the gelatin and set aside to soak for 10 minutes. In a large, heavy kettle, combine the sugar with the remaining applesauce and the salt; bring to a full boil. Add the gelatin mixture and boil hard for 20 minutes, stirring often. Remove from the heat and add the nutmeats, vanilla and rose extract; pour into a buttered pan. When cool, cut into small cubes and roll in powdered sugar. Do not refrigerate.

Note: Rose extract is available at Hickory Farms.

The candy will keep for up to 1 week, but do not roll in sugar until just before serving or packing in a gift box.

Jacque Cate
Nola Sears
Reservations

## Olympian Creams

3¼ cups sugar
⅓ cup hot water
¼ cup white Karo syrup
1 cup heavy cream

2 Tbsp. butter
1 tsp. vanilla
Nuts (optional)

Melt ¼ cup sugar in a heavy pan until brown, add the water and cook until the sugar is dissolved. Add the remaining sugar, the syrup, cream and 1 Tbsp. butter; cook, stirring, until the mixture boils. Cook to a soft ball stage or 230°. Add the remaining butter and the vanilla; do not stir. When cool, add nuts, if desired, and beat or mix on a marble slab. Roll into logs for slicing.

Note: These creams can also be made up for the center of pecan rolls or can be rolled in balls and dipped into chocolate.

Nola Sears
Reservations

## Caramels

1 cup broken nuts (optional)
2 cups sugar
½ cup butter or margarine

2 cups heavy cream
⅓ to ½ cup evaporated milk
1 cup white corn syrup

Place the nuts in the bottom of a greased, 11" x 7" pan. Combine the remaining ingredients in a heavy, 4½-quart saucepan. Cook over medium heat, stirring constantly. When the candy reaches the soft ball stage (230°), remove from the heat and carefully pour over the nuts. Chill until set. When set, cut into squares. Wrap in wax paper, if desired.

*Makes about 2½ lbs.*

Geri Shippee
Reservations

## Arlene's Yummy Caramels

2 cups sugar
½ cup butter
1 large can evaporated milk

½ cup light Karo syrup
1 tsp. vanilla
Chopped nuts

Boil the first 4 ingredients together, stirring often to keep the mixture from sticking to the bottom of the pan. When the mixture reaches the soft ball stage, add the vanilla and nuts and pour into a greased pan. Cut into squares.

*Note: For Turtles, roll the caramel into balls, add pecans and dip in chocolate.*

Nola Sears
Reservations

## Gumdrops

1 (1¾-oz.) pkg. powdered fruit
    pectin
½ tsp. baking soda
1 cup sugar
1 cup light corn syrup

2 tsp. imitation strawberry
    extract
Red food coloring
Sugar

Combine the fruit pectin, ¾ cup water and the baking soda in a medium saucepan. (This mixture will foam.) Combine the sugar and corn syrup in a large saucepan. Place both saucepans over high heat and cook, stirring alternately, until the foam disappears from the fruit pectin mixture and the sugar mixture boils rapidly, about 5 minutes. Pour the fruit pectin mixture into the boiling sugar mixture in a thin stream. Boil the mixture, stirring constantly, for 1 minute. Remove the saucepan from the heat and stir in the strawberry extract and a few drops of red food coloring. Immediately pour the mixture into an 8" x 8" x 2" pan. For fancy shapes, spoon the mixture into tiny tart or hors d'oeuvres pans. Allow to stand at room temperature for 3 hours or until the candy is cool and firm; do not refrigerate. Cut the gumdrop mixture into cubes with a knife dipped in warm water or into fancy shapes with small cutters. Roll in granulated sugar.

*Variations: Green Gumdrops: Substitute oil of anise or mint extract for the strawberry extract and green food coloring for the red. Yellow Gumdrops: Substitute oil of lemon for the strawberry extract and yellow food coloring for the red. Red Gumdrops: Substitute oil of clove or cinnamon for the strawberry extract.*

*Makes 1¼ lbs.*

Elaine Musselman
Reservations

## Mom's Marshmallows

*2 cups sugar*
*1 pkg. Knox gelatin dissolved*
*    in ½ cup water*
*2 egg whites, stiffly beaten*

*1 tsp. vanilla*
*Coconut, browned and*
*    crumbled*

Combine the sugar with ½ cup water and boil until the mixture reaches the soft ball stage (234° to 240°). Fold the dissolved gelatin into the egg whites and slowly pour in the cooked syrup, beating constantly until the mixture stands in peaks. Add the vanilla and pour into a greased pan. Refrigerate for a few hours. Cut the cooked marshmallows into squares and roll in coconut.

Nola Sears
Reservations

## Toffee Bars

1 cup margarine
1 cup light brown sugar
1 tsp. vanilla
2 cups flour

1 egg yolk
1 (8-oz.) chocolate bar
Chopped nuts

Mix the first 5 ingredients together and press into a large, lightly greased pan. Bake at 300° for 15 minutes. Melt the chocolate bar and spread on top while the toffee is still warm; sprinkle with chopped nuts. Cool and cut into 1" squares.

Jan Taylor
Reservations

## Chocolate Chips

¼ cup margarine, melted
¼ cup plus 1 Tbsp. cocoa

½ cup sugar

Mix together all the ingredients, spread on a cookie sheet and freeze. Break apart to sprinkle over ice cream, use in cooking or use as a garnish on cakes and cookies.

Kathy Morgan
Inflight Services

## Streusel Topping

1 cup butter
2 cups sugar

Lemon, vanilla, almond or
coconut flavoring to taste
4 cups flour

Cream the butter and sugar until light and fluffy. Add the flavoring and gradually mix in the flour. Refrigerate and crumble over dough (cake, cookie, etc.) or fruit (apples, cherries, pineapples, etc.).

Hubert F. Malco
Pastry Chef
Seattle Food Services

## Plain Pudding Sauce

2 cups sugar                                 Flavoring
6 Tbsp. to ½ cup cornstarch

Combine the sugar with 4 cups water and bring to a boil over medium heat. Cook, stirring constantly, until the mixture is clear and bubbly. Stir in a flavoring and cool before serving.

Note: Suggested flavorings include rum, cognac, liqueurs, wines, lemon or orange.

Makes 4 cups pudding.

Hubert F. Malco
Pastry Chef
Seattle Food Services

## Caramel Sauce

½ cup brown sugar                            ½ cup butter
½ cup sugar                                  1 Tbsp. flour
½ cup cream                                  1 tsp. vanilla

Combine all the ingredients in a saucepan over medium heat and boil for 1 minute. Serve warm with **Fresh Apple Cake** (see index).

Dottie Martin

## Fruit Syrup

4 cups fruit juice                           2¼ cups sugar
  (raspberry, blackberry,                    1½ cups Karo syrup
  strawberry, etc.)

Combine all the ingredients, bring to a boil and boil hard for 6 minutes, stirring constantly. Serve on pancakes and waffles.

Susan Warren
Reservations

## Fudge Nut Sauce

1 cup butter or margarine
2 cups chocolate chips

1 cup coarsely chopped
  walnuts or pecans

In a double boiler over hot water, melt the butter or margarine and chocolate chips, stirring until smooth. Stir in the nuts. Serve hot over ice cream. The sauce may be refrigerated and reheated.

*This sauce hardens on ice cream like the topping on a dipped cone.*

*Makes 2 cups.*

Judy Nott
Payroll

## Honey Icing

1⅓ cups honey
2 egg whites

Pinch of salt
1 tsp. lemon or orange extract

Combine the honey, egg whites and salt. Beat in the top of a double boiler over boiling water until the mixture stands in soft peaks, approximately 10 minutes. Add the extract.

*Makes 2½ cups frosting.*

## Peach and Pineapple Conserve

2 cups diced cling peaches
1 cup canned, drained
  crushed pineapple

3 cups sugar
Juice and grated rind of 1 orange
Juice and grated rind of 2 lemons

Combine and cook all the ingredients until thick and clear. Pour into sterilized jars and seal.

Catherine Lakey
Reservations

## Pear Honey

3 lbs. ripe pears
6 large slices canned
  pineapple

Juice and grated rind of
  1½ lemons
5½ cups sugar

Pare and core the pears. Combine with the pineapple and put through the fine blade of a food chopper. Drain and combine with the lemon juice and rind. Cook over low heat until boiling, stirring frequently. Add the sugar, bring to a boil and simmer for 20 minutes, stirring constantly. Ladle into sterilized jars and seal.

Lillian Warren

## Quince Honey

3 large quinces

7 cups sugar

Wash, pare and core the quinces; put through a food chopper. Combine and boil 2 cups water and the sugar for 2 minutes, add the quinces and cook slowly for 20 minutes, stirring frequently to prevent scorching. Ladle into sterilized jars and seal.

Catherine Lakey
Reservations

## Peach Marmalade

18 peaches, finely cut
2 oranges, grated

1 small bottle maraschino
  cherries, finely cut
Sugar

Combine and measure the first 3 ingredients and add an equal amount of sugar. Cook slowly for 2 hours, stirring often to prevent burning. Pour into sterilized jars and seal with wax.

Jan Taylor
Reservations

## Apple Butter

8 lbs. tart apples
2 cups apple juice
1 cup sugar

1 cup dark Karo corn syrup
2 tsp. ground cinnamon
¼ tsp. ground cloves

Wash and quarter the apples but do not peel or core. Remove the blossom ends and stems. In a large saucepan, place the prepared apples and apple juice. Cover and cook over low heat, stirring occasionally, for 1 hour or until the apples are soft. Press the mixture through a colander or food mill; discard the skins and seeds. Measure 3½ quarts strained pulp into a large kettle. Stir in the sugar, syrup, cinnamon and cloves. Cook over low heat for 3 to 5 hours or until the mixture is very thick. To keep the apple butter from spattering too much toward the end of the cooking, cook over very low heat and partially cover. Ladle into clean, hot jars leaving ¼" headspace. Seal according to manufacturer's directions. Process in boiling water for 10 minutes.

Makes about 12 half-pint jars.

Rick Sanders
Reservations

## Carrot Marmalade

4 cups raw chopped carrots
2 cups sugar
½ cup chopped blanched
  almonds

¼ cup lemon juice
1 tsp. salt

Combine the carrots and 2 cups water, bring to a boil and boil, stirring constantly, for about 30 minutes. Add the sugar and boil slowly, stirring frequently, for approximately 1 hour more. Add the nuts and cook, stirring, for another 10 minutes, then add the lemon juice and salt. Pour into small, sterilized jars and seal.

Catherine Lakey
Reservations

# CHEFS

**Alt, Erwin** Born in Austria, near the Olympic Village in Innsbruck, Chef Alt served his chef apprenticeship in his native country. He then worked for three years in Bogotá, Colombia, where he served, among others, the then vice president of the United States, Richard Nixon. Chef Alt immigrated to the United States in 1959 to work in Elkhart, Indiana, at the Palmer House in downtown Chicago and at Henrici's at O'Hare International Airport. He started with United Airlines in 1961 and currently is executive chef for their Chicago Food Services.

**Arquisch, Duri** Born and raised in Switzerland, Chef Arquisch served his chef apprenticeship at the Hotel Baeren in Baden and worked for seven years following at other first-class hotels in Switzerland. In 1962, he opened Hilton hotels in Amsterdam and London as chef saucier. From there he went on to work as chef *garde-manger* for the Hotel St. Gotthard in Zurich. Immigrating to the United States in 1965, he first worked here as assistant chef for Anthony's Pier Four Restaurant in Boston and then as executive chef for the Sheraton Hotel in Quincy, Massachusetts. In 1967 he began his work for United Airlines in Los Angeles. He was promoted in 1971 to executive chef in Boston and maintained that position when he moved in the same year to Salt Lake City. Chef Arquisch is a former president of the *Chefs de Cuisine* Association of Zurich and has won numerous first prize awards in culinary exhibitions held in such cities as Los Angeles, Boston, and Lausanne and Lucerne, Switzerland. In 1981, he was granted the rating of *Certified* by the American Culinary Association.

**Boyer, Jerry F.** Chef Boyer was born in Worcester, Massachusetts. He earned a chef's diploma in 1968 from the Culinary Institute of America and a bachelor's degree in hotel and restaurant administration in 1972 from the University of Massachusetts. His professional experience includes working as sous chef for the Eastward Ho Country Club in Chatham, Massachusetts, as executive chef for the Devon Yacht Club on Long Island and as assistant chef at Smith College in North Hampton, Massachusetts. He also held the position of food production manager for the Marriott Hotels. He started with United Airlines in 1973 in Chicago and was promoted to his current position, executive chef for Newark Food Services, in 1978. Chef Boyer's varied experience throughout the years has provided him with the opportunity to serve many political notables, among them Emperor Hirohito, Ronald Reagan and Henry Kissinger.

**Conrad, Rolf** Rolf Conrad was born in Amsterdam and served his culinary apprenticeship in Bad Kissingen, Germany, which was completed in 1955. He then worked in such famous hotels and restaurants in Germany as the Park Hotel, the House Mererbusch and the Zweibruecker Hof in Düesseldorf, and the Europaeischer Hof in Hamburg. He also worked for two years on a German ocean liner, the Hanseatic. In 1963 he moved to the United States to work in United's San Francisco kitchen. He was promoted there to sous chef in 1965 and to chef in 1971. He transferred to the Denver Flight Kitchen in 1973 as executive chef. Chef Conrad has earned many awards during his career including receiving a United Airlines rating of *Excellent* in 1981, as well as special recognition in various culinary art shows. He also had the honor in 1976 of preparing a special cocktail buffet for President Ford in Vail, Colorado.

**Cook, Lyell E.** A graduate of the Culinary Institute in New Haven, Connecticut, Chef Lyell E. Cook has held various positions such as cook, saucier and sous chef in restaurants and hotels in southern California and Colorado including the Broadmoor Hotel in Colorado Springs. He also held executive chef positions at the 26 Club and the Denver Athletic Club, both located in Denver. He joined United Airlines in 1967 as sous chef for the Chicago Flight Kitchen and moved on to become, in 1967, executive chef for their wide-body kitchen. He was promoted in 1972 to executive chef for Miami Food Services, where he later became operations manager. In 1977, he was appointed to his present position, chef manager for the Detroit Flight Kitchen.

**Delbol, Raoul F.** Chef Delbol was born in Bruges, Belgium, and raised in Knokke le Zoute, a vacation resort on the Belgian coast. He received the finest culinary education, serving apprenticeships under such French and Belgian master chefs as Pollet, Maxaire, Dupond, Carlier, Rabaux and Delmotte. After moving to the United States, he worked as sous chef for the Beverly Hills Hotel and then for the Chasen's Restaurant. He first worked for United Airlines in Los Angeles, moved to Newark as sous chef, then to Philadelphia as chef and finally returned to Los Angeles as executive chef. Chef Delbol has had the honor during his career of serving such political dignitaries as King Boudouin of Belgium and President Jimmy Carter. He holds membership in the *Société Culinaire Philantropique* of New York, the *Club Gas-*

*tronomique Prosper Montagne* of Belgium and the Epicurean Club of Los Angeles. He is also an active member of the jury to select the Belgian Chef of the Year. He has won several first prizes for his culinary exhibitions and competitions, and his executive chef's performance in Europe was awarded the *Chevalier de Saint Fortunat.*

**Dorfhuber, Erich**  Chef Dorfhuber, a native West German, served a three-year chef apprenticeship at the Hotel Krone in Hochenschwand, Germany, and also studied at the German Vocational School. He spent his journeyman years at various hotels and restaurants in Germany and Switzerland including the Gasthaus Drachenburg in Gottlieben and the Bahnhof-Buffet in Rapperswil. He prepared for his eventual position with United Airlines while in Europe by also working as lead cook for Lufthansa German Airlines in Frankfurt, Germany. He immigrated to the United States in 1964 to work for the Hyatt House in San Jose. The following year, he began his work for United Airlines in San Francisco as cook. One year later, he transferred to Denver as sous chef. In 1974, he was promoted to his current appointment, executive chef for Portland Food Services. Chef Dorfhuber is a member of the Chefs de Cuisine Association of Oregon.

**Gnigler, Oswald M.**  Chef Gnigler was born and raised in Austria where he began his cooking career in 1955. Working and studying throughout Austria and Switzerland, he completed his apprenticeship in 1961. Following graduation, he worked in some of the finest resorts and hotels in both of the above countries which included cooking for the Olympic athletes at the Olympic Village in Innsbruck. After immigrating to the United States in 1964, he worked at Le Hartford in Chicago and then for two years was assistant chef for the Arlington Park Jockey Club outside Chicago where he was in charge of all cold buffet and *garde-manger.* He was so favored there that during the off-season he was hired to be the private chef for the race track owner. For three years, he also worked as chef for Szabo Food Service which took him to various places throughout the United States including Spring Green's Frank Lloyd Wright Supper Club, Chicago's 91st Floor in the Hancock Building and the Midwest Bank Club in the MidAmerican building in Chicago. He joined United Airlines in 1969 and has worked for the company in Chicago, Honolulu and Newark. He is now executive chef in Las Vegas.

**Good, Bruno** Chef Good, a native Swiss, began his cooking career at the age of fifteen at a hotel in Geneva. He worked in many hotels in Switzerland, in such cities as St. Moritz, Lucarno, Arosa, Lenzerheide, Lausanne and Interlaken, before moving to Sweden for one year. His next position, one which he maintained for seven years, was executive chef for a hotel in Klosters, Switzerland. He moved in 1957 to New York where he worked at the Manhattan Hotel, Trader Vic's and the Savoy Plaza Hotels. Following that, he opened the Sheraton Hotel in Dallas and worked there for two years as executive sous chef. He moved to Seattle in 1961 to become executive chef for the prestigious Rainier Club. His work with United Airlines was begun in 1964. Now the executive chef for the Seattle Flight Kitchen, Chef Good directs 110 employees and the preparation of as many as 300 full-course meals and 900 snacks per day.

**Jantzen, Hans** Chef Jantzen was born and educated in Hamburg, Germany, where he served a five-year apprenticeship in the hotel industry. He then worked as first cook for the S.S. Bremen, a German passenger cruise ship. He came to the United States in 1965 where he gained professional experience in various New York restaurants including the Empire State Building and Longchamps Restaurant. He started with United Airlines as sous chef in 1969 and was promoted to executive chef in 1975. His present assignment is executive chef for New York Food Services.

**Kopleck, Helmut W.** Chef Kopleck's family owned and operated a hotel in Düesseldorf, Germany, where his great love of cuisine was sparked and nurtured. He completed his apprenticeship in Germany as cook and baker and, following graduation, enhanced his skills by working in Switzerland, France, Holland and England. He then ventured to the United States. In New York he worked for the Four Seasons Restaurant before United Airlines hired him, assigning him first to San Francisco. From there he worked for two years as sous chef in Honolulu and was then promoted to executive chef in Washington, D.C. Four years later, he transferred to Philadelphia. Because of his interest and abilities, Chef Kopleck is now not only responsible for United's Philadelphia Food Services, but also for food preparation and production for British Airways, Lufthansa German Airlines, Trans World Airlines, Mexicana Airlines, Eastern Airlines, Ozark Airlines, U.S. Air and Altair Airlines.

**LeBoulluec, Emile**  Chef LeBoulluec began his chef apprenticeship in Paris in 1948. He gained much of his professional experience working for the Sheraton Hotel Corporation in such positions as cook, *chef tournant, chef des banquets,* sous chef, chef and executive chef. He began his work for United Airlines as sous chef in Denver and is now executive chef for Boston Food Services. He has won many awards at culinary shows for food decoration and ice and grease sculptures. He is a member of the Vatel Club, a French chef, cook, pastry and baker association of New York. Chef LeBoulluec also holds an Associate degree in liberal arts from the Metropolitan State College in Denver where he graduated magna cum laude.

**Mendreshora, George J.**  Chef Mendreshora, who has been a chef for thirty years, was born in Montreal, Canada, where he served his apprenticeship. During the first ten years of his career, he worked for the Canadian Pacific Hotel and in Bermuda, Nassau, and Lausanne, Switzerland. He has been with United Airlines for twenty years, holding executive chef positions in New York City, Philadelphia, Los Angeles, Chicago and Honolulu, his present location. His career has been highlighted by serving such dignitaries as Queen Elizabeth, the Duke of Edinburgh, the Prime Minister of France, Dwight D. Eisenhower, Winston Churchill, Pierre Mendes-France and Princess Margaret. He has won prizes for culinary art in New York and Canada, and he has made great contributions to the Chefs de Cuisine Association of Hawaii, serving as its Chairman of the Renaissance Dinner for the past three years. In 1978 Chef Mendreshora was honored to be chosen one of seven judges for the United States National Professional Pineapple Cooking Contest, being the only Hawaiian to represent that group.

**Niederer, Willi**  Chef Niederer was born in Amriswil, Switzerland, and served his apprenticeship in St. Gallen. He then worked in many famous Swiss hotels, including the Grand Hotel in Montreux, the Hotel Trois Couronne in Vevey and the Belveder Hotel in Leysin. Before immigrating to the United States in 1962, Chef Niederer also worked on a Dutch ocean liner, the S.S. Rotterdam. He then worked at the Olympic Hotel in Seattle until 1964 when he joined United Airlines. He worked for them in both Seattle and Los Angeles before being assigned to San Francisco where he is currently in charge of preparing meals for the flights of wide-body airplanes. Chef Niederer was recently chosen by officials of Japan Airlines to prepare a special menu for the flight of the prime minister of Japan to Washington, D.C.

**Reichmuth, W.** Chef Reichmuth was born in Switzerland where he completed his apprenticeship program and several journeyman positions. After leaving Switzerland, he worked at the Queen Elizabeth Hotel in Montreal and then the Hilton Hotels in San Francisco. In 1965 he began his work for United Airlines in Honolulu and since then has worked in Los Angeles, Portland, Cleveland and Chicago, where he presently holds the position of executive chef. He is a member of the Academy of Chefs.

**Schmuki, Walter J.** Chef Schmuki, a native Swiss, has worked in many great resorts in Switzerland in the cities of Bern, Lucerne, St. Moritz, Grindelwald, Klosters and Zermatt. He also worked in Montreal, Chicago and Detroit before being hired by United Airlines for whom he is now a chef in Denver's Flight Kitchen. He has had the honor to cook for a large number of well-known individuals during his career, such as Audrey Hepburn, Mel Ferrer, Sophia Loren, Françoise Sagan, Konrad Adenauer, the Queen Mother of England, Werner von Braun, Ronald Reagan and Edward Kennedy. Chef Schmuki has participated in many culinary presentations and is a member of the Colorado Chefs de Cuisine Association.

**Steuri, Paul** Like so many of United's chefs, Paul Steuri is a native of Switzerland. He apprenticed for three years at the Montreux Palace Hotel and perfected his talents at world-famous hotels and resorts in Bern, Interlaken, Lucerne and Davos, Switzerland. He left Switzerland for Sweden where he worked at the Grand Hotel Royal in Stockholm. He later moved to Canada to work at the Royal York Hotel in Toronto and then the Chateau Lake Louise and Petroleum Club in Calgary, Alberta. He arrived in the United States in 1953 to become chef at the Hotel Jerome in Aspen, Colorado. He joined United Airlines in 1956 in Los Angeles and later transferred to Chicago. His current assignment is executive chef for Omaha Food Services.

**Wolfsheimer, John H.** Chef Wolfsheimer's talents and creative abilities come from a richly varied background which began in Lyon, France. He served his apprenticeship at Chez la Mère Brazier, a French restaurant which has held for many years a four-star rating in the *Guide Michelin*. He also served in Nice, on the French Riviera and at the old Ritz Carlton in Paris, followed by a brief period in Germany. In the United States, he has been associated with the Plaza Hotel and the Waldorf Astoria Hotel in Manhattan, the Piping Rock Club on Long Island, the Indian Harbor Yacht Club in Greenwich, Connecticut, and the Beverly Hilton Hotel and the Sportsman Lodge in Los Angeles. He joined United Airlines in 1957 and currently is executive chef in San Francisco. Chef Wolfsheimer has had the pleasure to serve such notables as Presidents Kennedy, Eisenhower, Truman and Hoover, King George VI, Queen Elizabeth and Chief Justice Earl Warren, in addition to other dignitaries. He is presently a member of the American Culinary Federation, the Chefs Association of the Pacific Coast and the Chaîne des Rôtisseurs. He is also president of the Gastronome Club of San Francisco and holder of the *Carême Medal*.

# RECIPE INDEX

# RECIPE INDEX

## Appetizers

Artichoke Squares .......... ... 27
Avocado Dip .................. 6
Bacon Roll-Ups .............. 18
Baked Oysters Maxine ........... 21
Bean Dip ..................... 7
Brandied Mushrooms and Cream ... 32
Bruno's Cheese Fondue ......... 3
Cheese Balls ................. 12
Cheese Delights .............. 13
Cheese Fondue ................ 5
Chicken Livers with Mushrooms .... 19
Chili Con Queso .............. 11
Chinese Barbequed Spareribs ...... 20
Crab Crunchies ............... 22
Crab Dip #1 ................. 7
Crab Dip #2 ................. 8
Crab Dip #3 ................. 8
Crab Fondue .................. 4
Crab Guacamole ............... 9
Crab Mousse ................. 21
Crab-Stuffed Mushrooms ........ 32
Creamy Chutney and Nut Spread ... 10
Deviled Sweet and Sour Eggs ...... 17
Egg Rolls .................... 15
Escargot .................... 27
Fiesta Dip ................... 9
Fillings for Stuffed Eggs .......... 16
Flintstone Bread .............. 14
French Bread with a Twist ........ 14
French-Fried Vegetables .......... 30
Ham-Filled Mushroom Caps ....... 31
Hot Crab Appetizer ............ 23
Hot Dip ..................... 6
Hot Pepper Bean Dip ........... 6
Hot Ryes .................... 13
Liverwurst and Beer Dip .......... 10
Lobster Pâté ................. 12
Marinated Bacon Wraps .......... 18
Mrs. Di's Antipasto ............ 28
Mrs. Ritchie's Hot Crab Soufflé ..... 22
Nordic Shrimp Delights .......... 23
Pepper Jelly Canapés ........... 14
Pineapple Cheese Spread ......... 10
Poor Man's Smoked Salmon ....... 25
Quick Chicken Pâté ............ 12
Rhinelander Cheese Fondue ....... 3
Salmon Cheese Appetizer ......... 24
Salmon Dreams ............... 26
Salmon Fritters .............. 25
Salmon Party Mound ........... 25
Salmon Sandwich Loaf .......... 26
Sausage-Stuffed Mushrooms ...... 31

Scotch Eggs .................. 17
Scottish Sausage Rolls ........... 19
Shrimp Dip ................... 8
Shrimp Fondue ................ 5
Shrimp Pâté ................. 11
Smoked Eggs ................. 16
Smoked Herring with
    Horseradish Cream .......... 24
Spinach and Cheese Squares ...... 28
Stuffed Celery Hors D'Oeuvres ..... 30
Stuffed Chicken Wings .......... 20
Stuffed Mushrooms with a View .... 29
Sweet-Sour Sausage Balls ........ 17
Taco Dip .................... 9
Voilà la Fondue de la Gruyère ..... 4
Zucchini Appetizer ............. 30

## Beverages

Champagne Punch ............. 41
Chevoney ................... 35
Crème de Cacao Nightcap ........ 35
Egg Nog .................... 36
Holiday Punch ................ 38
Hot Buttered Rum ............. 39
Hot Spiced Apple Cider ......... 40
Kahlua ..................... 36
Orange Julius ................ 41
Orange Liqueur ............... 37
Peach Margarita .............. 37
Punch with a Punch ........... 37
Rum Punch .................. 38
Schweizer Gluhwein ........... 40
Spiced Tea .................. 42
Tom and Jerry Batter .......... 39
Uncle Norm's Rum Slush ........ 38
Velvet Hammer Drink .......... 35
Wassail ..................... 41

## Breads

Apple Muffins ................ 312
Apricot Nut Bread ............. 308
Aunt Lulu's Rye Bread .......... 294
Banana Bread ................ 309
Beer Bread .................. 304
Birchermüesli ................ 316
Bran Muffins ................ 310
Breakfast Bars ............... 317
Butter Dips ................. 305
Carrot Loaf Bread ............ 307
Christmas Fruit Bread ......... 302
Cornbread Stuffing for Turkey ...... 318
Corn Spoon Bread ............. 304

Cottage Cheese Pancakes . . . . . . . . . 314
Date Nut Bread . . . . . . . . . . . . . . . . . 306
Dilly Bread . . . . . . . . . . . . . . . . . . . . 294
Edna's Yorkshire Pudding . . . . . . . . . 317
English Muffins . . . . . . . . . . . . . . . . . 310
German Pancakes . . . . . . . . . . . . . . . 315
German Pancake with Orange Sauce . 314
Gooey Rolls . . . . . . . . . . . . . . . . . . . 300
Gougère . . . . . . . . . . . . . . . . . . . . . . 304
Griddle Cakes . . . . . . . . . . . . . . . . . . 313
Gumdrop Bread . . . . . . . . . . . . . . . . 309
Honey Whole Wheat Bread . . . . . . . . 293
Hot Cheese Onion Bread . . . . . . . . . . 297
Hot Roll Monkey Bread . . . . . . . . . . . 300
Icebox Muffins . . . . . . . . . . . . . . . . . 311
Irish Soda Bread . . . . . . . . . . . . . . . . 303
Malco's Sourdough Bread . . . . . . . . . 296
Ninety-Minute Whole Wheat Bread . . 294
Pao Doce . . . . . . . . . . . . . . . . . . . . . 298
Peanut Butter Loaf . . . . . . . . . . . . . . 308
Pearl's Coffee Cake . . . . . . . . . . . . . . 307
Portuguese Sweet Bread . . . . . . . . . . 298
Pumpkin Bread . . . . . . . . . . . . . . . . . 308
Quick Hot Dinner Rolls . . . . . . . . . . . 297
Rhubarb Nut Bread . . . . . . . . . . . . . . 306
Robert Redford's Whole Wheat
    Quick Bread . . . . . . . . . . . . . . . . 303
Sally Lunn . . . . . . . . . . . . . . . . . . . . 299
Sour Cream Peach Muffins . . . . . . . . 311
Sourdough Starter . . . . . . . . . . . . . . 296
Stouffer's Pumpkin Muffins . . . . . . . . 312
Swedish Coffee Bread . . . . . . . . . . . . 302
Swedish Pancakes . . . . . . . . . . . . . . 315
Swedish Rye Bread . . . . . . . . . . . . . . 295
Washington Waffles . . . . . . . . . . . . . . 316
Whole Wheat Croissants . . . . . . . . . . 301
Whole Wheat Pancakes . . . . . . . . . . . 313

## Desserts

Banana Torte . . . . . . . . . . . . . . . . . . 338
Berry Blender Ice Cream . . . . . . . . . . 344
Blueberry Cobbler . . . . . . . . . . . . . . . 340
Burnt Cream . . . . . . . . . . . . . . . . . . . 347
Cream Puffs . . . . . . . . . . . . . . . . . . . 337
Crème Fraîche . . . . . . . . . . . . . . . . . 341
Danish Pastry . . . . . . . . . . . . . . . . . . 338
Deluxe English Trifle . . . . . . . . . . . . . 342
Fluffy Peanut Butter Dessert . . . . . . . 343
Four-Layer Dessert . . . . . . . . . . . . . . 343
Fresh Plum Tart . . . . . . . . . . . . . . . . 339
Lemon Mousse . . . . . . . . . . . . . . . . . 336
Lillian's Blueberry Delight . . . . . . . . . 340
Peaches and Cream . . . . . . . . . . . . . 341
Pistachio Dessert . . . . . . . . . . . . . . . 342

Rhubarb Crisp . . . . . . . . . . . . . . . . . 339
Rice Pudding . . . . . . . . . . . . . . . . . . 347
Rich Chocolate Mousse . . . . . . . . . . 336
Swedish Chocolate Roll . . . . . . . . . . . 344
Toffee Ice Cream Supreme . . . . . . . . 346
Vanilla Bavarian Cream . . . . . . . . . . 345

## Cakes:

Anne's Cheesecake . . . . . . . . . . . . . . 323
Apple Crumb Cake . . . . . . . . . . . . . . 327
Applesauce Cake . . . . . . . . . . . . . . . 328
Blueberry-Glazed Cheesecake . . . . . . 322
Carol's Carrot Cake . . . . . . . . . . . . . 328
Carrot Cake . . . . . . . . . . . . . . . . . . . 329
Cheesecake . . . . . . . . . . . . . . . . . . . 321
Chocolate Chip Date Cake . . . . . . . . 325
Chocolate Rum Cake . . . . . . . . . . . . 324
Cocoa Cake . . . . . . . . . . . . . . . . . . . 327
Crazy Cake . . . . . . . . . . . . . . . . . . . 326
Dark Chocolate Cake . . . . . . . . . . . . 325
Dinah Shore's Quick Cake . . . . . . . . . 332
Dump Cake . . . . . . . . . . . . . . . . . . . 331
Duri's Cheesecake . . . . . . . . . . . . . . 324
Fresh Apple Cake with Rum Sauce . . 327
Fudpucker Cake . . . . . . . . . . . . . . . . 333
Harvey Wallbanger Bundt Cake . . . . . 332
Mississippi Mud . . . . . . . . . . . . . . . . 326
Orange Carrot Cake . . . . . . . . . . . . . 329
Orange Walnut Cake . . . . . . . . . . . . . 330
Pig Pickin' Cake . . . . . . . . . . . . . . . . 330
Pineapple Caramel
    Upside-Down Cake . . . . . . . . . . . 331
Poppy Seed Cake . . . . . . . . . . . . . . . 335
Raoul's Cheesecake . . . . . . . . . . . . . 322
Red Velvet Cake
    from the Waldorf Astoria . . . . . . . 334
Sherry Wine Cake . . . . . . . . . . . . . . . 333
Virgins' Gold Cake . . . . . . . . . . . . . . 335
Walnut Cake . . . . . . . . . . . . . . . . . . . 335
Weehawken Cheesecake . . . . . . . . . . 321

## Pies:

Amazing Coconut Pie . . . . . . . . . . . . 349
Black Bottom Pie . . . . . . . . . . . . . . . . 350
Brandy Alexander Pie . . . . . . . . . . . . 352
Charlie Pie . . . . . . . . . . . . . . . . . . . . 347
Creamy Lemon Meringue Pie . . . . . . 348
Ginger Rum Pumpkin Pie . . . . . . . . . 349
Lemon Sour Cream Pie . . . . . . . . . . . 350
Paper Bag Apple Pie . . . . . . . . . . . . . 352
Perfect Pie Crust . . . . . . . . . . . . . . . . 353
Strawberry Bavarian Pie . . . . . . . . . . 351
Streusel Cream Peach Pie . . . . . . . . . 348

# RECIPE INDEX

## Cookies:

Almond Cookies . . . . . . . . . . . . . . . 366
Angel Bars . . . . . . . . . . . . . . . . . . . 355
Aunt Martha's Party Squares . . . . . . 356
Brownies . . . . . . . . . . . . . . . . . . . . 354
Butterscotch Brownies . . . . . . . . . . . 354
Butter Tart Bars . . . . . . . . . . . . . . . 359
Cheese and Pecan Diamonds . . . . . . 357
Chocolate Mint Bars . . . . . . . . . . . . 358
Cream Cheese Cake Bars . . . . . . . . . 357
Crispy Cookies . . . . . . . . . . . . . . . . 367
Diagonaler . . . . . . . . . . . . . . . . . . . 361
Dutch Anise Drops . . . . . . . . . . . . . 367
Famous Amos
    Chocolate Chip Cookies . . . . . . . . 363
Forfar Shortbread . . . . . . . . . . . . . . 360
Fruit Balls . . . . . . . . . . . . . . . . . . . 363
Glazed Brownies . . . . . . . . . . . . . . . 355
Hamilton Gingerbread . . . . . . . . . . . 368
Lebkuchen . . . . . . . . . . . . . . . . . . . 365
Lemon Bars . . . . . . . . . . . . . . . . . . 359
Little Gems . . . . . . . . . . . . . . . . . . 361
Lunch Box Cookies . . . . . . . . . . . . . 366
Melanie's Own Chocolate
    Chip Cookies . . . . . . . . . . . . . . . 362
No-Bake Cookies . . . . . . . . . . . . . . 366
Peanut Butter Surprise Cookies . . . . 362
Persimmon Cookies . . . . . . . . . . . . 364
Raisin Crispies . . . . . . . . . . . . . . . . 364
Raisin Energy Squares . . . . . . . . . . 358
Scottish Shortbread . . . . . . . . . . . . 360
Seven-Layer Cookies . . . . . . . . . . . . 356
Wheat Germ Brownies . . . . . . . . . . 353

## Candy:

Almond Roca . . . . . . . . . . . . . . . . . 369
Apple Candy . . . . . . . . . . . . . . . . . . 374
Arlene's Yummy Caramels . . . . . . . . 375
Caramels . . . . . . . . . . . . . . . . . . . . 375
Cherry Divinity . . . . . . . . . . . . . . . . 368
Chocolate Fudge . . . . . . . . . . . . . . . 372
Divinity . . . . . . . . . . . . . . . . . . . . . 369
Five-Pound Fudge . . . . . . . . . . . . . . 372
Glass Candy . . . . . . . . . . . . . . . . . . 370
Gumdrops . . . . . . . . . . . . . . . . . . . 375
Lemon Drops . . . . . . . . . . . . . . . . . 371
Maple Fudge . . . . . . . . . . . . . . . . . 372
Mom's Marshmallows . . . . . . . . . . . 376
Olympian Creams . . . . . . . . . . . . . . 374
Peanut Brittle . . . . . . . . . . . . . . . . . 370
Peanut Butter Chocolate Candy . . . . 373
Peanut Butter Fudge . . . . . . . . . . . . 371
Rocky Road Candy . . . . . . . . . . . . . 373
Toffee Bars . . . . . . . . . . . . . . . . . . . 377

## Sweet Accents:

Apple Butter . . . . . . . . . . . . . . . . . . 381
Brown Sugar Spread . . . . . . . . . . . . 300
Caramel Sauce . . . . . . . . . . . . . . . . 378
Carrot Marmalade . . . . . . . . . . . . . . 381
Chocolate Chips . . . . . . . . . . . . . . . 377
Cream Cheese Icing . . . . . . . . . . . . 329
Fruit Syrup . . . . . . . . . . . . . . . . . . . 378
Fudge Nut Sauce . . . . . . . . . . . . . . 379
Honey Icing . . . . . . . . . . . . . . . . . . 379
Orange Sauce . . . . . . . . . . . . . . . . . 314
Peach and Pineapple Conserve . . . . . 379
Peach Marmalade . . . . . . . . . . . . . . 380
Pear Honey . . . . . . . . . . . . . . . . . . 380
Plain Pudding Sauce . . . . . . . . . . . . 378
Powdered Sugar Frosting . . . . . . . . . 338
Quince Honey . . . . . . . . . . . . . . . . . 380
Rum Sauce . . . . . . . . . . . . . . . . . . . 327
Streusel Topping . . . . . . . . . . . . . . . 377
Toffee Crunch . . . . . . . . . . . . . . . . . 346

## Eggs & Cheese

Bacon and Eggs Crescent Sandwich . 184
Baked Eggs with Bercy Sauce . . . . . . 181
Baked Eggs with Sausage . . . . . . . . 182
Cheddary Creamed Eggs . . . . . . . . . 185
Cheese Soufflé . . . . . . . . . . . . . . . . 189
Eggs Baked in English Muffins . . . . . 185
8" x 12" Pan Breakfast . . . . . . . . . . 183
Poached Eggs Florentine . . . . . . . . . 182
Quiche Lorraine #1 . . . . . . . . . . . . . 186
Quiche Lorraine #2 . . . . . . . . . . . . . 186
Quiche Lorraine #3 . . . . . . . . . . . . . 187
Quiche Lorraine à la Suisse . . . . . . . 187
Roquefort Cheese Soufflé . . . . . . . . . 188
Seafood Quiche . . . . . . . . . . . . . . . . 188
Un Pan Kocha . . . . . . . . . . . . . . . . . 184

## Meat

Bali Hai Pork Pieces . . . . . . . . . . . . 136
Bali Miki . . . . . . . . . . . . . . . . . . . . 150
Baked, Barbequed Spareribs . . . . . . 145
Barbequed Double Pork Chops . . . . . 137
Barbequed Korean Kal Bi . . . . . . . . 143
Beef Filets in Flaky Pastry . . . . . . . . 149
Beef in Mustard Sauce . . . . . . . . . . 145
Beef Roulades . . . . . . . . . . . . . . . . . 152
Beef Sauté Stroganoff . . . . . . . . . . . 150
Beef Wellington . . . . . . . . . . . . . . . 148
Braised Beef Bourguignonne . . . . . . 160
Braised Brochette of Beef
    with Burgundy Wine Sauce . . . . . . 152

Braised Short Ribs of Beef
  with Horseradish Sauce ......... 144
Braised Veal Shanks,
  Osso Buco, Kalbshaxe .......... 176
Broccoli Wrapped in Swiss Cheese
  and Ham ................... 134
Broiled Top Round of Beef,
  Southern Style ............... 151
Carbonnade of Beef à la Flamande .. 143
Chiles Rellenos Bake ............. 168
Chinese Sweet and Sour Spareribs .. 142
Company Casserole ............. 166
Company Stew ................. 159
East Indian Curry .............. 161
Easy Forget-It Brisket ........... 154
Easy Pork Chops ............... 136
Filet of Veal Financière .......... 172
Fort Still Mexican Food .......... 169
Garden Patch Stew ............. 163
Glen's Chili .................. 168
Gourmet Calves Liver ........... 162
Grilled Salisbury Steak .......... 166
Ham and Cheese Pie ............ 133
Hawaiian Open Double-Cut
  Pork Chop Plantation .......... 140
Homemade Poor People's Salami ... 167
Indonesian Lamb Roast .......... 132
Irish Lamb Stew ............... 133
Joe Booker Stew ............... 160
Lamb Chops Marinated in
  Wine Sauce ................. 129
Lamb Chops with Rice and Onions .. 129
Lamb Shanks and Pot Roast,
  Lombard Style ............... 130
Larded Beef à la Mode
  with Red Wine Sauce .......... 159
Mandarin Pork à L'Orange ....... 137
Marinated Beef Roast, German Style . 156
Meatballs in Spaghetti Sauce ....... 164
Minced Beef à la Deutsch ......... 147
Minced Veal, Swiss Style ......... 175
New England Boiled Dinner ....... 155
Old Fashioned Meat Loaf ......... 164
Orange-Glazed Lamb Shanks ...... 132
Ossi Buchi Esterhazy ............ 177
Pepperoni ................... 167
Pepper Steak ................. 146
Piccata of Veal Zingara .......... 170
Polish Sausage with Apples
  and Red Cabbage ............ 135
Pork and Chicken Chop Suey,
  Canton Style ................ 140
Pork Tenderloin Piccata .......... 139
Pork Tenderloin Ziganne ......... 138

Pot Roast with Sour Cream Gravy ... 158
Roast Sirloin of Beef with
  Mushroom Sauce ............. 157
Sauerbraten with Red Cabbage ..... 155
Savory Roast Lamb ............. 131
Savory Scottish Sausage ......... 135
Sliced Veal, Swiss Style .......... 171
Spareribs Cantonese ............ 142
Spareribs with Ginger and
  Apricot Sauce ............... 141
Steak Diane .................. 153
Steak Hong Kong .............. 154
Stuffed, Baked Pork Chops ....... 139
Stuffed Crown Roast of Lamb ..... 130
Stuffed Ham Roll au Gratin ....... 134
Sukiyaki .................... 146
Sweet and Sour Pork Chops ....... 141
Taco Pie .................... 169
Veal Cordon Bleu .............. 174
Veal Côtelette Liègoise .......... 178
Veal Cutlets Saltimbocca ......... 173
Veal Oscar .................. 171
Veal Scallopini Sauté, North Beach .. 177
Veal Scallopini with Shrimp
  and Oysters, Monterey ......... 172
Veal Zürichoise ............... 174
Walnut Meat Loaf ............. 165
Zucchini Beef Pie .............. 162
Zucchini Lasagna ............. 163

## Pasta & Rice

Barbara's Fettuccini ............. 197
Best Yet Complete Spaghetti ....... 193
Brother Bobbie's Sketti .......... 194
Carbonara ................... 194
Chicken or Turkey Tetrazzini ...... 196
Fresh Pasta and Garlic Sauce ...... 196
Greek-Style Macaroni Bake ....... 199
Lasagna .................... 201
Manicotti Cheese Bake .......... 199
Million Dollar Spaghetti ......... 193
Paella ..................... 203
Pasta E Fagioli ............... 198
Rice ...................... 85
Rice Pilaf ................... 204
Spaghetti Pie ................ 195
Taglereni ................... 202
Tortellini Florentine ........... 200
Vegetable Noodles ............. 202

## Poultry

Almond Chicken ............... 100
Baked Chicken Breasts Supreme .... 94
Braised Chicken with Peanuts ...... 120

# RECIPE INDEX

Breast of Chicken Paprikash .......  91
Breast of Chicken Teriyaki .........  113
Broiled, Deviled Spring Chicken .....  96
Capital Chicken ....................  97
Chicken and Cashews ............  114
Chicken Breasts Eugenie ........  109
Chicken Breasts Piquant ........  92
Chicken Broccoli Casserole ......  101
Chicken Cacciatore .............  93
Chicken Canary Islands ..........  117
Chicken Cordon Bleu ..........  104
Chicken Delight ................  95
Chicken Enchiladas ............  110
Chicken for the Greek Gods ......  115
Chicken Fredericka ............  102
Chicken Hawaiian ..............  94
Chicken Hunter Style ..........  116
Chicken Mexicana ..............  112
Chicken 'N Cheese in Wine Sauce ...  102
Chicken 'N Rice Casserole ......  95
Chicken 'N Swiss Extraordinaire ....  106
Chicken Oriental ..............  114
Chicken Paprikash ............  118
Chicken Sauté Cacciatore ......  119
Chicken Sauté Hunter Style ......  118
Chicken Sauté Matador ........  112
Chicken Sonoma ..............  122
Chicken Stroganoff ............  108
Chicken Tortilla Casserole ......  110
Chicken Tremendous ............  91
Chicken with Artichokes ........  99
Coq au Vin ..................  116
Cornish Hens and Dressing
   in Wine Sauce ..............  123
Cornish Hens with Apricots
   and Brandy Sauce ............  125
Crusty Chicken Wrap-Ups ......  104
Delicious Chicken ..............  93
Fried Chicken Bits ............  108
Fruit-Stuffed Chicken Breasts ......  103
Grilled Chicken Breasts Hawaiian ...  92
Holiday Chicken with Champagne ...  106
Ken's Company Chicken ..........  105
Lemon Chicken ..............  100
Lemon Chicken Broil ............  97
Mexican Chicken and Rice ........  109
Mexican-Style Chicken Kiev ......  111
Pineapple Chicken with
   Sweet and Sour Sauce ........  121
Poulet Marengo ..............  98
Raspberry Glazed Chicken ......  101
Roast Cornish Game Hens ......  124
Roasted Chicken with
   Browned Potatoes ..........  98

Sesame Chicken ................  107
Sweet and Sour Chicken ........  115
Turkey Parmigiana ............  123
Twelve Boy Curry ..............  120

## Salads

Alaskan Crabmeat on
   Tomato Remoulade ............  230
Apricot Nectar Salad ............  245
Avocado Salad ................  246
Banana and Peanut Salad ......  241
Beet Jello Salad ................  243
Blueberry Fruit Salad ............  249
Broccoli Molded Salad ..........  244
California Chicken Salad ........  233
Chinese Chicken Salad ........  232
Cole Slaw ....................  235
Corn and Cabbage Slaw ........  235
Crabmeat Ravigote ............  229
Cranberry Ring Salad ..........  244
Festive Frozen Fruit Salad ......  245
Fruited Chicken Salad ..........  233
Fruit Salad ....................  243
Gazpacho Salad ..............  240
Golden Delight ................  246
Greek Salad ..................  240
Hot Chicken Salad ............  234
Hot German Potato Salad ......  237
Hot Green Bean and Bacon Salad ...  236
Hot Seafood Salad ............  231
Hot Sweet and Sour Cabbage Salad .  236
Lime Fruit Salad ..............  247
Marinated Carrots ............  236
Marinated Vegetable Salad ......  241
Mediterranean Salad ..........  239
Molded Pear Salad ............  248
Pineapple and Cottage Cheese Salad .  247
Seafood Tomato Aspic ........  231
Shrimp and Crab Surprise Salad ....  229
Shrimp Salad ................  231
Spiced Fruit Compote ..........  242
Spinach Salad ................  239
Spinach Salad St. Louis ........  238
Summer Fruit ................  247
Taco Salad ..................  234
Three Bean Salad ............  237
24-Hour Head Lettuce Salad ......  238
Waldorf Crown Salad ..........  248
Watergate Salad ..............  242

## Salad Dressings

Caesar Dressing ................  254

Catalina Dressing . . . . . . . . . . . . . . . 252
Celery Seed Fruit Dressing . . . . . . . . . 255
Dill Dressing/Dip . . . . . . . . . . . . . . 252
Fluffy Dressing . . . . . . . . . . . . . . . 248
Green Goddess Dressing . . . . . . . . . 255
Honey Lime Dressing . . . . . . . . . . . 257
Javanese Dressing . . . . . . . . . . . . . 250
Luscious Fruit Salad Dressing . . . . . 257
Orange Dressing . . . . . . . . . . . . . . 256
Oregano Salad Dressing . . . . . . . . . 250
Poppy Seed Dressing . . . . . . . . . . . 256
Ray's Special French Dressing . . . . . . 249
Roquefort Dressing #1 . . . . . . . . . . . 254
Roquefort Dressing #2 . . . . . . . . . . . 254
Rum Lime Sauce . . . . . . . . . . . . . . 256
Russian Dressing . . . . . . . . . . . . . . 252
Sesame Seed Dressing . . . . . . . . . . 253
Stone Jug Salad Dressing . . . . . . . . . 250
Sweet and Sour Bacon Dressing . . . . 253
Sweet and Sour
    Sesame Seed Dressing . . . . . . . . 251
Winter Salad Dressing . . . . . . . . . . 251

Meat Marinade . . . . . . . . . . . . . . . 284
Mornay Sauce . . . . . . . . . . 182, 200, 275
Mushroom Sauce . . . . . . . . . . . . . . 157
Paprika Sauce . . . . . . . . . . . . . . . . 91
Piquant Marinade for Beef Steaks . . . 283
Provençale Sauce . . . . . . . . . . . . . 276
Red Sauce . . . . . . . . . . . . . . . . . . 137
Remoulade Sauce . . . . . . . . . . . . . . 230
Rhubarb Relish . . . . . . . . . . . . . . . 286
Sauce Café de Paris . . . . . . . . . . . . 278
Sauce Poivrade . . . . . . . . . . . . . . . 278
Sauté Marinade for Chicken or Pork . . 285
Shirley Sauce . . . . . . . . . . . . . . . . 281
Sour Cream Sauce . . . . . . . . . . . . . 66
Spiced Marinade for Lamb . . . . . . . 284
Supreme Sauce . . . . . . . . . . . . . . . 109
Sweet and Sour Sauce . . . . . . . . . . . 121
Teriyaki Sauce #1 . . . . . . . . . . . . . 280
Teriyaki Sauce #2 . . . . . . . . . . . . . 281
Watermelon Relish . . . . . . . . . . . . . 286
Zucchini Hot Salsa Sauce . . . . . . . . 282
Zucchini Relish . . . . . . . . . . . . . . . 287

## Sauces & Relishes

Barbeque Sauce #1 . . . . . . . . . . . . . 282
Barbeque Sauce #2 . . . . . . . . . . . . . 283
Bearnaise Cream Sauce . . . . . . . . . 149
Bearnaise Sauce . . . . . . . . . . . . . . 275
Bercy Sauce . . . . . . . . . . . . . . . . . 181
Best Barbeque Sauce . . . . . . . . . . . . 283
Blueberry Sauce . . . . . . . . . . . . . . 78
Bordelaise Sauce . . . . . . . . . . . . . . 276
Brandy Sauce . . . . . . . . . . . . . . . . 148
Butter Sauce . . . . . . . . . . . . . . . . 70
Choron Sauce for Poached Salmon . . 280
Cranberry Relish . . . . . . . . . . . . . . 289
Cranberry Sauce . . . . . . . . . . . . . . 289
Cream Sauce . . . . . . . . . . . . . 46, 48
Cucumber Relish . . . . . . . . . . . . . . 288
Cucumber Sauce . . . . . . . . . . . . . . 73
Cumberland Sauce . . . . . . . . . . . . . 124
Elegant Sauce for Ham . . . . . . . . . . 277
Espagnola Sauce . . . . . . . . . . . . . . 279
Fresh Chutney . . . . . . . . . . . . . . . 285
Fruit Sauce . . . . . . . . . . . . . . . . . 103
Grandma's Hamburger Goop Relish . 287
Hollandaise Sauce . . . . . . . . . . . . . 277
Horseradish Sauce . . . . . . . . . . . . . 144
Lemon Butter . . . . . . . . . . . . . . . . 70
Light Supreme Sauce . . . . . . . . . . . 107
Macadamia Nut Sauce . . . . . . . . . . . 60
Marinade for Beef . . . . . . . . . . . . . 284
Marinade for Game . . . . . . . . . . . . 285
Martha's Cabbage and Celery Relish . 288

## Seafood

Baked Cod . . . . . . . . . . . . . . . . . 72
Baked Fish au Gratin . . . . . . . . . . . 74
Baked Fish in Mustard Sauce . . . . . . 72
Baked Scallop Casserole . . . . . . . . . 55
Barry's Baked or Barbequed Salmon . 62
Butterfish in Spanish Sauce . . . . . . . 74
California Seafood Stew . . . . . . . . . . 83
Cape Cod Scallops Denise . . . . . . . . 53
Cheese-Stuffed Baked Salmon
    with Mushrooms . . . . . . . . . . . . 64
Cioppino . . . . . . . . . . . . . . . . . . 84
Crab Broil . . . . . . . . . . . . . . . . . 47
Crab Imperial . . . . . . . . . . . . . . . 46
Crabmeat Dewey . . . . . . . . . . . . . . 48
Crabmeat Imperial . . . . . . . . . . . . 45
Crepes Diplomat . . . . . . . . . . . . . . 56
Dick's Favorite Seafood Stew . . . . . . 84
Filet of Red Snapper Palos Verdes . . . 81
Filet of Salmon Marguerite . . . . . . . 63
Filet of Sole Veronique . . . . . . . . . . 80
Finest Barbequed Salmon . . . . . . . . 62
Flounder Provençale . . . . . . . . . . . 76
Fried Mahi Mahi in
    Macadamia Nut Sauce . . . . . . . . 60
Golden Puffs of Fried Flounder . . . . . 77
Halibut Alyeska . . . . . . . . . . . . . . 77
Hangtown Fry . . . . . . . . . . . . . . . 52
Hawaiian Kabobs Teriyaki . . . . . . . 75
Jambalaya . . . . . . . . . . . . . . . . . . 85
King Crab Legs Parmesan . . . . . . . . 45

# RECIPE INDEX

Lobster Newburg #1 . . . . . . . . . . . . 50
Lobster Newburg #2 . . . . . . . . . . . . 50
Lobster Thermidor . . . . . . . . . . . . . 51
Mahi Mahi Espagnola . . . . . . . . . . . 60
Mahi Mahi Pacific . . . . . . . . . . . . . . 61
Mountain Trout Sauté Temple Square . 69
Ocean Perch Almondine . . . . . . . . . . 80
Poached Salmon with
    Cucumber Sauce . . . . . . . . . . . . . 64
Poached White Fish
    with Cucumber Sauce . . . . . . . . . 73
Potlatch Salmon . . . . . . . . . . . . . . . 66
Puget Sound Clams in Shells . . . . . . . 49
Quenelles of Scallops Nantua . . . . . . 54
Salmon Lasagna Pinwheels . . . . . . . . 65
Salmon Loaf . . . . . . . . . . . . . . . . . . 68
Salmon Loaf with Sour Cream Sauce . 66
Salmon Romanoff St. George . . . . . . 67
Salmon Steaks à la Crème . . . . . . . . . 65
Sashimi . . . . . . . . . . . . . . . . . . . . . 79
Sautéed Trout Bretonne . . . . . . . . . . 70
Scalloped Clams . . . . . . . . . . . . . . . 49
Scallops Meunière . . . . . . . . . . . . . . 55
Seafood Newburg . . . . . . . . . . . . . . 86
Seafood Redondo Beach . . . . . . . . . . 86
Shrimp Arnaud . . . . . . . . . . . . . . . . 59
Shrimp Casserole Harpin . . . . . . . . . 58
Shrimp de Jonghe . . . . . . . . . . . . . . 56
Shrimp Poulette . . . . . . . . . . . . . . . 59
Shrimp Saganaki . . . . . . . . . . . . . . . 57
Shrimp-Stuffed Flounder . . . . . . . . . 76
Smelt Almondine . . . . . . . . . . . . . . 68
Sole au Gratin with Shrimp Sauce . . . 82
Sourdough Fried Fish with
    Blueberry Sauce . . . . . . . . . . . . . 78
Stuffed Rainbow Trout
    with Mushrooms . . . . . . . . . . . . . 71
Stuffed Red Snapper . . . . . . . . . . . . 82
Stuffed Trout with Butter Sauce . . . . . 70
Sweet and Sour Shrimp . . . . . . . . . . 58
Trader Vic's Crab Crepes Bengal . . . . 46
Trout Almondine . . . . . . . . . . . . . . . 69
White Fish en Casserole . . . . . . . . . . 72
Zucchini Boats with Lobster . . . . . . . . 52

## Soups

Bay Scallop Chowder . . . . . . . . . . . . 265
Beef Bouillon or Stock . . . . . . . . . . . 266
Bloody Mary Soup . . . . . . . . . . . . . . 267
Bratten's Clam Chowder . . . . . . . . . . 262
Broccoli Soup . . . . . . . . . . . . . . . . . 270
Creamed Tomato Bisque . . . . . . . . . . 267
Cream of Cauliflower Soup . . . . . . . . 271
Fish Stock . . . . . . . . . . . . . . . . . . . . 264

French Onion Soup . . . . . . . . . . . . . 268
Fresh Seafood Bisque . . . . . . . . . . . . 261
Jim's Crab and Asparagus Soup . . . . . 263
Lobster Bisque . . . . . . . . . . . . . . . . . 262
Lobster Shrimp Chowder . . . . . . . . . 263
Martha Washington Crab Soup . . . . . 264
Mushroom Soup Supreme . . . . . . . . 268
Puree of Leek and Potato Soup . . . . . 269
Russian Borscht . . . . . . . . . . . . . . . . 269
Sicilian Meat Ball Soup . . . . . . . . . . . 265
Spinach Soup . . . . . . . . . . . . . . . . . 270

## Vegetables

Asparagus Soufflé . . . . . . . . . . . . . . 208
Asparagus with
    Almond Mushroom Sauce . . . . . . . 207
Baked, Stuffed Tomatoes . . . . . . . . . 221
Beans in Sour Cream . . . . . . . . . . . . 207
Beets with Orange . . . . . . . . . . . . . . 210
Bread-Stuffed Tomatoes . . . . . . . . . . 222
Broccoli Casserole . . . . . . . . . . . . . . 210
Cabbage Stir-Fry . . . . . . . . . . . . . . . 212
Calico Beans . . . . . . . . . . . . . . . . . . 208
Cantonese Cabbage . . . . . . . . . . . . . 211
Carrot Casserole . . . . . . . . . . . . . . . 212
Carrots Paysanne . . . . . . . . . . . . . . . 212
Cauliflower Polonaise . . . . . . . . . . . . 214
Cauliflower Steamed in Wine . . . . . . . 214
Cranberry Puff . . . . . . . . . . . . . . . . . 215
Creamed Mushrooms and Ham . . . . . 217
Corn Soufflé . . . . . . . . . . . . . . . . . . 215
Deluxe Potato Casserole . . . . . . . . . . 219
Eggplant Parmesan . . . . . . . . . . . . . 216
French-Fried Potato Puffs . . . . . . . . . 218
Green Beans in Sabayon Sauce . . . . . 209
Hawaiian Carrots . . . . . . . . . . . . . . . 213
Herbed Brussel Sprouts . . . . . . . . . . 211
Magic Yams . . . . . . . . . . . . . . . . . . . 222
Marinated Broccoli . . . . . . . . . . . . . . 210
"Mashed" Potatoes . . . . . . . . . . . . . . 218
Mushrooms and Sour Cream . . . . . . . 217
Mushrooms Parmesan . . . . . . . . . . . 217
Offbeat Carrots . . . . . . . . . . . . . . . . 213
Party Potatoes . . . . . . . . . . . . . . . . . 219
Potato Breakfast Casserole . . . . . . . . 220
Red Cabbage . . . . . . . . . . . . . . . . . . 155
Sautéed Spinach . . . . . . . . . . . . . . . 182
Scalloped Potatoes . . . . . . . . . . . . . . 220
Sweet and Sour Beans . . . . . . . . . . . 209
Sweet Potato Soufflé . . . . . . . . . . . . 221
Vegetable Medley . . . . . . . . . . . . . . 226
Vegetable Royal . . . . . . . . . . . . . . . . 225
Wilted Lettuce . . . . . . . . . . . . . . . . . 216

Yams Richard .................. 223
Zucchini Casserole .............. 223
Zucchini Cheese Bake ........... 224
Zucchini-Stuffing Casserole ........ 224

..........................................................

**Send a check for $11.95 plus $1.50 postage and handling for each book to:**

UNITED AIRLINES FRIENDSHIP GUILD
*PRIVATE STOCK COOKBOOK*
**2033 6th Avenue**
**Seattle, WA 98121**

**Send to:**

**Name** _____

**City** _____

**State/Zip** _____

Enclosed is my check for $ _____ for _____ copies.
*(Please remember to add $1.50 for postage and handling per book.)*
..........................................................


..........................................................

**Send a check for $11.95 plus $1.50 postage and handling for each book to:**

UNITED AIRLINES FRIENDSHIP GUILD
*PRIVATE STOCK COOKBOOK*
**2033 6th Avenue**
**Seattle, WA 98121**

**Send to:**

**Name** _____

**City** _____

**State/Zip** _____

Enclosed is my check for $ _____ for _____ copies.
*(Please remember to add $1.50 for postage and handling per book.)*
..........................................................


..........................................................

**Send a check for $11.95 plus $1.50 postage and handling for each book to:**

UNITED AIRLINES FRIENDSHIP GUILD
*PRIVATE STOCK COOKBOOK*
**2033 6th Avenue**
**Seattle, WA 98121**

**Send to:**

**Name** _____

**City** _____

**State/Zip** _____

Enclosed is my check for $ _____ for _____ copies.
*(Please remember to add $1.50 for postage and handling per book.)*
..........................................................

**Send a check for $11.95 plus $1.50 postage and handling for each book to:**

UNITED AIRLINES FRIENDSHIP GUILD
*PRIVATE STOCK COOKBOOK*
**2033 6th Avenue**
**Seattle, WA 98121**

**Send to:**

**Name** _____

**City** _____

**State/Zip** _____

Enclosed is my check for $ _____ for _____ copies.
*(Please remember to add $1.50 for postage and handling per book.)*

---

**Send a check for $11.95 plus $1.50 postage and handling for each book to:**

UNITED AIRLINES FRIENDSHIP GUILD
*PRIVATE STOCK COOKBOOK*
**2033 6th Avenue**
**Seattle, WA 98121**

**Send to:**

**Name** _____

**City** _____

**State/Zip** _____

Enclosed is my check for $ _____ for _____ copies.
*(Please remember to add $1.50 for postage and handling per book.)*

---

**Send a check for $11.95 plus $1.50 postage and handling for each book to:**

UNITED AIRLINES FRIENDSHIP GUILD
*PRIVATE STOCK COOKBOOK*
**2033 6th Avenue**
**Seattle, WA 98121**

**Send to:**

**Name** _____

**City** _____

**State/Zip** _____

Enclosed is my check for $ _____ for _____ copies.
*(Please remember to add $1.50 for postage and handling per book.)*